WILLIAM
BARCLAY
Prophet of Goodwill

WILLIAM BARCLAY

Prophet of Goodwill

———

The authorized biography
CLIVE L. RAWLINS

Fount
An Imprint of HarperCollins*Publishers*

Fount is an Imprint of
HarperCollins*Religious*
Part of HarperCollins*Publishers*
77–85 Fulham Palace Road, London W6 8JB

First published in Great Britain in 1998
by HarperCollins*Religious*
13 5 7 9 10 8 6 4 2

A catalogue record for this book
is available from the British Library.

ISBN 0 00 628097 8

Printed and bound in Great Britain by
Caledonian International Book Manufacturing Ltd, Glasgow

For Veronica

CONTENTS

ACKNOWLEDGEMENTS

It is a pleasure to offer these public thanks to the very many who made this book possible – both in the original edition of 1982 and this revised one.

Following the destruction of William Barclay's paperwork at his death, an immense correspondence developed, from around the world and from every continent. My generous correspondents are too numerous to mention here – though some are named in the text. I offer my warmest thanks for the time and effort they took, and for sharing with me – with us – their memories. (This correspondence led to the publication in 1986 of *Ever Yours: Selections from the letters of William Barclay*, edited by me. All this material has been placed on deposition with the National Library of Scotland, Edinburgh, though it will remain out of the public domain for thirty years, to protect confidentialities.)

Pride of thanks must go to the Barclay Estate, to Ronnie Barclay in particular, for many hours of interviews, and very many – perhaps sometimes impertinent – questions; and to Jane his sister, who also allowed me access to her own recollections. Many of William Barclay's friends and fellow students declared their respect and affection for him by responding similarly, as did various members of Trinity Church, Renfrew, whom he served between 1932 and 1946. Many of his former students were generous in offering details of him and his work, as well as countless cups of coffee. I am too aware that space considerations do not allow me a more personal acknowledgement.

Organizations to which William Barclay was close also helped enormously, not least his old school, DHS (Dalziel High School), the Boys' Brigade, the YMCA, the University of Glasgow, the Scottish Sunday School Union (now defunct), the Bible Society, the IBRA, and The Fellowship of Reconciliation. Sadly, this cannot be said for the Church of Scotland. None of my appeals for information received an official reply from them; those who did write made it plain that they were acting in a private capacity. The subject of this book would not have been surprised. William Barclay repeatedly drew attention to the way in which the Church had lost the sense of family and close relating which characterized its beginning years. Happily, this cannot be said of many of its members and ministers – the real Church. Alongside these I must place the ever-helpful librarians of Edinburgh, Glasgow, Fort William, Wick, Motherwell, East Linton and Haddington, Manchester, Birmingham, London, Oxford, Cambridge and Belfast. Some of these work in academic positions, some in municipal posts, others in private collections. They all went 'the extra mile' for me.

I must not forget William Barclay's publishers. Many of them provided unstinted information, making available letters, reports and minutes, etc. which have been a very great help: James Clarke & Co. Ltd, T & T Clark Ltd, Darton, Longman & Todd Ltd, Drummond Press, Epworth Press Ltd, Hodder & Stoughton Ltd, Labarum Publications Ltd, The Lutterworth Press, The Methodist Home Mission, A R Mowbray & Co. Ltd, The National Christian Education Council, The SCM Press, The Upper Room (Nashville), Westminster Press (Philadelphia), William Collins & Sons Ltd (now HarperCollins *Religious*). To these and their respective managers, editors and secretaries, I offer my heartiest thanks.

It is always invidious to select names, but a special work of thanks must go to Mowbrays of Oxford (now owned by Cassell PLC), to Evi Jesse not least, for permission to quote from *Testament of Faith*, William Barclay's autobiography, now sadly out of print – a very rich source of Barclayana, if sometimes inaccurate. Three newspapers hold very important information on our subject and his family: *The John O'Groats Journal*, *The Motherwell Times*, *The Renfrew Press* (which advertised virtually every sermon he preached as a minister); and three others were solid in their support of his writings: the *British Weekly* (now defunct), *Life and Work* (the monthly journal of the Church of Scotland) and *The Expository Times*. A special thank-you is due to their respective editors and former editors. I also thank the Publications Department (now the Department of Communications) of the Church of Scotland for the quotations from William Barclays' writings published by them. It should be noted that I have preferred to quote from the first editions of his books wherever possible – he himself rarely revised his work once published – as these often give a truer picture of him.

I must not omit to thank Bill Eerdmans & Co. of Michigan, the publishers of the first, huge, edition of this book, more a chronicle than a biography. When others' courage failed, Bill and his colleagues stood firm, ever enthusiastic. The editor Tim A. Straayer and my old friend Peter Cousins both supported the project with their editorial expertise. It is my pleasant duty to thank HarperCollins*Religious* and all its staff: its Publisher, James Catford, and Kathy Dyke, Lisa Brosnan, Elspeth Taylor and my copy editor, Bryony Benier.

Such names recall others who must not be overlooked: my friend and mentor of over thirty-five years, the late Professor F. F. Bruce, found time to read my original manuscript, and was a source of great wisdom and not a few pawky asides. Also to the Reverend Laurence Twaddle – which did not prevent me being 'scalped' by the *unco guid*! My parents, Mary and Leonard Rawlins (the latter sadly no longer with us) offered even longer support and encouragement; as did my sister and brother-in-law, Pat and Ken Jones. My wife, Veronica, has cheerfully and generously shouldered much extra work to make mine possible, also my sons, Stephen and Philip (I remember the logging, lads!) To them and, latterly, their wives, Gillian and Karen, I am greatly indebted.

It is not only the publishers of William Barclay's writings that I must acknowledge. From time to time I have quoted from others' works – but not, I fear, as copiously or as aptly as Willie did himself. To these and their respective authors I offer my thanks: Faber & Faber Ltd for the T. S. Eliot quotation from *The Waste Land* on p. 253; Pan Books for the Bernard Levin excerpt from *The Pendulum Years* on p. 216; Handsel Press for the Falconer piece in *Kilt Beneath My Cassock* on p. 233; the *Sunday Times* for the Peter Clark quotation on p. 257; Chatto & Windus for those from Aldous Huxley in Sybille Bedford's brilliant biography on p. 269. Some of my quotations come from old memories, their sources now long lost. Any inadvertent omissions in these acknowledgements will willingly be amended in any further editions.

If this biography has the effect of successfully taking its readers back to the writings of William Barclay, I shall be well content. Let my final thanks, therefore, be to him and his family, who sacrificed bountifully for us all, and now rest from their labours.

C. L. Rawlins
Easter, 1998

LIST OF ILLUSTRATIONS

Page 1
Bank House, Motherwell.
On honeymoon. Kate and Willie at Bournemouth, 1933.

Page 2
'Chaplain Barclay' (leaning to the left!), 1944.
Gathering of civic dignitaries at Renfrew 1942.

Page 3
Barbara Barclay and Rusty shortly before her death, 1956.
Commentator *extraordinaire*, 1957.
Barclay's room in the YMCA tower, 'the prophet's chamber'.

Page 4
The Dean in his office, 1968.
Readying himself the typewriter, c. 1970.

Page 5
Symbols of Barclay: blackboard, lectern and piano, c. 1970.

Page 6
Map-reading with French friends and with Ronnie, Kate and Jane,
    c. 1967.
Kate and Willie on holiday, c. 1970.
With his daughter-in-law, grandchildren, Kate and Jane, c. 1975.

Page 7
Kate and her Commander of the British Empire, a celebration, 1969.
Upper Room honours shortly before his death, 1977.

Page 8
A quiet break, on holiday with Kate, 1974.
The latter years, in pensive mood.
The author, delivering the William Barclay Memorial Lecture,
    Church House, London 1985.

LIST OF ABBREVIATIONS

ARP   Air Raid Precaution
ASRV *American Standard Revised Version* (of the RV; the precursor
      of the RSV)
AV   *Authorized* (or *King James'*) Version of 1611
BB   Boys' Brigade
BCC   The British Council of Churches
BD   Bachelor of Divinity
BFBS The British and Foreign Bible Society (now The Bible Society)
BIOS Greek for 'life'; the old Free Church students' acronym for
      British Israel Original Succession, a playful coup against the
      Auld Kirkers' stuffiness. They were also known as Uffies.
BLB   Barbara Barclay, William Barclay's mother
BW   The *British Weekly*
CoS   Church of Scotland*
DBR   *Daily Bible Readings*, a series of devotional commentaries on
      the New Testament by William Barclay, later published as the
      DSB, qv.
DD   Doctor of Divinity
DHS   Dalziel High School
DSB   *Daily Study Bible*, see *DBR* above
ET   The Expository Times
FoR   The Fellowship of Reconciliation (a peace movement)
FUME Federation of University and Ministerial Ethicists
IBRA International Bible Reading Association
IVF   Inter-Varsity Fellowship (see SCF below)
MA   Master of Arts
NEB   New English Bible
PE   Political Economy (i.e. Economics, which WB read at
      postgraduate level at Glasgow)
RE   Religious Education
RSV   Revised Standard Version
RV   Revised Version

SA   Salvation Army
SAP   Saint Andrew Press (latter name for the CoS publications'
        department)
SCF   Student Christian Fellowship (a conservative evangelical
        group operating in colleges and universities; predecessor to
        the IVF, now the UCCF)
SCM   Student Christian Mission
SNTS   Studiorum Novi Testamenti Societas
SSST   *Scottish Sunday School Teacher* journal
SSSU   Scottish Sunday School Union
STA   Scottish Temperance Alliance
ToF   *Testament of Faith*, WB's autobiography
TNT   Translators New Testament (part of the BFBS)
UCCF   Universities and Colleges Christian Fellowship (see SCF above)
UP   United Presbyterian (Church)
URC   United Reform Church (a union of the Congregational and
        the English Presbyterians)
WCC   World Council of Churches
WDB   William Dugald Barclay, JP; William Barclay's father
Y   or YMCA, the Young Men's Christian Association

* The nomenclature of the Church of Scotland is as distinctive as its history is complex. A daughter-church of the Reformation (of Geneva), and presbyterian in essence (Andrew Melville is called 'the father of presbyterianism'), it has fully shared and developed the genius of reformed faith, and those idiosyncrasies to which the Renaissance and the Reformation gave rise, namely the tendency to splits and schisms. Scotland has always been the cauldron of fiercely held viewpoints. In 1843 the most illustrious clash in the history of the Church since the Reformation took place, when Thomas Chalmers led 474 ministers out of the Church in what is known as the Disruption, protesting over the power of the Moderates (of patronage particularly). They became known as the Free Church of Scotland. In 1847 the UP was formed by the union of the United Secession Church (itself a union church from the previous century) and the Relief Church (another eighteenth-century protest group of churches). In 1900 the UP and the Free Church of Scotland were united, forming the United Free Church (of which the Barclays were members); a protesting rump was left which kept the original Free Church name, often referred to as the Wee Frees.

ONE

THE HIGHLAND BACKGROUND

The childhood shows the man,
As morning shows the day.
(John Milton, *Paradise Regained*, IV.220)

William Barclay was born on 5 December 1907, the only child of William Dugald Barclay and Barbara Linton Barclay (née McLeish), both aged over forty. They lived at Wick in Caithness-shire, but had been born and raised at Fort William (formerly Maryburgh, in honour of King William II's wife), regarding that former garrison town as their true home. They gravitated there for their holidays, and in its quiet environs they were eventually laid to rest.

Willie, as their son liked to be called by his friends (Bill to those closest to him), knew Fort William only from those holiday visits. He was impressed by the large house his maternal grandfather kept, the high esteem in which the town held him, and the Highlander stories he told. But his stay in the north was of short duration, though long enough to impress on him for ever the serenity and discipline of Highland life and its great differences when compared with that of the 'soft' southerners. Willie and his parents moved south before he was five years old, to the heavily industrialized centre south-east of Glasgow, to which he remained faithful for the rest of his life.

He was born in an age of transition and growing tensions. Change was in the air: technologically, politically, socially, commercially and industrially; not least religiously – which was to become his main sphere of work as a minister of the Church. This atmosphere of change was particularly apparent in Scotland, which has ever led the way in innovative thinking and doing. It was not so much an unresting ambience as warlike – in politics, industrial relations, and the Church. Church relationships were very complex, although they became somewhat clearer after the historic Union of 1929, when the United Free Church of Scotland (to which the Barclays belonged) reunited with the Church of Scotland (the established Church). The struggle for union had been long and bitter, involving social as well as theological and biblical issues, which continued alongside the West of Scotland's historic battles between Roman Catholics and Protestants: their way of demonstrating how seriously they took their religion. Into this embattled situation Willie was born, and against it he worked throughout his long career: a man of peace, a man of goodwill.

Willie's parents were themselves no strangers to those tensions, being keen church workers. And they knew familial pain and sorrow – as well as the more distressing personal opposition to their wish to marry each other. Their hopes were blocked by the strong-minded Daniel McLeish, Barbara's father, despite which they remained true to each other over many years of hardship and forced separation. The precise cause of the friction is unclear, though hints in Willie's autobiography, *Testament of Faith*, suggest that it was McLeish's *amour-propre*, particularly his class-consciousness, that was chiefly behind it. For William Dugald Barclay (we shall refer to him as WDB), William's father, was but the son of the local joiner. He was clever, if without higher education; short of stature and ebullient; and very ambitious. Moreover, for all his religious fervour, he had a detonating temper. There was much about the younger man that McLeish disliked – perhaps much that reminded him of himself – but more than that, he *resented* him and his outspoken, intrusive demeanour.

McLeish had arrived in Fort William from Edinburgh – there always was something of the dour lawyer from the capital about him – posted there by his seniors in the law firm for which he worked, to oversee and expand their work in the north-west. He was neither a graduate nor a formally qualified lawyer, as we know them today, though he described himself as a 'writer' (a synonym for lawyer, whose meaning we may trace in the word 'writ') on his marriage certificate. There is no trace of him in the records of the Writers of the Signet, but the recognition of such was more casual then than now.

He was the ambitious son of a Perthshire farmer, born at Dunkeld – 'the cradle of Scots' Christianity' – and proud of that fact. It lies about fifteen miles north-west of the city of Perth. He was probably indentured as a law clerk, and soon made good his energetic promise; so much so that he was sent north when still in his mid-twenties, principally to act as factor (i.e. estate manager) for Mrs Cameron Campbell of Monzie, recently widowed. It was a move that could scarcely have been more opportune, for he now had an entrée into the cream of local society, and a chance to make his impression on its commercial and financial interests, in which he did not fail.

He became a man of distinction, mentally and physically. Of more than average height, darkly bearded after the manner of the time and with a voice to match, he early bore the carriage of the Lieutenant-Colonel of the volunteer regiment he later became. His acute mind and decisive *mien* soon brought him wider approbation than that of Mrs Cameron Campbell. In the Census Returns of 1871 we find him described (at thirty-six years of age) as 'the Managing Law Clerk' in his firm's local office, and 'the Depute Clerk of the Peace' for the now important market town of Fort William. Following a revision of Scotland's policing laws in 1862, McLeish was appointed Chairman of the nine-member police commission. He was housed in the prestigious Parade Cottage adjacent to Parade House, now owned by the local doctor, which overlooks the parade ground that was the centre of the town's military and civic functions. It had formerly been the residence of the Governor of Fort William, a position that had lapsed a few years earlier (in 1854). Daniel McLeish enjoyed playing the Governor *manqué*.

He was a proud man, and traced his ancestry into the romantic past of Scottish history, unlike the upstart Barclay, his office junior, who was now essaying to match himself with his youngest daughter. McLeish was especially proud of Highland traditions and spoke the Gaelic with aplomb. Among his many attempts to preserve the language are four folktales in the archives of the School of Scottish Studies, the gift of WDB's nephew, I. M. Mackintosh of Troon, whose mother was McLeish's eldest daughter Jean (sometimes called Jane). The interest of these tales is expressed by their titles: 'Lochiel's Fairies'; 'Gormshuil, the Witch of Moy'; 'Ticonderoga, The Ghost of Inverawe'; and 'Mary of Callart'.

The most powerful symbol of his interests is the blackthorn stick he acquired. It was carried into battle in the '45 Rising by Macdonald of Kinlochmoidart, at the Raising of the Standard for Prince Charles at Glenfinnart, which is near to Fort William. It is one of the few artifacts to have survived the deliberate destruction of everything pertaining to that lost cause, which finds not a few adherents in Scotland even today. How McLeish acquired it is unknown – perhaps a gift from Cameron of Lochiel, for whom he later factored. After his death it was presented to the West Highland Museum by his sister, Isabella, who gave her address as Bank House, Motherwell: the home of WDB, McLeish's eventual son-in-law. In a sense that fact consolidates much of the background to our story, with its reflections of power, Highland pride, the victory of the heart, and the greater victory of reconciliation.

In 1862 McLeish married the daughter of a local landed farmer, James Linton of Coruannan, whose farm adjoined the estate of Cameron Campbell. Linton himself hailed from Broughton in Peebleshire, a lowlander. But he was not outranked by his Highlander son-in-law, nor by his passion for the past. Originally, Linton's family had worked the farm where 'the Black Dwarf' of Sir Walter Scott lived. It is doubtless from such roots that their respective great-grandson and grandson, William Barclay, obtained his own passion for literature and story-telling.

Sadly, McLeish's joys were not untrammelled. Having given him four children – a son and three daughters – his wife, Jane Scott Linton, died at an early age in 1870. He never married again. Some of the harshness with which he treated William Dugald Barclay may be put down to that searing loss. His wife's place was briefly taken by his sister-in-law, Barbara Linton; then his own sister, Isabella McLeish, splendidly sacrificed her own marital prospects – actually breaking off her engagement – to care for her brother and his children, then aged six (James William), five (Jane – or Jean – Scott), three (Margaret Ellen), and two (Barbara Linton). McLeish was the sort of man who felt himself worthy of such sacrifice.

He continued to make his successes. Not long after his wife's demise he was made 'agent' (manager) of the local branch of the Bank of Scotland, which did not lessen his other interests. In those days bank agents frequently undertook their duties alongside commercial enterprises, thus shouldering financial risk as well as administrative responsibility. Because of it they achieved mandarin status, and were very highly respected by the community, and feared by their minions – though, to McLeish's annoyance, not by the unfazeable WDB. An accountant would have been put in charge of the day-to-day functioning of the bank, a man chosen with great care for financial know-how as well as personable abilities. It says much for both men that, despite strong personal antipathy, the day would come when McLeish would recommend WDB to such a post, though his motives may have been self-serving, as we shall see.

By the Census Returns of 1881, the McLeish household had enlarged again, to nine people, comprising: himself, Isabella (housekeeper), the four children, Janet P. Mellie (governess), Hannah Cameron (housemaid), and Isabella McKenzie (cook). The man who was now factor to the great estate of Cameron of Lochiel lived in the style of his laird – as well as enjoying a well-earned reputation for uprightness and hard work. Such spare time as he found for himself he spent on his triple hobbies: Gaelic literature, antique watches and militaria (hence the blackthorn stick). In addition to these he was an elder of his local Free Church and its Session Clerk (i.e. Church Secretary).

The governess undertook elementary educational duties – the three Rs – until the children transferred to junior school. They were well catechized at the local Free Church, according to the demanding traditions of the day. Then the girls were sent to the Queen Street School for Young Ladies in Edinburgh, whence Miss Mellie had herself come. There they were submitted to a careful, socially oriented and very practical formation, which not only included the standard educational requirements of the well-to-do (not least in selected literature and music), but was also strong in social graces, deportment, and so on. The children who entered this school full of immature gaiety and enthusiasm departed as young women, well finished, and able to cope with the demands that were soon to be made of them, whether over the staffs of their husbands' large houses around the empire, or in the professional opportunities that were just beginning to bud. But there were other challenges, too, for this was the age of the suffragette; the McLeish daughters were not left untouched by its possibilities, as their careers demonstrate (Jean married Dr H. J. Mackintosh of Troon, following a period as matron/housekeeper during which she established a reputation for 'good works'; Margaret became an army nurse, served in the Boer War – she was at Kimberley when it was relieved by Lord Roberts, referred to ever afterwards as 'Bobs' – and was a friend of Florence Nightingale; Barbara became housekeeper to her father, as we shall see). Their family nickname was 'the three graces', a classical reference which was appreciated by WDB, whose heart was taken by the slim, willowy figure and devout elegance of McLeish's youngest.

The family's happiness was blighted again in 1894 when their brother, James William, died. It was an immense blow to the already afflicted Daniel McLeish, who nevertheless bore it with a stoicism fused with Christian hope and resignation that was common to his generation: 'the Lord has given, and the Lord has taken away...' His was an austere faith and a courageous one, as much a duty as a religious expression, given his many responsibilities to the local Free Church and before the town community. Each day his household gathered for prayer, a short Bible reading, and 'a word of exhortation' from its head, family and staff kneeling to commit themselves and their work to God before the long day's business began.

Barbara's own duties became increasingly heavy, as the youngest daughter's were wont to be in such a situation in those days. Whatever her personal interests, there was no question of her seeking employment elsewhere, as her sisters had done. Her father's reputation was increasing – as bank agent, factor of several large estates, sometime Sheriff Substitute, Colonel of the local volunteer regiment (the Cameroons), and church officer. The domestic staff coped with the running of the house, of course, but the social aspects fell more and more heavily upon Barbara. WDB was even more impressed. 'Bella', her very sympathetic aunt, was ageing; and her two sisters had long departed to the south. McLeish's youngest daughter was ideally suited for her work: not only efficient, but 'tall, fair, blue-eyed, gracious, beautiful; every inch an aristocrat', as her son recalled many years later, doubtless relying on his father's memories as well as his own.

William Dugald Barclay, Barbara's would-be suitor, was not so fortunate in his background, and we can readily imagine the concern 'His Honour, Colonel McLeish' had over the mutual attraction between WDB and his youngest. He combatted their relationship by every means, a task made more difficult by their several commitments to the local church.

When Willie referred to his father as 'the son of the village joiner' he was not actually being very accurate. He never showed real interest in his family roots – which WDB for his part may have been glad to forget, but which also reflected Willie's deep repugnance for class distinctions. His grandfather, also called William, was the equivalent of a civil engineer in the mid-nineteenth century, self-employed – with all the insecurity that betokens. He it was who built at Lochgoilhead 'Barclay's Jetty', an important way-station to which coal boats and other critical supplies made their way along Loch Fyne, from which local produce was exported south to Glasgow and beyond. It served a huge area, and the responsibility for building it well was a large one. Not that we can compare it with the great works which took place, say, at Aberdeen or Glasgow or Leith, of course. Compared with them it was a small undertaking, but it stood the tests and it never failed; it was only the arrival of modern transport – especially the growth in rail and road networks – which provoked the jetty's doom, and that simply by disuse. It now lies derelict and forgotten, its stones scattering in the currents, almost completely submerged.

William's father, Samuel Barclay, was not Scottish but English, born in Manchester. In the Census Returns of 1841, then aged sixty, he was described as a tailor, living at the prestigious Dramsynnie House, at Lochgoilhead on Loch Fyne. (The family appears to have had its roots in the English Barclays of Berkeley in Gloucestershire, whose progenitor was Jean, son of Roger de Bechelai.) Why Samuel left Manchester is not known, though we can guess it had something to do with his interest in wool and woollen cloth, for which Fort William was famous. Steamers plied between the two places, stopping off at Lochgoilhead, where Samuel met Jean, who became his wife. They had six children: Betsy (born in 1815, died aged three); Catherine (born in 1816, died at nineteen months); William (born in 1823); Samuel Jnr (born in 1826, died aged twenty-two); Joseph (born in 1830); and 'Dund' (born in 1844, died aged thirteen). The Barclays thus experienced their own intense sorrows – as many families did in those medically primitive days. Their memorial stands today, erected in 1854 by Samuel's 'only surviving sons', William and Joseph, 'as a tribute of dutiful affection', as it proudly states. Jean died in 1871, at the cottage of her unmarried son, Joseph, who now disappears from the scene.

In 1847, William (Willie's grandfather) married Sarah MacVicar in Glasgow. The family had obviously kept some southern links – William indeed had spent some time serving his apprenticeship there. It was usual for sons to follow their fathers' profession or trade, but the clothing trade was already changing, crumbling under the weight of the Empire's gains. Perhaps Samuel far-sightedly saw little future in it for his sons. Whatever the cause, Joseph went into farming, and William into woodworking (to which he added masonry).

The young couple returned to a new base in the north, to Fort William, where there was more work for William's trade. There they slowly re-established their roots. In the Census of 1861 we find them residing at 9 Low Street, Fort William, aged thirty-nine and thirty-six respectively, with their four children: Catherine (eleven), Jane (nine), Samuel (five), and Mary (one), plus a domestic help. The later clash between McLeish and Barclay may be said to be projected in these addresses: High Street versus Low Street!

William Dugald Barclay, their last child, appeared in 1864, and was named after his father (Dugald was Sarah's father's name, who also lived at Fort William). Anyone living in that former military town could not but be reminded of the historico-religious and personal references behind that name (i.e. William of Orange, who became William III of England, Scotland and Ireland. He married Mary of York, his cousin, in 1677. She returned to England in 1689 and frequently acted as Regent in William's absence. William replaced James II, a Roman Catholic, who fled to France). A little later his father described himself as a joiner – not even a carpenter now (who makes larger structures), and employing but two men: the effects of economic degeneration, no doubt. There were three other joiners in town, so competition for work was obviously stiff. Doubtless this struggle played some part in making what WDB later became – a tough-minded and ambitious man.

TWO

FORT WILLIAM AND WICK

> In the Highlands, in the country places,
> Where the old plain men have rosy faces,
> And the young fair maidens
> Quiet eyes.
>
> (Robert Louis Stevenson, *Songs of Travel*)

When WDB started school, only his sister Mary was still being educated. Catherine and Jane had married, and Samuel had gone off to teach in Glasgow – in those days 'all roads led to Glasgow', not least for this family – a throw-back to their earliest days in Scotland, perhaps. Samuel's teaching career is the only indication of formal academic interests in the family to this point.

WDB showed himself a hard and serious worker, intellectually able and athletic to boot. He was driven by a natural curiosity and had a high degree of native shrewdness. An avid reader, he early joined the Subscription Library at Fort William, whose most prized possession was a twenty-six-volume set of the works of Sir Walter Scott, signed and donated by the author himself. The day would come when he could boast of having read every one, several times, and very much more besides.

Unlike his brother Samuel, WDB (who had that Scottish didactic turn of mind) did not go into teaching. Banking became his interest. We do not know his motivation for this – perhaps his father's struggle to keep his business going, or the growing recognition that the world of finance offered better prospects. Whatever the impulses, his entrance examination (in arithmetic, writing and dictation) confirmed his aptitudes and he was indentured in 1879. Thus he became a trainee under the eagle eye of Daniel McLeish, who had doubtless watched him grow up, not least in the local church and its activities, unaware that one day he would rue his encouragements. Such young men had recently become an identifiable group in the banking world which, recognizing its need to prepare for the future, began to install systems for training and moulding promising young men.

Training lasted three years, for which WDB was paid a pittance. His father had to offer a personal bond against any defalcation his son may make. Even after the training was over, the financial rewards for the lower ranked employees were unremarkable, and the system was harsh and rigid. Bank employers were paragons who brooked no excuse. Remuneration was low and increments infrequent – the wily managers preferred bonus schemes. There were no less than five thousand clerks by now in the industry, and a thousand seniors. Beyond the walls were long queues of hopeful men, waiting their chance to enter, keen-eyed for someone else's downfall. It was a rough and competitive world: a managers' market. Promotion came only through long hours – years, indeed – of zealous loyalty amid very strong competition. Male employees were not allowed to marry before twenty-six, and few could do so honourably even then thanks to poor pay and prospects. As one economic historian commented, 'banking in Scotland was popularly regarded as the most dismal of respectable professions'.

But its potential was great, for those who did manage to get ahead, and WDB was the sort to make progress. He earned his promotion by constant application, slow and resolute, during which time Barbara and he – already church friends – became seriously attracted to each other. McLeish was not amused. It was probably this that caused WDB's transfer from Fort William to Pitlochry in Perthshire. It was only seventy miles away as the crow flies, but a good many more by road, and very difficult to travel in those restricted days. WDB thus got his much hoped-for promotion; and McLeish got his much desired separation. Far from family and friends, with more time than ever before on his hands, WDB's interests increased, especially in literature, alongside his developing religious inclinations.

During his time in Pitlochry WDB met and listened to some of the greatest preachers of his day. Just a little further north, at Bonskeid in the Tummel Valley, was the Barbours' country house. The Barbours were merchants who had made their wealth in Manchester (no doubt a special point of interest to WDB), and thus introduced a wider world-view to those whom they benefited by their generous hospitality. Their son-in-law was Alexander Whyte, one of the most influential Free Church preachers of the time, whose appropriation of the mysticism of William Law and an informed love of literature made him an immensely popular figure. Like many wealthy Edinburgh folk the Barbours divided their time between the capital and Bonskeid, which enjoyed a high reputation as a most desirable watering hole. Their home became a centre for the well-to-do people who frequented such places, not least religiously, to which many preachers and teachers were invited. From this time dates WDB's reputation as a notable sermon-taster (not then a pejorative term). Attracted to the eminent preachers who were introduced to the area, he soon developed biblical and theological acumen, and was encouraged to develop this in work among children and young people, thence adults. In this he showed himself especially gifted, not least among 'working men' – like Arthur Samuel Peake (the Primitive Methodist scholar who became Professor of Biblical Criticism and Exegesis at the University of Manchester; alongside his academic work he produced many volumes of popular theology which attained extraordinary sales).

It was here that WDB first heard Henry Drummond, a minister-cum-scientist *manqué*, a one-time co-worker with the American evangelist D. L. Moody. Drummond's book *Natural Law in the Spiritual World* became (in 1883) a best-seller and remained such for over eight decades. In this extraordinarily gifted young man WDB found a soul-fellow and journeyed far to listen to him, later collecting and disseminating his books. Drummond, having given up his theological studies for mission work – and to extend his knowledge of the natural sciences – was ahead of his time in theological circles. His chief intellectual stimulus (in the wake of Darwin's *Origin of Species* of 1859) remained in the natural world and was uniquely wedded to a firm evangelical conviction. It was heady stuff to one such as WDB, who had been denied advanced education but was untiring in his intellectual gropings. That influence did not pall with the years, even though Drummond himself died early (in 1897). WDB passed his curiosity (and much more besides) on to his son, Willie, in whom it became an important element – in his preaching and theology both. Knowledge for its own sake became a dominant passion with him, but it nevertheless had to have a practical end. (Willie even entered the evolutionary fray, as we shall see.)

It has been said that the work of such men as A. S. Peake, a Primitive Methodist and a biblical scholar of great distinction, prevented a conservative-versus-liberal split in the United Kingdom such as rent the USA in 1926 and since. But the work of Drummond was possibly more decisive, for his unchallenged evangelicalism (bearing the *imprimatur* of Moody, no less) was geared to important scientific (i.e. botanical and biological) work, which may have led its author to distinction had not an early death intervened.

WDB developed his skills as a communicator very much under the shadow of such men. They were first tested in the Bible Class and

Young Men's work in Perthshire, in local church groups and in the YMCA (the latter a great passion for WDB and others), for which he became well known. Then a new promotion took him back to Fort William, which gave him further opportunities to develop his teaching and preaching talents, as he tried to do for the rest of his life; at first verbally, but then by using every mechanical and electrical invention – such as the 'magic lanterns' – that came his way. In this also he paved the way for his son's own eagerness to discover fresh methods and styles, also among young people to begin with.

WDB was not in the first bracket intellectually, but there was a natural smartness, a keen logic and robustness, that quickly established him as a leader of men. He combined this with a genuine thirst for knowledge which the young found very appealing, as did older men and women. His attitude was not only open and receptive, but 'masculine', and proud of the term: combative; unafraid of asking hard questions; ever seeking better answers. 'Masculine Christianity' became an in-word of his day. Yet there was within him a hard core of conservatism, which he never yielded, especially in matters of religion. He appealed to people on a broad front, and worked contentedly beyond the barriers that denominational tradition and theological prejudice had built up. The day would come when he was a welcome preacher in thirteen out of Motherwell's fourteen churches (the fourteenth being the Roman Catholic). In this he was upheld by his obvious successes and his upright stance in the world of finance.

It did not happen – given their strong personalities, it could not happen – but at times one thinks that McLeish almost began to like him. Something more than a grudging respect surfaced, which was demonstrated in WDB's recall to Fort William. Their natural dislike – it was mainly on McLeish's side and defensive, for his sister Isabella regarded WDB highly (she secretly played postman between the young couple) – was not merely a matter of class-consciousness. There was a politico-physical element: the patrician against the plebeian, the tall against the short, the slim against the corpulent, the professional against the worker, the employer against the employee, higher middle-against lower working-class, even old world against new world. They were both Free Churchmen, but the one was less 'free' than the other, more concerned with external things, driven not so much by goodwill as by duty and law – those twin Kantian pillars which too often undermine the ethic of love. McLeish was dutiful in his commitments and devotion; more ready to warn than encourage, to blame than to understand; a latter-day Pharisee who exerted great pressure within his church and beyond as a man of 'stern duty', a man of the establishment – and too often religiously sterile. It was not only the poet Burns who saw the true nature of the *unco guid* (the excessively moralistic). WDB was making much of himself, but the gap between him and McLeish was still very great – unbridgeable as far as McLeish was concerned.

It was in 1891 that WDB secured promotion to teller status and returned to Fort William, now a man recognized. But it was not for long. The attraction between him and Barbara, which McLeish had thought 'cured' (not knowing his sister's duplicity), soon showed itself – and to Glasgow he was sent. For WDB it was a major move professionally; it became such personally, too. Glasgow has ever been the capital of the people's Scotland, and WDB quickly warmed to its great heart. Now senior teller at the Anderson branch, he had his work cut out in this thriving industrial and maritime city. Its urban warmth, its exciting civic spirit, the sheer dynamic of its churches and its lively cultural interests, overcame any sense of homesickness. Like his brother and his father before him, he felt at home among the lowlanders; never more so than in the religious work to which he put his hand in his spare time. His sermon-tasting reached new heights, his love of books new depths, and his evangelical fervour new strengths. To them was now joined a maturer biblical and theological awareness, somewhat liberated – but by no means completely – from the harsh Calvinism of his upbringing. As a young man his chief area of interest naturally remained with young men. He proved indefatigable in the cause of the YMCA and its doctrine of 'Christian manliness' – another aspect passed on to his son; and to his church, too, in its Bible Class work and the Boys' Brigade. But his deeper affections and needs remained in Fort William, with Barbara, a stalled fairy-tale romance.

The day of 25 July 1905 was one of WDB's best, when he learned at last that he had been appointed Manager at the Wick branch of the Bank of Scotland, in the far north-east. His goal had been reached. Sadly his parents were not alive to savour its joys with him. But Barbara was there, and so at forty-one and thirty-eight respectively, they announced their engagement and began planning their long-delayed wedding. Colonel McLeish's strictures were no longer valid; his future son-in-law had reached his level, in one area at least. Their invitation to him to share their joys in marriage was turned down flat. He churlishly refused to have any part in it. Was WDB's promotion so far north his last gambit – a forlorn attempt, once and for all, to have him moved away from his daughter's affections? His hardness of mind, of soul, suggest as much: such was the nature of his 'Reformed' Christianity; his inadequate 'understanding' of the Golden Rule; his self-interested love for his daughter. It burned a permanent scar into WDB's mind. It closed down any chance of an amicable relationship – in the short term at least. It undoubtedly influenced WDB as to the power and prevalence of *social* sin – an influence he and his son were ever to emphasize, not least through the national poet's mocking versification of the *unco guid*. WDB and Barbara married a year later, on 26 July 1906, 'according to the Free Church form', the Reverend John McIntosh (of Fort William) officiating, which must have caused some embarrassment to the inflexible father.

The word Wick comes from the Old Norse *vík*, meaning 'little bay'; and such it is – though it was then the busiest fishing port in the far north, a 'new town' that had been established in the eighteenth century to further the exploitation of the herring industry. Ancient rocks, sparse natural resources, scant population and remoteness, are the aspects which come to mind when one thinks of Caithness, the most northerly county of the mainland, nearly four hundred miles from Edinburgh, a thousand from London, only three hundred and fifty miles from Bergen. There is very much more than this to it, however, not least its open skies, broad vistas and an incredible, ethereal light which is almost tangible, as well as a soft-spoken, kindly people. The sombre mountains of the Highlands recede as one skirts Dingwall and the Black Isle, and the small triangle of mainland (delimited by John O'Groats, Thurso and Dunbeath, Wick being central to them) becomes an attractive coastal plain. Its light is not the brilliant light of the Aegean or southern California; it is almost a dawn light, somewhat cool and still, yet inspiring. It inspires not to the physical frenzies of bacchic mysteries, but to the quieter, more socially responsible issues of faith and works, to which WDB now gave himself zestfully.

Wick was once 'the herring metropolis of the world'. (The word 'daunted' derives from its practice of 'pressing down' fish into barrels.) But by the time WDB arrived much of it had gone, along with its many support industries. There is a sad comparison with today's even more rigorously run-down fishing communities: the fishing stocks had been depleted, the fleet run down – by over 90 per cent; the casual workers no longer came, the average age in the community was increasing, and their capital was being exported. Tourism had not yet begun – it was never to become very big, thanks to the great distances between it and the south. WDB was out on a limb, and WDB was undeterred. He loved it, and made it his home, his workplace, his mission field. He had arrived; and he had a beautiful and intelligent wife to prove it.

Barbara's new home was very different from that of Parade Cottage. It was not a centre of social prestige, but of work; without historical interest, or any other beyond the personal and the financial. For it was over her husband's bank, in the middle of the busy High Street – yet *High* Street at least, WDB may have thought gleefully! It was a two-storeyed, spacious and comfortable flat, with a small rear garden, and pleasant river walks which led to the sea. But that sea was very different from the one with which she was familiar. Now she gazed over the cruel North Sea, nothing separating the stone flags on which she stood from the coast of Norway. Harshness is its dominant feature, a grey, cold sea quite unlike the waters of Loch Linnhe which led out through Loch Lorne and the isles, gently warmed by the Gulf Stream that flows around Ireland from the south-western Atlantic. Yet, warmed by new love, the hearty greetings of their new neighbours, and stimulated by the picturesque town with its beautiful little harbour and the challenges of their new appointment, this world was their oyster. To it they devoted their energies and talents, prodigiously.

Their first year was naturally one of settling in, getting to know their new neighbours, making new friends, establishing themselves in the business, civic and religious life of the area. And discovering each other, after so long and so fraught a courtship, so much of it clandestine. It was an exhilarating time for them, culminating in their greatest joy, on 5 December 1907, with the birth of William, their first and only child. His birth certificate was the best Christmas greeting Barbara had ever received, despite the physical demands made on her at such a late stage in life. No fewer than eighty-eight William Barclays were registered that year, but none was more welcome, more loved or cossetted. And none was to be more famous – 'useful' to use his preferred word – in the service of God and humanity in the twentieth century and around the world. The real meaning of Christmas sounded as never before in their hearts and minds:

> To us a child is born
> To us a son is given...

It is sadly significant that, unlike his father and against Scottish tradition, Willie was given his father's but not his maternal grandfather's name. It must have been an especially sad moment for Barbara; and it is doubtful that she ever came to terms with her father's rejection. It was hard for WDB, too, who had done so much to win her heart and his father-in-law's approval. (Such accounts for Willie's own wrathful rejection of 'social' sin in all its forms.) Once again pain entered their lives. So they celebrated the occasion together and with their new northern friends.

It is often stated that the famous laird, Cameron of Lochiel, was Willie's godfather, but there is no evidence for this, and it is unlikely on every count. WDB was effectively unknown to him, if Barbara was not, and the antagonistic Daniel McLeish was merely the factor of his estate, not a personal friend. Further, Sir Donald Cameron had died in 1905, and was succeeded to the title by his son who was a serving officer in the Grenadier Guards. His disinterest in the child was shared by McLeish (though contacts between him and Willie's parents did become more frequent at a later stage, in fuller family holidays at Fort William, when a measure of superficial friendliness was achieved). WDB, for all his attempts to be otherwise, was too different. Tragically and paradoxically, he reminded his father-in-law of the son he had lost; unhappily and unforgivably, he was the one who had deprived him of his darling daughter.

Lord Moran commented of Churchill, one of Willie's great heroes, 'To understand Winston, you must go back to his childhood.' It is so with the subject of this book, William Barclay. The man he became, the great-hearted servant of God, the intellectual-cum-popularizer, the sportsman who became desk-bound and overweight, the workaholic who braved excruciating loss and personal calumny in the cause of his work, who loved comfort yet denied it to himself so often, who displayed charm and graciousness yet courted vulgarity, all find their roots in this time at Wick and his ensuing early years at Motherwell, with WDB and Barbara – sometimes to their grief. It was not merely the person who was nurtured and developed in these years, but the essential theology of the man, too, whose beliefs stood the test of time and the ferocity of assaults, albeit redefined here and there. As another of his heroes, J. M. Barrie, acutely remarked, 'the God to whom a little boy says his prayers has a face very like that of his mother'.

For all WDB's influence, and it was very great, it was *Barbara's* spirit and instincts that were written largest in their son; *her* faith and stability that saw him through the agonies that were to disrupt his life and expectations, personal and professional; *her* God was his God, born of faith and hope and love – the three graces, which she epitomized: goodwill incarnate, ever in action, a working faith.

If there was shortness of stature, a certain coarseness of feature, an aggression borne of inferiority in WDB, the very opposites were true of his wife. With her at his side he was twice the man, and he knew it. Yet it was her temperament that chiefly moulded his son; her theology that Willie took in with her milk; her fine principles that were bound up in the bedtime stories with which she regaled him; her patience that aided his growth, mentally and physically; her graciousness that reinforced his character; and her sense of social decorum that underscored – but not always! – his life. If he reflected in any way the One who came 'full of grace and truth', and tens of thousands bear witness that he did, then it was very largely thanks to her, despite his harsh voice and craggy features. She, above all, was the rock from which he was hewn; it was her blood that flowed in his veins; her sweetness that characterized his life – until, maturing among the students and local football supporters, he presented a new persona and a tougher attitude. His autobiographical comments from *Testament of Faith* are worth quoting:

> Whatever I have done in life it is because I have stood on the shoulders of my parents ... [Chesterton's] father had unlocked for him so many doors to wonderful things – and I too can say that of my father. My mother ... she *was* a saint ... She could write, she could paint, she could play the piano, but above all she was kind ... My mother, lovely in body and spirit, good all through.

Willie rarely spoke of his mother. His last memories of her were too painful, as we shall see. But in these few words he owns his deepest debts, her gift to him, and through him to the world: Scottish womanhood at its finest. WDB was a fortunate man, and William Barclay an even more fortunate son.

Within months of arriving at Wick, WDB had made his mark on the town, not only in his professional sphere but also religiously and culturally. While sifting through some old newspapers and magazines in the storeroom above the Carnegie Library at Wick, I chanced upon an old notebook, unkempt, uncatalogued and long disused. It turned out to be the Minutes of the old Wick Literary Society, a rich source of Barclayana. In it WDB's great love for English Literature was displayed; his first public pronouncements on it are recorded there. (His last was in the setting up of a school prize in his name at Motherwell.) One of the most interesting was made in December 1906, in a paper read before the Society, which had the title 'Tennyson's *Idylls of the King'*. The Society met in the Free Church Hall, its Committee (on which WDB quickly obtained a place) met in the Manse itself. Before the lecture WDB had already been busy nominating new members to the Society. Were they bank customers, one wonders, inveigled into literary pursuits for services rendered? It may not sound quite professional, but it rings true of WDB, ever energetic, ever the enthusiast. He lectured 'in a masterly fashion', the Secretary recorded, on the stories of Tennyson *'with their spiritual significances'* (his italics); he recounted each of the stories comprehensively, *'dwelling upon the characters and their allegorical meanings'*. This is pure Alexander Whyte, who was famous for such treatments – to which we may compare Henry Drummond's. It became pure Barclay – *père et fils*; but most tellingly *fils*.

WDB was a man who loved his Bible above all else. He was a great believer in the maxim of D. L. Moody: 'Either this Book will keep you from sin, or sin will keep you from this Book.' He had long been a member of the Church's *Daily Bible Readings* scheme, a practice he inculcated among the young people of his Bible Study class Sunday by Sunday, as well as those in the local YMCA and within his own home. Mrs Barclay was at one with him in this. But WDB had another tool in his fire, no less important: the Brotherhood organization. (Mrs Barclay was an enthusiastic worker for the Sisterhood.) This was also a movement with the stamp of Alexander Whyte and Henry Drummond *et alii* upon it, along with Arthur Samuel Peake, whose 1904 Hartley Lectures, *The Problem of Suffering in the Old Testament*, had been enthusiastically taken up by it. A little later, in 1908, Peake published his *Christianity, its Nature and its Truth*, which was so successful that the Brotherhood organization commissioned a special edition for its members. WDB, already a very serious bookman, thanks now to a salary worthy of the name (£120 p.a.!) and great personal contentment, filled his house with books – on literature, history, travel, poetry, but above all on biblical studies and theology. Not only was his house filled up with books, but it became an unofficial distribution centre for them. Not a few of my correspondents have recalled his prolific habit of giving books to ministers and young men. Peake's five-volumed work *The History of Christianity* became a regular gift to Willie's friends and others on ordination.

In 1911 the *John O'Groats' Journal* reported a celebration of the Wick Brotherhood. Now its President, WDB heralded the *six hundredth* member's admission (in a town whose population was nine thousand) – by announcing that its target membership for the next session had been increased by 33 per cent – to eight hundred. This is an indication of the vision and energy of WDB, which he also displayed in business, the Church and his social life. On 7 April of that year the same journal numbered him among the five Conveners of the United Free Church, and spoke of his chairing the Band of Hope (anti-alcohol) meetings – yet another strong interest – in which he was referred to as its founder. A few days later he was giving a magic lantern lecture, one of his favourite forms of address and in the van technologically. Meanwhile, Mrs Barclay went off with a posse of her friends: the local delegates to the General Assembly. Then WDB is found taking the General Salute alongside the Senior Scouts' Commissioner for Scotland and Ex-Provost Nicholson at their annual event. So it went on, night after night, week after week, month after month. Young Willie, his fair hair hinting auburn, growing delightedly and in the safe keeping of his governess, went from strength to strength. If not always the centrepiece of their attention, he was never very far from it.

An announcement on 30 August 1912 created a minor depression in the town. It was declared – typically by way of a public invitation from him to the members of his Bible Class – that WDB was moving on. The high summer advertisement explained that he wanted to meet them to say goodbye. A week later the *Journal* published a piece in praise of the Barclays. It was republished enthusiastically a week later in *The Motherwell Times*. Valedictory meetings sprang up from the many organizations in which they were engaged, at which speeches were made, telegrams of greetings and commiseration were read, and many gifts were offered. Among the latter was a fine silver inkstand and a solid silver sovereign purse given to WDB; Mrs Barclay was presented with a solid silver tea service; Willie got a silver chain. The only words on record left to us from Mrs Barclay derive from this time. Typically, they were of gratitude: 'I thank you very much for your beautiful gifts.'

THREE

MOTHERWELL SCHOOLBOY

Farewell to the Highlands, farewell to the North,
Birthplace of valour, the country of worth!

(Robbie Burns, *My heart's in the Highlands*)

Bank House, Motherwell, was as different from Bank House, Wick, as that had been from Parade Cottage, Fort William; and the town itself offered fewer comparisons. The Barclays had exchanged the rural beauties of the Highlands for the urban and industrialized lowlands, just fourteen miles from Glasgow, the third city in the United Kingdom.

The Motherwell atmosphere could scarcely have been more different from the crisp dawn light of rural Caithness, its clean air, its healthful climate. All this was surrendered for the smoke of Lanarkshire's largest town; fragrant ozone gave way to sootiness; fish and fresh produce to imported goods; cattle and poultry to coal and iron; the softly murmuring waters of the River Wick to the noisy turbulence of the Great Western Railway – only three hundred yards from their home; the clip-clop of horses' hooves on cobbles to the relentless clank of trams; the unhurried, quiet flow of Highland life to the stresses of an industrial bedlam.

This was now their home town and Willie never ceased to regard it as such, for all his pride in being a Highlander; ever faithful to what he believed to be one of its greatest assets: its football club. For the next seventeen years he and his parents lived there in happy and fruitful endeavour. His memories of it formed the backcloth to all that he knew of family and social life, and of the religious life, too. Whenever Willie referred to love of home and family, to parental harmony and mutual trust – WDB's 'explosive temper' notwithstanding – it was to Motherwell that his mind naturally turned: with strong memories of his loving and honoured parents, at the centre of the town's business life, prominent in its church life, privileged by emotional wealth and monetary sufficiency; to which should be added his own rich talents:

a phenomenal memory, a canny intellect; so many gifts, of mind and body. Here he sank a deep taproot, from which he drew sustenance for the next sixty-five years.

Yet from the first – no doubt resulting from the pampering he received at Wick and the effects of the very different southern climate – Willie became a sickly child. Unprepared for the onslaught, he became a prey to every militant microbe. In addition to the usual colds and sore throats, toothaches and tumbles, he became the victim of seven major children's diseases in five years. These problems mirrored those of other children at large, of course. In this respect Motherwell was more fortunate than neighbouring Glasgow (which gained its first Health Clinic as late as 1912), but life was still medically crude. In addition to many more positive things, the town thus endowed him with two health legacies: his early deafness, which has been ascribed to a bout of scarlet fever in 1913; and his harsh voice, which is said to result from similar causes in which his vocal chords were damaged. Neither of his parents suffered from deafness, and their voices were clear and melodious, such as the broadcasting world has learned to respect in Highlanders.

The latter problem was undoubtedly worsened by his heavy smoking from an early age, though in this we have the advantage of hindsight. The medical effects of tobacco were not very well known until the late fifties, by which time Willie was truly addicted. We should not forget that many evangelical clergy had smoked – for example, Charles Haddon Spurgeon, whose sermons were another great influence on WDB and his son.

Willie, it has to be said, became successful in spite of some harsh natural disabilities: he was virtually stone-deaf by his mid-thirties. His voice became a matter of concern to his parents, as did his Motherwellian (not Glaswegian) accent which he deliberately fostered. The former became a bigger problem on its 'breaking', which created a marked self-consciousness on his part. It was abetted by rampant acne, from which his father had also suffered, and which left his face pock-marked. It is doubtless from such influences that his profound shyness obtained; that and the overdominant WDB and his forceful attitudes.

He loved his new home town. Many years later he admitted missing the noise of Motherwell: 'the rattle of the tramcars, the sound of the railway engines, and the noise of the traffic'. By now a majestic silence had fallen on his world, a silence which penetrates his writings. It may be seen in his mystical aptitudes, his preference for solitude, his romantic spirit – made concrete in the complete absence of auditory ry in his written work: the sounds of nature (birds, bees, wind, ...ooks, etc.), much as he enjoyed its beauties, even the idiosyncrasies of human speech and song are missing, though he loved song passionately. This was compensated for by his love for literature – poetry especially – and music. As with many deaf people, he enjoyed the latter immensely, and enjoyed producing it – though some musicologists cringed. His early piano-playing and his parents' love of concerts broadened into a passion; his marvellous memory kept alive in his head tunes and rhythms and their meanings, not least those of Gilbert and Sullivan, which he knew in their entirety.

His age was Edwardian, proud of its Victorian links – of humanity's unlimited capacity to progress, its power over the natural order, its culture, its empirical prestige, its literary and scientific successes. To these were added its comfort, esteem, confidence – and optimism; stimulants by which he grew up, reinforced as they were by a solid, dependable society, and his family's prominent place within it. From this developed his goodwill ethic, which demanded that if you believe in man and his God-given status and potential, you must recognize this in your attitudes to all people. To love became his most prominent ethic, and kindness was its most practical by-product, which often got him into trouble for its universal commitment. His father's position in the community and his mother's almost regal demeanour – supplemented by their live-in maid, Rebecca, who was decked out in black-and-white lace and finery – did not deter him from this. Nor did his boyhood summers, which were memorably spent at his grandfather's cottage, now even more prestigious and interesting to the growing lad fed on tales of derring-do, the '45 revolt and the famous blackthorn stick.

Modelled on the lifestyle of his father-in-law (despite their estrangement), WDB's home reflected that Victorian elegance expected of the successful men of the day. Some of Willie's former friends have spoken of it with awe – in addition to the warm welcome they received into an obviously 'high-class', if classless, home. WDB wore the accustomed 'uniform' of his type: morning suit, frock coat, wing collar, gold Albert, bowler hat, and spats. Willie's friends noted it, and Willie never forgot the effect it had on them – and on him in observing them. Mrs Barclay was dressed to match, demure and perfectly soignée; ostentation was never present; quality and excellence were never absent. Cleanliness and neatness were founded on the more visible aspects of her spirituality (in the French sense of that word), heightened by their solid oak furniture, silver plate and superb china. They were aware of their high position, but we err if we imagine them aloof or starchy. They were not. Willie's ability to be 'all things to all men' lay at the heart of WDB's views, and his insistence on serving his fellow citizens. He met civic leaders with ease, minor royalty with grace and aplomb; he played golf with the Secretary of the Bank of Scotland; and he dined – never wined, for he was enthusiastically teetotal – with the captains of industry.

Tough WDB could be when required, principled he ever was; people of all sorts were welcome to make their approach, and did so. He might be found in a high-class office or at a hotel reception in the morning; he was just as likely to be in a hovel in the evening, comforting its family in their reduced circumstances, and generous to them to boot. But it was chiefly his conversation that did the trick. Alive to a full humanity, his talk was full of anecdotes, *jeux d'esprit* and *bons mots*. Improving tales were slipped in, not least the maxims of the Haddington writer, Samuel Smiles, whose best-seller *Self-Help* had aided WDB himself in his developing years. (This book was chosen – in 1870 – to aid aspiring Japanese to attain western know-how and powers of success. It was one of the first books to be translated into Japanese. By the end of the century it had sold almost a quarter of a million copies; it was last reprinted in 1996.) Some of Smiles' key phrases very adequately sum up WDB's attitudes – and those were passed on to, and imbibed by, his only son: e.g. ceaseless resolution, unflinching diligence, invincible determination, strenuous energy, unflagging persistence, indefatigable zest, ardent exertions. They provide an accurate portrait of William Barclay.

Bank House was naturally full of books, and splendidly representative of the standard authors of the day, alongside – never far from Willie's reach – the 'kailyard authors': Ian MacLaren, J. M. Barrie, S. R. Crockett, and Annie S. Swan. The name of William Robertson Nicoll, a fellow Highlander and leading member of the United Free Church, was soon to echo throughout the land, and well beyond it, through his roles as editorial advisor to Hodder & Stoughton and founder of one the most illustrious weeklies in the history of publishing: the *British Weekly*. In all these names we may see influences on Willie. Nicoll's views became a touchstone of literature, secular and religious, a literary mentor to the masses – foremost among whom was the avid WDB. Fortunate the boy brought up in such a household, as Willie well knew. Questioning WDB one day, he asked, 'Daddy, when you're dead, will all these books belong to me?' The answer was affirmative, of course, and in time many of them did become his – as many a visiting Professor covetously noted.

In the meantime he was wisely pleasured on more suitable fare for a young boy: Bunyan, Defoe, Swift, Scott and many more, much of this at his mother's side, their readings and piano duets – for she taught him herself – now being central features of his life. Did he suffer from this closeness, as John Buchan (another of his favourite authors) suffered from his? The suggestion has been made that Buchan's natural development was stifled by his mother's overcaring. I do not think that this can be applied too much to Willie. Barbara Barclay was too intelligent for that, and the presence of the masculine-minded WDB and the down-to-earth Rebecca were balancing mechanisms.

Apart from the aspects already mentioned, WDB, for all his seriousness and businesslike demeanour, was a great human, and humane, character. He maintained his sporting interests until late in life: golf and football notably, but also shinty, rowing and cricket. Willie and he even played football together on Fort William's steep hillsides, portly as he was. He projected an all-round personality that was the pride of Willie and the grudge of his friends' fathers. There seemed to be nothing that he could not do, and do well. His son was proud to have stood on his father's shoulders. His friends and their fathers were in awe of WDB – not least as banker and school governor – whose 'manly' emphases ran harmoniously through his life and preaching.

As at Wick, so at Motherwell. WDB threw himself with bold panache into everything within reach, civic, religious and educational. He applied for the post of School Board Treasurer within five weeks of arriving in the town – but was unsuccessful, a rare event in his life. (It was an elected position and he was virtually unknown.) A little later he was at the forefront of a public debate about a female teacher's rights to continue to teach after her conversion to Roman Catholicism, a very bold move from someone with his Free Church background.

For the next five years WDB was caught up in torrential activity outwith his banking work, which makes one marvel at his conviction and energy. As we noted earlier, he preached regularly in thirteen out of the town's fourteen churches, to children as well as young people and adults. He was an elder of – and a very conscientious visitor for – his local church, Dalziel United Free Church. His activities in this regard remind me of a deacon in a church of which I was minister who refused to visit people precisely because he was a bank manager! WDB had no such falsity; nor did he hide his light under a ledger, still less a profit and loss account. His faith was active and took first place: his first love. He worked assiduously for Women's Meetings, local and national Brotherhood groups, the YMCA, various Bible classes,

Christian Workers' Association meetings, Christian Unions, Band of Hope societies, Bible Society meetings, good-cause concerts, and literary and musical associations: a man of many parts.

These all claimed his time and energy, as did the treasurerships of not a few organizations, including that of his own church. No barriers were raised by him as to creed or dogma – he was found at the Hallelujah Mission Hall as much as he was found at the Church of Scotland, though Free-Churchmanship was his deepest conviction, to him a style of life, of belief, not just an accident of birth. These were the years when the churches of Scotland were hammering out the reunion which eventually took place in 1929, a long hard road which tested the people's patience as well as their convictions, forcing them to argue against the malicious chatterings of misrepresenters amid downright abuse. It is a measure of the man that he could entertain in his house leaders from all sides supporting church reunion, and their highly vocal opponents. His Christianity was muscular and well informed, biblical and charitable, like his son's later: a gospel of goodwill.

He never lost the Moody touch, nor was he defensive about it; evangelical earnestness was his hallmark. Phrases like 'the common touch', 'a gifted children's speaker', 'stories tripping out of him', are scattered throughout the press comments on this extraordinary lay ministry. The evangelists Chapman and Alexander swept through Scotland in 1913/14, as Moody and Sankey had done many years earlier. WDB threw himself into their work, whipping up support, arranging meetings, raising and donating money, diluting scepticism, negating criticism, handing out hymn sheets – and sitting on platforms.

One regret that WDB had long held, which McLeish vaunted over him, concerned his lack in speaking the Gaelic. No true Highlander could fail to do so, and this troubled him, even after his move south where he was a very active member of Highland societies and meetings. So, at fifty-five years of age, he took up its study, astonishing everyone by his application and success. He became so fluent that he frequently chaired and spoke at meetings of the local Highlanders' Association; he was never happier than when reading the Gaelic Bible to them at their meetings, as he did at home with his wife.

These were halcyon years for the Barclays. But the shadows of war changed things. Soon the first zeppelin raids on Scotland were made, and the civilized world lurched into madness and obscenity. In this, predictably, WDB found a part to play, lecturing wherever there was

need on 'the German menace', magic-lantern-style and otherwise,
calling attention to the justice of the Allies' position. In this the
Brotherhood meetings offered a special opportunity, as their cause
was torn apart at the hands of men of indifference and questionable
principle. There could be no doubt that the old order was disappearing,
and WDB – an arch exponent of it – fought for it with all his powers.

An important family event of this time was the death, at eighty,
of Daniel McLeish, amid civic and other honours. His youngest
daughter's husband was, ironically, the administrator of his estate,
and of many of the public proceedings. A fine marble stele was
erected by WDB in his honour, next to the (even taller) Linton
memorial. It was positioned facing west, towards Loch Linnhe, yet
with a good view to the north-east and Ben Nevis, which McLeish
had climbed several times – as had WDB, one of his many successful
uphill struggles. It was at this time that 'Aunt Bella' came to live with
the Barclays permanently, increasing their small household to five.

During all this Willie himself made good progress, justifying earlier
hopes of his parents, and developing his precocity and talents at
school. No information has been preserved about his elementary
schooling – overseen by Barbara – which was much disrupted
through illness, but his junior and senior phases are very different.
WDB had refused to send his son to one of the elitist schools of
Glasgow or Edinburgh for politico-religious reasons, rejecting elitism
in every form. So to Dalziel High School Willie went. It was, he said,
'comprehensive long before that term was ever used'. This went
against his wife's view, but WDB 'ruled' his house; his son was left to
make his own way by dint of hard work – and every conceivable
parental encouragement and pressure.

DHS, as it was known, had a modest but solid reputation for getting
the best out of its pupils, not least in sport. Its nearby neighbour and
staunch competitor, Hutchinson's Grammar School, was the real leader
educationally; it was the sort of school – it was the sort of age in
Scotland – where copies of the *Hebrew Concordance* by Brown, Driver and
Briggs (over a thousand pages long) no less were given as prizes. Even
theological students today would have to decline such a volume. In the
examinations for 1920 Willie was placed first in English (always his best
subject at school), also in History, Geography, Mathematics, Science,
French and Latin. He was unplaced in German – and never reached
real proficiency in it – perhaps influenced by the anti-German feelings
of his time. Whenever he wished to impart a 'continental' attitude, it
was to French that he gravitated, as university library records and his

own writings show; a curious attitude, as Scots were then in the fore-front of popularizing German ideology and learning. These results were thereafter repeated with slight fluctuations until his school days ended, though classical Greek was added to them, in which he also excelled. Indeed, it took over from the others and became his real subject – the language of his heart as well as his head, as we shall see.

It was during this summer of 1920, aged thirteen, that he decided to become a minister. It followed a sermon he heard while on holiday at Fort William. After it he took a walk along High Street, sat down on a stone placed there to aid horse-mounting – which for ever after-wards marked his private Bethel – and dedicated himself to God. Some sermon! From its challenge millions around the world have benefited, though we should not forget that behind it lay the unrelenting influence of his father and mother.

By the time Willie reached the senior level, aged sixteen, the school was attracting some criticism. Its rector (headmaster), David Grieg, was unwell and nearing retirement, and things began to slip. His character was said to be humourless – which did not go down well with such of Willie's temperament. Worse, discipline began to slacken, taking the intellectual and sporting standards with it. This changed radically in 1923 when David Anderson MC took over. The school was literally revolutionized. Discipline rose overnight, and with it fear – the fear of the tawse.

To Willie's regret the school was made coeducational. He soon changed his mind, however, doubtless to his father's displeasure, and befriended a number of young females. Some of these became mem-bers of a group known as 'Barclay's harem', a non-sexual group which obtained cigarettes for him, among other things. (He used to blow the smoke up the chimney when his parents were out, which signifies a change in his relationship with them familiar to many parents of teenagers.) From this point on a clash of wills developed between him and his father. This grew more heated as time went by, and as WDB saw, or thought he saw, his treasured ambitions being dashed. The peacemaker was Barbara Barclay, ever applying oil to the troubled waters that for so long had been serene.

This change in headship had an immediate effect on Willie, whose work rate increased decisively, his results accordingly. WDB was delighted – and offered an annual prize for excellence in English in response, though he held it back until after his son had left to safe-guard himself against embarrassments: there was no question at the time as to who towered over the student body in English Literature.

We know that on at least one occasion the ebullient Willie fell foul of the rector and his dreaded tawse. Despite his emphasis on masculinity and 'masculine Christianity', Willie hated authoritarianism and militarism in any form. It was perhaps this which alienated him from Anderson – though he also hated corporal punishment. Significantly, the rector does not get a single mention in Willie's glowing description of his schooldays – a Freudian omission.

He was again placed first in the boys' section, though annoyingly pipped for the top position, not for the last time, by Irene Tyrrell – emphatically not a harem member. One of Anderson's most celebrated actions was to introduce the music of Gilbert and Sullivan to the school, which captured Willie's heart and imagination, though he overstates its influence on him in his autobiography. It was only introduced in his final year. About this time a German measles epidemic swept through the school: 'That is another grievance we have against the Germans,' growled someone at the School Board Meeting. Shortly after this followed the death of Samuel Dugald Barclay, WDB's nephew, whose boat was torpedoed while on active service. It was Willie's first encounter with violent death.

Despite his ministerial intention, Willie's religious interests were not overdeveloped. Church attendance was *de rigueur* of course, as was his membership of 'Sabbath School'. He knew his catechism inside out, and fared well in Bible knowledge and such-like competitions, as well he might. He had read the usual 'improving' books of the time, and warmed to the tales of the Covenanters and the early missionaries, such as David Livingstone, who hailed from just a few miles away. As a member of the Boys' Brigade he was enthusiastic, and soon gained his stripes and badges. Alexander Whyte called that organization 'a youth's entrance to manhood'. In this Willie surpassed himself, and he remained a lifelong supporter, eventually becoming one of its national Vice-Presidents. But sport was now his great passion, in and out of school, and that in profusion: swimming, tennis, cricket, golf and especially football. Indoors, he played a good game of billiards – not approved of by WDB – as well as table tennis. And then there was the dancing, even less approved of as the gateway to worldliness and much worse: the harbinger of the 'twittering twenties' and its superficiality.

Willie was wont to overemphasize his sporting abilities. He was not chosen to play in the Schools' football cup final, and reports of his other abilities are not ecstatic. But he made his mark, and was commended mainly for his exuberance. Take this, for example: 'Barclay is wholehearted and fast; can cross a nice ball, but his ball control is weak.' Another match proved 'that Shaw was not a forward, nor Barclay a half-back'. When chosen to play for the YMCA he failed to get any mention, though his team won. However, in his final year school sports day, Willie, who had always shown acumen in running, came first in the 100-yard (at 11.2 seconds) and 220-yard (at 26.2 seconds) races. He was placed third in cricket ball throwing. It was not a bad show for one described by his friends as 'Bun Barclay', who justified the nickname by the sustained enjoyment of his food – not least from Rebecca's abilities in the kitchen – which led to its enjoyment on an even more lavish scale in later life.

He gave high praise to some of his teachers: among them Geordie Robertson for Latin; Jimmy 'Monkey-Brand' Paterson for Greek (the epithet comes from the tobacco he used; he was one of the youngest members of staff); and A. D. Robertson for English Literature. But it was the school experience itself that he recalls most vividly, especially following Anderson's arrival. In addition to the changes mentioned, the rector introduced two further aspects: 'At Home' meetings, which were thrown open to friends and parents, and which increased the popularity ratings of the school dramatically; and a school magazine – *The Dalzielian* – on whose board staff and students sat together. Willie had already caught the eye of the rector and was accordingly appointed Coeditor, his first literary appointment, aged sixteen.

During these days nothing is mentioned of his ministerial ambitions; they were almost certainly eclipsed by his teachers' and rector's enthusiasms for his pronounced abilities in English Literature. Even his friends have reported that this was the direction they expected him to take. Proofreading, however, was obviously not his forte, as we may see from a number of slips in *The Dalzielian*, including the misspelling of Julian Huxley's name. The magazine did give vent to Willie's prose and poetic inclinations, with the following piece appearing in the second edition, when he was about to leave:

> Within these four gray walls for twelve long years
>   The even tenor of my way has lain.
>   I have been bound, in youth, by learning's chain
> To tread instruction's tortuous path with fears
> And in my conquests I have laughed, and tears
>   Have been my only mead, when I would fain
>   Have sent my cheerless tasks to Pluto's reign.
> But now the hour to quit thee, school, appears
> I sport no more in careless joys of heart.

> To learning's business must I turn, from play,
> From youthful joy to manhood's sterner day.
> Alas! I find it wondrous hard to part.
>   I never saw thy pleasures till they fade away
>   The days are unappreciated while they stay.
>
> The stony paths of Maths I've trod with fear;
>   At French's tasks I've labour'd late at night
>   That I may gain upon its myst'ries, light;
> Among the whirling eddies did I steer
> Of thy forgotten tongue, O Latin, dear
>   To pedants, with thy tales of blood and might.
>   No less I've journey'd through Greek's Stygian night
> Until with Xenophon, I seem'd to cheer.
> The sea! the sea! With poets I have soared
>   To Elysian fields, in fancy's highest flight,
>   Whilst over wrong, the victory of right
> As all day long the crash of cannon roared,
>   The book of history to me has shown
>   As I approached the steps of learning's throne.
>
> The dawn of schooldays was to me a pain,
> Their sometimes weary course I did disdain;
> But now I ask to prolong, in vain,
> The way which I alas! did often stain
>   With hours of idleness and wasted time.
>   But now the final bell's last ring doth chime;
>   The curtain's down; and this the youthful mime
>   Is finished, and I tell in faltering rhyme
> My last regrets, my many hopes, my fears
> For times that are gone by, and future years.

Other pieces by him were offered, but this is useful in manifesting his
state of mind, his approach prior to going to university. The triple aspect
of fear is surprising in one renowned for his confidence and optimism; and we may wonder from whence came his reference to mead
– a cigarette-like delinquency, or merely a literary artifice? Another piece
he offered was titled 'Regret'. The beginning of his schooldays, he tells
us, was 'a pain' – as was their ending. Pain, we shall see, came to be
written deeply into the texture of the life and theology of this young
man, who even then was nonetheless asserting his goodwill.

FOUR

GLASGOW GRADUATE

'There were debts, and there was a fellowship.'

(William Barclay)

Prior to matriculating, Willie was required to sit the all-Scotland examinations which not only determined university places but also some important bursaries. Thus, on 3 July 1925, over five hundred young people sat down to several hours of crucial testing. DHS had good cause to congratulate itself on the outcome. Three of its pupils were placed in the first twenty, and six in the first hundred – results that put it on an equal footing with Hamilton Academy, with which it had broken many a competitive lance. Willie himself started 'learning's business' with great aplomb.

The local paper commented that it was 'probably the best representation from any school in the west of Scotland'. Among the DHS pupils, Willie came second; Laura Bowyer came first – beaten by a female yet again. It was sweetened by his old rival, Irene Tyrell, coming six places below him, though she had taken the much coveted position of *dux* at DHS, with Willie as runner-up. He was thirteenth overall, an impressive result. For this he gained the Biggart Memorial Bursary of £25 per annum – no mean amount in those days – which added to his kudos at home. It was his first earned income, a good start to his undergraduate years.

He registered for his Arts course on 5 October, a week before classes were due to commence, just short of his eighteenth birthday. His form shows a confident, neat and legible hand, full of character. It was soon to deteriorate. He stated in *Testament of Faith* that the over-scrupulous Professor Macaulay used to make him read his papers to him because of his poor writing, but it was not the whole matter. Additionally, the Professor told him that unless he got rid of his 'Glasgow [sic] accent' he would never get anywhere in the Church; a comment soon emptied of point. But there is reason to believe that 'the great theologian' was especially interested in him, and hopeful of developing his gifts to good use. 'I was very close to him,' Willie remarked, admitting to being on first-name terms with him.

His second task was to acquire the recommended textbooks and notebooks he needed. He enjoyed the thirteen-mile train journey into Glasgow, shortly to be his daily activity in the company of a few friends – and the more open enjoyment of his cigarettes. It was part of the London–Glasgow line; travelling on it gave them a sense of cosmopolitanism which they cherished. Willie – ever an exuberant train spotter – was able to develop his hobby yet further in journeying to the university. By this time he was the acknowledged 'leader' of the small gang from Motherwell, and enjoyed the extra status it gave him. He made one of his rare political moves by joining the Liberal Club, an influence obtained from his father whose great idol, William Robertson Nicoll, was a leading figure. It was his first social commitment, which was to grow over the years and become more and more dominant, though he never became a party man politically.

By contrast with this, neither of the Christian societies – SCM (Student Christian Mission) or SCF (Student Christian Fellowship) – gained his membership. He was already well occupied at home with the BB and the YMCA, as well as his local church generally, and those societies' interminable internecine war (largely over the interpretation – conservative versus liberal – of biblical and doctrinal texts) he found wasteful of time and effort. Theological squabbling never interested him. He was tolerant towards others' beliefs – a key part of his goodwill attitude – but in matters of biblical interpretation he was still very much under the influence of the (more or less fundamentalist) Free Church, and of his father particularly. He did attend the Religion and Life campaigns, which were backed by the SCM (and rejected by the SCF; instead it held its own miniscule prayer meetings in protest at the dangers of ecumenism and false doctrine!). His main 'extramural' interests lay in the preaching of such eminent thinkers as Dean Inge and William Temple, who spoke adventurously to packed halls of young people.

Such free time as he had was spent in games of billiards with Duncan Black and others in the Students' Union, and in lively conversation. Nearer home he founded, with Willie Bishop and others, the Twenty-Five Club. It met in Fraser's Tea-Rooms, in Muir Street, Motherwell, and flourished for five years, an ad hoc discussion group which occupied itself with the day-to-day issues: of politics, literature, music, film and sport; always sport. Willie was naturally a leading light in this group – as he tended to be whenever he turned his hand to anything: a WDB trait. In Glasgow this same habit took him to the Eldon Street coffee-shop, where similar joys predominated. Later, he was to transfer his affections to Craig's Tea-Rooms, as we shall see. Such activities should not veil his essential shyness. With friends and in familiar places he was the soul of the party, ebullient and extrovert; with strangers he was reticent and very careful of observing the maximum courtesies: Barclay's antisyzygy (to use David Daiches' splendid word; in psychological terms, cognitive dissonance), the contrast of opposites.

His principle first-year subjects were Honours Latin ('Humanity' as it was called) and Greek. English Literature was also offered, but now began to take a back seat. For Latin he was in the hands of the polymath, John Swinnerton Phillimore, a renowned scholar and the successor to the great Gilbert Murray. Phillimore had, in addition to his scholarship, a pronounced teaching ability, and an immense rapport with his students. He believed that the teacher's main job was to instil a love for his subject in his students, and he did so. Three-hundred-plus eager listeners would pack into his lecture room, and they not only learned assiduously but often broke into boisterous song, Phillimore's own voice holding its own among the delighted songsters. One of their favourites was, perhaps oddly, 'Ye mariners of England'. Willie was entranced by such virtuosity. Here was a scholar indeed, who wore his great learning lightly – yet preserved that common touch which gilded life with special meaning. Tragedy soon touched Willie in this, however, for in his second session his new-found hero contracted the terminal illness which took him to his bed, from which he never rose. Heroically, he offered to mark his students' papers from his sickbed. It was under Phillimore that Willie won his first undergraduate prize, for which he had to visit the Professor in his sickroom, an unforgettable experience. There is not a little of Phillimore in the later William Barclay.

In Greek, which was beginning to claim stronger affections even over his beloved Latin – there is so much more of real life among the Greeks than their more austere neighbours! – he sat under the teaching of Gilbert Austin Davies, 'the most fastidious and meticulous scholar' he had met to date. It was Davies who took his nascent love of linguistic nuance and meaning (imparted by Paterson in the tower-room at DHS), and raised it to new *and dynamic* heights, thus begetting one of Willie's most favoured teaching methods, reflected so usefully in his classwork and books. From this time dates his use of notebooks (long lost, alas), which he always carried with him as *aides-mémoire*, in

which he captured the erring minute – a habit some of his friends
found irksome. But it paid off, as did his conscientious set work which
usually gained him top marks. Unlike some students, he never cut this
homework; rather, he excelled in it, delighting in the joys of surprise
and discovery. He was usually found happily ensconced in his bed-
room-cum-study above the bank, if need be late into the night – but
more often in the early mornings – surrounded by his large collection
of books, and a biscuit or three to encourage the mind's appetite. Free
of the wrong sort of competitive edge, he made it his business to help
his fellow students, even those who preferred to spend their time
in less scholarly ways; more than one gained good marks through
Willie's help, and one actually put the gaining of his degree down
to him. Naturally competitive (in the right way), he never allowed
such rivalry to prevent him helping someone in need: goodwilling all
the way.

In English Literature, his former first love, Willie sat under
Professor MacNeile Dixon, famous in that and subsequent generations
for his book *The Human Situation*. If Willie was entranced with Terence
and Cicero, Catullus and Horace *et alii* under Phillimore, and a like
range of literary greats under Davies, he now fell willing prey to
Chaucer, Spenser, Shakespeare, Milton, Dryden and others under
MacNeile Dixon. This was an area in which his father and mother
had large interests, and soon Willie's shelves were graced with first
editions, and rare copies at that – to the admitted envy of his friends.
It was particularly from this popular Irishman, MacNeile Dixon, that
he learned the secret of clear writing, as well as the importance of
humour, both of them key aspects in his later work (and not always
noticed – still less understood – by those who criticized his tongue-in-
cheek style). As with Humanity and Greek, so with English: Willie
came top, gaining the English Literature Prize alongside the Latin and
Greek; prizes, he said, that were infinitely worth the hard work 'when
I see my mother's face'.

The second year was little different. Latin authors and Roman
history were now his chief delight – that and cycling around the
countryside, shouting mischievously in passing to his friend Duncan
Black (who objected to Willie's early-morning routines) such comments as, 'Fifty lines of Ovid this morning!' This second year was
notable for something outwith his university work, an indication of
his interior interests which were never paraded by him, and later
surprised even some of his friends: he conducted his first church service and preached his first sermon, at the local Baptist church. He had

already spoken at Young Men's Guild meetings prior to this – but that is a very different thing. The day would come when he would fill the most important Baptist churches, as well as those of other denominations as well as his own, but this 'first' was very special. Fifteen years had passed since he decided to be a minister; many were the occasions when his parents wondered if his decision had gone by the board. Now it reasserted itself. Willie had found his *métier*; his parents were delighted.

In his third year the range of academic interests increased with the addition of Moral Philosophy, which he read alongside another William Barclay (of Troon), to the perplexity of the tutors. His Professor in this subject was Archibald Allan Bowman, whose life was also claimed by early death – another unnerving blow. Willie found in Bowman more than an encouraging ally, so much so that Duncan Black (later Professor of Mathematics at Cambridge) contended that Willie had been 'spoiled' by this Professor's fulsome compliments and 'excessive proximity'. But Willie, who loved and even needed such encouragement, was not the sort to have his head turned by it. He gained more than philosophical information and discrimination from Bowman, for the Professor was an addict of the writings – philosophical and other – of William Temple, later Archbishop of Canterbury. His influence encouraged the deepening of Willie's philosophical base, which many have failed to see. The man who could feed tasty snacks to multitudes shaped his beliefs among the great systems and problems that have challenged mankind from the beginning.

One aspect of Temple in particular struck home, and became a key element of his thinking: that of the universe as 'sacramental'. If WDB's influence had erred in placing too much emphasis on the spiritual in his son's development, here was a concept that challenged and rectified it; which agreed with Willie's exuberance for everyday life and living; which argued for the unity of secular and sacred, the world and God – a truth which ran ever more strongly in his life and work from now on. In *Testament of Faith* it actually led to the espousal of a moral dynamic in the concept of evolution – which some have judged merely an indulgence in kite-flying, a favourite game of his. But it was more than that: behind it lay his understanding of the nature of God and thus of the world.

In due course Willie sat his most important examinations to date, ones that would determine his entire future: his finals. A first-class pass was essential to one such as he, and he prepared for it as never before. Happily he was victorious, and gained not only the coveted place in the First Class but a clear victory over those girls who had competed and won so often against him. Sweet victory! The rest of the summer was spent in a delicious haze of joy and contentment, recovering from his exertions by idling around town, lazing in the parks, random reading, and – best of all – tramping and cycling with his friends, largely from the YMCA. He had developed another passion: he took pleasure-trips up the Clyde with the boisterous citizens of Glasgow – of which his father vehemently disapproved – enjoying its stunning views, the thrill of travel, the singing and laughter of the crowds, their essential camaraderie, that particular evocation of joyous humanity.

The Barclays decamped to Glasgow on 1 July 1929, following the retirement of W. D. Barclay JP from the bank, after fifty years' service. They took a rented flat at 198 Wilton Street, in a three-storeyed block which was shared with four other tenants. This was Willie's first experience of such communal living – only the stairs were truly communal, of course – and he liked it. It gave him an extra insight into humanity (Glaswegians are ultra-human) that was to become his essential field of work. WDB's retirement was one of great joy, the completion of work well done. It was embodied in the happy receipt of many gifts from countless sources of work and influence, and was celebrated with a round of parties and farewell speeches. It marked a turning point in the small family too: WDB was settling down, and WB was setting out – but not before completing the long training programme to which he had committed himself.

It was not all enjoyment and hope, however. A deepening shadow now lay across them. Mrs Barclay had not been herself for some time. Uncomplaining, she had typically overlooked her symptons and turned aside their concerns. Worrying questions were nevertheless left in the minds of her menfolk and her sisters. The shadow was all too soon to turn to a midnight darkness.

Willie's academic interests also took a sharp turn. The Church of Scotland had recently introduced a ruling by which students intending for the ministry should take a course away from the traditional arts-plus-divinity qualifications, in order to acquaint them more closely with modern society, a view WDB favoured enthusiastically. It was a first-rate innovation, given the increasing technicalities of modern life. Thus Willie registered for a course in Political Economy, in the process upsetting one of his best friends, Duncan Black, who now woke up to the clear and disturbing religious aim of his friend. He is adamant that the idea of Willie entering the ministry 'had not previously been mentioned'; he was very upset to hear of it, not least because 'the one genius I knew was abandoning his genius for the sake of gain'. A rift developed between them. How could Bun, with all this linguistic ability, with such a superb mind, overstocked as it was with data and promise, opt for parish cares and an outworn theology? The years went by and the rift happily healed. Professor Black came to reverse his judgement, admitting that 'on the contrary, his genius used Bun for its own ends'.

WDB never had any such misconceptions. Unable to keep pace with his son linguistically, he was now delighted to find him coursing through subjects he had himself long delighted in, and was able to add a practical touch to the economic arguments and theories Willie was mastering. Little did he realize that, one day, they would be celebrated civically as a monumental contribution to the nation's war effort. So, in place of the delights of Homer and Shakespeare, Cicero and Wordsworth, and a host of others, Willie now substituted Adam Smith and Sydney Webb, and above all, Alfred Marshall the Cambridge economist – exchanging the nectar of the gods for the sometimes brackish water of industrialized accounting: a sobering challenge to his one-world ideology. It was a year of unusual and intense discipline, into which Willie plunged himself, measuring and weighing questions of value, agents of production, distribution and exchange, and pondering the full range of economic theorizing, its history and its geography. He gained his certificate in PE with distinction and was again awarded a prize, from which he swiftly moved on to the things which really excited him, which mattered most. 'Manhood's sterner day' was completed; it was now time to immerse himself directly in the things of God.

FIVE

THE SCHOOL OF GOODWILL

'Glory to God, and ... goodwill towards men.'

(Luke 2:14; trad. tr.)

For a good time now I've lived by this law:
the good man is born to serve others
The man who devotes himself to his own advantage
is a dead weight in any common enterprise
a useless burden, good for nothing but himself

(Euripides, *The Children of Heracles*)

The 'School of Goodwill' may seem an odd description of a man's post-graduate course, in this case the specific training for his future work. It may seem an even stranger description for Divinity, 'the Queen of Sciences', given the modern more politicized ethics and behaviour of some of its proponents; but if self-sacrificing love was ever the hall-mark of Christianity, then it is apt. It is certainly so of 'Bun Barclay' who, after his privileged undergraduate years, now garlanded with success, stood poised at the door to his future. The message of the heavenly host uniquely recorded by Luke, the most *human* of the Gospel writers, was fast becoming Willie's professionally – as it had long been his personally.

He had shown this from his earliest days. Nothing has been recorded of him which in any way suggests less than a full personality, characterized by respect, thoughtfulness and consideration for others, one identified by the most practical expressions of it even when his own interests were at stake. From here on it hallmarks his character: in his maintaining a positive and robust attitude towards life and humanity; in his readiness to share what he had; in his turning aside from anything that was patronizing, cheap or small-minded. Unlike his critics, who all too often took goodwill for weakness – even his family doubted him at times – he opened his heart as well as his mind; he refused to sit in the seat of the scornful and, as a result, began a ministry whose fruitfulness was notable for its adhesion to the New Testament, a nobility of mind and a largeness of heart.

His one-time hero, Winston Churchill, once suggested that there were four components which constituted greatness in a nation: 'in war, resolution; in defeat, defiance; in victory, magnanimity; in peace, goodwill'. They are a good description of personal greatness, too. Willie was resolute when faced with conflict, defiant when under attack, magnanimous when successful, and ever goodwilled. The latter point is out of fashion today, as are good manners and respect for others. Television 'soaps' and modern humour are the pre-eminent example of its negation, and reveal what excites people today: one-upmanship, nastiness, self-interest. Smartness rules. Cyril Connolly defined the concept by coining the neologism 'smartistic', which is more precise, even if it never caught on. It is the trademark of the upwardly mobile, the Sloane Ranger, the yuppie, of 'Essex man' (as the modern materialist is now called in Britain): the first-born of Thatcherism – and the smug self-centred behaviour that flows from it; the ultimate deceit of the mindless view that there is 'no such thing as society'.

William Barclay's life and work is a denial – a denouncement rather – of that poisonous lifestyle, whether found in politics or in church life. Goodwill is its opposite, and it is unpopular because it is costly. The Bible is rejected by such 'smartistic' people and its central message, 'peace ... goodwill towards men', is deliberately smothered. We should remember that biblical 'peace', *shalom*, is the satisfaction of that which is necessary for a full life, not just the absence of anxiety or conflict. It also means goodwill. At its simplest, it is the Great Commandment, of love to God, to one's neighbour, to all people. Willie spent twenty years learning it, and over fifty years practising and preaching it. Whatever else we may say of him, he was a man of consummate goodwill, to friends and enemies alike, known and unknown. In this, his final course, he was able to plumb its depths biblically and theologically. In so doing he began to realize that the term 'servant' is more appropriate than 'Queen' for his great subject, to which aspect he now gave himself completely.

His matriculation form of October 1930, by which he registered himself for the Degree of Batchelor of Divinity, is in handwriting much reduced in style and character from that of four years earlier: by then it had become a scribble. Its deterioration was due to the incessant scramble of note-taking in lectures and among his textbooks, the quick writing of historical and linguistic pieces, term-essays and translation notes. In filling out the form he made a curious mistake,

giving his age as twenty-three – it was not that until the following
December. Doubtless he already *felt* twenty-three! The new course was
funded by two of his prizes: the Stevenson Scholarship of £32 p.a.,
tenable for two years, and the Ainslie Bursary, of £25 p.a., happily
administered by the Deacons' Court at Fort William – a source which
gave particular pleasure to his parents. (When WDB retired, his salary
was said to be a mere £120 p.a.)

The Divinity course was offered at Trinity College, dedicated to
the training of men for the ministry of the now united Church of
Scotland. (1929 had seen the great Reunion of the Church of Scotland
and the United Free Church of Scotland, the latest of many such movements.) The exertions and traumas of the reunion debate were slowly
becoming a thing of the past, though some sorting out remained to be
done. For example, there were 'two Professors of everything', as one
former student stated of the new course they now embarked upon – the
legacy of combining the divinity colleges. The two presbyterian
churches now joined became the established church in Scotland. Willie
was not therefore ordained as minister in the tradition of his father and
its great influences, but in the mainline tradition of 'the daughter
church of the Reformation', whose interests were locked into the
nation's, and to whom he dedicated himself wholeheartedly.

There is no evidence that Willie resented this move away from
his family traditions, and much to suggest that he revelled in it: it
gave him so much more opportunity and influence, in which he
delighted. But he never succeeded in throwing off the mantle of
Free Churchmanship, which dogged him throughout college and,
indeed, his life. Many of his characteristic traits and activities derive
from this background; he is not, indeed, fully understandable without it. It forms part of his sense of freedom – his sense of religious
freedom especially.

WDB could not have been happier; the hopes, prayers and labours
over the years for his son were now coming good. But he was also
concerned. He was fervent for theological education: knowledge of the
Word of God was supreme. He also knew that theological education
could undo men as well as make them. He was not a little concerned
that his and his wife's care and guidance of the last twenty-plus years
might come to nothing, a fear he shared with several friends, both
ministerial and lay. His friends – men of the calibre of James Barr (an
anti-unionist and father of the brilliant Hebraist James Barr who
wrote a provocative book on fundamentalism) and A. J. Gossip (shortly

to be one of his son's Professors) – agreed with him. Moreover, though in broad agreement with the reunion (he later became a member of one of the reunited Church's main committees, the Highlands and Islands Committee), he was also concerned that some of the essential tenets over which the Scottish Church had formerly split and split again might be forgotten or diminished, a fear shared by not a few. His anxiety was therefore twofold: theological dilution and ecclesiastical compromise.

The Church of Scotland, he knew only too well, was a broad Church within the reformed tradition, in which certain compromises were doubtless necessary. To some minds a measure of rank worldliness was also apparent. Still aflame with the ardent spirituality of Moody and Drummond, WDB feared that such worldliness would contaminate his son. Would Willie resist it? Or would he bend to its demands and appeals? How would he cope with the biblical criticism now being presented to him? Would he continue to uphold the faith committed to him? Or would he weaken in his understanding and witness of it, as others had done? A ditty did the rounds which sums up WDB's fears precisely:

> There was an old fellow of Trinity,
> A Doctor well versed in Divinity.
> He took to free-thinking,
> And then to deep drinking,
> And had to leave the vicinity.

Such worries led to what his son called the 'explosive rackets' between him and his father, to which he refers in *Testament of Faith*. We should remember that WDB was not only unsettled by the marked changes in his own circumstances and his wife's increasing ill-health, but by the double temptation in his son's life.

On the one hand WDB saw him becoming detached from the narrower forms of evangelicalism he had himself upheld. A fervent disciple of A. S. Peake, who had imbibed the faith and the Christ-mysticism (to use James Denney's term) of the Primitive Methodist scholar, WDB refused to follow him in the not less important matters of biblical criticism and exegesis. A surprising example of this was given by the newspapers: on retiring from the Motherwell Brotherhood presidency, the organization asked him what he would like as a parting gift. He asked for the *Scofield Reference Bible*, which is noted for its fundamentalist outlook, its naivety, a fixation on the

Authorized Version, an attachment to a dispensationalist view of history, a negation of critical scholarship, and a stress on typology and analogy (which Alberto Soggin brilliantly defined as 'historic sublimation'). This at the very time when his son was being immersed in a totally different approach – in a critical and a theological awareness far removed from such obscurantisms. His son was not only being immersed in it, but was obviously loving every minute of it, agreeing with very much of it, actually revising attitudes which he had long held under his father's assertive vigilance. It was a revolutionary time for the son, and one of great anxiety for the father. As Willie admitted, he had himself been so thoroughly conservative in his approach to the Bible up to this point that he denied the legitimacy of even the omission of a comma from the *King James' Version* at Isaiah 9:6. Now, while Willie delighted, WDB writhed. 'We fought,' his son commented forty years on, 'for my theology was if anything even more to be suspected than my dancing.'

On the other hand, this latter 'worldliness' – as WDB saw it – was becoming more prominent. In smoking, dancing and associating with those who had no thought for the Church, who enjoyed the raucous behaviour of the Clyde cruises, the weekend drinking and more, Willie's very spiritual commitments were thought to be at risk. It all played on the older man's imagination. Where would it lead? The rackets got worse, even as Willie – his humanity now fully entered – recognized more and more decisively that Jesus did not cut himself off from people but got alongside them, shared their humanity, refused to condemn them, except when dealing with the self-appointed poseurs who usurped the prerogatives of God and led his people by the nose for their own ends.

To Willie, the biblical inconsistencies, the alternative readings, the new emphases that sounder learning discovered via his new mentors, rang true. He saw the force of their arguments, and came to a more historically aware and a more dynamically historical view of Scripture and doctrine; one that recognized the revelation as ongoing, to which the Bible itself bore witness. He came to understand that the dispensation-ridden interpretations of Scofield and his followers were out of kilter and insupportable. Their hearts were right, but their intellectual attitude was inadequate. Even his father's beloved Puritans, venerated for their godliness and tenacity, were now relegated to a position below that of the modern commentators. We may even see a certain gleefulness in Willie in this encounter with his father: he was throwing off the yoke of youthfulness, gladly shouldering the burdens of manliness. Much as he respected WDB, it was time to try his own strength, to flex his own mental and spiritual muscles, and combat untruth from that new perspective. The rackets increased yet more.

What WDB regarded as danger, Willie's Professors regarded as discipline: the subjecting of our preconceptions of the Word of God to the proper processes of linguistic and historical transition, to which all historical documents are subject; whose careful understanding *aids* their internal and external reality and *frees* them from the accretions of history – of human traditions and councils, the sheer inertia of tradition. None of this painful process was taken lightly by those who pioneered the new sciences. Some even suffered great loss in doing so. Men such as Professor William Robertson Smith of Aberdeen were hounded from their jobs and livelihoods, but it was a necessity laid upon them: the search for truth, no less, which was rediscovered and underpinned by the new linguistic, literary, historical and archaeological awareness that was daily being furthered. The faith had to be refined, readied for a more dynamic exposure and a clearer proclamation to the modern world. It was theologically justified, as well as necessary evangelically, pastorally and apologetically. In Jesus the Word of God had become incarnate. He *was* the incarnate Word, a Word that needed to be given form in modern understanding and related to modern experience – which could only be done by the most careful historical criticism, to which Willie now energetically set his heart and mind. In the face of his father's and his father's friends' arduous pleadings, Willie pledged himself to this undertaking. He spent the next forty-eight years working it out, an inseparable part of his life and work.

On 26–7 September 1930 Willie presented himself for the Postgraduate Entrance Examination, which was in two parts. The first concerned four compulsory subjects: Scripture Knowledge, Hebrew, Greek and Moral Philosophy; the second entailed a single subject selected from eight: English, Latin, French, German, Maths – pure or applied – Economics, or Gaelic. Willie remained faithful to his first love, choosing English. The examination cost him 2/6d (12.5 new pence). He passed easily, and was admitted to College. His professional training had begun.

To help him achieve this, a solid array of scholarship was offered in the persons of Professors W. D. Niven (Church History), John Edgar M'Fadyen (Hebrew and Old Testament), W. M. MacGregor (New Testament), A. B. Macaulay (Dogmatics and Philosophical Theology), and A. J. Gossip (Practical Training, i.e. preaching and pastoral care). There were others, but these were the key men. Between them the Bible was minutely investigated, its anatomy rigorously studied, its physiology carefully analysed and described. Its historical processes were followed from oral tradition via papyrus and codex to printed book – noting the perils risked through copying, habit and accident. They scrutinized it in English, Hebrew, Greek and Latin, and in some of their cognate languages; they examined its differing and essential themes, and its social and historical contexts. Willie thrived.

Church History was treated likewise – the story of the People of God; their geographical and historical expansion; their need for accurate doctrinal and moral definition; their spiritual prescription; the processes that were pursued to secure them. From this immense labour Willie graduated with distinction (there was no honours system for theology at that time), his faith stronger than ever, his mind more certain, his resolve to serve more firm: goodwill unimpaired.

It was more than an academic formation. Moral, social and religious aspects were all at stake. Willie himself registered changes, as we saw. Now a man of twenty-five, who had never worked commercially, who had always lived at home, who had been so carefully groomed for the ministry of the Church, he now groomed himself – deliberately moving away from the easy, affluent, privileged context of his upbringing; making time to wander around Glasgow's less salubrious parts to study its people, noting their joys and sorrows, weighing their hopes and fears, observing their needs. He now saw with kindlier eye the unfair mess that is called the human condition; he learned to pick up the drunkard, to respect the fallen woman, to love his fellow citizens in all their need.

Not a small part of that training was in College itself, in meeting with other men of different backgrounds and persuasions. There was, for example, a *social* difference between many of the 'Uffies' (as the former Free Church men were called) and the Auld Kirk students, as well as a theological, even a political one. In the wake of the illustrious Reunion there was an ongoing debate, as there is in every open theological tradition. At one extreme the primitivism of the New Testament and the early Church were urged, at another the catholicism of the Church – its complexities, its ever-increasing legislation, its fuller 'order' and its doctrines, its state involvements, matters which the Uffies sometimes felt neutered 'the freedoms of the Spirit'. The debate was ethnic as well as theological. Books and articles proliferated, one of the best being Charles Warr's *The Presbyterian*

Tradition of 1933, a powerful exposition geared to 'the traditional character of the Scot'. Warr epitomized it as 'simple, reserved, robust, and austere'. This obviously had a social slant, but was not exclusively that. Willie's maternal background was nearer socially to the Auld Kirkers, and sometimes showed through. He was easy with both parties, though more at home with the *spirit* of the Free Churchmen, which never left him. Warr's epithets, the austerity apart, are as good a summary of Willie's character as can be found.

The Reunion matters affected the relationship between Faculty members and the students. Two examples may be offered. One day Willie and his friends were caught in Craig's Tea-Rooms (an Uffie haunt) by Professor Niven, 'cutting' a lecture by an Auld Kirk Professor. Niven demanded to know what they were doing. They explained, naming the lecturer, guiltily admitting the reasons for their rejection of him. 'Ah!' exclaimed the professor knowingly, and ordered another pot of tea for them before going on his way. Again, one of the Auld Kirk Professors used to invite groups of students to his house, where they were regaled with tea and uplifting tales, plus some old songs sung by the good man's wife at the piano, an embarrassing soirée for the young men. Such stuffiness was not foreign to these Free Churchmen, but the ambience was still unacceptable, and so the well-meant soirées became a matter of fun-making.

Another curiosity of College life was the annual appointment of a Moral Censor, whose job was to oversee the students' behaviour. It was not taken very seriously by men of Willie's ilk. He did not hugely respect conformism or entertain judgemental attitudes towards his colleagues, and regarded the 'moral censorship' as the very essence of pharisaism, the *unco guid*. That function also became a joke. On one occasion a student, George Fraser, was taken to task by the Censor for wearing a brightly coloured pullover, judged unsuitable for 'robust ... and austere' ministers according to the pretentious self-regard in which some held themselves. Fraser's reply was apt: despite what the Censor said, he declared, it was desirable for the student body to be well-knit.

The Free Churchmen founded a party known as BIOS, an acronym for British Israel Original Succession. The name means little today – it meant little *per se* then – but for the party's members it urged one of the basic convictions of Free Churchmen: their inalienable and historic continuity with the early Church, free from man-made restraints and ecclesiastical correctness. The letters of BIOS form the Greek word for 'life'. That was their point. Real life in religion, not its dead letter;

life which could grow and express itself freely; life which obeyed the promptings of the Spirit – open and flexible, unconstrained by article or tradition; listening, not always-speaking; volunteered, not ordered by authority or enacted by law. It was a minor protest, not a revolution; a gambit, not a programme; and it very soon wilted as an organization, as it was expected to do. All its members eventually took their positions as ministers of the Church of Scotland. They were proud to do so, but some of their contentions were long in dying, and some never did, in fact, die out entirely.

The reality of *bios* never left William Barclay, not as an ecclesiastical matter (in which he was actually little interested), but as one which took life – human existence and spiritual freedoms – seriously. This rapport with people in general accounts for the way he determined the outcome of his life and his work. He once said, having by then written over eighty books, that he never wrote one that was not asked of him; he wrote them as a service *for* people, as all his ministry was. His books are replete with quotations from other books, from other lives and others' experiences: windows into reality, into ultimate *bios*. He particularly loved 'men of action', and quoted them repeatedly. André Reymond's description of Teilhard de Chardin he found to be particularly apt, 'vibrant as a flag fluttering under the Asian sky, energetic, lively, generous, tireless, greeting each day with a burst of joyous enthusiasm'. It is a perfect description of his own character.

Willie shared a desk (and much else) with Merricks Arnot, whose drawing skills delighted him. He also admired his socialism – an undercurrent in BIOS – and with that some of his favourite authors, such as Wells and Shaw, who were definitely not found in the Barclay household. But Arnot judged Willie's political opinions to be disconcerting; in his phrase, 'they swithered about'. It is one of those classical denouements that we see repeatedly in William Barclay, when the old order and the emphatic idealisms of his father's circle, engrained in his consciousness since his earliest days, come into flat collision with new, equally impressive ideas. His antisyzygy increased. A Liberal in politics, to WDB 'liberal' in terms of theology meant the denial of much that was life-preserving: a renouncement of the authority of the Bible and its evangelical message, a resiling of the faith, a denial of the Church's most sacred task, of its Master and Lord. The evangelicalism he had nurtured for decades, which had so often taken the nation by storm and redirected it; which he sought to preserve in the face of Edwardian disenchantment, through the war years and their aftermath, was now under dreadful attack – from within; even from his own son.

To men such as Arnot 'liberal' meant, or was coming to mean, something quite different: a new spiritual liberation, the adoption of science in all its facets and disciplines, a new hope for humanity. Merricks Arnot saw the evangelicals as offering outdated views, siding with the established order, which was dreary in its analyses of what was required to set the nation alight, unimaginative, weary in its responsibilities, stained by failure. (For all this he was a keen participant in the Billy Graham campaigns of the fifties.)

Willie was intrigued, inspired – and converted, yet not all at once, for the old still held him: one day he would see its gains, another its losses. If PE had added anything to his mindset, it was the reasonableness of some aspects of socialism, already encountered by him through French literature (e.g. Molière and Voltaire) and Scottish history (e.g. Keir Hardie). He also saw its vibrant congruity in his growing understanding of biblical ethics. After all, if he was to preach that all people were equally treated by God, should that not affect how they treated each other? The twin doctrines of the liberals were the Fatherhood of God and the Brotherhood of man. It rang bells and it made sense; more importantly, it redefined the man/God and man/man relationships as seen in the Bible. The need to find a competent reply to the burgeoning communism – not least in the west of Scotland, where tempers over inequality and unfairness had been fraying and signs of civil disorder had been mounting – was oppressive. Their discussions were intense, and Willie learned, argued, and swithered yet more.

Other memories of these days come from Willie's fellow students, and paint a picture of a well-read, refined, if boisterous man, aglow with his new-won knowledge, triumphant in it, impatient for the opportunity to express it. Sometimes he expressed it in ways not wholly approved by the Faculty, aiding some students who found the minutiae of Hebrew and Greek (the latter especially, for Willie himself was never fond of Hebrew) too much. James L. Dow described Willie's efforts like this:

In the last year the student had to prepare a New Testament exegesis, which is a full analysis and interpretation of a passage of Scripture. He is supposed to look up all available manuscripts, and make his own translation of the Greek. He then writes down all the variants, which are the textual differences between one [manuscript] and the others. Having completed this useful and, no doubt, necessary task, he then examines carefully the background of the book, the authorship and the rest, and finishes with a homiletic expansion – which, in plain language, is a sermon ... Willie

MacGregor handed out the passages one morning, and after class
Willie Barclay asked me what I had got in the draw. I told him ...
There may have been a trace of gloom on my face, for the next day
my friend handed me a foolscap sheet with all the variants written
on it ...

The best of such stories regards Harry Cummings, who had been
delayed by (nervous?) illness on his way to the examination hall for
one of the BD examinations. Arriving late, and fearing the worst, he
was surprised to find Willie outside the hall, pacing up and down in
agitation over his friend's failure to appear. In so doing, he risked
failure himself. Nevertheless, he waited, goodwill personified.
Cummings was greatly moved by this – invigorated. They went in
late together, and passed (Willie gained the equivalent of a First
Class). That was true friendship, and it culminated several years of
comradely behaviour entirely free from the more aggressive forms
of competition, even though it was known that Willie was hopeful of
gaining an academic appointment by his results.

Alongside such stories we have to place memories of this buoyant
man banging away at the piano, singing ditties which would have
graced the decks of the Clyde steamers – the SS *Ivanhoe* or the SS *Lord
of the Isles*: 'You may have Rose/With the upturned nose/But you
won't have Lulu!' Not one his Professor's wife would have sung at
those soirées, nor the type of song WDB would have allowed in his so-
sanctified drawing room. It was a time when Willie and his entourage
frequented the music halls of the area – The Metropole, The Pavilion,
The Princess – which frightened his father, and doubtless would have
incurred not only the interest of the Moral Censor but the wrath of
some Faculty members as well. Willie's rejoinder to any criticism was
that he was studying people as well as theology. He enjoyed studying
people! Like Ezekiel of old, he had to sit where his people sat – and
what was wrong with sitting with the 'under-classes', the outcasts of
society even as Jesus, their declared example, had done? Willie was
content to emulate the friend of sinners. He continued to sing duets
with his fellow students, such as George Boyd, in a voice that was
nothing if not stentorian.

In February 1932, after an agonizing illness for which there was little
relief, his mother died, aged sixty-five. Willie and his father were all but
torn apart by the slow, cancerous and degenerative process, which
threatened their concepts of an all-wise and loving God. How could

such things happen? And to the very best of people? Why was there such suffering? What was its function? Did it have a function? Why was it permitted? Was anyone in control? Such questions, and many more, were not the theoretical demands of the lecture room or the textbooks, but the stern reality at the centre of their lives, now all but broken; lives drenched with the hot tears of their grief, and those feelings of inadequacy which accompany the bereft. 'You'll have a new note in your preaching now,' WDB wryly commented after they laid Barbara to rest in 'God's Acre', the little cemetery at Corpach, overlooking Loch Eil at Fort William. It was only a few miles from the proud memorial to Daniel McLeish, but a universe away from Willie's comprehension of divine love and providence. He swithered yet more, and differently.

In his finals he gained a number of prizes, as well as the distinction he had sought so industriously. But there were only muted celebrations, the agonized satisfactions of two men who had been too often at war. He would never see the contented face of his mother again; it hurt unspeakably. It was the ultimate disciplining of his faith, its reorientation indeed, her last – perhaps her greatest – gift to him. In learning to let her go, he learned much of the human condition, the obedience of faith, the reality of trust in God, the nature of his world. From now on a leather sermon-case, the most prized of her gifts, went with him wherever he preached, a continual reminder of the grim realities of life as well as that triumph of hope to which he ever bore witness. It finally fell apart as he was nearing his own retirement, but he never threw it away.

Following his graduation as Batchelor of Divinity, he who had little German went to Germany for a semester, following an old tradition. Scottish divines had long looked towards Germany – as, indeed, many did in the south – for its penetrative scholarship and broad cultural balance. Thus Willie found himself at Marburg, one of the most famous of its universities, recently notable for the high distinction that von Soden and Rudolph Bultmann had given to it, at whose feet Willie himself now sat, at least ostensibly. He does not appear to have gained much from the German experience, though we may well imagine his delight among the boisterous crowds and the splendid cultural opportunities, even at that time being overshadowed by the growth of Hitlerism. Of Bultmann he commented in 1966, 'I was a pupil of Bultmann but never a follower.' He was not the following sort. Perhaps the chief value of his stay in Germany lay in the opportunity to reassess himself, recharge his batteries, and face the future.

SIX

RENFREW – THE MINISTRY BEGINS

'Nothing is difficult – if you only know how.'

(Jewish Proverb)

Willie had a choice of two for his first church. The charges on offer to him were Saint Andrew's at Kirkintilloch, near the site of the Antonine Wall, and Trinity Church, Renfrew, six miles to the south-east of Glasgow.

The former had been 'dry' by public vote since the twenties, an inimical disposition to Willie's way of thinking (which in this respect was *laissez-faire*, not prohibitionist), a church of mixed fortunes and average size. The latter was within the heavily industrialized area of the Clyde, more than twice the congregation of the former church, three times that of its Sunday School, seven times its Bible Class, and nearly twice as many elders. It was keen and active, open and resolute – perhaps too resolute, for they called it 'the fechtin' [fighting] church'. Even as Willie considered his future, two of its elders were involved in an argument which left one of them seeking to unchurch the other for his alleged insults. (The Minutes relating to the incident were later scored out!) No minister had stayed there for more than four years since 1919.

Some thought it too big a challenge for a young minister. But Willie, whose father had both sparked and defused many an angry moment in his own life, knew the mechanics involved and perceived its talents and potential. He felt compelled to serve it, not least because other ministers refused – a telling insight into his character. Red meat was always more enticing than milk to him; milksop Christianity was an aggravation, no matter how genteel its perpetrators. Family friend Professor Gossip, who was behind the award to Willie of the Dykes Prize for Practical Training in his final year, perceived that he was the man for the job and so recommended him.

On 9 January 1933, Willie made his first appearance in the church's pulpit as sole nominee. *The Renfrew Press* reported that he made 'a most favourable impression'. The next evening he was presented to the vacancy committee, who 'agreed without a single dissenting vote to present an unanimous call to him to be minister of our church'.

The photograph of him on page 1 of the picture section suggests why: a man of low to middling height, slim and athletic, handsome, of broad brow, reddish-brown wavy hair, a steady and purposeful gaze, slightly sensual lips – and a very determined chin. They knew his outstanding academic record; they pondered the strong recommendations with which he came; they heard his prayers and listened to his sermon (his voice had especially impressed them, as it rang out 'clearly and confidently' in the large church); they believed him to be the man to give their church the lead it needed; a man with a practical turn of mind, human and spiritual both; and, not least, he was the son of W. D. Barclay who was well known to them. The formalities leading to ordination were put in place; his 'proving' (from the point of view of character and qualifications) was noted, to which was added the further note that 'W. D. Barclay, ruling elder [a significant description!] of Stevenson Memorial Church and Parish ... father of the Probationer ... was associated with the Presbytery'. The 'form of call' was signed by 594 members and 64 adherents of Trinity Church, laid before Presbytery along with his Extract of Licence and Presbyterial Certificate, plus a letter – now unfortunately lost – from Willie himself. The Students' and Ministers' Committee of the General Assembly added its bit by declaring itself 'highly satisfied with the exercises submitted on trial for ordination'. The Call was placed in Willie's hands; the resolution was seconded; the matter was carried unanimously.

On the evening of Wednesday 22 February 1933, William Barclay MA BD became a Minister of the Church of Scotland, a role he never surrendered and a commitment from which he never withdrew. He was 'preached in' by A. G. Fortune of Saint George's East Church, Paisley, the most recently inducted minister in the area, as custom happily demanded. Fortune used Paul's words in Ephesians 4:13 as his text: 'Till we all come into the unity of the faith, and of the knowledge of the Son of God, unto a perfect man, unto the stature of the fulness of Christ.' The four main components of his text and sermon – unity, knowledge, manly perfection, and Jesus as Christ and Son of God – had been the central emphases of WDB's life over many years. They now became his son's and were to remain and develop, on a worldwide platform of incredible proportions. It was a prophetic address.

At his ordination ceremony the Preamble concerning the Church's authority to ordain was read; its doctrines were emphasized as those found in the Word of God and the *Westminster Confession of Faith*; and the Avowal was made, followed by Willie's signing of the Formula and the actual Act of Ordination itself. For this Willie knelt and the formal laying on of hands was undertaken by the Church's representatives. The Declaration of his new status was publicly announced.

The church was especially full for the occasion, causing one visitor to remark, 'Do they aye turn out like this?' It was indeed one of Trinity's outstanding abilities to organize church functions. Its socials were unrivalled in the area. The next day Willie saw for himself how well they did them, and how long they could be, too! We should remember that these were the Depression years, but that did not stop the church from providing tables of plenty and great enjoyments, which reinforced that unity to which Willie was committed. As a well-read student of Church history he knew only too well what emphasis the apostolic Church itself placed on such communality (i.e. its 'love feasts'), though he later confessed to David Anderson, a former student, that Trinity's abounding enthusiasms sometimes worried him. Few at the time have any recollection of such concerns; indeed, he is remembered as an enthusiastic and supremely effective leader on such occasions.

We can be sure that he did not offer any criticism to the organizers at Trinity – a veritable army of stalwart, hard-working men and women (many of whom were out of work) who had helped to build the church up to what it was. The church hall had just been renovated, so there was an extra sparkle to the festivities, which comprised the tea itself, a number of anthems and songs by the choir – secular and sacred, English and Scottish, and some of his favourite 'Negro Spirituals' – followed by the communal singing of 'Auld Scotch Sangs' which reminded Willie of those gleeful days on the Clyde. (It is curious that only in recent years has British television found such Scottish *caillidh* a formidable festive attraction.)

This was followed by the presentation of his pulpit robes, hand-made by a member of the congregation. Willie's speech in reply reflected on the seventy-two-year history of the church, and audaciously asserted that 'its greatest days – are ahead'. This was to be a constant theme of his for the next fourteen years, emphasizing his native optimism as well as his faith in the power of the gospel when plainly preached. No less than ten speeches by fellow ministers followed this, among them one from Merricks Arnot who darkly warned them, 'William Barclay was a man as well as a student and a minister; they would soon discover that' – the theme of manliness ever recurring. Some speeches by the lay leaders of the church were added, as were two closing prayers by neighbouring ministers, A. W. Sawyer and Lewis Sutherland.

In moving to Renfrew Willie rooted himself in the fourth and penultimate area of Scotland that claimed his allegiance: from Wick to Motherwell; Motherwell to Glasgow; Glasgow to Renfrew. The young Highlander had now become the urban – and urbane – low-lander, and with this urbanity went a resolute spirit to serve his people where, when and as he found them: in their homes, on factory floors, in shops and offices, in the dockyards and the parks, at work and at play. His first pastoral letter to them pledged this, 'My time will always be yours, and it will be my privilege and my honour to serve you at all times in every way I can. You have chosen me to be your minister, and now I want you all to make me your friend.' His message of goodwill was sounding out.

One of the titles of the Heir Apparent is Baron of Renfrew, a royal connection of which its people are very proud. As the visitor enters the town a conspicuous sign declares it to be 'The Royal Burgh of Renfrew, Cradle of the Stuarts'. One can almost see the late Daniel McLeish waving his blackthorn stick in its honour. Other than this, the town has little to offer by way of attractions. The Clyde is hidden from view behind docks and their termini; and the proximity to Lanarkshire's coal and iron works and the industrial expressions of them (a senior manager of which, William Braidwood, later became one of Willie's closest and longest-lasting friends) have also charac-terized the town to its disadvantage. The Argyle Stone and the Blythswood Testimonial School buildings are justly famous to the local people, and – a late addition – Renfrew Airport (which was built over Willie's favourite golf course) offers extra transport facilities alongside those of the later motorway. The 'airfield' (as it became known) – a runway and some hastily erected buildings – soon drew Willie, as train spotting had in former years (in which he remained exceptionally well-informed as to recognition, timetabling and so on). He soon became expert in aircraft design and recogni-tion, and in payloads, ranges and services. But he never overcame his fear of flying! It was partly this that kept him almost exclusively within the UK, as we shall see.

The town's history long antedated the Stuarts. Signs of the old Roman occupation are nearby, recorded in some of the local names, such as Oakshawhead, Castlehead and Woodside – fertile places for Willie's classical imagination. Cotterall is probably correct in suggesting that a series of Roman forts and fortlets were built along Renfrew's coast, for they certainly planted many orchards there, though there is tantalizingly little evidence of them now. The area later became known as Strathgryffe (Valley of the Griffin?), guarded by the legendary eagle-beaked animal. It later formed part of the Kingdom of Strathclyde, which stretched from Cumberland in the south to beyond the Clyde in the north, centring on Dumbarton Rock. It became a regal burgh under the ancient kings of Scotland. Under the Stuarts – from one 'Walter, steward [thence Stuart] of the king' – it became a Burgh of Barony, hence the modern Barony of Renfrew. Walter's grandson gained the hand in marriage of Robert the Bruce's daughter, and thus access to the throne. It was made a Shire in 1404. On such reminiscences was the pride of its people rightly built. When Willie moved in, the town had a population of about forty thousand, but much of its former wealth was now being savaged by the Depression.

Trinity Church was a former United Free Church establishment, so there was no need for Willie to feel defensive here about his Uffie status. His people welcomed it. Prior to that, the church had been within the United Presbyterian (UP) tradition, one that stood for the separation of Church and State – a voluntarist tradition, which was closest to Willie's deepest convictions (akin to the English Free Church ideologies he would shortly encounter; and had already encountered, in fact, in his involvement with Baptists and others).

The sharp differentiation between Church and State in UP doctrine was reflected in Trinity Church's internal organization which he inherited, and was a cause of its infighting. It was thoroughly presbyterian, its authority being divided between the church's elders (spiritual aspects) and its managers (secular aspects). The leader of the elders was the minister, a 'first among equals'; the Preses (from *praesidere*: to preside) was the managers' leader; the managers held their meetings separately from those of the elders. The Session Clerk (i.e. Church Secretary) managed the Minutes and other such formalities, and acted as the minister's right-hand man. At the Annual Business Meeting of the church, both groups came together: the Minister presided over the first 'sessional' part, the Preses over the second 'business' part. All very Acts 6:2, from which principle Willie did not deviate, though he came to believe that it was not the best form of leadership. He preferred a single hand at the helm, as we shall see.

The strengths of the form are obvious. The 'division of labour', if we may use Adam Smith's economic term, required everyone to fulfil their own gifts whether 'sacred' or 'secular' – a division Willie came to repudiate as artificial and therefore wrong. (The 'therefore' is important.) But its potential for trouble is also patent. In the hands of a wrong-headed leader – Fortune's emphasis on unity was not ill-advised – divergent policies could arise, and with them tensions and actual splits. It is to Willie's great credit that, with the exception of one incident, he held this church with its history of sharp divisions and headstrong personalities together for fourteen years – a period of unparalleled growth and activity, and another angle of the 'manly perfection' of Paul's vision of the church, and of Willie's goodwill ethic.

Following the Crash of 1929 and the subsequent Depression (it had really begun much earlier), unemployment in Renfrew was very high. Without a National Health Service scheme to speak of, and very little by way of social security, needs were many and sometimes dire. Nineteen of his twenty-six elders were out of work at one stage. Much was done to cushion people by the voluntary organizations – of the churches, old peoples' and youth groups, women's organizations, the Salvation Army, the Quakers. Trinity Church was to the fore in this locally, and Willie did not hesitate to stimulate it even further. Having so many of his elders out of work was actually a blessing in disguise. With time on their hands they were ideal leaders for community activities; they had the church's well-being in mind; and they could fill their long days of forced inactivity with good works, which to their credit they did.

Thus entertainments and good-cause activities proliferated, and 'resting facilities' were provided for people to meet, sit and talk together, read, or listen to music. Simple pleasures, but immensely important. Tea and biscuits were also cheaply provided in the church halls, into which the bustling, energetic figure of the young minister would burst, never afraid to roll up his sleeves and work – or take off his dog collar, though some frowned at that! He would offer a game of table tennis or billiards, sit down and discuss the news of the hour, swap stories, advise, and pray with his people: he was there for them. Additionally, the Trinity Church Players, as the church's drama group called itself, put on much appreciated comedy and drama shows. Some of those out of work were skilled craftsmen, who made sets for the Players which were the envy of many churches around the district. Various choir groups offered concerts and other forms of entertainment.

The thirties have been dubbed 'the Devil's Decade', and such it was, for a variety of reasons. At home, pressures on families created heart-breaking problems which led both to human heroism and its opposite; lives were made and smashed in the process. Food was scarce and expensive, inflation soared, and ill-health and premature death were daily realities. Unburied corpses were not a rare sight on nearby Glasgow's streets. The tradition of British humour was born of such times, and few knew its beneficial and recuperative powers better than Willie, whom death had touched closely and grievously. It can take years to recover from such a death; all the evidence is that Willie, despite his bravado, was still hurting. The 'new note' was there, underpinning his pastoral sympathies and attitudes, and quietly working at his theological awareness. He eschewed the hurt by working harder than ever. He officiated at others' losses and burials with great sympathy, supporting them in the dark hours as best he knew how, but he could not escape the pain he shared with his people, and they were quick to notice this. Their bonding became extraordinary and deep.

Further afield the growth of Hitler's Germany continued menacingly. (Churchill's 'Little Corporal' became Chancellor of Germany in the month of Willie's ordination.) There the 'unfinished business' of the Great War was wedded to a sense of national betrayal and a maniacal sense of injustice. Unreason took hold of the nation, which had once been to the fore in its opposite; its great humane culture was ignored; violence and vengeance took to the streets, as did a rabid anti-Semitism. In the west of Scotland it produced acute nervousness, and anti-war marches and peace demonstrations took place in Glasgow, led by the 'Red Shirts'. Goodwill was coming into short supply.

I have a list of virtually all the sermons Willie preached at Trinity Church, thanks to the assiduous reporting of *The Renfrew Gazette*. They cover ten double-column pages and run into dozens of series and hundreds of titles. Alas, he destroyed their manuscripts (which he was careful to write out in full, by Thursday of each week). The titles were wide-ranging, ear-catching and provocative, suggestive of his careful planning and a systematic teaching objective. They were thoroughly biblical, too, in content if not in title. The social activities of the church were 'earthed' by the high voltage of this preaching. It was their justifi-cation: a sort of parallel to what in earlier generations had been achieved by other means. The church thus established itself as the vital heart of the community – even of the town (to the distress of other ministers).

At the heart of it all were Willie's Sunday services. There was an architechtonic quality about them, from the introit – beautifully prepared and sung by the choir – to the Scripture readings, which he read with almost thespian skills and evangelical fervour, to the prayers – *long* prayers and earnest, which transported the congregation – to the sermon and its very practical applications, and the prouncement of the Blessing at the end. The congregation was borne on a wave of spiritual energy – true *bios* – and reacted accordingly, in phenomenal growth.

This was an apostolic ministry ('of one sent'), and the congregation, the town, knew it. It offered 'knowledge' – that second element to which A. G. Fortune had bound Willie when he preached him in, as well as uplifting guidance and help. Willie's head was full of knowledge, in four cultures: Hebrew, Greek, Roman and modern; it was full of their history, their social mores, their literature; it was full of doctrine – biblical and reformed (there is an important difference!); and full of life, from the refined tea parties of his mother's set to the loud revelry of the Clyde steamship tours. But more than all this, it was full of 'the knowledge of the Son of God ... the fulness of Christ'. *That* was the secret of his power, from which he drew his imaginative schemes and to which he pointed his hungering, attentive listeners.

Attention must be drawn to one technique of his sermons from which he never deviated, which is classical, and pure WDB. Willie's sermons were usually three-tier, not only in their general structure, 'like a good book' as it has been said, with beginning, middle and end, but in their triple saliences: points 1, 2, and 3, plus their subordinate points A, B and C, even their sub-subordinate points i, ii, and iii. This structure echoed and re-echoed like a hammer drill throughout his work, and is found in much of his published exposition of Scripture. But the clarity of his structures, and of his teaching and preaching, should not obscure from us the essence of Willie's spiritual power: he was a man of prayer, a man obsessed with the need to serve God, but a man's man, for all that.

By the time of his first Communion Service, the congregation was topping the six hundred mark – a record – and the place was buzzing with enthusiasm. A few days before this, Presbytery had announced a grant of £327 to Trinity Church which cleared it of all outstanding debts, a great boost to the new beginning. The Communion Service is a special event in every minister's work, in Willie's not least. He received unstinted praise for the devout and sensitive leading he gave to it. This first one was special to him for another reason: alongside him in the evening service was James H. Gillespie, Parish Minister of Dundonald, shortly to become his father-in-law.

It was all happening, much of it very well publicized. A week after his first Communion he undertook his first baptism, initiating Colin Campbell *Barclay* McMaster into the Christian family, the parents thoughtfully giving their child the young minister's name. A little later WDB himself occupied the pulpit, inspiring the press to release one of those panegyrics that had so often accompanied his work – whether for the Church, the business community, literary and debating societies, or young peoples' organizations. It was the happy culmination of a busy life for WDB, now aged almost seventy: to stand in his son's pulpit, to hear of his congregation's esteem for him.

The pleasure was strengthened by Willie's first venture into journalism since his schooldays: an article in *The Renfrew Press* called 'On the Secret of Happiness: taking life as we find it'. It is an instructive example of his approach to the community outside the Church. It was Willie's entrée to what would be called 'threshold evangelism' – a quasi-secular mode of outreach similar to that used by Jesus in his parables, in which spiritual meanings are introduced and deduced from secular entities. We see it also in Paul's preaching to the Athenians in Acts, in which the great apostle assumed little religious interest or knowledge above the perfunctory or superstitious in his listeners, but latched on to their basic human instincts and inclined them (via a quotation of one of their own philosopher-poets) to that other great instinct, man's fear of death, and the Christian hope which overcomes it.

In this first journalistic piece Willie used mankind's instinctive pursuit of happiness as his 'handle', quoting – entertainingly – Hilaire Belloc, Plato, W. L. George, Abraham Lincoln, Hartley Coleridge, Jeremy Taylor and a Chinese proverb, to make his points. Unlike his sermons, not a single Scripture was quoted; yet in a sense it was full of Scripture, or at least full of the themes of Scripture. His stock rose further in the community. They were hearing things they wanted to hear, things for which their souls cried out; hearing them in a way they could understand, and to which they could respond. They were finding out what sort of man Merricks Arnot's friend really was, and they liked him, and his message. His abundant goodwill was winning friends and influencing many, not least because of its intelligent, down-to-earth spirituality.

SEVEN

MARRIAGE, FAMILY
AND MINISTRY

'Whoever finds a wife finds a good thing, and obtains favour...'
(Proverbs 18:22)

Happiness became William Barclay, even given the hard knocks he took. He was essentially a happy man who believed in a positive, outgoing, 'masculine' and joyous faith, unlike some who seem to prefer the *via negativa*, a sombre world-view and a judgemental attitude towards others (the *unco guid* of which the Church is full). In a sense his joy was constitutional, born of that social and personal contentment his parents had long demonstrated – hard won by WDB, but a natural element of Barbara's more serene personality. Willie set the seal to this outlook by translating the now largely unmeaning word 'Blessed' in the Beatitudes from the Sermon on the Mount as 'O the happiness of ...'

He refused to accept easily the material handed to him by his father and tutors; he fought to make of them his own thing, sometimes through an agonized questioning of meaning and direction – but he tried, and he won. It was never an easy path. He determined to examine everything through the newer perspective of modern man: at first pre-war man, thence war-torn man, and finally post-war man – man allegedly 'come of age'. He chose to define 'the iron rations of the soul' (see pp. 173 and 179), and lived by them. He examined them in the intensities of a full-blooded life, of pain and suffering and death – not only at a distance (such as all ministers and chaplains live with) but also within his own home, notably within his own body. He made light of his own sufferings; he never showed pity for himself, let alone wallowed in it; he never allowed his difficulties to interfere with the overpowering ethic of goodwill – through which God was served and man was welcomed: all people, equally.

Fortunate as he was with his parents, WDB was a hard taskmaster, and extremely ambitious for his son. Barbara, the ever-dutiful wife, was careful not to contradict or oppose her husband – in public at least. With the privileges went the responsibilities, and they were added to year by year, each parent having contributed in different ways to their civic, religious and domestic bliss, to their son's advantageous growth and nurturing. From them Willie inherited his extraordinary energy, but he was expected to use it for positive ends; from them came his fine intellect, but woe betide him if he was found reading or indulging low-mindedness; from them came his highly retentive memory, but it was expected to be stocked with good and useful things; from them came his love of social gatherings and enjoyments, but there were many painful clashes when he sought to express these in his own way – a way more befitting the 'twittering twenties' – which was not his parents' way, who had stoically defied the 'naughty nineties'.

He had been well catechized in his childhood and youth, a very great boon despite the misgivings of modern educators, for it laid in a stock of knowledge – even if some of this had to be relearned and reinterpreted later. At times his efforts to escape the straitjacket of an uncritical biblicism had resulted in Vesuvius-like eruptions from his father, who regarded it as an attack upon Scripture itself. The war-zones had multiplied as Willie grew: smoking, dancing; his non-judgemental acceptance of his fellows' failure and farce; the love of the music halls (abominated by his parents and especially relished by Willie's broad mind); even a Rabelaisian sense of humour. 'Neither do I condemn you' had already become one of his watchwords; he never saw such activities as gross sin – unlike his clear perception of pomposity, pride, haughtiness, one-upmanship and elitism. 'The gentleness of Christ' had early seized him.

His mother's death from an excruciatingly painful spinal cancer had wrought a great effect in his life – his *de profundis*. For a time it blackened his consciousness and threatened his faith; it also brought him closer to WDB, as father and son were caught together in the inevitable and distressing progress of the illness. Their lady, who epitomized Paul's model character of Philippians 4:8 – expressing all her life 'things honourable, just, pure, lovely, gracious, excellent and praiseworthy' – was forced to suffer one of the most degrading of health breakdowns and unspeakable pain, then much less controllable than today. Willie eventually overcame the trauma, though it left him scarred. His triumph lay in the hopeful convictions which emerged from it – though he knew the force of the desperate cry, 'Lord,

I believe. Help my unbelief.' It became the strength of his joy: tested and invincible, but always open to human suffering and doubt.

Helping him through the latter stages of this by her tender support was the College cook, Catherine Gillespie of Dundonald, a village about thirty miles south-east of Glasgow. She was ideally suited to do so. Her father, as we saw, was the Reverend James Hogg Gillespie, who had married Mary Muir Ferguson, daughter of the Registrar of Glasgow, in 1902. He was not brought up in the Free Church tradition, but in that of the high church, at the Barony Church in Glasgow, whose minister had been Marshall Lang, father of the then Archbishop of Canterbury, Cosmo Gordon Lang. The family was well connected, even beyond Scotland. Gillespie, a parish minister of the old type – the backbone of Scottish presbyterianism – had the scholar's touch and reflected men of Ruskin's disposition in his love for the classics: 'I must do my Plato. I'm never well without that.'

There was a squire-like atmosphere about the manse at Dundonald, surrounded by its glebe from which much of the family's provisions were obtained. At its rear were stables which gave the children an ideal play area in inclement weather. The minister ran a pony and trap, and even used an ancient phaeton for special occasions, at which parishioners would doff their caps or curtsey as it passed. Adjoining the stables were barn, hay shed, pig house, byre and henhouse, in which Mrs Gillespie – his 'squiress', and the business brain of the family – raised her chickens and sorted her eggs when not involved with parish and family work. It was not unknown for her to bring some of the weakest chickens into the manse, nursing them with brandy and milk, and keeping them warm in her armpits. The range and quantity of their produce was extraordinary: grains and cheeses, meat and a wide variety of fruit and vegetables, and home-made produce. By the end of the summer their larder shelves groaned under the weight, a crucial contribution to the family's income as the stipend was not always paid on time. (Once it was delayed by the gambling debts of the heritor, i.e. the landowner, which no doubt fired a polite sermon.) It was a lifestyle loved by the Gillespies, and one they shared for fifty years. WDB knew how to hold his head high, but he never lived in such a style. Being of the people, among the people, was an essential part of his persona; he was not cut out to vegetate in a quiet country living, least of all philosophically. Still less would it have suited Willie.

The Gillespies had five children, all daughters, of whom Catherine (Kate or Ka to her own family) was the youngest. Her sisters were schooled locally to start with, but were later sent to Troon, four miles away. Kate, a sensitive and highly strung child, did not follow them. She was schooled privately at Milngavie, then attended Troon High Grade School, and finally went to Glasgow where she stayed with her uncle, James Muir, a Professor of Mathematics. Naturally gifted mentally, if more sensitive than her siblings, she benefited from this personalized academic treatment. Many years later her former teacher, Robert Houston, at ninety-three, recalled to me the brightness of his former student who had showed particular accomplishments in English, Maths, Science, French and Drawing. She gained results in these subjects on her School Leaving Certificate, adding History and Latin to them in the following year.

She was not interested in an academic career, so she was sent to the Dow School in Glasgow (now part of Queen's College) where she took up Domestic Science. No doubt this interest stemmed from counting all those eggs, preparing and preserving all those vegetables and fruit, helping to make the cheeses and cure the bacon, and the general administration of the busy manse. She did not then realize how well this was preparing her for a brilliant service in her own right. Having successfully completed her course, she became Assistant Cook at the Erskine Hospital for the Limbless, and then moved on to become governess to the sons of Sir Charles MacAndrew MP, Ronald and Colin, in yet another busy household. She spent much time travelling between Newfield and Westminster. In 1928 she moved yet again, becoming Cook at Trinity College, at the young age of twenty-three.

Here she was in charge of the kitchens, under the watchful eye of its Committee, which was not entirely at ease with so young a woman being given the job. Its members included the Principal, W. M. Macgregor, Professors Macaulay and Niven, Mrs MacGregor and Miss Buchanan. But Kate Gillespie was her own person, and she knew her job and set out to prove her competence. Within three months she had convinced them; her probationary status was lifted and her job was made permanent. In addition to the Committee's watchfulness, she naturally had to endure a good deal of interest and banter from the students, not only over the food (especially the size of the portions – she considered them adequate for the subsidized thirty-five shillings, i.e. £1.75 in new pence, they were charged per term), but from the leavening mix of students, not least across the denominational divide they were all seeking to bridge.

Kate Gillespie was a committed Auld Kirker, who stood her ground. She enjoyed the joke of BIOS, and had little patience with it as making a serious point. The Reunion was delicately poised, but relationships at grass-roots level 'were not always very religious' as one of her sisters shrewdly commented; a polite understatement. The following year Kate proudly observed her father escorting the Moderator of the Church as his Chaplain in the great Reunion Walk, a fitting tribute for his long years of service and his great sagacity.

If some of the students liked to rib her over her Church of Scotland status – and over a certain aloofness that she thought proper to her rank – others quickly realized that this was a gifted and astute woman. She had a sharp sense of humour as well as a sharp tongue, to which the students warmed enthusiastically. Very soon a guessing game commenced as to which student would be lucky enough to catch her eye and win her heart. Everyone knew, from the Principal down, that it was only a matter of time before one did. They knew, too, that he would be a special man.

Willie arrived at the College in 1930, naturally irrepressible, the First Class Honours tag adorning him lightly, and soon assumed the lead in conversation, in College sports (especially football and billiards), in the classrooms – and in baiting the Auld Kirkers. They made him Dinner Convenor, which entailed keeping discipline in the Dining Room – a Refectory Censor, if not a Moral one – to ensure that good order prevailed and the students were as satisfied as possible. It involved liaising with the catering staff, notably with the Cook, which is how he met Kate. 'What could be more natural,' questioned Professor Galloway forty years later, 'than that the Cook and the Dinner Convenor should strike up a partnership?' What, indeed? And what a partnership!

It is arguable that they were genuine soul mates. Perhaps they were, in the Platonic sense – of finding their other, opposing, halves. They were certainly very different personalities, from very different backgrounds, with quite different outlooks. It is obvious that, for all their similarities, Kate was and remained more practical and worldly than Willie; and that he was more devout and bookish than she. She was a great believer in the established order of things; Willie was ever a questioner, a natural iconoclast, always returning to the fundamentals, looking for the best way to get things done, despite the past and its traditions. Kate was naturally conservative in such matters – 'why mend it if it ain't broken?' as our American friends might say; Willie a natural 'liberal', ever urged forward by the new and becoming. Yet their differing attitudes merged brilliantly – they worked hard at their merging. They struck up a dynamic partnership which none can deny, in which both were stretched and fulfilled, serving their generation together in ways beyond full telling.

'The only truly happy man,' Willie once opined, 'is the man who finds the other half of himself.' A Platonic concept, to be sure, which he knew at the beginning of their partnership, and reaffirmed forcefully at the end of his life, writing in *Testament of Faith*, 'She has all the qualities I do not possess ... I do not know how she has put up with me for forty years ... I have been cared for and protected all my days with a care and a protection which no man can deserve, and for which no thanks are adequate.' It was particularly obvious in their pastoral years, in which Kate showed all the knowledge and wisdom derived from life in her father's manse, bringing with it a narrower ecclesiastical background if a broader experience than Willie had known. For his part, he offered breathtaking vision and commitment, and an energy and determination to match. He managed to combine all this with a writing career which set records in the history of parish work, in religious education, journalism and biblical literature, in which Kate helped to no small degree, not only by freeing him to write, but in actively helping him by providing criticism and comment.

The match occasioned surprise to some onlookers; others were against it from the start. Willie, well-built, athletic, intellectual, very physical, ebullient, courteous and humble, his wavy hair and broad brow framing a handsome face, if partly deaf. Kate, auburn-haired, slim, short, vivacious, her acquiline features warning of her serious disposition, but ever ready to burst into fun and laughter; tense, intelligent and talkative, fond of the social life. Willie was able to ascend the spiritual paths, even to a point of mysticism (a characteristic little spoken of by him, even less noted by his unseeing commentators), always laid back. Kate was ever down-to-earth, full of the day's needs and responsibilities, fussing even. Willie was a genuine scion of the United Free Church, an Uffie protagonist (of its freedoms rather than its institutions). Kate was a proud member of the Auld Kirk, defensive of its reputed place in the nation, its contributions to the history and people of Scotland – and far beyond. He was the single product of aged and doting parents, their pride and joy, somewhat spoiled by them, not least by Rebecca, their maid. Kate was anything but that: one of five, brought up to the rearing of pigs and chickens and horses, who knew the arts and labour of cheese and jam-making and everything beyond that. He was two years younger than she, less mature, at times more fun-loving, almost loud with it, verging on the irresponsible, untrammelled by convention. Their relationship was the subject of many a conversation by staff and fellow students, and not a few of the latter were quietly jealous. It was 'love at first bite', as one wag commented.

They were ribbed mercilessly, of course. He was charged with being overfavoured by her; she with doting on him, offering more than his fair share of food – a man who was graduating from Bun Barclay to *bon viveur*. One student noticed that there were actual peas in *his* soup. 'Favouritism!' he yelled, and the rest joined in. His was a smart move, they conceded, not a little impressed by Kate's and Willie's ability in working so smoothly together. No matter how demanding the week-end duties, travelling around the churches, supplying pulpit, taking Bible classes, no matter how dense the studies became. Even with his mother in terminal decline, he was always found in the kitchen early on Monday mornings, chatting to Kate, catching up on the news, describing his travels and visits, his bookish discoveries, ensuring that the week's duties were in hand.

The time came for them to introduce each other to their respective families, a move bound to arouse natural concerns for both. Willie was now within sight of his accomplishments. The word was out that he was a student well above the ordinary, a man with a future. Mr Gillespie warmed to him, and was glad to note Willie's love of learning as well as his other gifts: here was a man who could discuss with him the minutiae of classical tradition; who could talk to him man to man; whose conversations were rich in knowledge as well as cautious in judgement; the son he never had. Willie was amazed at their parish life, and listened and watched assiduously. Mrs Gillespie, however, was of a different opinion. She could see the strength of character that lay in Willie, and guessed how difficult life with him might be. His enthusiasms were becoming well known, his rate of working exceptional, his need for sleep well below the average. She was aware of Kate's purposeful commitments, of her vulnerabilities as well as her strengths. She knew, as few others did, the trials and pressures of parish life. And she had real doubts over WDB, whom Willie (she thought) too closely resembled.

It was there that she sensed the real problems would be encoun-tered. And in that she judged rightly. WDB had become even less flexible of late, more withdrawn – worried about his wife's declining health, even more so about his son's activities, particularly his choice of wife. Blessed beyond measure himself in this regard, he had seen many a man's work and potential ruined by an unhelpful or uncom-prehending spouse. This slight, garrulous, sometimes frenetic young woman of Dundonald concerned him. He was not the man to hide his concerns. He saw tendencies in her he had long combatted in Willie; the writing was on the wall for a disastrous turn to his hopes.

Kate, contrariwise, saw no need to apologize for herself and did not do so. She was an accomplished and professional woman in her own right, unusually so for those days – a matter that WDB did not entirely favour. It was an era of accepted chauvinism, of male pre-eminence, in which WDB led, his son aptly following him. Kate had no interest in becoming 'the little woman' at Willie's beck and call; still less of becoming subservient to his wishes. But she was in love, and she was determined. Reciprocity was her understanding of their future together, and she meant to achieve it.

Further, Kate, like her parents, did not like WDB's evangelicalism, his Free Churchmanship. She did not like its enthusiasms, its 'easy believism' (as she saw it). It was too cloying. He was too opinionated; he was too fluent and wordy for her tastes. He was simply too much. She preferred her father's quieter, more measured attitudes. Her father was a real minister, WDB merely aped one. There were other differences, not least the physical. Her father was tall and slim, ascetic even, aristocratic in bearing – curiously like Daniel McLeish. She found WDB small and portly, and not only in stature. She found his face unattractive ('like a bottle of port', as one of her sisters tartly described him to me), though he had never drunk alcohol and was indeed a combatant against it publicly and privately, which was also very much to Kate's distaste. Why did he have so many rules? The chemistry was simply not there, and they never really got to *like* each other. Even when WDB tried to be friendly he came across as patronizing. Worst of all, he could not admit Willie's faults!

Kate and Willie were not put off by such problems. They had each found their ideal, and they were content to weather the problems and get on with their lives. They did so for three happy years. In this time Kate discovered some amazing things about Willie. She never lost her awe at his abilities and enthusiasms, his strength of mind as well as his strength of body, his incredible memory as well as his breadth of outlook. One surprise was that she discovered he had never really left Motherwell – an unattractive place to Kate, full of noise and dirt. He loved it. It was *home*. He idolized its football team. He was crazy over its railway yard, its engines; its proximity to Glasgow. As ever, he 'kept his friendships in good repair', some of which she was none too keen about. They were not her type, town-people.

They married on 30 June 1933. The wedding took place at Dundonald, Kate's father officiating, her unmarried sisters Mary, Elspeth and Alison as bridesmaids – a big celebration for the locality, for the family was immensely popular. A big day for Willie, too; at long last, aged twenty-six, he was taking leave of what was left of the family nest, making his own. John Smith, a former DHS schoolfriend, acted as best man. Willie was determined not to upset things by having 'a ministerial type act for him' (he later confessed to being anti-clerical, as we shall see). The ever-faithful Rebecca undertook his grooming. John collected him from Wilton Street in his Morris Cowley. (WDB and Rebecca made their own way to Dundonald.) The two ex-schoolboys stopped at a small village for refreshments on the way, causing something of a stir as they were both done up to the nines, Willie clerically collared.

Following the service, Kate and he set off in John's car, which they had borrowed for the occasion. They had set their sights on Bournemouth for their honeymoon, and to it they proceeded happily, Willie singing rapturously into the wind, as was his wont. Only one record has been publicly preserved from their honeymoon, a photograph of them walking happily along the front, hand in hand – *several books under Willie's arm*! The pattern of his batchelor days was thus continued even on honeymoon, and well beyond it: 'Love me, love my books.' It was to become a source of irritation to Kate, who wondered why he could not do without books, just occasionally.

They were received into his parish with enthusiasm, and Kate took over from Mrs Cameron who had looked after Willie in the manse until now, very content to have her own things, her own home. Among the gifts they received were a fine gate-leg dining table from the church and a study chair from the Sunday School, which served them and many others for years. The routine Willie had established at the beginning continued, if anything more dynamically than before with Kate at his side, as she was able to release him from the domestic duties he was forced to attend to when single. The church organized two 'Welcome Meetings' for Kate, at which Willie introduced his new bride, who was eagerly adopted by them into their vibrant family. And so the Winter Session got under way.

One of the most fruitful expressions of Willie's ministry lay with young people, not least in his relationship with the Y (as the YMCA was called). He was placed – to WDB's delight – on its local list of accredited speakers, thereby adding another arrow to his already bulging quiver. It was to be an association which was to last until the end of his life, in which he was to form a part of its history. As I write this, the Y's specially bound presentation volume in honour of his great service for them sits alongside me; it is signed by twenty-two of their most senior officers and is beautifully illustrated. Additionally, the Presbytery of Paisley made him the Liaison Officer with the Scottish Temperance Alliance, a role he was able to throw his weight behind thanks to his father's heavy influence, the YMCA and Trinity Church, which were all anti-alcoholic. This task he shouldered willingly, though his views on the subject were somewhat different from theirs. He would 'give them what they wanted to hear'. In St Paul's words, he would be 'all things to all men, that he might win some' – antisyzygies prevailing.

The essence of those days may be summed up in a sermon he delivered at the end of August: 'Onwards, not Backwards'. It was to become a sort of leitmotif in his ministry, like his emphasis on goodwill, recurring again and again in his sermons and writings. Strong churches are proud of their traditions and successes. It was part of Willie's genius to take this church and its past and fire it again for the future: 'The best is yet to be,' he had declared at his ordination. He did so by reminding it of its fundamentals – in solid week-by-week teaching and preaching – and by externalizing its vision by pointing it towards society, away from that self-absorption to which so many churches fall victim. Renfrew was their mission field, as he never tired of reminding them; to lead the way whenever an opportunity presented itself was now his mission.

He was not allowed to forget the wider Church. In addition to becoming Liaison Officer with the STA, he was appointed to serve on the Presbytery Committee on Foreign and Jewish Missions and Colonial and Continental Affairs – i.e. its world mission. References in his books to missionaries and missionary endeavour show just how well-informed he was in this respect, having been brought up on a diet of missionary biography and enterprise. But he soon showed that he had very little time for mere attendance at committee meetings – the 'talks about talking' that often characterizes them, their ability to proliferate minutes and waste hours. At times he did not much enjoy meeting even with his fellow ministers; he particularly disliked their jargon-filled talk and jockeyings for position. As he was to admit in *Testament of Faith*, 'I take no delight in saying so – I am ashamed to say so – there is in me a strain of anti-clericalism.'

His own activities were well rounded and balanced, recognizing the differing interests of his large congregation, and of the larger civic community he sought to reach beyond it. Music, he knew, was one of their greatest joys, which he shared. This was, of course, long before television, even radio, gained their strangleholds on society; a time when many people could not afford such, or only sets of inferior quality, when records and radiograms were still quite primitive. Willie firmly believed it was one of the Church's functions to offer people the right sort of entertainment – on the principle of Philippians 4:8 (see p. 60). Accordingly, music nights became a regular feature in this music-loving church, the first of which was a 'Sankey Night', based on the hymn book of Ira D. Sankey, a partner in the D. L. Moody campaigns of fifty and more years before: another reflection of WDB's great influence. Hymn sheets were supplied at first, but the evenings became so popular that they soon had to purchase proper hymn books. The style of the hymns is vigorous, the tone fervent, the theology not always strictly biblical, and some of the hymns are pure sentimentality. But that was of little concern to Willie. 'The theology can always be straightened out later,' he argued. What mattered was the hymns' ability to rouse and sustain devotion by poetic force and rhythmic verse – with ditties for choruses and refrains, and bold musical strains to carry them through.

No one who has been at such hymn-singing nights would controvert their power, though today other emphases are called for, as Willie later conceded. But it was a true 'form' for that age and it worked brilliantly. The Anglican theologian, Charles Raven, no lover of the evangelical tradition, called attention to this quality when he contrasted Sankey's work with 'the desolating Protestantism' of so many hymns. Willie knew it, too, and used it as one weapon among many in his armoury.

Alongside this, and in bold contrast, went his growing interest in the work of the League of Nations, as concern over Germany's plans and fulminations grew, the religious and the secular ever hand in hand. A convinced pacifist – to the scorn of some fellow ministers – he hoped that talking would preclude warring. He was particularly glad to read that Chancellor von Papen of Marburg University, his own for a brief time, was one of those who dissented from the Reich-Chancellor's crazed ambitions.

Nothing can replace the regular and systematic teaching of Scripture, however, and Willie embarked on the first of a large number of sermon series. This first concerned 'The Seven Churches of Asia' from Revelation 1–3, and was delivered on a fortnightly basis. The church warmed to these lively (and short) expositions, and their appetite for them increased. The local newspaper, out of its depths in such matters, announced the third in the series as 'The Letter to the Church at Pajamas' instead of Pergamum, to Willie's amusement and the Editor's embarrassment. The day soon came when the announcement of another series was met with enthusiastic pleasure. Some members of the congregation made their own requests for this or that passage or theme to be dealt with, which he was happy to oblige – once again 'giving them what they wanted', what they needed. Thus a 'working-class' and worldly church was turned into a studying and Bible-loving community, and grew accordingly.

The Editor of *The Renfrew Press* asked for a second article from Willie. 'The Art of Forgetting' came almost by return, another example of his 'threshold evangelism' technique, also replete with provocative quotations, a call to understand and make use of one's time, of one's responsibilities for the present and future – as against dwelling on the past. 'The task that is given to man is not to think of what is gone, but to get up and work in the present,' was a lesson Willie obviously believed the historic and royal burgh needed to take more seriously. The point was given a practical airing at Presbytery at this time. Willie's response shows that he had his own view of what constituted present need. Presbytery called for a consideration of the place of women in the Church, and it voted in favour of their being ordained to serve the Church ('in a certain proportion'!) as elders. Willie, for once the traditionalist, disagreed with this measure, as he did when the question of ordaining them to the full ministry came up some ten years later.

Written all over Willie's concept of home life is that of man as bread-winner and woman as homemaker, an experience that had been idyllically successful with the Barclays senior, as with the Gillespies, and which had still given their womenfolk abundant opportunities to serve the Church in women's groups etc. (The largely female-dominated congregations still have implications to teach their opposite gender.) It was repeated with the Barclays junior, Kate playing a formidable role alongside her husband, not least as President of the Woman's Guild. Willie was simply out of tune with his generation's mind and needs on the issue. Otherwise, it was 'all systems go'. On one occasion Kate mentioned to Jean Haggard that between 10.00 and 12.00 hours she had answered the telephone twenty-two times: i.e. once every six minutes – while Willie calmly wrote his sermons in the vestry, in peace. Kate was frequently left to attend to all her own personal and household duties as well as those for the Woman's Guild, *and* was expected to have his lunch on the table just after noon so as not to delay *his* afternoon's work. It was never different, and they both paid the price, as we shall see.

We should note how well Kate managed all this. She was by common consent the perfect minister's wife, ever available, ever courteous (well, usually!), ever encouraging of her husband's interests and duties. In one week in December 1933, to take an example, she organized a baking competition (who better than this skilled cook?) for the Guild in collaboration with Brown and Polson Ltd, the food manufacturers. She also chaired a meeting at which Willie spoke on 'Impressions of Germany' – an account of his Marburg days; and she prepared for the congested Christmas celebrations. As proof of her leadership qualities we must note that within a year of her arriving in Renfrew the Guild's membership rose from 180 to 262 – nearly 50 per cent. She was very largely responsible for this upturn of interest; she knew every member's name, and their family details, and would often be found visiting, freshly made cakes or scones in hand, to be left as parting gifts to those in need.

In his turn, Willie knew how to lead and work with men, despite his strongly individualistic turn of mind. He now called the attention of the Kirk Session to what he considered to be a lack of cohesion among the elders and managers. Some were doing things 'off their own bat', not in conjunction with the leadership of the Church. The gentle reprimand was well received. He led where it was his duty to do so – but was content to take a back seat when others suitable to the occasion were present. He invited a succession of popular preachers to address his church from time to time, which in turn allowed him to preach well beyond his own parish. Sermon-tasters from all over came in response to the (astutely placed) advertisements that were made. It was another way of keeping things on the boil, and one which left him free to do other things.

These were days of unremitting activity. He sought to 'fence' the morning hours in his amply equipped study or the vestry of his church. (It is significant that he wrote his sermons, not among his books – his photographic memory easily catered for the appropriate point or quotation – but in the vestry; close to where his people sat.) Here his sermons and letter writing were undertaken at full throttle, as the almost illegible handwriting shows. Ever a gadget-man, like WDB, he started to use a typewriter early in his ministry, and he claimed to be the first minister to have used carbon paper: all 'mod cons' in the service of the gospel. Additionally, he kept up with his reading and studying and a host of pastoral and parish activities, not least with the needy visitors who came in a continuous stream to see him.

His afternoons were spent visiting – in homes, hospitals, institutions of various sorts – as well as being present at a wide range of meetings where he preached or lectured as the occasion demanded. One of his primary principles was the old adage that 'a house-going minister makes a church-going people'. During his Sunday services he was able to note who was present and who was absent in his congregation. A superbly retentive memory enabled him to do this, and he never forgot where each person sat. One of them returned after many years' absence, and was enthusiastically greeted by Willie at the door. He commented that he had noticed him during the service, adding that it was nice to see him sitting in his old seat.

The fine detail of his congregation's lives and families was also remembered by him. Any prolonged absence merited a visit, in which he expressed his regret at not having enjoyed their company. Willie claimed in his autobiography that 'he dreaded pastoral visitation'. Some of his former parishioners were astonished to read this. They had not noticed that he feared anything or anyone. Essentially a shy person, this was never allowed to obtrude on his work – rather the opposite, in fact. His visits were red-letter days for his parishioners, always uplifting, not without a humorous note. One recalls his following her – though unbeknown to her at the time – up the stairs of her maisonette. A piece of coal fell out of the bucket she was carrying, and bounced dirtily on every stair until it reached the bottom, which produced an unpresbyterian expletive from her. It was then that she noticed the Minister, the offending lump now in his clean hand. The embarrassment was soon passed off with jovial comments and an astute change of subject – and a prayer for help in days of stress.

Alongside this work were 'the sacraments of the home', the weddings and the baptisms which often took place in members' own houses, or even hotels. These required preparation as well as execution, a demanding role in such a large church. Not the least of his duties lay in the 'death and disposal' aspects of life which often culminated long months of sickness, though sometimes in that catastrophe of sudden death which spares no one. In this experience humanity confronts its fragility in a way that is unappreciated by those who diminish the importance of pastoral care as merely being 'at the edge of existence' or 'in the gaps'. Nothing is more needful than helping a distraught and death-ravaged person through the lonely, hurt, bitter and angry hours – sometimes the weeks and months, even years – of loss.

Willie took this duty, as he took all duty (a Barclayan keyword), very seriously. It is the operational key to his 'all things to all men' principle; serving *their* needs, not what he chooses to call their needs; genuine service. He was well known for his ability to sing and laugh and enjoy himself with his people, but he could also weep and mourn with them, and not a few saw him shed tears at their suffering. With over a thousand homes to visit, he was rarely without pressures of this stricken sort, which he sustained by assiduous caring and a careful prayer life. James Martin is wrong to suggest that Willie's first priority was 'his ministry and its obligations': his priority (and this echoes throughout his life) was his relationship with God, his prayers and his reading. He was not one to spend hours on his knees, but there were very few hours in which he never prayed; it was a life of prayer, rather than a prayer life that he exercised. Unlucky the ministerial colleague who was found guilty of neglect in this pastoral area, especially if he was known to prefer the easy life of committee attendance to that of exposure to raw, unhealed emotion. William Barclay's every sympathy was with the suffering parishioner, church attender or not, and not with the responsibility-evading parson. Unlike theirs, his ever fuller congregations proved the point. (One must be careful here. He was frequently critical of ministers, but he also knew how hard and demanding the ministerial life is. Just as forcefully did he criticize congregations for *their* failure to work, to adapt, to spend themselves and their privileged resources. He well knew that many a brilliant minister's work was broken on the anvils of congregational apathy and selfishness.)

Among those now needing extra care was WDB himself. Aged seventy and without the help of Rebecca, who had found employment in a hospital management post, he was finding life lonely and difficult. He kept up some of his speaking and lecturing, fulfilled his role as a member of the General Assembly's Highlands and Islands Committee, but he missed the rich home life that he had enjoyed with Barbara for nearly thirty years. Several times Willie invited him to join them at the manse, but everyone knew that it would not have worked. Instead father and son opted for a telephone conversation *every* evening, which did nothing for Willie's careful budgetting. 'Oh, those phone bills!' he would exclaim as they dropped through his letterbox and reduced still further what little free money Kate and he had. A servant – especially to him in this cradle of Stuarts – was a steward above everything else. Stewardship of time was just as important as that of money, and a number of sermons were geared to that principle. He was extremely competent in such matters, as many observed. One of his favourite prayers was that of Sir Jacob Astley, spoken as he went into battle: 'O Lord, Thou knowest how busy I must be this day; if I forget thee, do not thou forget me.'

'Mr Barclay is to be congratulated upon his first Annual Congregational Meeting,' the editor of the church magazine commented, noting with surprise that it had finished by 21.00 hours, a record in this talkative and fretful church. Willie's use of his own time was a matter he prided himself on, that of others even more so. The day was to come when, as Dean of Faculty in the University of Glasgow, the same compliment would be made of him. It was one of the big secrets of his busy and successful life. At the time of the quinquennial visitation by Presbytery, he and his fellow leaders were praised for the orderliness with which matters were done – another aspect on which he prided himself, though they had their knuckles rapped for not using a fireproof safe, a complaint that proved prophetic, for a few months later part of the church's records were destroyed by fire. Up to this point Willie's attendance at Presbytery had been acceptable. Alas, it was not to last. His first year saw ten attendances at its *sederunts*; his second but three; from whence it got very much worse.

Pressures of a different sort began to pile up as his church and reputation grew. Invitations began to pour in for him to take part in civic and other churches' special events, with Willie usually being described as 'the well known minister of Trinity Church, Renfrew'. Among these, for example, was his role as Special Summer Preacher at the fashionable Rutherford Memorial Church; and then Main Speaker at a united churches' open-air service. He was also called on to act at the Prize Giving at Renfrew High School, when some of his young people saw him in a very different light as he recounted some of his own, less than ministerial, exploits at school. 'I have enjoyed living,' he wrote at the end of his life, and he had. Observers saw it, and wondered. More seriously, he won an important argument in the Church Session when he succeeded in obtaining its agreement to affiliate the Sunday School with the Scottish Sunday School Union, thus delivering it from its traditional insularity. Little did he realize that this move was to pave the way for a whole new career – in a sense, two careers – that were, literally, to change his life.

It was not all seriousness. At the Sunday School outing he caused consternation among some of the fuddy-duddies (old and young) – when he took off his clerical collar and ran a race for a dare. In truth it did not take much daring. The old DHS finalist leaped at the opportunity to put aside his decorum and whoop with glee as he came in first over the line, if a little slower than hitherto.

The SS *Queen Mary* was launched from the nearby dockyards, the King and Queen attending, escorted by the Baron of Renfrew who was shortly to make his own impression in a way that Willie thought the antithesis of public service.

The Session at Trinity was asked to sit for a photograph. As the editor phrased it, 'it was asked to descend from the pinnacle of solemnity on which it is believed to stand – or sit'. 'Stooping even lower,' he continued, 'the Session challenged the Men's Club to a bowls match,' deftly adding, 'the results may be published, as the Session won.'

Work for the Sunday School was always one of Willie's most important responsibilities, but this year (1934) Kate did not accompany him as usual to the Annual SSSU Convention. She was busy about other matters. On his return she presented him with their first-born, named William James Ronald, the names representing her husband's family, her own, and that of her former charge, the late son of Sir Charles MacAndrew, whose photograph had hung in the manse since his premature death. A more historic touch for the name's influence might be that of the Clan Ranald, which hailed from the Lochaber District of Fort William. It had joined the Macdonalds and Prince Charlie in the '45 Rising:

> No more we'll see such deeds again
> Deserted is the highland glen
> And mossy cairns are o'er the men
> Who fought and died for Charlie.

Commented the magazine editor, taking up Willie's now often expressed wish for an assistant, 'A small assistant has come – Barclay Tertius – and before long the little fellow will no doubt make his presence felt among books and papers.' WDB was overjoyed; Kate had finally conquered.

Willie was conquering too. On 7 December an article appeared in the prestigious *British Weekly* over the initials 'A. G.' (i.e. those of Professor Arthur Gossip), dealing with Willie's ministry and hinting at greater things yet to be realized. It reviewed his career to date, spoke rapturously of his gifts and accomplishments, mentioned the high esteem in which he had been held by students and Faculty alike, in particular for his preaching ability and his voice 'of more than usual strength' ('like an Ayrshire farmer', one fellow minister commented). It was a good note on which to close the year for the young minister, husband, and now father – and on which to look forward to even better things, which was ever his style.

EIGHT

TRANSFORMING THE DEPRESSION

Augustus John, answering W. R. Rodgers' question, 'What do you
think of life?' replied, 'There's nothing more terrifying.'

(*Sunday Times*, December 1963)

'Going to Trinity Church on Sunday was like going to the pictures,' a
former member commented. She was referring to the tide of people
who thronged the streets on their way there; the sense of excitement
which was always present and which Willie later called 'an uplift of
expectancy'. Excitements of another sort sometimes broke out in this
'fechtin' church' – for example, when a quarrel broke out between
the elders and the managers as to whose duty it was to greet people at
the church doors: was it a spiritual or secular function? This sort of
argument exasperated the new minister.

By 1935 the congregation had grown so large (it regularly
stood at something over seven hundred, and was soon to go into four
figures) that it was felt the Annual Meeting had to be held in three
groups, based on elders' districts, an idea drawn from the At Home
Meetings of the YMCA which Willie had recently introduced into the
area with great success. There *was* excitement at Trinity; usually
of a serious and disciplined sort. 'We are Christ's folk,' the minister
now wrote in his pastoral letter, 'and the view of that great spiritual
pilgrimage into which we can enter will surely refresh us.' A refreshing was certainly obtained, not only through sound words and uplifting prayers and sermons, but in song and drama, debate and study,
games and sports – and simple, genuine friendships: life in the round,
goodwill among men.

Early that year the cryptic intimation made by Gossip in his profile
of Willie became clear. It was announced that Willie, aged twenty-
nine, was to give the prestigious Bruce Lectures for 1936–7. These
celebrated the work of Alexander Balmain Bruce of Perthshire, New
Testament Professor at Trinity College from 1875 to 1899, with
which subject he combined Apologetics (i.e. the reasoned defence of

Christianity). Like William Robertson Smith, who had been removed from his Chair at Aberdeen for his 'advanced' views on the Bible, Bruce had come under suspicion from his ecclesiastical confrères, as many more were to do, including Willie himself.

'He cut the cables and gave us a glimpse of the blue waters,' said Willie's mentor, Garth MacGregor, of Bruce's liberating work. He was one of the few Scottish divines to have delivered the prestigious Gifford Lectures on Natural Theology, which sought to emphasize the legitimacy of reason for the understanding of God. The Calvinist-Puritan tradition has tended to minimize this and stress instead the 'revealed truth' of Scripture, to which it annexed its own compilations of doctrine, *The Westminster Confession of Faith*, ('the subordinate standard [of doctrine]' of the Church of Scotland) and several others. But many have failed to remember that it *is* subordinate to Scripture, i.e. the whole of Scripture. Many have jettisoned the understanding of John Robinson, the Pilgrim Father who sailed in the *Mayflower*, who declared that, 'the Lord hath yet more light to shine forth from his holy word'. Willie never did so; he never fell into the trap of minimizing the truth of God on behalf of a creed or standard: 'the Word must out', was his lifetime belief. He early learned the truth of J. B. Phillips' criticism of conservatives: 'Your God is too small.'

Trinity Church was delighted to hear of this academic appointment. 'Knowing our Moderator and the earnestness with which he prepares his work for the ministry, we are certain that the honour will not have been misplaced,' records the Session Minutes. Perhaps surprisingly, in view of his later concentration on New Testament studies, Willie did not choose a specific New Testament subject for these lectures, but one related to Church History, to its Apologetics (Bruce's secondary preoccupation). The title of his lecture series was 'The Use of the New Testament in the Early Apologists'. The Apologists were the immediate successors to the New Testament writers (their dates vary between AD 120 and 220), men who enjoyed ministering to the increasingly educated classes of the Roman Empire, facing up to the objections to faith, the challenges of the current philosophies, the implications of New Testament doctrine, and the increasingly thorny question of Church–State relationships among both Jews and Gentiles.

The choice is an important indication of Willie's mindset at this time, undoubtedly engendered by his position as a newly ordained minister in a State-established Church (though free from its control), with responsibilities beyond those of his former Free Church convictions. For example, its courts are courts of the realm, whose authority can be called on when necessary. It is extremely doubtful if William

Barclay ever accepted this beyond nominal acknowledgement. For him the Church was *essentially* a family organization – the family of God, for which legal concepts were out of place, formal non sequiturs in the religious framework. Further, his choice of lectures betrays the *practical* aim of his work, from which he was never deflected, as we shall see.

He spent the next few months strenuously scouring the Fathers' writings and their methods – such men as Aristides, Justin Martyr, Tatian, Athenagoras, Theophilus, Minucius Felix and Tertullian. It is not inappropriate to note that with the exception of Tertullian, none of these writers was a theologian in the technical sense. This is to risk creating a distinction where no difference exists. Theology is 'words about God', though it has been developed into a highly technical, multi-disciplined subject. It has a very important part to play in rationalizing faith, examining its essence and attributes, its strengths and weaknesses, and what constitutes a true theological method.

The lectures were highly praised by his former tutors and mentors. Through them he reached the second rung of the academic ladder, following his brilliant degrees. Talk of his place in academia began to circulate, as Gossip intended it should. No one imagined that it would be fourteen years before he achieved the next step, or nearly thirty years before he would gain the title of Professor – and that after a humiliating and semi-public ordeal. The measure of the man may be assessed in the sheer persistence and grace with which he survived this quasi-political delay, in his ready shouldering of the second place in the academic echelons. Willie ignored the chance to have these lectures published, itself an indication of his practical priorities at this time; their publication would have substantiated his application for an academic position, though they may well have sent him down a road essentially foreign to his gifts and real interests.

Given his practical orientation, we may ask what actually was his preferred subject? His mentors were curiously unclear on this, even when they enthusiastically gave him references for an academic position. Commented Professor A. B. Macaulay, 'His work in Systematic Theology was so excellent that, had his attainments in Classics not been so distinguished ... I would have urged him to devote his life to the study of the Philosophy of Religion and Christian Dogmatics...' He added contradictorily, 'The New Testament was conspicuously his province.' Professor G. H. C. MacGregor, cousin of W. M. MacGregor, who had recently taken up his own appointment at Glasgow and chaired the lectures, stated, 'The treatment indicated skills in methods of research and a profound knowledge of the field, while the lecturer's vigorous and attractive delivery held the interests of the students to the end.' Professor John Mauchline, who had been a minister at Motherwell and thus knew our man and his family well, commented, '...with the exception of one man, William Barclay is the ablest student to have passed through my hands ... He did not content himself with mere linguistic mastery, he pressed through to essential meanings ... He acquainted himself with the range of Early Christian Literature ... He delivered an important course of the Bruce Lectures in which his mastery of the subject and his power of lucid exposition were apparent.'

We should note the subjects: Church History, Apologetics, Systematic Theology, the Philosophy of Religion, Dogmatics, Linguistics, the New Testament. His range of abilities gave his mentors – academic mentors, not mere friends or well-meaning advisors – cause for doubt. Where would he be most useful? Where did *he* think he could do most good? What were his intentions? Do we see here another aspect of Arnot's criticism, that he 'swithered about in his convictions'? Or do we see a multi-talented man zestfully encountering every aspect of the gospel, alive to its varied facets and developments, who was seeking to understand and apply it in every direction that was germane to his service of it? This latter comes very close to the matter, in my view. Forty years on we find David Edwards, the doyen of religious book publishing in the UK, saying that Willie had never turned down a book suggestion 'so long as it was *useful*'. (By when Willie had added Communication and Ethics to his interests, and committed himself to writing commentaries on the Old Testament.)

Whatever their hopes, Willie's mentors failed to realize them at this time. A few months later Willie was informed that he had been refused the Chair of Divinity and Biblical Criticism at Aberdeen for which he had applied (despite the very strong recommendations from these and other scholars). It was his first rejection. He set it aside, content to take up the challenge of finding 'the essential meanings' of his text, and to define and refine them as was indeed his forte, offering them week by week in carefully reduced density at Trinity Renfrew – and to a widening audience across western Scotland. Kate, 'a home-girl', never keen on wandering far or for long from her roots, was not unhappy. She – who was enthusiastic for him to apply to Aberdeen – had her family, the unstinted praise of the community, and her beloved Woman's Guild. It was enough, and they got on with it, together.

The widening audience showed itself when the senior minister of Renfrew, John F. Marshall, spoke warmly of Willie's 'high scholarship and intellectual powers' which had been 'proved, not only in his preaching, but more particularly in the training class [for teachers] which he has conducted at the request of the local [Scottish Sunday School] union'. This had always been of immense interest to Willie. He knew from his own youth the importance of learning in the early, formative years, and he now gave himself more and more to it. One door had closed; another was opening, and with it a career and an influence that was to be greater than any university post could have offered – in religious, thence secular, education.

His work for the SSSU, for Sunday and Day School religious education, has been hugely underrated. Astonishingly, it was entirely omitted in his obituaries, official and otherwise. We shall return to this subject, but we do need now to bear its importance in mind: literally tens of thousands of children and young people around Scotland and across the world have benfited from this extraordinary facet of his ministry.

Trinity continued to grow, and its influence expanded. The Annual Meeting heard reports of this from all its organizations: Sunday School, Bible Class, Senior Bible Class, Choir, Musical Association, Girl Guides, Brownies, Boy Scouts, Wolf Pack, Rover Scouts, Woman's Guild, Women's Foreign Missions, Men's Social Club, Badminton Club, Trinity Players' Club, etc., all representing over a thousand enthusiastic families.

It was the pulpit, however, that dominated. Sermon series came and went, prayers by the hundred were composed and offered, Bible readings were introduced and illustrated, all geared to a meticulous pastoral activity – challenging the young, encouraging the old, cheering the sick, exhorting the slackers, strengthening the defeated, supporting the bereft: goodwill to all. Amid it all Willie rushed serenely about, pulpit robes wafting behind him as he walked – never sedately – behind his beadle, the more mischievous in the congregation hoping they would catch on the corner of the pulpit steps as he flapped by. To their voiced regret they never did. Appropriately, perhaps, this was the year in which the government introduced a speed limit (of 30 mph) on the roads; none such was observed by Willie in his ministry. He took the pulpit steps two at a time, a single piece of paper in hand – the latest news of members of the congregation and its affairs at the ready. The rest had been laid out carefully for him in advance: order of service, sermon notes (in that sacred leather case, the gift of his mother), intimations, prayers and hymns.

A deeply moving experience now became the congregation's – for its dynamic minister, too. As he once confessed, 'Sometimes, as I stand in the pulpit, and hear the wave of sound come up to meet me as the people sing, I am more deeply moved, even to tears, than at any other time...' And, hurrying away from any egotistical reference, as was his wont, he continued, 'That fervour and that excellence of singing is largely due to the teaching that Mr Mitchell [Choir Master] has given to generations of young people ...'

In May 1936 WDB died after a short illness. Newspapers, local and national, offered their condolences and many comments about his extraordinarily active life: fifty years in the Bank of Scotland, an unparalleled lay ministry among young and old in several denominations, a singular Committee man, a Justice of the Peace, popular leader in the Brotherhood movement, a powerful mover in the cause of alcoholic abstinence, a great bookman and literary taster, a superb organizer, devoted husband and father, and so on. He was 'a fine type of north country gentleman,' *The Motherwell Times* reflected, 'possessing special sagacity, perseverance and native ability ... His name was a household word among us.' His obsequies took place in the Stevenson Memorial Church, Glasgow, and at his home church in Fort William (the Mackintosh Memorial Church), from thence he was laid to rest alongside his wife at Kilmallie Cemetery, Corpach. It has often been said that a man matures on the death of his father; hereafter, for certain, a richer, bolder, maturer note now characterized Willie's ministry. Parentless himself, he set about being a devoted father to his children ('He was a wonderful father,' his son recently wrote of him), his congregation, and many more beyond them.

The church halls had recently been closed to allow for further refurbishing and other necessary work. They were reopened in September 1936, £1,200 having been spent on them – no small amount for those days. In addition to the hall floor being relaid, the walls were repanelled, parts repainted, a new lighting system introduced, the organ overhauled, pews and seats revarnished, the driveway relaid, and the exterior of the church repainted. Delighted with the new effect, the minister warned his congregation that these were merely cosmetic aspects; the inner reality – their unity, knowledge and their 'manly perfection' – was what really mattered. Stressing the reality of the *spiritual* successes, it was announced that the Senior Bible Class, now under Willie's personal control, numbered seventy-nine members; unusually the boys outnumbered the girls, at a ratio of 44:35. That was *his* style of manly perfection, written in human terms on young lives. The refurbishing had been undertaken for the church's seventy-fifth anniversary which was joyously celebrated in 1937. Thus Willie had outmatched his previous four predecessors' records of a maximum stay of four years; typically, he was looking forward to the next four – and more – with firm resolution.

Several offers of larger churches, richer livings and greater influence came his way, but he and Kate had found their niche and they were happy in it. His congregation was glad to hear this reaffirmed, alongside his perpetual motto: 'The best is yet to be.' The church officers reported that the church was in fine feckle, not least in its youth organizations – which were to Willie the hope for the future. It now had no less than sixty-eight Sunday School teachers (also under Willie's personal tuition), with a waiting list of others who wished to take part; the Bible Class then gained another four members, making eighty-three in all. Moreover, they added a football club and a stamp club to the long list of societies operating under the church's auspices. Willie himself lectured to the latter with a masterly knowledge which he illustrated by his own extensive collection. These interests were not entirely self-serving: the local newspaper announced that this new club had given 18,000 stamps to the local Deaconess Hospital in aid of its funds. The football team did so well that it was able to enter the Scottish Football Association (via the Paisley YMCA League). Its minister was often seen careering up and down the line urging his players on in tones that could almost be heard back in Motherwell, whose team he continued to support.

The church took steps to abolish seat allocations, thus doing away with the rent-pew system – one of Willie's *bêtes noires*, with which he had lived uncomfortably for over four years. He used the excuse of the church having only had 690 seats, with 1,200 in membership; 'standing room only' had become a literal fact, and the problem was not helped by 'paid seats'. It is a strong indication of his voluntarist thinking. So the church reformed itself yet again, and went on to celebrate three new records: heightened membership figures, raised Communion attendance (rated as the most moving of all Willie's activities), and increased 'congregational liberality' – i.e. its collections. The liberality of a church is a good barometer of its spiritual temperature. His ministry had not only touched their hearts, it had opened their pockets in a most difficult economic period; many were the richer for the church's generosity: goodwill expanding. The church advertised for a new church officer and 120 applications were received. Trinity was now *the* place to be.

In June 1937 a sister to Ronnie arrived, named Barbara Mary after both grandmothers. A raise in stipend was discussed by the church managers (the level had actually been reduced prior to his coming to Renfrew), but Willie refused it. He insisted on remaining on £450 per year, quite content, though far from rich. It was all part of his private PE – his consciousness of economies, seen as an integral aspect of his Christian commitment. His children were often amused (Kate less so) at his going around the house – and sometimes the church – switching off unwanted lights, closing doors, creating a general atmosphere of careful stewardship.

Their family unit was now complete, and life was sweet. Time was found for visits to Dundonald to see Kate's parents, still ensconced at the large manse, and other trips took them to the nearby parks and the seaside, mainly for Ronnie's enjoyment – at least that was what his father said, who was often to be observed with socks and shoes off, trousers rolled up, collar undone, joyfully paddling or playing football with him. Other outings took them to Glasgow, to hear the Scottish National Orchestra and other musical treats, such as the operas of Gilbert and Sullivan, the latter a demanding passion of Willie's.

The 'thin-faced thirties' had started to flesh out; the economic outlook was becoming brighter than for many years; but the international tensions were growing, and rumblings of war were increasingly menacing. Acute observers knew that it was only a matter of time before the rumblings became actuality. Air Raid Precaution (ARP) notices began to appear around town, and military training was observed nearby. At the nearby shipyards HMS *Forth*, a mother ship to eleven submarines, was launched, shortly followed by the destroyer HMS *Jackal* and the cruisers HMS *Kenya* and HMS *Duke of York*. Neville Chamberlain was still being praised for his 'statesmanship'. But all that was soon to change.

Willie's activities in society increased. Some of these were of a negative but important nature, reflecting his deepest convictions – such as the part he played at pacifist meetings. 'War is mass murder,' he thundered on one occasion; to which was added his conviction that the Church was apathetic about the subject. He also spoke at temperance societies and protested the sanctity of the 'sabbath' (a misnomer for Sunday), if guardedly: 'wherever Sunday is being used to the ultimate good of men it is being used well.' Such activities were matched by others of a lighter and more positive bent. For example, he gave a lecture in WDB mode at the Literary and Debating Society of one of the largest local manufacturers, Babcock and Wilcox Ltd, on 'The Life and Work of J. M. Barrie', in which the work of the play-wright provided spiritual hooks – reminiscences of Drummond's *Natural Law in the Spiritual World*, which continued to influence him.

One of his most important activities was a new service for fellow ministers and teachers, which was to continue for over thirty years and produce more than three hundred written pieces: his monthly contributions to *The Expository Times*. These were mainly reviews of important new books, though he also supplied some articles, including two important series. I had the privilege of editing these pieces for A. R. Mowbrays of Oxford twenty years ago, when they were published as a companion volume to Willie's autobiography under the title *Men and Affairs*. In this work his goodwill principle came to the fore. His reviews were positive and *kind* – he was not afraid of that word (a Barclay keyword, akin to goodwill), nor was he in need of asserting his superiority as many reviewers do by saying how much better they would have written the book. The invitation to write for the journal came at the behest of his champion, Professor A. G. Gossip. Unlike the earlier one, this move did not fail, and so Willie joined the ranks of some of the best theological minds of the day, under the skilled editorship of Dr Edward Hastings and his sister, Ann.

His first piece was a full article. It reminds us of his Bruce Lectures (and may well be part of them), and was titled 'Church and State in the Apologists', which shows again that the New Testament was not at the centre of his intellectual activities. The Church and its functions were at the centre of his thinking and were to remain so throughout his life, despite his huge contributions to biblical commentary: his was a practical intellect.

This was not the only such event that year. A crucial meeting took place when he met Andrew McCosh, a minister of the Church of Scotland whose reputation had gone before him. Described as 'one of the most brilliant men of the church', McCosh had already made his reputation on both sides of the Atlantic. He was now set to do more, not least in collaboration with William Barclay. This early encounter was, significantly, made under the aegis of the YMCA and established a rich friendship between the two men. But the benefits went way beyond them. Soon the Church worldwide would feel the results of their conversations – a point that would have astonished them both had it been suggested at the time.

Celebrating Willie's sixth year at Trinity, the magazine editor commented, 'a tug of war has been going on recently, but the prize is still ours'. Once again tempting offers had been put to him to move, and once again he and Kate firmly refused them – despite the church's wearying reputation as 'the fechtin' church', Willie ever mollifying hot tempers, ever aware that the precious unity he sought could so quickly be ruined. 'That was a rare discussion tonight, Mr Barclay!' was a phrase he heard all too frequently. It was their euphemism for another tough debate (for which read 'argument') as elder opposed elder, and manager opposed manager. Much of it was the result of the church's own success, its growing interests colliding, its premises now too small, its large workforce too busy. At such times the minister's firm chin would stiffen, his powers of compromise and conciliation be stretched to the limit: goodwill and iron will working in tandem.

War fever increased, and the first Registration Day was set for 3 June 1939, when men of the prescribed age lined up following the enactment of the Military Training Bill, knowing that the writing against peace was on the wall. Willie lined up, too, joking with the nervous, debating with the serious, consoling the fearful, and calming the belligerent. His increasing deafness – it was now almost total – was to preclude him from active service, as his pacifism would have precluded him from taking up arms, but he was determined to play his part.

'THERE WILL BE NO WAR' promised *The Daily Express* in a faux pas of classic proportions. Its hopes were as false as the appeasers' logic. On Sunday 3 September, in the middle of the morning service, the church officer made his way up the pulpit steps, unusually interrupting the minister in full flight. Willie paused, read the slip of paper handed to him, and curtly announced, 'I am sorry to tell you that war has been declared between Great Britain and Germany. Let us pray.' With that the service ended, and an amazing new opportunity for a different kind of service opened, the effects of which were to be even greater than anything William Barclay had done hitherto. His ministry of goodwill had transformed his people's Depression; it was about to transform their war, at home and abroad.

NINE

PACIFIST AT WAR

'I am an absolute pacifist ... the murder of men disgusts me.'
(Albert Einstein, 1929 interview)

The first bombs fell on Scotland five weeks later, when the Forth and Kincardine bridges were attacked and an air battle took place over Fife and the Lothians. In the west of Scotland people were put on alert, but nothing came of it. A prescient report of atrocities in concentration camps (not yet of an anti-Semitic nature) was published in November, provoking comment about the 'descent into barbarism' of the German people, and provoking that righteous anger which carried the nation through the war. News of Hitler's escape from assassination a few days later did nothing to calm their fears or reduce their pessimism; it was going to be a long hard slog before peace was achieved, and then at a fearful price.

Willie's most conspicuous act at this time was another piece of 'threshold evangelism'. It was published under the title 'A calm spirit in troubled days' in *The Renfrew Press*, and was a portrayal of that state of mind which can prosper even in crushing adversity. It is curious that only American reviewers picked out my emphasis in the first edition of his biography on this principle of 'threshold evangelism', and some of them did not get it quite right. But Barclay made it his own – and was well criticized for it by the uncomprehending. Loren M. Scribner's review defining it as 'his way of relating the gospel to the modern world' is suggestive, but inexact. The essence of the method was simply to 'catch the ear' of the unchurched; to arouse interest and stimulate need in outsiders; to point to Christ tacitly, not to 'relate' the modern world to the gospel *per se*. 'Grab their attention' was his first law of communication, but he was well aware that much was required beyond this. We may see it behind Paul's statement at 1 Corinthians 3:6, where the apostle divides the church-making process into planting, watering and increasing. Threshold evangelism is not one of these three; it is the preparation of the soil that precedes

them, a prelude in which he sought their attention by alluring, sometimes contradictory statements and gadfly questioning.

Willie had been sheltered by his parents from the more hideous
effects of the Great War, though he soon repaired that omission – not
least through Robert Graves' best-seller *Good-bye to all That*, published
in 1928, which resulted in a successful film. In so doing he hardened
his mind against the blundering decisions of the establishment which
had so lightly used human life, and softened his approach to those
who were forced to fight 'for King and country'. Additionally, the film
All Quiet on the Western Front had gone the rounds in the cinemas and
halls recently, another reminder of the horrors of war and its futile
barbarities. Now, as the father of two, and the spiritual supporter of
many hundreds, knowing that the local dockyards, industries and
airfields would be targetted by the enemy, Willie knew that life would
be anything but calm. He had talked and preached against war very
often, and was militant against the destroyers of peace in any form,
domestic and social. Now he had to sort out a different message, one
which was more constructive, which would support those actually
engaged in war, which would deal with grief and loss on a scale
unimaginable hitherto.

This was not the only doctrine of his which changed its emphasis
at this time. It would be years before he parted company publicly with
the doctrinal tenets of his ordination vows, but changes there were,
not so much in essence as in emphasis, though he was not afraid to
repeat questions others raised and use them as pegs on which to hang
his statements – especially for those who found themselves on the
threshold of the Church. His conservatism was undoubtedly giving
way to a greater liberalism; the purely intellectual arguments of his
undergraduate years had now been lived and worked out arduously
within a parish situation. His people had little time for nuance and
theory, yet had shown definite understanding of the problems raised
by dogmatic questioning (as Sir George Adam Smith had discovered
many years before, when he was reprimanded by a fisherman for
being superficial). So lingering traces of 'easy believism', which had
never been a key part of his gospel, were rooted out; and a greater love
for humanity in the round – and in the raw – was born.

It is not easy for a refined man 'to get dirty his hands at the bench
of human frailty'; it takes time and sacrificial effort, and a true
sympathy. All the evidence suggests that by now Willie had done so. He
was thoroughly at ease with his work, unshocked and undaunted at its
challenges. He *was* a refined man, for all his displays to the contrary, as

his schoolboy, satirical essay 'On taking tea [in his mother's salon]'
revealed. By now two streams had become confluent in him:
first, his responsibility to make the gospel acceptable, to communicate it
accurately to his largely working-class, blue-collar congregation; second,
to free his mind from the credal straitjacket of WDB and his Motherwell
minister, Thomas Marshall, which had resulted in his own early (at
times aggressive) conservatism. If 'swithering about' can be discerned, it
was because he took both responsibilities seriously. Of a tolerant, open-
minded disposition himself, the weight of this responsibility could not be
dismissed; he wrestled with the conflict continuously, to the end of his
life, sometimes emphasizing this aspect, sometimes that one (to loud
criticisms of inconsistency).

His pacifist principle reveals this process. In 1936 his former tutor,
G. H. C. MacGregor, had published *The New Testament Basis of
Pacifism*, which Willie used in his own pacifist declarations. A stout
believer in and worker for the League of Nations, he had – like WDB
– been unremitting in his anti-military stance. 'War,' he roundly
declared, 'is not the answer.' This had aroused great opposition, even
from ministerial colleagues. One, in the neighbouring parish of
Inchinnan, had publicly declared him unfit to be called a Christian.
Willie took no heed of such attacks. He knew that people only had to
look at the evidence of his ministry to realize where true Christianity
was manifesting itself: 'By their fruits shall you know them.' It is an
interesting exercise to compare the congregational statistics of such
critics with Willie's; they reflect the withering influence on their
congregations of the little minds that attacked him – then and later.
Yet, in the light of actual war, and the criminal acts and heinous
behaviour of the Germans, Italians and others, he recognized that a
new situation had been created: a different emphasis was called for.
He was not afraid to answer the challenge.

Merricks Arnot, his best friend at Glasgow University, failed to
perceive this ability to understand both sides of an argument and
work with mutually contradictory precepts: it worried him. He was
also worried by his friend's apparent lack of concern over putting
such contradictions across, and said so. Willie's reply, often repeated
here, was 'I give them what they want to hear.' Arnot was distressed
to hear this apparently easy view of it from the man, the mind,
he so much admired. Willie was not put out; he believed that he was
meeting people where they stood, in their need, at the vital point of
their felt ignorance and (mis)comprehensions. A complete pacifist
view was no longer supportable. 'Offering the other cheek' was not

a message he could deliver to soldiers, airmen and seamen about to embark on dangerous missions. They had to be comforted, strengthened and made to see that the defence of justice sometimes required violence; that present-day fighters would not be cut off from the love of God when called to fight in a just cause. They needed friendship and assurance and pleasurable diversions 'before going out to die', as Willie once dramatically framed it.

Nothing dramatized his change more clearly than the requisitioning of the YMCA building in Renfrew and of his own church hall, in which Willie was a positive participant. Within a month, *The Renfrew Press* announced, 'the Reverend William Barclay has been doing a considerable amount of welfare work for the army, chiefly arranging concerts ... and now he is doing the same work for the Church of Scotland Canteen Scheme for soldiers established in his church.' In this he not only displayed a totally non-judgemental and fully caring attitude for some fairly rough types with little or no education, many of whom had never stepped inside a church, but did so naturally and enthusiastically, to the chagrin of not a few who were concerned over lesser things than people's need, such as buildings, fixtures and fittings.

He was not merely there for these newcomers to Renfrew, to Scotland (for most of them were English), but alive to their needs, providing for them by offering food, stationery, cigarettes; banging away at the piano, and leading them in song; swapping stories and anecdotes; playing billiards, darts or card games with them, or carpet bowls or table-tennis, and so on. He was unabashed by what J. R. Ross ('Lawrence of Arabia') called 'the rude maleness which is the serviceman's repute ... his f and b adjectives'.

His goodwilling for God was both a continuation and a breakthrough. It certainly owed much to his father's methods and his own involvements with the YMCA and other organizations, but it also marked a development from them, and that in two ways – a fuller appreciation of the sacred and secular as not two entities but one; and the realization that in the incarnation, death and resurrection of Jesus Christ, the sacred and secular, God and man, become one: the ultimate discovery. Peace was not just a happy emotional state but wholeness; reconciliation was not merely a legal formality but the restoration of a personal relationship – of fullest life, of deepest *bios*: an enjoyment of the life of God itself. It was a dynamic discovery, which carried him through the war, and far beyond. As Proust saw it (in a quite different way), 'The real voyage of discovery consists not in seeking new lands, but in seeking with new eyes.'

This revelation now energized and inspired his work anew. He learned to trust his message – the simplicity of the Good News; and refine his medium – dispensing with the inessential. His prayers thus became even more workaday, his sermons shorter, his language plainer – this was the real birth of the 'plain man' theme he made conspicuously his own – yet, contrastingly, his message became more forceful, more 'evangelical', and his church became even fuller. The idea of Good News (i.e. gospel) really *meant* something now. People were hungry for it. Forgiveness, not least self-forgiveness, became a live issue as men were trained to do and see things which would live for ever in their worst nightmares. Hope asserted itself over dire need.

One letter of thanks for this ministry (from a slightly later time) came to him from the front; he kept it for over thirty years, deeply moved by its comments:

> ... the Church has always stumped me ... Now I can honestly say I look on the Church in a different light ... Next Sunday I shall take the oath, stating that I believe in God and Christ, and that I shall strive to uphold his Church with all my power...

That was worth all the spiteful criticism, the narrow-mindedness, the paltry visions of little minds and the jealous expressions of the withered spirits of his detractors. One can face Heaven – and Hell – with such a trophy.

Amid all these demands he showed himself yet again to be a superb organizer. He was made the convener of the local committee dealing with the soldiers, but it was a committee that *did* things: concerts and other functions were arranged with bewildering speed. Kate was drawn into this via her presidency of the Woman's Guild, organizing her volunteers to make clothes and offer refreshments on a gargantuan scale. The church kitchens were kept open, providing tea and sandwiches, jam tarts and cake, and whatever else it could find and offer as supplies tightened and rationing took hold. Furniture ('comfortable!' insisted Willie, aware of how hard it was to relax on a wooden seat) was begged and borrowed – and books galore. To the horror of some of his friends, even his own valuable first editions were not exempt from this, as were many from WDB's prized collection, now steadily depleting. Games were gathered and played incessantly. In such a time the days of the week melted into one another; any day could be a soldier's or an airman's last; every day had to offer relaxation and spiritual sustenance, even if at threshold level. It was not unknown for the minister to carry a soldier or airman back to his barracks, having found him the worse for drink, in danger of being rounded up by the military police. He worked through the week, and often through the night. Their need was his call; goodwill consuming him.

Nor did this happen without criticism, of course. Some members of the congregation showed their anxiety – over his 'defaming God's house'; over the occasional damage to repanelled walls and revarnished seats; over the strong language heard, the occasional fisticuffs that broke out. They were quickly silenced by seeing a thousand troops bowing their heads in prayer or listening wide-eyed with astonishment as the mentally nimble, spiritually fervent minister-cum-jazz-pianist turned the parables into stories of applied grace. (Not that Willie would have used such language to them, of course!) In his second volume of autobiography (*The Mint*), T. E. Lawrence referred to the Sunday Parade services he was forced to endure: 'unreal service' was his description; the troops 'singing ... with the voices of their everyday blaspheming. There was no contact between these worlds.' But Lawrence was too hard, and too unknowing. This was precisely where God's goodwilling triumphed. Here was that 'contact' that mattered, as the soldier's letter above confirmed. These hardened men, often half- or even uneducated, were delighted to hear old, misunderstood precepts transformed into bright, hopeful possibilities of everyday living, even of dying. They did not get the old paradigms, still less chunks of the *Shorter Catechism*, but parables, everyday stories with spiritual meanings, dextrously fashioned and with the moral equivalent of a mule's kick at their application. Even the weeknight activities were concluded with a short prayer, an epilogue, and a hymn or chorus – often enough requested by the troops themselves.

A rumour went around town, ending in an anonymous letter to the press, to the effect that only married women could work in the canteens. It quickly boiled up into hot resentment. Willie, in a rare letter to the press, reacted with despatch, disclaiming interest (for which read 'expressing anger') in anonymous stories, asserting their falsity. It is easy to see how such a rumour could start, how careful the organizers had to be with so many single men and women thrown into each others' company, when sensibilities were heightened by vigorous training and fear. Willie scotched the rumour with his statement, and followed it up by an invitation to its writer to come and see him – and a challenge to join in the work. Inclusiveness, not rejection, was his principle for dealing with opposition.

Beside all this the normal work of his church went on, though its members were becoming somewhat scattered as the demands of war service spread. This allowed the younger ones to have more say, a thing their elders sometimes resented, which also contributed towards change. Willie took on extra duties belonging to those posted elsewhere, as well as helping embattled members and comforting those who felt excluded by the needful emphasis on war work. He became Sunday School Superintendent, Leader of the Junior – and then the Women's – choirs. The sick and lonely continued to be visited, and were found jobs to do in their homes; the straying were rounded up and brought back; the fallen were raised; the young were taught. Sermons and sermon series continued to proliferate, as did Song Nights and Music Nights. A late-night service became especially popular.

Not least of Willie's duties was the monthly pastoral letter which reflected something of what was going on back home to distant and absent members. It never weakened in its supportive and exhortatory roles and was usually accompanied by chocolate and cigarettes.

In 1939 the records show that Willie had 62 requests for 'special functions' outside his church duties; they rose to 93 (up 33 per cent) in 1940, and 127 (up 34 per cent) in 1941. Each of them required special preparation (sometimes many visits) and follow-ups.

Christmas came soon enough, Willie being found with the Provost and other dignitaries sitting down with 150 soldiers to a special dinner put on by the Woman's Guild – the first of a series of such dinners, which sought to rescue the spirit of Christmas (i.e. goodwill) from the bedlam of war. They could not manage turkey, but a fine meal of steak pie, potatoes, vegetables and dumplings was provided, followed by fruit and custard, cakes and tea. Behind the scenes, and contributing to its great success, was Kate – now cook *extraordinaire* to hundreds, who revelled in her easy expertise. It was followed up by a concert of music and song, the civilians being allowed to join in with the soldiers and airmen. Local boys on active service were not forgotten. The Woman's Guild had already, as the press reported, 'like the genie of the lamp, [which] can produce anything from a play to a haggis', sent over forty assorted parcels of socks, scarves, writing materials, cigarettes, chocolate and toffee to them; a practice that became regular as the war wore on.

John Kidd, the magazine editor and one of the stalwarts of the church, a great friend and ally of the minister, did not allow Willie's seventh anniversary to go by unnoticed, nor the incredible change in the church's affairs:

Seven years ago we did not think anyone could achieve such a record – we had become accustomed to the maximum of four years. We congratulate Mr Barclay on his success; no minister ever put more work into his first seven years than he has done. We congratulate ourselves on having been able to hold him; and in spite of war-time difficulties we are determined to do all we can to encourage him in his work.

At Presbytery – it had not seen Willie for some time, and was going to see him even less in future – there was much concern about the effects the war was having on church finances, now decidedly reduced. It offers an interesting view of the bureaucratic versus the spiritually alive principle (*not* that presbyteries are the problem *per se*!). At Trinity giving was *up* by almost 25 per cent and its expenditure was *down* by nearly 15 per cent. Indeed, the only rise in expenditure was that demanded from the church by Presbytery, a fact the young minister found supportive of his less than enthusiastic views regarding church bureaucracies.

He was an enthusiast for inter-church relationships, church unity and the like, but an implacable opponent of the churches' tendency to develop committee-riddled establishments – any establishment, indeed, that placed a higher value on tradition than life, on talk than action; that generated symbols of power and structure over the hopes and needs of people. He especially criticized the minister-lawyer type under whose influence (can it be called ministry?) the Church was visibly waning, whose religious *vade mecum* (handbook) was not the Bible but Cox's *Practice and Procedure in the Church of Scotland*, and whose stance was merely 'upright' – as opposed to 'kneeling'. To Willie the genuine minister was the one for whom visiting and praying, encouraging and expounding were the real duties, the specific components of his call, training and pastoral work.

He who respected all people had scant regard for the religious careerist whose fine sermons and prayers sailed over his listeners' heads, to whom a life of prayer was a conundrum. It is significant that some of his most favoured organizations – YMCA, BB, SSSU, Salvation Army, Baptist, Methodist, SCM, etc. – placed less emphasis on order and ordination, and more on the personal qualities of spirituality and leadership, though he would have been the first to say that they should not be mutually exclusive. Indeed, as we shall see, he thought the genuine Church of Scotland minister potentially superior to others, given his rigorous training.

We shall fail to understand William Barclay if we do not see in this a *principle* and a *devotion* at work. This was a man who took his classics seriously, his Bible too. The Church has contributed magnificently to society, but it has also negated it, over and over again, in pettiness and squabblings and irrelevant rule playing. It has tied itself up with State affairs, and sold its spiritual birthright to maintain its position of power and influence. Willie knew that the early Church minded these things not at all. He began as a Free Churchman, an Uffie, and he never sold the pass; rather, he reinforced it. He never forgot that the early Church did by the Spirit what others seek to do by schemes, legislation, articles, motions and minutes – and fail. He could not see the biblical basis for classifying church meetings as 'courts', or why its ministers should wear lawyers' wigs, or why its Moderator had to dress in outmoded (seventeenth-century court) dress or be afforded pseudo-court style. If he criticized his Church, its departments, its publishing house, its ministry, as he did, it was because he saw with great sadness that it was failing – betraying its inheritance, cause and ends; that it had become more concerned with tradition, with mammon, than faith and the work of the Spirit. He had listened to too much speechifying, too many empty – if beautifully written – sermons, too many prayers from which the reality of God was absent. He was ever ready to change and reform himself – some said too ready – but he also recognized the mere fidgets and decorators. He wanted, knew, and practised the reality. He knew that 'where the Spirit of the Lord is, there is freedom', and he knew that 'the apostles of freedom are ever idolized when dead, but crucified when alive', as James Connolly the Labour leader once remarked. Willie was determined not to be a pot-boiler.

He was not a natural maverick. He believed in good order and ran a tight ship, at Trinity Renfrew and later at university. But his imagination was not restricted by form and tradition; and his gospel was not emasculated by self-seeking, pride or class. He delighted to don the boilermaker's image of the shipyard people of Renfrew, use their language, get his message over to them. He was obsessed by that need, his *duty*. He regarded it as more important than laying down credal exactness or defining moral correctness, though he could express those when necessary. He was willing to minister under any conditions – in the open or at church, at a football field, a park, on a boat, a hillside, in the house of a known sinner; whether by music or dancing, singing or mourning, eating or drinking – so long as he *served* his people and supplied their spiritual needs. He was a true servant of goodwill, whose ethic is so much higher than mere duty, powered by love. In method he firmly believed that 'wisdom is justified by her children' – as many, unwisely, did not, and their emptying churches and fossilized traditions proved it.

Work among service men and women – there was a camp for the latter now locally, and they manned the batteries of searchlights and undertook communications and similar work – took a great deal of his time. But he had time and energy to give. Were there not 168 hours in the week? Only thirty or so were set aside for sleeping; a few more for family and personal interests. The rest was theirs: over a hundred hours, which he filled unstintingly. He never forgot that the work with young people, even in these fraught circumstances, was a primary responsibility of the Church. 'Let the little ones come unto me' was not a baptismal platitude but a dominical demand, to be interpreted in flesh and blood, in sweat and tears, laughter and gaiety – and positive goodness.

His responsibilities overflowed the boundaries of his church and district and found fulfilment at a national level. Willie became a co-opted member of the National Executive and the General Council of the Scottish Sunday School Union, a movement which had begun in nearby Paisley in 1797. For the next fifteen years his name was to appear regularly in its minutes, as his influence was to spread through their local unions. It was a work of unprecedented success, no less noteworthy for the fact that, amid trained teachers of distinction, he was able to redefine and redirect the Union's course, and supply much of its teaching's actual content. In this he was no formal committee member. The acme of courtesy and charm, he knew how to recognize and break through corporate waffle and reach new and specific decisions quickly, calling for the delegation of responsibilities and the trust that such implies in those so delegated, thus obviating waste and repetition: his applied principle of economy.

He delivered the Annual Address at his first involvement with the SSSU, an unusual honour. He did so with such ability and panache that his address was circulated around the churches. In it 'average church members' and 'average church officials' were taken to task; he offered a new vision of their work by exhorting them to take themselves more seriously, and God even more so – a prophetic word made brilliant by flashes of humour and insight, as well as his characteristic choice of quotations. Here preachers like Hutton, Tillotson, Martineau and Spurgeon are placed alongside *littérateurs* like Gibbon, Jerome K. Jerome and Carlyle, as well as old favourites such as Virgil or newer ones such as Richter – to say nothing of Isaiah and Amos, Paul and John, even Pilate, and, above all, Jesus himself. 'The great characteristic of Christianity is that it is all or nothing,' he roundly declared, totally committed as ever, if freshly anointed – and returned to Renfrew to manifest his own dedication, on four hours' sleep a night, the new work of the SSSU added to his already overfull schedule.

We get some idea of the mood he evoked by the phrases he used: 'clamant need', 'intensity of purpose', 'penetrate every fibre of one's being', 'the gift of enthusiasm', 'the man who matters most is the fanatic', and so on. Little wonder that he frightened the conventional and upset the apathetic. Comments such as 'This man is fantastic' and 'This man is dangerous' fluctuated. It was precisely the sort of thing that produced the death of the prophets, and of Jesus himself, as the staid and the proper, the curriers of favour and privilege, the unadventurous (a moral fault in Willie's eyes), reacted in shock to their own mediocrity, now fully exposed.

In the wake of this came Sunday School Week, on the first day of which he spoke, setting the theme: 'The Challenge of the Present Situation to the Teacher'. He got an accolade from the editor of *The Scottish Primary Quarterly*, who picked out a curious phrase in his talk, namely, 'the crucial importance for future history ... of our Sunday Schools'. It is worth noting again, for he was well-known for this concentration on 'what lies ahead' and 'the best is yet to be'; appreciated for his exhortations to honour yet remain unshackled by tradition – 'hats off to the past, coats off to the future' – and admired for emphasizing the religious intensity which was meant to charge their motives and work – 'stretching forward to that which lies ahead'. He knew he was preparing them for the future; he did it with a consummate abandon – goodwill asserting.

Dunkirk came and went, darkening the hour and suggesting that the war-cry, 'one People, one Reich, one Führer', might yet echo within Britain's unconquered shores. To the fray had been summoned Winston Churchill, aged sixty-five, whose lonely and passionate voice Willie had long admired. 'All my past life,' the former commented, 'has been but a preparation for this hour and this trial.' It was sufficient stimulation to turn disaster into victory, albeit with 'blood, sweat and tears', and certainly sufficient to encourage our minister to redouble his already heroic efforts.

Another of his rare letters to the press now sought to contradict a published criticism that the churches were not doing enough, in which he pointedly drew attention to the facilities at Trinity Church. The canteen was open, he declared, from 18.30 to 20.15 hours each evening. It offered billiards, carpet bowls, darts, draughts, dominoes and other games, as well as supplying tables and free writing materials, with subsidized refreshments. No less than 1,600 teas had been served in the past week – i.e. 73 an hour. He again called for help, not allegations. It is typical of Willie, who would count the verses of the Bible to make a point, to have counted the number of teas served, and he undoubtedly compared this number to the amount of tea, sugar and milk used in order to maximize economy. W. W. Braidwood, a manager of the largest industrial firm in the vicinity and one of Willie's closest friends, emphasized the point that he would have made a superb industrial manager had his leanings been in that direction.

A little later he was found writing to the press again, this time to protect the Town Hall from some 'ill-founded attacks' on its personnel. He went on to praise it for its support and generosity, not least in the light of 'our own hall [i.e. Trinity's] ... rapidly becoming completely inadequate to house the men who wished to attend our concerts'. Success breeds success, even as it evokes opposition. The result was that the authorities offered him the free use of the Town Hall – and so 'Impresario' Barclay emerged! The problem of overcrowding evaporated, and not a few thought that this was a timely fulfilment of the saying, 'Where there's a Willie, there's a way.' The concerts increased – in attendance, in the range of items offered, and in their influence for good. Willie's stature increased likewise.

One of the latest ideas of this proud Scot was 'to show something of the beauties of our native land to Englishmen stationed in Scotland for the first and perhaps the only time'. The result of this bright thinking was 'the now famous Three Lochs Tour' (at 1/– to 1/6d each – i.e. 5 to 7.5 new pence), which did indeed introduce many to those beauties for the first time – and sadly some for the last time, as they went out thence to their deaths. That sense of urgency prevailed; they were, indeed, 'living in the last times'. A letter under the signature of an old trooper from the last war appeared in the press, angry at the petty criticisms, appealing for 'all honour to the Reverend William Barclay, for the good work he is doing among the troops'. Many added their names to it. No biographer likes to be accused of compiling mere panegyrics in honour of his subject, but in this case criticisms are very rare, and then usually from withered minds, all too conspicuous for their unfruitfulness for good – for their consummate lack of goodwill. By far the greater proportion of onlookers were in awe of Willie's work and held him personally in the highest esteem. They were frequently shocked to learn that he was a man disabled by an almost total deafness.

Operation Sea-Lion, Hitler's plan for the invasion of Britain, was called off in August 1941 and a new phase of battle commenced – aiming to liberate Europe. Great Britain presently stood alone. Poland and Czechoslovakia had long gone, along with other East European countries; the Netherlands had fallen, as had Norway and North Africa; Belgium and France had capitulated, Italy and Spain had made their nefarious deals; only Greece had stood firm – David-like, its great stoical tradition undergirding it until the weight of the German army crushed its heroes (in which died men such as John Pendlebury, one of our best archaeologists, assistant to Sir John Evans of Knossos fame). A 'formidable army' was now assembled in Britain, and the counter-offensive went into action – 'one of the most fertile days of my life', to quote the Prime Minister. Horrendous attacks on the British population were still made – the 'Moonlight Sonata' blitz on Coventry on 14 November was one among many, and all but laid flat that city from which came a number of Willie's temporary charges.

Yet another of his innovations now appeared: the introduction of the 'Talkies' to his concert nights. A great buff of the silent film, he was delighted to introduce this new type to his area. At the same time the Committee on Church and Nation of the Church of Scotland notified the press, the presbyteries and the individual churches of its concern that 'the entertainment and social amenities' being offered to the troops were too secular in tone. To Willie it was yet another sad reminder that at some levels of church life men old before their time cannot dream dreams, and myopic young men fail to see visions. The negativism and idleness behind the committee-chair criticisms were not, in Willie's view, the way to press forward, even if some did (unlike him) emphasize entertainment without a balancing spiritual input. He ignored them, as he ignored all such tedium, now a stranger to Presbytery, pressing on regardless: pastorally, evangelistically, expositionally – ever entertainingly – Sunday by Sunday, evening by evening, in song and prayer and preaching.

His work thus proliferated still further among children, youth, the middle- and the old-aged, around his church and around the community, among civilians and in the armed forces – hundreds of whom went away declaring that at Trinity Church, Renfrew, their lives had been touched by God. Nothing moved Willie more than receiving letters from such, from bunkholes and battlefields, in health and *in extremis*, in freedom and even in captivity; who, in thanking him and his hardworking fellow labourers, thanked God for their posting to that small town in the west of Scotland.

There is almost an element of the comic about some of the enthusiastic statements made of him at this time – that sense of humour for which the British were rightly noted. Commented the editor of the church magazine, 'While crowned heads fall and states disappear, the Junior Choir keeps moving steadily on, unperturbed by the events of history.' It *was* funny to think that; but the point could not fail to be made. And the Junior Choir, after all, was making its own bit of history in the young lives it was directing and moulding. As were sixteen other vital departments of the church's life, all of which Willie kept under close supervision.

Versatility was the key – being all things to all men, that some might be gained: the predicate and the purpose. Versatility was in generous supply at Trinity Church, as the editor announced yet again. His point concerned another change, not in direction or goal but in means. With a sense of pride and undisguised affection, he commented:

> Some churches have singing ministers; some are proud of their play-acting minister; but our minister can do almost anything. He can play centre-forward when called upon; best members of his Kirk Session on the golf course; talk with philatelists; play the piano and organ; train and conduct choirs – even ladies' choirs; and lecture on any subject one cares to select. In addition to the many duties that come to him from a congregation of over twelve hundred, he has found time to attend to the welfare of the soldiers stationed in the district, and for this he has been thought worthy of being selected *as an Army Chaplain*.

An ardent pacifist, Willie was now in uniform, perhaps the least military-minded man ever to don it, but energetic in the responsibility now formally devolved upon him. The only photograph regarding this duty that has been preserved dates from this time, a formal photograph following a civic event. Willie is one of four uniformed officers (one of the others is the local BB chief, happily the smartest of them all), and Willie is easily the youngest on display, aged thirty-four, and definitely not the smartest in appearance. The mayor is with them, in chain of office, surrounded by other dignitaries. Willie's wavy hair has now receded by 50 per cent and is raked backwards and upwards to reveal a large pate, his right shoulder sags four inches below the left one, his right hand appears to be in his pocket, and he has forgotten to put his beret on. Moreover, he was not in fact an Army Chaplain, but appears in the famed blue of the Royal Air Force – the culmination of all those hours spent gazing over the airfield, his mind replete with payloads, distances, speeds and other vital statistics of flight; his heart full of ambition to serve still, in this new venture. Another phase had opened up for him, which would also continue long after the cessation of hostilities.

TEN

TOWARDS VICTORY AND CHANGE

'The Future is purchased by the present.'
(attributed to Sam Johnson)

Seventy thousand incendiary bombs fell in a single night on London during this time, which opened a new and horrific phase in the war. Thus it was that fire-watching was added to Willie's multifarious duties. He worked in ten-hour shifts with a number of his local friends, from 22.00 to 08.00 hours, a gruelling obligation for those whose energies were already reduced by overwork, fear and inadequate food.

In addition to his own stints of duty, he regularly visited the various observation centres, usually around midnight or later, to take a cup of tea with those on duty and chat for an hour or more, relieving their tedium and catching up on the gossip. Sometimes he even wrote his sermons, lessons and prayers while with them – to their amazement, for he did so without a book or note in sight. Sometimes Kate's welcome cakes were on hand, though these were curtailed when, shortly, she and their children were sent away to Dundonald for reasons of safety.

Some admitted that they learned more about the Bible and Christian doctrine from these ad hoc sessions, often on a one-to-one basis, than in the many more formal services. Their 'mental hikes', as one called them, were immensely invigorating. Willie would bounce them energetically around Scripture, history, philosophy, linguistics, literature and dogma, sometimes in formal expository style, sometimes in friendly banter, always goading them to *think*, ever the Socratic gadfly. The 'closed mind' was anathema to him, which he assailed at every opportunity, deliberately seeking to provoke those who enjoyed what he derided as 'the certainty of ignorance'. He knew that truth, whatever its cost, and true religion were fellow servants – as the Mishnah states, 'No ignorant person is pious'.

There were some narrow escapes for them, for manse and church as well, both of which suffered from superficial bomb damage. Others were not so fortunate and lost everything and everyone. It was one of

Willie's most painful duties, this wartime visiting. He would simply sit
with them, being there for them, saying little – having little to say;
simply sharing the pain of their torn hearts and shattered lives. Then
he *knew* that war was the ultimate madness, the obscenity of ugly,
calculating minds, and that physical opposition to it was a necessary
evil: a change indeed. He always finished such visits with prayer,
aware that too many ministers fail in this regard.

He was now even more a man of prayer – 'prayer on the wing',
amid frenetic activity; prayers to quieten minds and inspire hope;
prayers to foster love for God and humanity. It was not unknown for
him to pay more than one visit to some households as recurrent raids
added disaster to disaster, a second night's bombing finishing off what
was left of the first's. During some air raids Willie would go outside,
into the danger, and insist that passing people share the security of his
manse and air-raid shelter. On one occasion two Polish army officers
were invited to do so, but refused. They wanted to observe the raid
from outside – and died at his gateway for their folly. On another
occasion, a disabled German bomber deliberately flew down the path
of one of the searchlights which was tracking it. This resulted in
scores of deaths for the local WRAFs, whose screams were clearly
heard by the distressed Willie. Death stalked him daily, and still he
worked on, goodwill prevailing.

Presbytery did not forget him, even if he forgot it. It now nominated
him for two quite different committees: Life and Work and Public
Questions (of which he himself had many, over which he deeply cared);
and Ceremonials (of which he had none, and cared but little). It is hard
not to criticize the sort of mentality that would do this to such a man,
when people were suffering, desperate for his pastoral care. There was
irony in it, too. Willie did not reject such things outright – in the right
place, and at the right time, for those gifted to do them, they had their
worth. 'Due order' he held to be right and proper, but to put aside
war work and argue about ceremonials and such-like things he found
indecent. It suggested a level of ethical mindlessness beyond credulity;
it deeply offended him, as it offended others. Presbytery, accordingly,
saw nothing of him for the next fourteen months. He voted against
their irreligion (see James 1:27) with his feet, even refusing to send in
his apologies for his absence.

As if not wishing to be spurned, Presbytery voted him on to another
committee which was to consider the Baillie Report: *Interpreting God's
Will for the Present Crisis* – a considerably more important undertaking
to his mind than 'ceremony'. Willie's group was delegated to discuss

Sections 1–13, but no record has come to light of their meetings (if they did meet), still less of any conclusions they might have reached. The Report itself, he stated, was an important piece of work by an outstanding theologian. He introduced some of its material into his sermons and study groups, and he got some of his people to reflect on its findings. But to spend time during this crisis period 'discussing discussions', playing pitch-and-putt with concepts, arguing possibilities, he found inimical or worse. He ignored it, unceremoniously.

Willie's own interpretation of the will of God for the present was demonstrated when he founded an Old Men's Club in December, speaking to it 'in a racy and appropriate manner', according to the pressman who now found it necessary to follow him about. Willie suggested that his own name be put on the roll – a confession as to how he felt! Every day these aged men of the parish had the run of the church hall from 10.00 to 17.00 hours (the servicemen were now fully employed in training during the daytime, but their night-time activities in the Town Hall and in his church continued). Willie acknowledged that his helpers were 'hard-pressed at times to cope with their numerous customers'.

On 7 December 1941, the Japanese attacked Pearl Harbour, which marked a turning point in the war. Many restrictions were now in force, such as food rationing and other shortages (fuel, petrol, clothing, paper, etc.) which made life difficult, but a sense of victory was apparent, and thus their plight was made less severe. The stress was clearly showing on Willie. For the first time since his childhood health problems arose, mainly of a dental sort, which necessitated a leave of absence for two months from his beloved pulpit; the other work he kept going, toothless. (It was from this time that his habit of tapping his teeth before going into his pulpit developed, thanks to the inadequacies of wartime dental work; another problem added to his acute deafness.) He could not be said to be slowing down, but he was putting on weight, his voice was thickening, his cigarette smoking increasing; some noticed that a more abrasive tone was creeping into his statements. As Lord Moran said of Churchill's own attitude towards his health, 'a fine disregard for common sense has marked his earthly pilgrimage'.

At his tenth anniversary at Trinity he was given a new set of pulpit robes, which gift was momentarily checked as they had forgotten the clothing restrictions. These were overcome by a bedridden member of the congregation generously offering her own coupons. In celebration the Session asserted that they had made 'a wise decision' in calling him. Willie agreed – he had loved every minute of it. Every department of the church mattered, but his Young People's Society did so more than others. It was the future church, and had grown through Sunday School and Bible Class and was becoming a major force in the church, aiding its financial burdens with special functions and taking seriously its potential for the coming post-war society. Some of its members were fire-watchers, and those nocturnal debates fired their consciousness and their energy in a way that would last for decades. They had much fun together, in sports and drama, music and debate, as well as flowering courtships and homemakings. They gave the minister a book token in appreciation. It was decorated with a picture of a single tulip growing on a bombsite. Willie retained it for years as a bookmark. 'Can spring be far behind?' it questioned, and set the mood for their continued activities: winter was over; spring was coming; beauty was rising out of ugliness, life out of death – the Christian message in action.

Springburn Parish Church in nearby Glasgow was three times the size of Trinity, also with great traditions. It now made an offer to Willie which it thought he could not refuse. He was sorely tempted. He was tired; he needed a change, as Kate did, too. Some members and church officers were beginning to take him for granted, relying too much on him. And some were testing their strength against his. It was probably time to go. Both congregations were in suspense. What swung it was a single thought: his sense of *duty* towards the servicemen and -women to whom he had bidden Godspeed as they went to war. He could not leave. He had to be there for their return; it was incumbent upon him that he should welcome them home. It is appropriate to recall Lawrence of Arabia's sense of duty as 'the shallow grave'. Willie had no such shallowness – except in the Pauline sense of not living to oneself, of denying oneself. Thus Springburn, for all its prestige, was turned down. 'I burned my boats completely,' he confessed, 'and told the congregation at the evening service that I was staying.' One of those impressed by this principled attitude was Professor J. G. Riddell, Convenor of the Glasgow church's vacancy committee. The point was not allowed to become lost, as we shall see.

In early 1943, with a balance in hand and all debts paid, the church made a generous increment of £100 p.a. to Willie's stipend. This time he accepted. Change was in the air, and some of it was not popular. A. M. Ferguson, Preses for many years, resigned dramatically after a collision of opinion with his minister, who wanted the joint meetings between elders and manager that had been introduced as a wartime expedient to continue, with the minister presiding. Ferguson wanted to resort to the old separation between Session and Business matters. It was the first really serious problem Willie had had to face, and the contretemps was made public when the whole Ferguson family took off to another church. It put at risk much of his work to date, but Willie, greatly regretting it, remained adamant. With a single controlling authority the work had proceeded unhindered; misunderstandings were minimized; he was able to steer the ship from a single helm and not risk someone else altering course from a different wheel. He was now looking to the future and its needs, rather than the past and its traditions – 'forward, not backward'; even if this meant reshaping the system and losing valuable personnel.

He let the dissenters go without more ado, but wrote a warm and generous tribute to the former Preses in the church magazine. Another change at this time concerned Communion attire. It had long been the tradition for elders to wear white ties, a habit now contested by Willie in the name of modernity (and rationing). They agreed, and black ties became the rule: his only recorded move to date concerned with 'ceremonials'. It was the precursor to a more public debate about dress in church. The next time he had to face such an issue would be in the full glare of the press, and at a national level. Mitchell Ramsay, the Session Clerk and a tower of strength to Willie, now retired and was duly fêted. His retirement was followed by that of John Kidd, the magazine editor, a stalwart defender of Willie's leadership. 'The times, they were a changin' indeed.

Salute the Soldier campaigns were now being organized to reinforce morale and urge people to greater effort. The battle was still less than half won. Operation Overlord, Churchill's 'majestic plan' to recapture Europe from Nazism was got under way: two million men with all that entailed in supplies, transport, and communications, quite apart from the actual fighting, were now readied. Willie made his own contribution to this by yet another series of sermons, called 'Men of Destiny'. Churchill, Roosevelt, Chiang Kai-shek, Gandhi and Smuts were all portrayed in this role and the first proved much the most popular. His monthly pastoral letter disclosed in a brief sentence the goal of such secular themes – and of his whole motivation: 'Fundamentally and essentially our task is to make God's kingdom come within this place.'

A change everyone welcomed was the removal of blackout precautions from homes, car headlights and street lighting. Darkness, they felt with relief, was giving way to light. Domestically, things were changing too. Kate's mother had died some months earlier. Her father, now in his seventies, having celebrated his fiftieth anniversary as a minister, announced that he was to remarry. Willie, aged thirty-seven

– Lord Beaconsfield's 'fatal age' – was astonished. 'Gad! he's got a big heart!' the son-in-law exclaimed to Braidwood, who had also moved away, a change Willie regretted particularly. He felt such losses deeply. He was a sensitive, even a sentimental man, who liked to sustain his friendships, who disliked having the personal furniture of his life changed, his habits remade – for all his emphasis on the future. More evidence of antisyzygy.

One change noted by members of the congregation concerned Kate herself, who began to appear less and less at the church, save for its morning service and her beloved Woman's Guild meetings. Their children were growing up and needing more attention; her husband was unstoppable in his exertions; and she was exhausted. But these, the observing felt, were not the only reasons. We shall probably never know the full truth, and there are several possibilities: delayed grief at the loss of her mother, her father's remarriage, the stark evil of war, the dreadful sufferings they encountered, the short friendships (often broken by death), her overwork, definite malnutrition (she gave unstintingly to her children and Willie), the stress of partnering a man such as he, possible early menopause. These all played their part, but one cannot but feel a yet deeper struggle going on within her, one that had a definite effect on their future life together, leaving Kate drained, at times virtually collapsed, with no one who really understood her or who was prepared to help at the level that mattered.

Her husband, it has to be said, was not often there for her. He took her for granted, as he took himself for granted, an important part of his commitment ethic: all or nothing. It was not how she saw Christian devotion; sadly, she came to despise some elements of it. I raise it only because William Barclay's life cannot be viewed accurately without its being taken into account. It was part of the price they both paid in their astonishing devotion and hard work. Willie later confessed that he had been an unthoughtful husband, though it was not quite like that. He was not so much unthoughtful as committed; he *assumed* their commitments were equal. He could not change himself. He could see that Kate had changed, that life was now more of a felt burden than before, that much of her spontaneity and joy had been eroded, that she was now more critical – cynical even – of men and women, of the Church, and less trusting of God. But what to do? Stop he could not.

Her burden was his, one too heavy for him to bear alone; one that he could not but share with others – which worsened matters for Kate, for he did begin to share it with others, even certain of his young people. It was not sympathy or 'solutions' that she needed, but relief; a relief Willie could not offer. She would have agreed with Annie S. Swan, a favourite 'kailyard' author of WDB, who retold the words of one theologian's wife: 'It is possible to love your husband dearly, and yet wish, quite often, to throw him out of the window.' Kate was not the sort of person merely to think such things; she would state them, too. It is probable that the fullest happiness had deserted them both by this time, at least momentarily, as it does many couples. It was not 'the seven-year itch', but the ten-year exhaustion. Members of Willie's Young People's Society recalled it clearly thirty-five years later. Alive themselves to the wonders of young love, they could not but ask why he stayed around longer than usual, appearing not to want to go home; why a certain defensiveness about home-life showed itself; why Kate's Christianity now took the form more of heroic effort than loving spontaneity. They did not realize how utterly exhausted they both were.

A look at a typical Sunday timetable shows what they faced every week: Morning Service 11.15–12.15; Sunday School 14.30–15.30; Bible Class 15.45–16.45; Evening Service 18.30–19.30; Young People's Society 19.45–22.00 (and later, often going on after 23.00). These are minimum times. Sundays started early, in preparation for the exertions of the day. He would arrive at least twenty minutes before these meetings started, discuss whatever matters concerned them with his elders and managers, find time for personal discussions with his parishioners and young people afterwards, and only then think of going home. He: an absentee husband, wedded to his work. She: a devoted wife and mother, wedded to unending, thankless toil. We are talking of not less than ten hours' almost unbroken commitment each Sunday, after which he was naturally exhausted. Monday he tried to take off – which he usually failed to do, unsurprisingly, though he found time for a round of golf on occasion. Kate meanwhile was tied down – and tied to – duties at home: cleaning and washing, preparing and cooking, reading to and playing with her children, answering the persistently ringing telephone, and so on. Once Tuesday came, the week (which had not really stopped) started in earnest – morning, afternoon and evening.

As Willie remarked to Braidwood, 'I am trying to do a hundred-and-one things,' which he went on to list, admitting that it was a fortunate night which offered him five hours' sleep. One may well pose the question: Why? Was it pure devotion to God and his people? Or was there some 'workaholic' mechanism at work, which prevented him from relaxing with his wife and children more often?

His works of love had now become his love of work, to which he had chained himself – and Kate not less.

The Renfrew Press never failed to detail his exertions. Neither did *The Motherwell Times* ignore them, whose editor was kept up to date each Monday morning on the top deck of the bus as he went to work, by 'an enthusiastic boiler-suited individual' who detailed the sermons and goings-on for him. One particular exertion had caught the editor's eye: Willie's almost too thorough enjoyment of Burns' Night celebrations (another was his golf club dinner speeches). This was one of the literary aspects that had not commanded WDB's approval; one that he did not enjoin Willie to follow. His strictures of Burns regarded not only his use of alcohol and women, but subtler aspects as well. He appears to have felt somewhat endangered by the poet's eruptions against the *unco guid* mentality, which his son did not – the opposite rather. WDB was not to know it, but alcohol had found an increasing place in Willie's life. The much laboured paternal principle was forgotten, even rejected, if somewhat guiltily.

With Willie's developing enjoyment of 'John Barleycorn' went an increased enjoyment of Burns, including some of Burns' more outré habits of thought and versification. Like the great poet, plunged into a thoroughly 'working-class' parish, to which soldiers and airmen of all sorts and descriptions had been added, Willie had come to realize that the 'social' sins – snobbery, disdain (he preferred to call it contempt), class-consciousness, an unsympathetic and unloving disposition, naked ambition, the duplicities of office, venality, worldliness in every form – wreaked more evil, and that more insidiously, than the more obvious fleshly failings. He could not see why an adulterer, for example, should be denied Communion or put out of church membership while a smug manipulator of people and parish, whose attitudes stifled the work of the church, went uncensored; still less why the obsequious toadyings of some towards the establishment should minimize Christian ethics. Such manipulations, he believed, needed to be recognized for what they were: a great sin.

Social propriety becomes especially important in such circumstances, and 'success' in the Church is geared to it. Hypocrisy thus becomes its besetting sin – as it did in the Jewish Church. Willie had to contend with this social posturing himself. He was criticized over his voice (see Macaulay's comments on page 31), but especially over his egalitarian ethics and attitudes. The hypocrisy of Burns' Willie Fisher (the sin of the *unco guid*) – *the* sin for Willie, which he defined elsewhere as 'play-acting', i.e. playing a role unreal to oneself – he judged severely. It was 'the most savage piece that Burns ever wrote', he commented, and applauded the poet for being 'utterly passionate in his sincerity', a prophetic trait.

Further, and well ahead of his time (cf. Bonhoeffer or Gregor Smith – though Willie was not as formal as they in his statements), he was becoming more secular by allowing the secular a greater place in his theology and ethics, and the surface expressions of religion a lesser one. Threshold evangelism was beginning to give way to over-the-threshold, frankly secular, appreciations. Or so it seemed to some. In reality he was seeking to *integrate* the two, making of the whole of life a more rounded experience – a process which was to continue to the end of his life, though not without diversions, some of them of immense value, others less so. Pulpit or lectern; church or Town Hall – what did they matter, intrinsically? God's work, Willie was learning, was being done equally in both areas; his Kingdom was being established through both.

The separation of sacred and secular, God and society, he found to be wrong in concept, a throwback to medievalism. We owe to both, he would urge, we owe to God and goodness in both. The demarcation which WDB and others had long striven to impart to him was now seen to be false, as Willie embraced the secular more and more – recognizing it to be as much the place of God's activity as the Church. That was where he found the people, where they could be contacted, where they were. The war and its challenges to traditional forms and practices, the relationships it engendered and their challenges to Christian community – these were the engines which drove this change. Other changes would follow, but their full espousal would be long in coming and some never fully came.

Amid all this, his private yet professional war, the other more wasteful war reached its joyous conclusion for the Allies. And with it came Willie's great hope: the return of his young men, now battle-hardened and mature; some of them – such as Joe Kidd, who had met General Paton, to Willie's great glee ('pearl-handled revolver and all'), actually ex-POWs – heroes, requiring a hero's return. They got it at Trinity Renfrew, in a great celebration bash that was talked about for years – with which went an unseemly row largely between the minister and 'the worst labour type and the communist element', as he defined his opponents, his own middle-class predilections showing. (It is not inconsistent to juxtapose this and the foregoing: he was 'swithering' still, yet always making ground, always advancing.) They had wanted to raise a fund of £20,000, to be given to the soldiers equally, but Willie would have none of it, and listed his objections: i) because he knew that they would never raise that sort of money at this time; ii) because 'it is too much like giving them a tip; and you cannot give a tip to soldiers and sailors and airmen'; iii) because it would be 'blown' in a couple of nights. He had worked out that even if they did raise it, there would only be about £12 per man. 'What use was that?' he demanded. Behind these reasons lies a fourth, the real reason for his totally dismissive attitude: he wanted a community centre built in Renfrew – even two (he suggested the other should be built at nearby Moorpark) – to continue the work he had started, as the fulfilment of his (secular) vision.

The debate rumbled on; the soldiers returned, the celebrations were made, the flags and bunting were packed up and stored away. And the great idea perished. 'I am physically and mentally weary,' he declared in a rare admission. With it something of his vision and its present all-out commitment died – or at least went into hibernation. What he had espied from afar, what he believed to be right, was at risk of being crushed.

ELEVEN

'THE LAW OF COSTLY SERVICE'

'God ... Whose service is perfect freedom.'
(The Second Collect of the General Confession; for peace)

At the General Assembly of 1941 John White, the architect of the great Reunion of 1929, called the attention of the Kirk to the heavy decline in church membership. His statement (already adumbrated by Professor John Baillie's report) sent a ripple of anxiety through the Church, occupied as it had been with more pressing matters. In 1943 the Church of Scotland produced another report, *The Church Faces the Future*, which again centred on the problems it would encounter in the post-war period. The ideas were not new, but the accelerated pace of such reports, and the concentration they elicited, was to become a feature of the post-war period: the Church was now becoming preoccupied with itself to an unprecedented degree.

In America, the Church historian Scott Latourette was similarly emphasizing the problems; in particular, he was isolating the growing influence of secularism as one of the chief factors of religious change in society. His judgement was that 'the Church will be less a community institution and more an organized minority ...' It is doubly significant that he saw this occurring particularly in those societies in which Church and State were closely intertwined. The *British Weekly*, ever in the van of such movements, called attention to the breakdown in parish structures, especially in urban situations, and to the shortening duration of ministries which added to the communal sense of social instability. If civilization came to its watershed in the period 1939–45, the Church reached its own in 1945. Its need to act purposefully, adventurously, had never been greater.

William Barclay was never given the opportunity to theorize on these matters, though we shall see that he eagerly sought a position which would have allowed him to do so, believing – which few at that time noticed (or wanted to notice) – that he had something to offer in their cause. He had worked long and arduously on practical matters, and very successfully; his ideas had been developing for years. They were essentially community related, for all his Free Church predispositions. The modern awareness cut clean across this view. He felt it was necessary to think, and rethink, both ground and goals. But it was not to be. His enthusiasms put some people off; his boldness to move in uncharted areas frightened others; and those who had the say could not see beyond the obvious and the conventional. Structures became more important than people from now on, the Church's identity more important than the Spirit who inspired it. The foundations of the present failure of the Church were laid at this time. Our own loss rests on that inadequate vision – on that exhaustion, too.

Willie came under criticism from Presbytery, which was not pleased by his failure to pull his weight for its institutions. To use language of a more recent period, those in power were uneasy over 'loose cannons', even – perhaps especially – if they were highly successful ones. Willie's view of the Church, of its growth and unity, was localized and spiritual, yet more widely universal (i.e. 'ecumenical') and outward looking than many realized – or wanted to know. Presbytery's view was nationalistic and bureaucratic, very largely self-centred. But the differences must not be overdrawn. He was a committed presbyterian; he did have a vision of his own church allied to theirs which he served strenuously. But at this time he was not so much interested in the 'here and now' as in the 'what next?' (to use the title of Professor George Knight's excellent autobiography, another who found his Church stuffy and staid). Willie was ever working for the best that was yet to be, believing in the possibilities of the unexpected. He was a man of faith and prayer – and action.

He listened to their criticisms – and he amended some of his ways, if but briefly. To the three committees named earlier a fourth was added, one much more congenial to him, one in line with his gifts: the Students' and Ministry Committee. A fifth soon came his way: the Youth Committee, also highly congenial to him, and he acceded to its Convenorship with alacrity the following year. Things were beginning to move his way. Moreover, he had been appointed one of the ten Presbytery representatives to the Paisley and District Sunday School Union in March 1944. Along with matters concerning youth, Presbytery also required him to be an ex officio member of its Business Subcommittee – which occasioned an outright and public attack by him on the General Assembly. He regarded its funding of youth activities as unjust, and said so plainly. If they wanted him to serve, he would do so – but according to his own lights.

The Life and Work and Public Questions Committee had also appointed him to one of its subcommittees, whose task was to make something of a report from the General Assembly *On Returning Service Men and Women*. This was a very important initiative, behind which he threw himself with the greatest possible vigour. Much of the past five years had been spent in the company of service people. He had been one of their chaplains; he had served brilliantly their spiritual and recreational interests; he knew the scars that war service made – of broken bodies and unhinged minds, of destroyed hopes and relationships, of lost faith. He cared for these people – his people. Never was his goodwill more deeply touched; never did it inspire more self-sacrificing commitment, not least for his wife and children.

He commenced by publishing an Open Letter, in which he welcomed them back. He warned them of the great changes that were taking place, of the new internationalism that was emerging, of what the Church stood for, and what it could offer (somewhat idealistically, it has to be said). Significantly, he spoke of its secular role in the world and isolated five aspects – social security, working conditions, housing, a more equitable distribution of the world's goods, and a crusade for a better world – as its key issues. His politics were now undeniably 'pink', which also raised nervous questions in some minds.

These issues, he urged, were not to be dealt outwith 'any particular party or programme'. The Church, he affirmed hopefully, 'realizes her function to be conscience to the world'. He closed his letter with an invitation to join the Church on the even more optimistic note that 'she will leave no evil uncondemned and no good unsupported', and asked for the names and addresses of every returning service person, undertaking to write to them individually in the name of the Church – which he did month by month, a labour of extaordinary tenacity, and expensive to boot.

In so writing he had formally moved beyond his parish work to that of the Church at large, a move which took place hand in hand with his rapidly growing influence in Sunday School and youth work. His parish work had succeeded by personal charisma and sheer spiritual exertion; he was about to find that wider Church interests were not so easily moved, that corporate apathy and self-interest were intransigent, and alternative opinions and vested interests were to question his idealism and openly seek its destruction. Such matters did not represent the full range of his emphases. Alongside his secular appeal went a sharp evangelical emphasis on winning people for God, and for their need to demonstrate the life Christ demanded of them. He knew that if the Church was to do anything remarkable, it was from that combined base that it would arise. Some of his colleagues expressed the one side, some the other. Few expressed both, and fewer still sought to grapple with both simultaneously, as he sought to do.

Meanwhile the popularity of his training lectures ('at least once a week' he told Braidwood) and the Summer Schools grew apace. One secretary declared at the end of one such, '... he has managed to give us his wonderful guidance and encouragement, and above all his friendship'. He gave them much more. Every session was thoroughly biblical, the application was welded to careful exegesis at varying levels, according to the group's needs. This activity developed into another national platform for him when George S. Stewart relinquished the directorship of the SSSU Correspondence Course for teachers.

Willie had already given them one course in 1940 under the title 'Our Faith Today'. Now he had to distribute Notes and Questions on that course, the completion of which would result in their teaching diploma. They sent their answers back to him, which he marked and entered into personal correspondence with the course members as required. Seventy-seven had enrolled, to whom 924 letters were sent in the first year: slightly more than one per month for each of them. The Convenor at Presbytery commented, 'The number of enrolments has been increasing steadily – indeed, alarmingly, when one considers the amount of work that has to be done in reading and correcting papers.' In another letter to Braidwood, Willie admits that it was gruelling work, undertaken alongside much else – and with 'another big job on': his first book. The book itself (*New Testament Studies*) turned out to be 'a slight thing', as he later acknowledged, published at 1/6d (18 new pence) each, but it introduced the newly launched Diploma students of the Sunday Schools to some of the disciplines and emphases of modern New Testament study. 'The rest of the time,' he added airily, 'is my own.'

He took his place alongside eighteen members of the SSSU at the Lessons' Committee, which met in Glasgow. His first involvement in such lesson-writing had been for two lessons which he contributed in 1934, to which he had added a few more from time to time over the intervening years. They were anonymously printed, as were those of all the contributors. But the Secretary sometimes put Willie's initials against his own copy of the lessons – exclusively so, perhaps suggesting how impressed he was. Willie's style is in any case distinctive. In April 1944 he was asked to provide specimen notes for a six-month series on 'Thou art the Christ'. Most biblical work was based on the

Authorized Version at this time, of course, and all prayers used the second person singular, 'Thou', etc., as Willie was to do for some years. The Committee asked him to stand by in case they needed him for the following six months, the person previously chosen having indicated that he might be too busy to fulfil his promises.

He did both, and to such acclaim that between 1947 and 1953 he was asked to undertake *all* the Senior Notes single-handed, thus serving every Bible Class in the Church of Scotland, and many elsewhere: two hundred and fifty or so thoroughly written lessons in all, with prayers and other practical suggestions such as hymns and drama included. It was an unparalleled achievement in the history of the SSSU, and very successful. Sunday School and even day school teachers around the country loved them; they simply could not get enough. Here was a thoroughly informed mind operating at a level open to all, offering not only sound exposition and clear definitions of the themes and passages, but excellent ancillary material too. All aspects were concisely handled: introduction, background, exegesis, illustration and application, plus worship aids, prayers and hymns. As with the scribe of the Kingdom of Heaven, 'things new and old' simply poured from him. Not a few teachers admitted (to his consternation) that they merely read his Notes to their young charges; they could not reproduce them better themselves and so chose this questionable method so as not to omit anything.

He had become a teachers' teacher, and a national luminary to young people. It is not easy for us today to realize how significant this work was – even later associates such as James Martin completely ignored it. It was a service of historic proportions and a high spiritual challenge. Willie's work may be summed up in his own words when speaking of the teachers' responsibilities: 'We shall keep *that law of costly service* as we have a new vision of him who loved us and gave himself for us.' As always, one piece of work led to another. Thus the Minutes of the Presbytery of Paisley for 11 September 1945 recorded that, 'The congratulations of the Presbytery were extended to Mr Barclay [on his] appointment as Editor of *The Teachers' Magazine*.'

It is surprising that in the many articles and obituaries which surfaced following his death, this aspect – rigorously fulfilled over several years – never got a single mention. When one considers that the Magazine went to 23,000 teachers, one can weigh something of his influence. It is impossible to overstate its importance. Quite apart from the routine – and demanding – work of editorship, he wrote 250 lessons for it. Put together in book form, they would make a volume of over 800 pages, almost half a million words, covering every aspect of Sunday School work. Over half a million young people were influenced by him in this way every month. Unlike those who found themselves too busy to do it, Willie himself never minimized such work. On the contrary, he magnified it, and served its need in a way truly costly to himself and his family. He worked hard at it, honing his language, clarifying his concepts, adjusting his statements, ensuring their true biblicality, yet always keeping in mind the need to be intelligible, relevant and modern – an apprenticeship (if we may call it that, though it was more a consummation) for the books that were to pour out from him across the world in due course. It had one unexpected result: it made him more conservative in his statements, less liberal, and certainly less radical. We shall see that now and then he even wrote against his own judgement and position (e.g. regarding alcohol): being 'all things to all men, that he may win some'.

Thanks to all this he was now a marked man, sometimes criticized, usually respected, but not entirely accepted – Macaulay's warning was still in force (that he would get nowhere in the Church with his 'Glasgow' accent), to which others added their own, quite different, doubts. Yet it was obvious that he was 'a coming man', and so the Nomination Board of the Presbytery of Glasgow – the largest in the world – wrote to him, suggesting he apply for two different posts: the Chair of New Testament and the Chair of Christian Ethics and Practical Theology, both at Glasgow.

Is it not curious that two such different posts should be offered at once? Where did he fit? It was apparently far from clear to them, though *his* mind was quite certain, as we shall see. Perhaps theirs were, too, but they feared the consequences... His brilliance in New Testament matters had been manifest since the early thirties. Gifted above the average linguistically, he knew the New Testament almost by heart, in Greek as well as in English, enhanced by an unrivalled knowledge of its Jewish and Hellenistic backgrounds (the latter more evident than the former as he never learned the actual language Jesus spoke – Aramaic, a cognate of Hebrew). His knowledge of the Holy Land was second-hand, but accurate according to the general knowledge of his day – and brilliantly employed by him. (He never went there, and later refused generous offers of expenses-paid trips, for example, from Bob Kernohan, the esteemed editor of *Life and Work*.) His attitude reminds one of the Chinese scholar and translator, Arthur Whaley, who did likewise regarding China – for the express reason that he feared its present reality would destroy its mystique.

Further, Willie had made a careful study of the Greek and Latin literature of the time; he knew its main authors extremely well and possessed a detailed knowledge of the writings of the early Church Fathers which astonished even the experts. It was also evident that he had great powers of oratory, a charismatic pulpit presence, a marked ability to lead by imaginative proposals, and a tenacious spirit. The problem lay in his versatility ('our minister can do almost anything' had its drawbacks; it was not the age of polymaths): a First in MA Classics; a prize winner in PE; a Distinction in Divinity; a practised journalist; a highly praised Bruce Lecturer; a very successful minister; reputed Chaplain to HM Forces; an able editor and lesson-writer; a teacher to thousands. How best could they use such talents? Willie knew. At least, he knew what he *wanted* to do. Commenting on the proposals put to him, he said:

> I don't want the New Testament one. I don't want to teach technical Greek. It is too soul-less and I have worked too long in the warm intimate contacts of a congregation ... To be honest, I would give my eyes for the Practical Training job. It means practical training for the ministry.

The choice – and we must presume the competing pressures – left him with what he diagnosed as 'a mentally unsettled life ... I am filled with horror,' he wrote, 'at the thought of leaving my church.' The swithering intensified, a condition that was to continue for some time. He wrote to Braidwood again, 'It is with my entire good wishes that someone else will get the NT appointment.' But, he added, 'I would give my ears to get the Practical Chair.' He continued, with his usual modesty, 'Although an entirely unsatisfactory minister myself [sic] I think I could tell other people how to do the job.'

His autumn pastoral letter reflected something of this unsettled state, though not a word as to its reason. To make matters worse, his children became ill: Ronnie (who 'has turned traitor' – i.e. swapped football for rugby at school) had been hospitalized; Barbara was in bed at home, the victim of poor diagnosis. Kate, as ever, simply endured. Willie catalogued the series of problems she faced, the effects of deprivation during the war and the stresses of manse life. Shortly after this, she also was hospitalized. He now *knew* that the only safe respite for them would be a change of location. Unusually, he admitted of himself, too, that 'I can only be said to be hanging on at the moment.'

New Testament Studies appeared in December 1945, his first book, a very simple introduction of eighty-two pages for Bible and Sunday School teachers. It provides an interesting insight, if not into his deepest convictions, then at least those he offered to be instilled into the young. It was weighted towards the Gospels and the life of Jesus (ever the real focus and fulcrum of his thinking and teaching), and bears all the signs of haste and uncareful planning. Indeed, one gets the strong impression that it was half finished; that the author possibly meant to continue the 'studies' (the word is almost too strong for the book's content) to cover the whole of the New Testament, but stopped at Acts, perhaps defeated by pressure and time. It is extremely conservative – in matters of doctrine and in its critical appraisals. It was based on the *Authorized Version*. The miracles are accepted literally, without qualification, as is the physical resurrection of Jesus, and the 'perfect identity' between Jesus and God is maintained. It was not a book made to last, and it did not.

One of the many reasons for this failure was that Willie was being taxed by two other literary demands: the New Testament section of the 1947 *New Syllabus for Day Schools* (it was so successful that he was invited to write two more sections – for the 1948 and 1949 syllabuses); and his initial appearance as a playwright, with the first of a series he wrote for youth under the title *Scotland for Christ*, which had its debut at a Parents' Night at Trinity Church. For this he acted as producer, his daughter Barbara featuring in the cast, according to an admiring report in *The Renfrew Press*. His avid reading of James Agate's drama reviews over many years were now bearing fruit. Alas, the plays have long disappeared.

Willie's career was altering shape – being reformed by events and pressures rather than by careful appraisals and resolution. In April 1946 Presbytery was asked to grant part leave of absence for him from Trinity Church due to an emergency: the need for a preparatory lectureship 'for demobilized men intending to enter the ministry', as he explained. It acceded to the request, and his classes were held at Trinity College on Mondays, Wednesdays and Fridays, from 14.00 to 15.00 hours. It is obvious that by this appointment his mind was being made up for him: the field of New Testament studies was clearly beckoning. Despite this, he still told his friends that he hoped to get Gossip's *Practical* Chair.

He wanted to plan, he wanted to venture, he wanted to experiment for Christ in the broader Church. He got what he did not want; but, being William Barclay, he accepted it with goodwill and fulfilled more than their expectations of him. He described his latest work with demobilized men as 'very interesting'. It involved the preparation of untutored and war-experienced men, now recruits for ministerial training, which was due to start in the autumn; a sort of dummy run at the subject to see if they were up to it. 'If they got through that class,' he informed Braidwood, 'they were to be allowed to start the course in October.' Other lecturers held different classes.

John Graham, one of the students, said he was 'by far the most interesting lecturer in the college', and many have repeated the comment. They remarked that he was 'not a professional lecturer', i.e. one content merely to churn out his notes in an academic way; still less was he a member of the ivory-tower style of lecturer. He was *engaged* with them on a path of discovery – of Jesus and themselves and their mission in the world. He shared their problems; his focus was always practical. The range of students served was impressive: his youngest was twenty-eight, the eldest forty-six. He himself was thirty-nine. It was not an easy job for many different reasons. Two of his students were father and son; others had problems associated with war mania; some had joined the course simply out of a lost sense of direction, not knowing what to do with their war-ravaged lives. Once again Willie became an outspoken pacifist. Some, not knowing his background, were far from impressed. They were also staggered to find that he was stone-deaf. He had difficulty in hearing them even via a huge and primitive hearing aid, whose battery was so heavy he was visibly relieved to place it on his desk on arrival.

He had one supreme virtue, however: he would *listen* to them; and he would talk with them as could no other teacher – at their level and about the things they had lived through, about planes and tanks, arms and armaments, war movements, strategies, tactics, the smell of fear, of death; about the leaders of the nation, the world, the Church, and where they were going wrong. Best of all, he could talk about football, stories of great matches, cameos of brilliant players; about railways and railway engines, films and theatre, books and music. He did not spend all his time with them, naturally; other matters were pressing in upon him – not least his own ongoing studies, his SSSU lessons, his sermons for Trinity Church and elsewhere. The students were amused to see him sometimes slip away into a corner, take a seat facing the wall, unplug his hearing aid and work – oblivious of everything and everyone while he typed incessantly.

Two different career opportunities were offered during this period, in addition to the two Glasgow posts, which stirred his hanging hopes.

The first was a nomination to the Chair of New Testament at
Edinburgh, where he would undertake 'all the inhuman things', as he
called them, that were necessary for graduation in Divinity. It was a
plum appointment, but he – with a known penchant for the west of
Scotland and its people – confessed that he only expected to be runner-
up. He was not disappointed. Edinburgh played safe, as it is wont to do.
He was again rejected, this time in favour of James S. Stewart, for long
years one of the most gifted and influential preachers in the Church,
to whom Willie was glad to accede the honour.

The second opportunity surprised even Willie. It sprang out of
the teaching work he had been doing in both secular and religious
spheres. He was asked to apply for the post of Lecturer at Jordanhill Training College, Scotland's largest. After a little thought, and
some reflection on its potential, he was raring to go. He was very
disappointed not to get this job, and said so. To his present work and
overfilled diary he returned, somewhat deflated and still exhausted.
It was all proving too much for him – a rare admission he made in
August: 'I can't go on indefinitely doing my own job and doing odd
jobs at the university.' Nevertheless, he did go on, because that was
his way: goodwill ever prevailing.

Things were going on behind the scenes, however. The situation
changed suddenly in the autumn. The shortest, most poignant of
records appears in the Session Minutes of 13 October 1946:

> Today, after the Morning Service, Mr Barclay intimated to the
> congregation that he had been appointed Lecturer in New
> Testament Language and Literature in Glasgow University, and that
> he would be relinquishing his charge as Minister of Trinity Church,
> Renfrew, at the beginning of the New Year.

The church magazine responded to this crushing news a
little later:

> The announcement made by Mr Barclay on Sunday 13th October,
> that he had been appointed Lecturer in Glasgow University on New
> Testament Language and Literature, did not come as a surprise to
> many of us. His lectures throughout the country during the past
> few years, particularly in connection with the Youth Movement,
> brought him very much prominence, and the appointment which
> he has accepted is just the sequel to the enthusiasm and energy he
> has put into that work. We had not realized, perhaps, the value set

on Mr Barclay as a lecturer and author, but those prominent in Church affairs are unstinted in their praise of him and his work.

His appointment is unfortunate from our point of view, but we rejoice to know that such an honour has been conferred on him, and we extend to him and Mrs Barclay our heartiest congratulations. Our hope is that he will be as happy in his new sphere as he has been in Trinity, and that he will impart that enthusiasm, which is characteristic of him, to the students of his classroom so that they in turn will pass out from the Divinity Hall zealous preachers of the Gospel of Christ.

For nearly fourteen years Mr Barclay has been our Minister, sharing with us our joys and our sorrows – the period of unemployment, the six years of war, and the days of final victory. The Session and Managers feel that they would like Mr Barclay to take away with him a token of their esteem, and it is the expressed wish of many in the congregation that they also should have an opportunity of showing their appreciation...

It has been decided to hold a congregational meeting of a social nature in the Church on Friday, 27 December, which will take the form of a Concert and Presentation. Because of the large attendance anticipated ... it has been deemed inadvisable to serve tea. For the event a souvenir admission programme priced One Shilling will be on sale early in December.

No one was surprised that the event should be celebrated by a concert, Trinity Church's hallmark in social terms. The formal announcement caused them all pangs of regret, not least Willie and Kate. 'To tell you the truth,' he wrote to Braidwood, in the realization of what he was going to do, 'I feel I need sympathy as much as anything else. It is going to be a tremendous wrench to go away from Renfrew after fourteen years of almost unbroken happiness.' That said, his mind quickly turned from the past to the future, as was his wont:

There is a job to be done up there. There are fifty-five students in the first year and most of them are demobilized men. Up till now there were two professors of New Testament. One [W. M. MacGregor] died; they have not enough money to fill his Chair with a real Professor, so they are giving me the job to do but calling me a lecturer and paying me as such. But it is the kind of job that will almost inevitably lead to something else.

The matter was formalized in a Presbytery Minute of 3 December as the 'Demission of Mr William Barclay'. There was laid on the table an extract of the General Assembly of 20 November, stating: 'The Commission of Assembly resolved to confirm the nomination of the Reverend William Barclay to the Lectureship in New Testament Language and Literature in the University of Glasgow ... and instructed the Presbytery of Paisley to declare the charge vacant.' Less formal and more moving was Willie's last pastoral letter to his people, which is typical for the warmth of his expressions and for his emphasis that what had been accomplished had been done through their support and encouragements. It is worth reprinting in part here:

My dear friends,
...It can have been granted by God to few ministers to have fourteen years of such unbroken happiness as I have had at Renfrew. It would be utterly impossible for me to set down what I owe this congregation ... One thing is true – this congregation taught me my job, and whatever I am or whatever I will be I owe to Trinity...

Never was a minister blessed with so loyal and understanding a band of office bearers who so lovingly and so wisely upheld his hands. Never had a minister such a band of young people around him who opened their hearts to him and who so generously gave him their friendship and made him one of themselves. Especially dear to me was the work amongst the boys and the girls.... Never had a minister a more loyal congregation. What I shall miss most of all is the feeling that around me there is a circle of homes, hundreds of them, into any of which I can go and find a welcome. And never was there such a congregation to preach to. Of late years my work has taken me to many places, but there was none like my own pulpit, no congregation in which there was such an uplift of expectancy, no congregation which so helped, nay compelled a man to preach with all his might and all his heart. [He described its huge increase in membership, the 'overwhelming' task it laid upon him, his indebtedness to it; which experience and knowledge he will pass on to his students, and so continued]

No matter where I go and no matter how long I be spared to live I shall never forget this congregation ... I envy with all my heart the man who will succeed me ... I hope that sometimes I may be allowed to come back to you and once again stand in the pulpit which is so dear to me...

Ever and always and very sincerely yours,
William Barclay

The 'congregational meeting of a social nature' lived up to expectations. Soloists, the full choirs and organist led the way, happily under the chairmanship of A. G. Fortune who had preached Willie in fourteen years previously, who had called on him to give 'decided answers' to the questions people were then asking. Other ministers attended, as did Professor J. G. Riddell of Trinity College, who was clearly taking a close interest in Willie's work. One of the ministers, D. M. Swanson, said that Willie was 'a problem minister': he worked too fast, he had gone through too many motor cars [which provoked much knowing laughter], and he had exceeded even Trinity's capacity for organizing events. He added the comment that not a few ministers were relieved to see him go; it was not fun constantly being compared with their whirlwind colleague.

Professor Riddell spoke of his academic successes, the brilliance of his Bruce Lectures, and the *excitement* he had engendered among the returning servicemen in the spring. He explained that there had been discussion as to who the right man was for this new post, but he had no doubt of this himself. Another spoke of Willie being 'one of the leaders of the Church of tomorrow'. Kate was praised for being 'one of the most bright and gracious ladies' of the times. Mr Kidd disclosed that Willie had been expressly advised *not* to go to Trinity Church; their church was regarded as 'a battlefield', prone to making casualties of even experienced ministers. Nevertheless he came – and flourished; they were immensely sad to see him go. The report of the proceedings in *The Renfrew Press* ran to over thirty column inches. It pointed out among many things that it was 'the largest congregation ever to assemble in the Trinity Church'.

Representatives from the elders and the managers spoke and gave their gifts, as well as those on behalf of the congregation: framed photographs, a radiogram and a wallet with a large cash donation. The Young People's Society gave him a radio and a new study chair. Willie replied on behalf of himself and Kate – 'All the good things that you have said about her are not half good enough,' he said. He thanked them for their encouragements and help, and urged them to support his successor equally well, and not consider how he would have done things had he stayed: 'When you shut the gate, shut it.' He, too, was shutting the gate and moving on.

TWELVE

BIBLE TEACHER
EXTRAORDINARY

'Open your discourse with a jest, and let your
hearers laugh a little; then get serious.'

(*The Talmud*, Shabbath)

Once again members of the Barclay family made their home in
Glasgow — that 'lovely, ugly town' as Dylan Thomas described it, 'the
centre of the country's vitality' according to John White. It was a
homecoming for Willie, who had shared the elegant apartment in
Wilton Street with his parents, and who shared much more with the
city's amiable people.

They established themselves on the southern edge of the city, in a
very modest house at 87 Vardor Road, Clarkston. Willie described it as a
place 'where people buy their homes, but not in the expensive bracket'.
Kate was delighted. Her first 'own' home ever, free from public pressures
and impingements, private, *theirs*. Willie was pleased, too, but his
conscience smarted at the cost, which was inimical to his careful habits
and attitudes. (WDB had refused to buy his own house; it is interesting
that his son, the unprofessional economist, gauged better the economic
realities.) 'There are plenty of houses here in Scotland,' he wrote to
Braidwood, 'but their owners seem to think that they are made of pure
gold judging by what they want for them.' However, a small legacy from
Kate's aunt and Trinity's cash gift more than half made up the asking
price, and they moved in with glee.

It was a three-bedroomed terraced dwelling, which lacked both the
style and the space they had enjoyed at the manse. They both felt 'that
if you stretch you will knock the place down', but its size suited Kate,
who was exhausted physically and mentally, and 'worried sick' over
Barbara's now indifferent health. Ronnie's school was happily 'a
minute from our door', and Willie's work 'a short bus ride away' —
though he used his car when petrol rationing permitted. What more

could they want? 'I live surrounded by gifts from Renfrew,' Willie commented, which diminished the pain he felt on leaving the place he had made his home for so many years. Their biggest problem was his library. Despite the sacrificial pruning to which it had been subjected during the war, it was still a large feature of their possessions. Books now occupied three walls of their lounge, from floor to ceiling, and spilled over into every other available space.

There was no time for him to reflect on his disappointment at not getting Gossip's 'Practical' Chair, still less on why they should not have wanted him in it – a rejection of his style as much as his attitudes and views – or on the fact that he had not got any Chair at all. 'There is a job to be done up there' remained the compulsive reality, and he got down to it in earnest.

As his record proved, he was a man who could accept a commission and rise to its challenge: ever goodwilling. In accepting this post he became supercharged by it, the proof of which may be seen in the eighty-plus books that now came from his pen (I include all spine-bound material under this term, as is usual, but not stapled material), the scores of lessons and articles that he wrote, the incalculable hours he spent behind lectern and pulpit around the country, in front of radio microphones and television cameras. If this is not apostolic ministry, what is?

His General Course lay in three areas of study. First, a general introduction, which was based on the old volume by F. B. Clogg, *Introduction to the New Testament*, a workmanlike if dull treatment of its subject which Willie successfully made less dull. In those days its competition was thin: Dods' volume was considered too brief, McNeile's too detailed. His course included an outline of each of the books of the New Testament, plus matters relating to authorship, provenance and chronology. An introduction to the text and canon of the New Testament complemented this, which followed the works of Lake, Souter and Kenyon. Second, the study of prescribed texts: Matthew 5–10, Acts 1–9, John 1–4 and 12–14, and Galatians. For this he prescribed ten commentaries. As he averred at the end of his life, 'I believe in work.' The third area concerned a more concentrated study of the Synoptic Gospels (Matthew, Mark and Luke) and the Catholic Epistles (James, Peter, John and Jude). A mere three textbooks were prescribed for these, the 'Cinderella books' of the New Testament. Honours students were given extra texts which sought a yet deeper penetration of the Gospels: John's Epistles and the Apocalypse, for which a further ten books were required reading. They were also given a choice of two extra subjects: the Hellenistic Background to the New Testament, or Aramaic (this latter not being within Willie's province, as we have seen).

He spent two days moving house, on 23 and 24 December, and filled the Christmas hours sorting out his library, delighting – as a confessed enjoyer of 'luxury' – in the comfort of his new study chair. He commenced lecturing in early January 1947, often completing the preparation for his lectures shortly before they were delivered; a hand-to-mouth existence. He had already done similar courses himself, of course, and preached and lectured on much of their content at a very different level. Now he had to write and deliver intellectually challenging material, as well as acquit himself of several other responsibilities – for the SSSU notably, and more specialist work for the Church of Scotland which we shall come to. He also had to settle into university life again, getting to know his new colleagues, acclimatizing to his changed routines. His official assignment was for five hours of lectures per week at the ordinary level, and two extra hours at honours level. Additionally, there were papers to mark and he had to make himself available to the students, some of whom had exceptional needs resulting from their war experiences.

He began a regime which was to amaze everyone who heard of it: he rose at 07.15 hours; arrived at the university at 08.20; worked at his desk until 11.00; lectured until 13.15. He lunched until 14.00, when he saw students personally until 16.30, after which he would attend to any pressing work, then think about going home, which he reached about 18.30. After a meal and the BBC news (always a critically important duty for him, for he did not think that one could preach effectively without 'the Bible in one hand and a newspaper in the other'), he would settle down to work, taking a catnap at around 23.00 hours, then resuming work until 02.00 or even 03.00 hours, when sleep claimed him – though it was not unusual for the local night watchman to see him driving off into town before this to catch the early postal collection from George Square Post Office.

His chief in the department, Professor G. H. C. MacGregor, was fond of travelling and did so avidly. A good case can be made out for his having taken advantage of his new assistant, but charity suggests that we should regard it rather as his confidence in Willie's energy and ability. The department gave a total of eleven hours of lectures per week, of which Willie took seven, scarcely a fair apportionment, especially for a man in his first year and known to be burdened with important Sunday School and Day School obligations. Willie was the (good)willing horse in this, positively devouring the opportunities that came to him, totally dedicated to preparing his students for their life's work.

The two got along well, and admired each other. 'When I die,' the older man commented to Willie at the end of his life, 'they will find your name written on my heart.' He was a Highlander, with the Gaelic, a description which Willie (without the Gaelic) loved to claim himself. He was 'the mystic and the scholar', which aspects Willie greatly admired. Part of his antisyzygy (Arnot called it swithering) lay in his being a this-world person with a marked ethereal bent.

They were well matched. MacGregor had been publishing learned articles before Willie had even matriculated. He was one of the great influences on Willie's life, and deservedly so. Listen to this from Principal Mauchline: 'A cold intellectualism was foreign to his nature; in him heart and mind did not coexist in mutual isolation, they were in deep harmony ... He longed to see a ... deep harmony in others.' It could equally have been said of his new assistant. As Willie informed Douglas Millard of James Clarke & Co. of Cambridge, 'True scholarship should be real and wide *but unobtrusive.*'

Willie was content with his lot. He wrote to Braidwood:

> Better yet, my chief tells me that one of us should do the work of the department in the summer term alone. That would mean that every second year one would have to work like a black doing the whole department alone but that in the alternate years one would have no set lecturing between 20 April and 20 October or thereby. That would leave one of us free to go to America or Germany every second year. It sounds good. How all this works out I will tell you.

It did sound good, but it did not work out. More often than not, Willie became the single-handed lecturer of the summer term – and of others besides – and never once did he find time to go to America; he only managed infrequent visits to Germany, and then not to research. He went to lecture to Service Chaplains, fearing the RAF flights that took him there, despite his passion for aircraft, in odd weekends squeezed into all the other pressures on his time. Not that this was entirely of MacGregor's devising. He was 'a martyr to asthma', frequently bedridden for weeks, when the smooth running of the department fell entirely on his 'untried assistant' (Willie's self-description), who ran it as smooth as silk despite the many post-war problems. 'Not a real professor' indeed – still less a properly paid one, but doing the work of one, and more than one. Kate was not amused.

Dreams of a quiet academic life were evaporating before her eyes; she was beginning to think his goodwill a constitutional weakness.

It is not surprising to find the biblical passages of his set books, above, forming the basis of much of Willie's extramural work as well as his formal lectures from now on. The care and enthusiasm with which he fulfilled his duties can be seen from the Shelf Register records at the Library. For example, during 1947 thirty-one books were borrowed by him, all of them in addition to the recommended textbooks which he possessed, with many others, in his own impressive library. He was getting through them at an average pace of at least three a week (to say nothing of the detective novels he enjoyed reading for relaxation, another aspect of *bios* for this deeply involved man). He and the Librarian, James Mackintosh, a former missionary to India, formed a deep and solid friendship. Willie had always admired such 'doers' of the Church, and continuously praised them for their sacrificial work. Mac, as he was known, was not only a doer but a man of extraordinary intellect and practicality – Willie's type of man.

Another friend he made at this time was the College janitor, Collins by name. One of his duties was to clear 'the debris' that surrounded, and sometimes engulfed, Willie's desk – the full ashtrays were a notorious item – as well as fetch and deliver books from the Library for him. Willie was a tidy and meticulous worker, but the circumstances within which he worked were far from adequate, so books and papers proliferated without anywhere to stack them. Arriving at College early each morning, he would spend a few minutes chatting with Collins, sharing his cigarettes with him – and deliberately forgetting to pick up the half-filled packet, aware that the janitor lived on an even lower income than he did. He always showed careful consideration for the workers who looked after his car, office or house.

Neil Alexander was one of those who studied under him at this time, and went on to become his Faculty colleague in 1964. He wrote a portrait of him in 1980 as scholar and colleague in *William Barclay: The Plain Uncommon Man* (ed. R. D. Kernohan). He enumerated three qualities that made Willie an outstanding lecturer: one, 'impeccable linguistics' (we should add: Aramaic and its cognates apart); two, 'an immense background knowledge of ancient literature and culture'; three, 'a passionate love of teaching'. But his general comment is more important than the specific: 'Mr [sic] Barclay had – toward all the students – a forthcomingness and positive friendliness that

Bank House, Motherwell. Scene of his growing years.

On honeymoon. Kate and Willie at Bournemouth, 1933.

Gathering of civic dignitaries at Renfrew, 1942. William Barclay in second row rear, far right.

'Chaplain Barclay' (leaning to the left), 1944. Rear row, third from left.

Barbara Barclay and Rusty
shortly before her death, 1956.

Barclay's room in the tower, known
'the prophet's chamber'.

Commentator *extraordinaire*, 1957.

The Dean in his office, 1968.

'Symbols of Barclay', blackboard, lectern and piano, c.1970.

Readying himself
at the typewriter,
c.1970.

Kate and Willie on holiday, c.1970.

With his daughter-in-law and grand-children, Kate and Jane, c.1975.

Map-reading with French friends and with Ronnie, Kate and Jane, c.1967.

ate and her Commander of the British Empire, a celebration, 1969.

pper Room honours shortly before his death, 1977.

A quiet break on holiday with Kate, 1974.

The latter years, in pensive mood.

The author, delivering the William Barclay Memorial lecture, Church House, London, 1985.

marked a new departure in staff–student relations.' He was a man *for* people, preaching the Good News – 'the God-with-us' event. Principal Allan Galloway later emphasized the teaching element, too, speaking of Willie's 'charisma for teaching'. The word is now hackneyed, but it cannot be avoided here; it is a true description of William Barclay: he was one anointed for teaching. The result was almost a poetry of action and greatly inspiring. It could not have been successful without that open, friendly, non-judgemental approach, his *goodwill* ethic, which lies (as Luke emphasizes) at the very heart of the gospel.

'The life of discovery' was how Professor W. R. Ramsay described his own teaching work, and that was especially true of Willie. Ramsay was a considerable classicist who evolved from liberal to conservative. Willie, nearly fifty years later, evolved from conservative to liberal. It is arguable which is the more difficult route. They both sought truth according to their lights, according to a person's ability to understand. Willie, too, was passionate for reading, enquiry, discovery. Theodoros says in the *Moralia* that discovery rests on two important attributes: a sense of wonder, and a sense of curiosity. We may even translate this latter term as doubt: the humility of the questioning and the adventurous mind. He preferred active doubt to supine belief, exploration to reiteration.

We see this discovery-sense frequently in William Barclay, and in all the great exponents of theology – from the psalmists to Karl Barth (whose sense of wonder demanded a book on the subject). It is not so with the ivory-tower scholar, happy to forage among dry Hebrew or Greek roots for private nourishment, pedantically scouring the material, a dispenser of form without life, a mechanical discoverer without wonder, a doubter without adventure: the 'grey men' of our churches and their dismal literature.

Willie was a colourful adventurer among his books and texts; a man with a true sense of wonder; a man curious to know and never afraid to doubt – but in his doubting devoted (never 'devout'), always positive: goodwill assertive. He was necessarily more the teacher than the researcher. He loved to have things 'to pass on' to his students and readers, bubbling with the delights he had found. Willie imbibed huge amounts of information – and retained it. But he *had* to give it out: 'Woe if I preach not...' His students sensed the thrill, the wonder, which energized his work, and many sought to make it their own. 'Education is a second sun to its possessors,' effused Heraclitus, and Willie passed this on, sunnily.

But there was more; education alone could not suffice. Relationships had to be struck and made good. W. M. MacGregor, his old tutor – whose personality he did not very much like, thanks to 'his terrible silences, a man with a tongue dipped in vitriol' – once spoke of 'the unforced interest in the men and women about us, without which no minister can ever do his work aright'. William Barclay had that 'unforced interest' to an unlimited degree. It set him apart from the merely ambitious, the string pullers, the social climbers. He had learned it from the Golden Rule – to love one's neighbour as oneself – and had long practised it: ever goodwilling.

Stewart Borthwick, another student of this time, who had served as a detective with the Glasgow Police Force before war duties claimed him, spoke of his avid humanity. Willie was *alive* to men and women and sought their good, which included their enjoyments as well as their more sombre needs. He was alive to the physical world, and sought to emphasize it not only as 'the arena of faith', as his father had been ever careful to emphasize (something he had learned from Browning *et alii*), but also as the expression of God himself, his gift – a concept which was but a step away from the ecological awareness that he later espoused.

Of late he had found (we do not know the exact date of this) an increased pleasure in the use of alcohol. This is a subject which has pained many – even to the point of their denying its actuality – and given smaller minds a rod with which to beat him. But Willie was concerned about it, as all those brought up under a strict teetotal regime tend to be on changing their position. So he sought out not the leading ethicist or biblical pundit, but the more worldly, experienced man: his student. Stewart Borthwick was struck by his lecturer's humility, his willingness to ask basic questions, to seek guidance. Willie expressed his gratitude. He was comforted by Borthwick's view that it *was* right to indulge (to a certain level), and went off determinedly to say so – to a meeting of the Woman's Guild who had asked him to address them on the subject! Borthwick, a man's man, loved his style, which was unapologetically human and 'gutsy', 'always bristling with anecdotes and experiences'. He warmly reciprocated the friendship that was offered to him – over a convivial dram or two.

Not all Willie's students could keep up with his pace of working. He crammed 'sixty seconds of distance run', and more, into each unforgiving minute, as became a former schoolboy sprinter. The problem for his students, indeed for most of his colleagues, was that he had the heart and stamina of the long-distance runner as well as that of the sprinter. His lectures (often from a single sheet of paper, and sometimes no paper at all) were thus marathons of endurance for the less well equipped. He spoke as he thought – which was very fast, with total recall – and he expected them to keep up with him, though he sometimes switched into slow gear when the struggling made their problems known. He expected them in those early years to take down his notes verbatim. This irked the more able men, some of whom dared complain.

He was the truest of practical bookmen. He could not live without books – not just textbooks, theological books, books of devotion, but every sort of book. He loved them because they offered him *life* in every form: poetry and prose, history and fiction, functional and pleasuring. They were not sacred to him, but tools, instruments of *bios*. He used his books, even to the point of writing (illegibly) on them in ink, even on their covers. A number of those came to me; they were all so marked. But they also demonstrate the important point that he never stopped learning. The life of discovery went on, in which he kept his basic texts in focus: the happy wonderer. Moreover, he had the ability to be able to rethink his positions, albeit not systematically.

A good example of his love of and care for books comes from this time. At the end of 1940 the College buildings were requisitioned by the military – the Royal Army Pay Corps actually, a typical expulsion of God by mammon – with the exception of the janitor's house, the Library hall and the chapel. But soon the Library hall fell prey to the war effort, and so the thousands of precious volumes that filled it were boxed and stored. At the end of the war, after derequisitioning and following the necessary repairs and alterations, the Librarian had to reconstitute his Library. It was too big a job for the retired missionary alone, and so Willie – despite his overwhelming work pressures – found time to sort, shelve and recatalogue the precious stock, which included such treasures as the Tischendorf Collection, the Fairburn Collection, and several others. For this service Willie was formally made Assistant Librarian in December 1947. By February 1948 – i.e. within just two months – they had reshelved over 3,500 volumes, nearly sixty a day, all of which had been indexed, crosschecked and referenced.

In *Testament of Faith* Willie describes James Mackintosh, the Librarian, as 'one of my closest friends', and dedicated two of his books to him, identifying him as 'Mac. Keeper of Books'. There was a deeper reason for their friendship than the love of books, however. It was the love of knowledge for its own sake. He called the Librarian 'the most erudite man I ever met', and he had met many, some of the best thinkers of his day, in fact. Willie once said that he could not have written any of his books without Mackintosh, a pardonable exaggeration, but it shows the partnership that was developing between them. It was Mac, he said, who found those errant quotations and references, so much the despair of scribblers; it was Mac who became his confidant and counsellor; and it was Mac to whom he unburdened himself when the going got rough. Until the lessening of petrol restrictions they usually had to take public transport to get to their work, but thereafter the older man travelled in Willie's car, affording them many hours of conversation and comment, discovering life together in their life of discoveries.

Mac is one of the underrated influences in Willie's life, a fatherly figure if not quite in the mould of WDB, an anonymous sustainer – and constrainer – of his younger colleague. 'He lived close to learning; he lived close to nature; and he lived close to God,' was the fitting trinity of compliments Willie offered of him at the end. 'There are few, very few, people with whom I am really friends,' he remarked, when many were overclaiming on his friendship. Mac was not one of them. But he was a friend, and more than a friend: the elder brother Willie never had.

The screen that hitherto had sheltered the precious boxes of library books now sheltered Willie, who would usually be found behind it when not otherwise engaged, hearing aid disconnected, hammering away at his typewriter. A two-finger typist, he was heavy-handed on the keyboard, working from the elbows rather than the wrists. As he once remarked – in the light of the many and diverse errors that frequented his typed work – 'the typewriter was never conquered by me'. In the course of his ministry he wore out several machines completely. One endearing fault was that he failed to realize how difficult the noise of his typing made life for the students – and his neighbours in Clarkston, thanks to his nocturnal habits. He had no office of his own, nor would he have one for many years – 'the lecturer without a side-room' in Richard Baxter's phrase – a cause of discontent for some, but one which he ignored, content simply to get on with his work.

When not in the Library or behind his screen, he was usually at lectures, shoulders back, gown flapping, covered in chalk, his increasingly husky voice now ringing, now modulating to make a point, ever brisk. He makes a statement. He offers a pastoral point. He throws in a joke – they were sometimes a little risqué, thanks to a full-blooded humanity that did not see 'dirt' in physicality. (Anyone familiar with Greek literature soon comes to terms with such. Even Paul risked them occasionally, as those who know their Greek New Testament can confirm. They are little different from the bucolic language of Martin Luther and others, the down-to-earth language of land and farm workers.) He pauses to write a keyword on the board, then sweeps on, quoting Greek, Latin, French, even Hebrew and German; suggesting parallels, contrasting opposites, ever expounding. He offers an illustration, and amplifies his point; the truth is driven home. His material was always well analysed, clear in its structures. His method was numerate as well as literate – he loved to count points, or occurrences, like the old rabbis. His arguments proceeded logically and were well articulated. Students noted that he had a predilection for threes – trinities recurring – as we also see in his sermons and even his Bible notes.

The lecture begins promptly, usually with a short prayer. He immediately drops into top gear and proceeds apace; time is short. Just as suddenly it stops: the fifty-five minutes are up. He collects his papers, his Bible, and is gone – to other work that cannot be kept waiting. He had that ability to change subjects quickly, almost without a pause. He accepted questions, and was always ready to provide answers – fulfilling Fortune's original challenge – but he did not much like the seminar method of teaching. They were there to listen and learn! The catechetical attitude of his own upbringing was not forgotten, even if he rightly rejected the method itself.

His lectures were thus a fast and uninterrupted flow of information: facts, theories, sources, linguistics, dates, viewpoints, customs, geographical, historical and cultural tidbits. What did he himself think? What was his preferred solution to an argument? His students were not sure; each possibility suggested was offered with equal force. He is now conservative, now liberal; now believing, now doubting. It is for *them* to make up their own minds, in which cause he leads them on, sometimes positively, sometimes sceptically; sometimes humorously, sometimes Socratically, always earnestly. They are pressed, challenged, cajoled, dared; his spectacles glint in the artificial light, his face opens up in a broad smile; he casts his bread upon the waters ... a man at ease with his subject, with himself; a man enjoying life.

A lectures 'pool' was started by the students. Some of the faster note-takers offered duplicated copies of his lectures; some of these still exist. Some took old copies to the lecture room with them and noted that, even when he was lecturing without his notes, he followed the pages before them almost identically, not infrequently word for word, illustration for illustration: an awesome feat of memory. It is suggestive of how his mind worked. He seemed to 'switch on' subjects and reproduce them effortlessly from this gargantuan memory base – large swaths of material, like frames in a lantern show. Frame followed frame; idea suggested idea. Here their point matters little – whether a list of football cup-winners, the dimensions or mechanical data of railway engines, of aircraft, Latin or Greek verbs, their declensions, roots and occurrences, biblical passages, textual difficulties, reasons for denying Pauline authorship to the Letter to the Hebrews, commentators' views – whatever. It is his method of delivery that amazes. His lectures were a great contrast to Professor Riddell's, for example, which were notoriously hardworked, disorganized and indigestible – the lecturer drowning with his hearers in a veritable soup of information, as many students complained.

That is the word for Willie's matter and style: digestible. He refined his flour, he was careful to have it sieved before use, he baked carefully and well, he broke his bread small, he offered it in bite-sized pieces, made tangy with spicy flavourings, delectable nuggets all, a full meal. It reminds us of the great French chef, Alexandre Dumaine (he who once refused to serve a Prime Minister of France because he arrived late), who said, 'The art is the setting in value of the ingredients to be cooked. If one just cooks, it is not worth the trouble.' With him, as Robert Carrier is at pains to emphasize, 'one experiments with flavours, textures, and above all, heat.' So with Willie, a master craftsman in 'dividing the Word', in communicating it. The 'pure' form of the detail was mixed with the 'applied' in delectable style. He dealt with life, not mere scholarship: the Gospels were living organisms, the Epistles far from dead letters. The students caught his fire. He made them want to share it with others.

They contrasted their lecturers as well as the way they lectured, as students do. Professor Riddell did not come out of this too well, as we saw. John Mauchline, known as 'Yahweh' (not disrespectfully; but because he resented the mistranslation 'Jehovah' in the old versions and sought to weaken its popularity by constant emphasis on the more accurate rendering of the Tetragrammaton), faired better, imparting his learning in aloof, measured phrases. 'Daddy' Niven was even more popular, still going strong after all these years in his beloved Church History – to some a dull subject, and perhaps now even to himself, as he allowed himself constantly to be sidetracked. He became famous for these asides; the students who led him on were not always clear as to what they were 'aside' from in the first place. The 'most impractical practical professor' was Pitt-Watson, a victim of his own philosophical mien, and unbending withal, yet still 'a theologian's theologian'. This inhuman style was too much for Willie, this air of intellectual superiority. He forgot protocol and dared to prick it publicly – to the shocked delight of the students. The subject at issue was pacifism, a cause reborn in Willie thanks to the A- and H-bombs and their gathering menace. It is not certain that he won the argument, but he won their hearts, as was ever the case.

One of his early absorptions was the College choir, his Trinity Church habit resettling on Trinity College. It was not unusual for the choir to give six or seven concerts each year, nor was it a completely religious repertoire that they offered – another species of Willie's 'threshold evangelism', in which pure enjoyment was always to be found (after the manner of Philippians 4:8). Such songs as 'The tickling trio' and 'Loch Lomond' – and later 'Raindrops keep falling on my head' – were sung gaily and strenuously, the silly combining with the sentimental, but never unseriously. It was huge fun, but he never trivialized their aims. Sentimentality was never less absent than in their evergreen renditions of 'Crimond' or 'When I survey the wondrous Cross', favourite hangovers from the 'Sankey Nights', his parents' presence in them, when tears would never be far away, sometimes coursing down his cheeks. Despite his deafness he was a good choirmaster at this level, waving his arms vigorously when he was not at the piano (and sometimes when he was), seeking rhythm, tunefulness, expression and enjoyment: goodwill in song. The musical perfectionists, needless to say, had another view.

Though privileged himself in his student days, he knew the anxiety of the penniless pocket and the sacrifices some students (and their parents or their wives) were making. He was deeply moved at their efforts. As a Junior Lecturer his salary was about the same as his ministerial stipend, except that he no longer had free accommodation, so he had to be careful – as he was used to doing, sometimes to Kate's and his children's annoyance: leave a door open, he closed it; leave a light on, he switched it off. Rationing was still in force – of food and clothing, petrol and paper – and his children were growing rapidly. Yet many and hilarious were the suppers he and Kate put on for the students in their wee home, bulging with books and their much-loved furniture, mainly old, which had too many associations to be discarded. These times were hugely popular with the students, but not so popular with the staff; envies arose. It is arguable which was the greater attraction – Willie's bonhomie or Kate's whisky cake. They went extremely well together, and they could not but notice that here was a man, and more than a man, more even than a man of God – a friend who had no airs; who loved them in an entirely unsentimental way; who was discovering life with them, preparing them for it with great absorption.

For all the fun, however, he was nothing if not strongly principled. One student was caught cheating in an examination. He was returned to civilian life almost before he had time to draw breath, Willie himself triggering the mechanisms which ousted him through College, university court and Presbytery. Integrity was all. An inveterate book collector, he was shocked on another occasion to find a number of nearly-new textbooks relevant to the College courses at one of his favourite second-hand bookshops. They had obviously been handed in at the completion of the course. He confessed to having felt 'daunted' (see p. 14) and said so caustically: 'It was as if … farewell to college meant farewell to study' – the ultimate betrayal.

The very nature of Christianity, he held, was discipleship, *mathēteiē*, from which we get our word mathematics: something learned, a science, a divine work. The Christian man (he usually spoke in these 'sexist' terms, though he was far from sexist in many of his attitudes) was the *learning* man, by definition. To follow Christ was to learn of Christ; to discover him from whose school no one graduated, for none could attain – in this life. He rejected the sophism that this learning was a purely 'spiritual' process, as many evangelicals maintained. The object of Christ's coming, he ardently believed, was to make full men of us, to extend our humanity, our mental as well as our spiritual life – the *manliness* of the BB and the YMCA. Not that he agreed with such compartmentalizations – he was holistic long before the term became prevalent. He refuted the artificial delineation between the physical and the spiritual, the secular and the sacred, and was to do so more decisively in later years. Of course, there were the Brother Lawrences, whose gifts and mental capacities were limited, whom he esteemed, yet insisted that they too could – and should – grow within their own capacities, forwards, not backwards: 'use it or lose it', as he would say.

A similar attitude is seen in his response to 'the closed mind', one of his blackest *bêtes noires*. Because of his background and his own struggle to free himself from the mental straitjacket in which his father's evangelicalism had bound him, his sallies against such were particular and fierce – but never personal. Evangelicals were his people, insofar as any one group could be so called. He felt a lively need to help them towards a broader, richer world: God's world. Idleness in that matter he warned against, remembering that Bishop Barnes' taunt, 'an evangelical not by conviction but by lethargy', was all too often true. How could anyone who knows God be narrow-minded? The very notion is nonsense: 'For the love of God is broader / than the measures of man's mind...' as the hymn says. How dare one shadow God's light by a lazy obscurantism? How could one be afraid to think when 'perfect love casts out fear'? He strove to make their world larger, more luminous, kinder. It was not always appreciated, still less understood.

In *Testament of Faith* he refers to the students (one notes the plural) who came to him 'after their first month of classes and apologized, and when I asked them what they were apologizing about they said that, before they came up, they had been warned against me'. Such reaction started early – in the clashes with his father and his father's friends, whose conservatism he quickly realized was based on ignorance and fear, by definition antithetical to 'the wisdom of God'. How often he referred to the *twelve* gates into the Heavenly City, and its enormous proportions (see Revelation 21:10ff) which symbolically offered room for all! 'There are many ways to God.' 'All truth is God's truth.' 'Truth', he would emphasize, was not different from 'reality' – the same Greek word serves for both our English words. The reality of the world cannot be different from the reality of God by which it exists. The truth of the world – the whole truth – cannot be different either. Theologians and scientists, preachers and researchers, were all about the same thing; were all in their very different ways servants of the divine. There *is* unity, if only one could discover its fullness. Willie found it in Christ and the incarnation, in the Word made flesh: the living, creative principle of the universe. It came to superlative expression when he came to expound John 1:1–14, and the cosmic Christology of Colossians and Ephesians, etc. The true disciple had to be a truth-seeker, which has no bounds, dogmatic or otherwise. It fed his ethics, too, and that in quite contentious ways.

Nowhere is this more plainly demonstrated than in the disputed passage of John 7:53–8:11, which received special emphasis in his two-volume commentary in the *Daily Bible Readings* series. His division of John here is artificial – in order to make the point. The passage occurs in the middle of a section generally recognized to have taken place at the Feast of Tabernacles (i.e. 7:1–8:59). Yet he splits his material at 7:52. This makes 268 pages of the first volume against 338 pages in the second, a very uneven treatment. Had he kept to the natural division, the first volume would have split at page 313, and the second one at page 293 – a more balanced allocation. We are bound to ask, 'Why'?

The answer points up Willie's *principled* position on this meaningful point.

He deliberately chose to commence his second volume with this disputed passage (relegated to the margin in several modern translations; one of them relegates it to the end of the Gospel) in order to highlight its teaching. To this he offers a triple commentary of ten pages for its eleven verses, its title 'Wretchedness and Pity' (as opposed to the more general, and negative, 'The woman taken in adultery'). The fact that it concerned adultery and a nice matter of law was secondary to the realities expressed by his title: the *human* realities at stake. In that he saw the very essence of the gospel – the essence of its ethics, too: the triumph of goodwill. He recognizes the unsatisfactory nature of the textual evidence of this passage, but nevertheless argues that the answer to the problem text does not lie within textual criticism and should not sidetrack us. The spiritual reality – a paradox to be sure – is the main point.

The first volume went out accompanied by an 'IMPORTANT NOTICE' (his actual emphasis). This advised that the *promised* division of the volumes in the advertising had been altered – another indicator of his determined emphasis. Its publishers, the Church of Scotland Publications Committee, curiously stated that the new division agrees with 'the usual division of this Gospel' (an untrue comment for several reasons). The technical problems at 7:53ff threaten to obscure the deeper, more substantial point Willie was at pains to make. Whatever its textual status (he offers a rare two-page explanation of it even at this devotional level of exposition), the importance of the narrative is emphasized by him as 'one of the loveliest and most precious stories in the Gospels' – a prime example of his habit of using superlatives to make his points.

The reason why translators and copyists omitted it, he argued, was because of the *moral* problem the passage gave the Church and its leaders, and its apologists too – cast as they were as 'a little island in a sea of paganism [for which read "immorality"]'. Within this sea, and against that defective morality (not least, we might add, in Ephesus, a key centre for the infamous Diana/Artemis cult, where this Gospel probably originated), the Church strove for purity, especially sexual. Here, some thought, was a story which downgraded sexual impropriety and therefore the law of God, making light of its precepts and strictures. Their response was to get rid of it: the easy way out, too often the churchman's way. Willie faced the problem without allowing it to disturb the solution provided by Jesus – which rejected the judgementalist approach. *That* was the point. And that was why William Barclay refused to go along with those who relegated the passage to the margin of their Bibles or placed it within brackets.

Many have found this passage profoundly disturbing: not merely embarrassing, but scandalous – as did the scribes and Pharisees who sought to entrap Jesus by bringing this woman and her behaviour to him. Many still do today. A 'fallen woman' finds few places of friendship, even – sometimes especially – in the churches. (We should emphasize that this took place long before the gender war got under way. Today Willie would have been more discreet.) Jesus forgave the woman without a single word of condemnation; indeed, he refused to condemn her, wishing on her the peace she so much needed – goodwill triumphant.

This is pure Barclay, as it is pure New Testament; we might add pure Paul, Augustine, Luther, Booth, *et alii*. But it is not standard Church tradition or Church authority except in word, still less is it Church practice, which has often been offended by it – to the point of erasure. It has been a scandal to late Christianity as much as it ever was to Paul and his followers. It still embarrasses Church leaders and ethicists, too many of whom lack the heroic element in their souls. They acknowledge its theory, of course, but too often ignore its practice, or leave it for others more willing 'to get their hands dirty', such as the Salvation Army or the 'rescue missions' – as if the Church itself is not meant to be that. Their words as to its theoretical place are too often drowned out by their avoidance of its practical reality. It is never so avoided as when the Church finds itself in a 'middle-class' situation, attuned to the much 'nicer' A, B and C social stratas, but rarely any lower. Who wants to work in the downtown parishes? In the Piltons of Edinburgh, the Moss-sides of Manchester, or the Saint Pauls of Bristol?

In this situation the scandal of the cross is moral and social, not theological. It faces us with the demand: What sort of God did Jesus reveal? The gospel opens the doors to sinners, the outcast, the underprivileged – merely to state that in some circles is to evoke a negative, Pavlovian response. Its greatest thinkers and leaders are those 'who did likewise', who went and sought 'the lost', and among those great leaders stands William Barclay.

His position was misunderstood and opposed, not only by the more pharisaic of his colleagues – I use the term only of those who emphasize law and social positioning to the detriment of humanity, and make of it the aim of their lives – but also by some of his less mature students, who were offended by his attitudes, and by those who naively made fun of them. To fail to understand his position in this matter is to fail to understand William Barclay, who made the plain, the common man, the centre of his work. Some reject this deliberately, including some who wrote most about him; others merely ignore it. Some patronize him in order to excuse him. It was not a failing of his, but a strength; not a pandering but a principle – a bold risk for Christ and his gospel in which humanity was sought and very often won (though sadly they often found no place to go beyond him).

There is another dimension to all this. No one with any knowledge of Greek and its philosophies can read John without being upended by the sheer daring of its writer. Here we are not confronted with a mere 'Gentle Jesus, meek and mild', but with the *Logos* of God, the principle behind the universe, to use Paul's term: the Cosmic Christ. As Willie commented in *Testament of Faith*, 'For me Jesus is the centre and soul of the whole matter.' Ten years or so after Willie's exposition on John, the works of Teilhard de Chardin became known. He was, says Willie, 'at one and the same time in the first rank of the scientists and the mystics'. 'His great aim,' he continued, 'was to *Christify* everything.' This was Willie's point, too. He was fired by Teilhard's view that 'Christ is the organic centre of the entire universe': a brilliant recapturing of the *Logos* doctrine.

We have come to the core of Willie's new task. 'My years in Renfrew were *a training in the obligation of intelligibility*,' he said. Some professors believe that obfuscation is their calling; that they should speak only to the intelligentsia; that obscurity is a standard of profundity. Willie specifically rejected this. He abhorred retiring into the ivory tower of academic life, becoming remote from ordinary life and living. He said, 'The greatest of all temptations was to think of nothing but what other academic teachers and experts ... think.' He would have no truck with such 'inhuman things'. He still coveted the Practical Chair. He was concerned that the work done in the colleges and the universities 'never seemed *in any sense* [his emphasis] to penetrate to the pew'.

This is undoubtedly an exaggeration, but it is all the more valuable for highlighting his burden, for when he talked of these things he frequently used the verb 'to worry'. He was *anxious* about the problem of communicating the gospel – a rare thing in Church circles! – not self-satisfied with his successes to date. The need to get across the meaning of Jesus and his coming, of humanity's need and Christ's 'sufficiency' (to use an old word so much misunderstood), lay on him like a heavy weight, daunting him – and to achieve this he was prepared to sacrifice academic reputation and much else besides.

He had more than doubled his congregation; he had widened his ministry to a national degree (imminently international); successes had been registered among all ages, from children through to the Old Men's Club. He met people where they were, mentally, culturally and morally. He spoke their language; he used their thought-forms. Evangelism for him was not just a slogan, a device, a tactic: it was *the* spiritual reality. It was what he did; it was how he lived; it described the nature of his work, how people may be won for God.

Towards his students he did not weaken the need for the fullest, most careful intellectual preparation. He challenged and guided them, leading them through facts, theories and ideologies; testing and examining them, always careful to make *practical* points. His goal clarified itself by reason of his persistent interest: 'The problem of communication [was] the problem which first came to my thoughts,' he told Stanley Pritchard some years later, adding that he could never have been a great technical scholar – a view his Professors disagreed with, which was contradicted by their response to his Bruce and other public lectures, such books as his *Educational Ideas in the Ancient World*, and international experts like the Master of Christ Church, Oxford.

Curiously, not a few were annoyed that he used his great gifts in this way. Brought up in a tradition that valued learning for its own sake, influenced by his father's friends and library, in which the distillations of scholarship were highly treasured, he wrote: 'I began to think that I might become a theological middleman, to take the results of scholarship, to take the things done in the classroom, to take the great books the scholars have written, and to restate them in ordinary non-technical language which ordinary people understand.' The judgement on him of the General Assembly in May 1948, that he had given 'inestimable service' to Scotland, is proof enough of the success of this 'theological midwifery'. Now aged forty, he was about to do so much more.

THIRTEEN

JOURNALIST AND WRITER

'The man is to be found in his book.'

(Jean-Paul Sartre)

The *British Weekly*, for so long in the vanguard religiously in those days, started to speak in the late forties of the 'ecclesiastical Springtime' and 'the renascence in theology' that was coming. Its prognosis was not ill-founded. Theological colleges were filling up; mass evangelism was stirring the populace (and the staid religious); youth movements like the BB, and various Bible classes, registered new growth; ecumenism was becoming buoyant; a great explosion of religious and theological writing – conservative and liberal – began; and the door to continental and transatlantic scholarship swung open, not only to their publications but to the theologians themselves. Willie thoroughly enjoyed sitting in some of the latter's lectures, and heard with delight a few of the most gifted minds of the twentieth century such as Martin Buber, Emil Brunner, Karl Barth and Albert Schweitzer. But his focus was elsewhere.

The appearance of popular religious publications – thanks to the introduction of the paperback – under such names as C. S. Lewis, J. B. Phillips, C. H. Dodd and Leslie Weatherhead (to name but four) soon became a flood. Old firms like Hodder & Stoughton Ltd and William Collins & Co Ltd increased their religious lists, while new companies such as Inter-Varsity Press appeared and flourished. Publishing departments of religious denominations also awakened to new life, as did religious trusts and specialist organizations like the National Christian Education Council and the International Bible Reading Association, London Bible College, Moorlands Bible College, and many others.

Similar advances were being made in religion in the secular universities, a most important breakthrough. For example, Matthew Black was appointed to a key New Testament post at Leeds; F. F. Bruce left his beloved Classics post at Leeds to found a Biblical Studies Department at Sheffield; D. M. G. Stalker moved to Edinburgh; and

William Neil established himself at Aberdeen. Willie, of course, was part of this movement, at one time very hopeful of landing a secular appointment himself, though eventually settling for a church position. His good friend Andrew McCosh was appointed Manager of the Church of Scotland's Publicity and Publications Committee, destined to play an important role in extending his career. J. W. D. Smith became an official advisor to the Church of Scotland on educational matters. Even more importantly, a strong emphasis on lay education and ministry developed.

In line with this latter, a School of Study was set up in Glasgow, attached to its university, as many were around the country. The first two lectures were given by Willie – at 2/6d (12.5 new pence) for the course. His subject was 'The Teaching of Jesus'. At a different level he was delighted to be made a member of the Studiorum Novi Testamenti Societas (SNTS), the most distinguished society for New Testament study in the world, and even attended its conferences from time to time, strangely (to the mind of some) staying in local hotels rather than billeting with the other members in college dormitories. He needed to be kept alive to the ongoing status of his discipline; but he did not have much personal interest in its proponents, which annoyed some of them. He was too busy. Not once in his thirty-plus years of membership did he offer a paper to this august society. Few would doubt his ability to do so, but his interests lay elsewhere: the role of 'middleman' had taken over. No one contended that it was a matter of ability: it was one of choice. He had little desire to speak to the converted, to enlighten the enlightened.

Despite his emphasis – an important interpretive key to his work – that 'theology is grammar', at best a half-truth, he agreed with the view of A. S. Peake that 'grammatical terrorism' was a sterile practice. He had parted company with 'the soul-less things' of pure research ('grubbing in the empirical ditch' as Drummond and Bulloch, the Scottish Church historians, described the researcher's work), though he did offer something like it in his Kerr Lectures of 1959. Nor did it stop him from asserting that he was 'a dictionary, not a theologian'. His role, however, was 'applied', not 'pure'. This interest is seen in his review (for two different journals) of the *Greek–English Lexicon of the New Testament and Other Early Christian Literature* by Arndt Gingrich. It was an important research tool: the good news must out. By now book reviewing had become a serious part of his métier, both keeping him in touch with developments and expanding the 'middleman' concept for ministers and teachers – a crucial service.

Some questioned his academic equipment. Some simply disliked his theology – accused him indeed of not having one worth the name. Some, such as Ian Henderson, who joined the Faculty at about this time, charged him with theological naivety, a curious charge against a man who could weave his way expertly around Greek and Jewish philosophers and early Church thinkers. Some charged him with superficiality – but rarely face to face. This was a man who could quote Greek and Latin authors all day long when he wished to, who knew his Bible back to front. Woe betide anyone who crossed swords with him unprepared – as some did, to their discomfiture. The *Expository Times* reviews show just how much he was prepared to handle, and what big books and big ideas (one of his regular counsels to his students, which he practised throughout his life) he delighted in.

How we handle the text of Scripture was Willie's passion. He never condoned the easy use of Scripture, the preacher who took a text out of its context and made it a pretext for something different: this was a cardinal sin. The historico-critical method was basic to his hermeneutic. But he did indulge at times in what we may call a single-dimensional use of some biblical statements to make doctrinal assertions. His unpublished, 'unintelligible' book on Christology (his phrase, see below) is an example of this, in which an adoptionist view of Christ was argued. We should note that it remained unpublished – by his choice. His approach was often descriptive rather than analytical, for all his emphasis on clear structures. It was based on an intimate knowledge of the Greek – the *koiné* Greek of Hellenism, of which he was an expert – plus as many additional sources and aids as he could get his hands on, as his well-marked copies of Hunt's and Edgar's two-volumed *Selections from the Greek Papyri* show. But even in this there were gaps. For example, he virtually ignored the *Corpus Hermeticum* which is of inestimable value for an understanding of Hellenistic Judaism and John's Gospel, as C. H. Dodd argued as far back as 1935; and he acted similarly towards the emerging *corpus* of the Dead Sea Scrolls, a focal point of public interest from 1949 onwards.

His expertise in Hellenism was recognized by the University when he was appointed Lecturer in Hellenistic Greek in the Faculty of Arts, which added a punishing four hours' lecturing per week to his workload. No one could compete with this. He loved it and was never happier than when exploring such matters. As he wrote to a retired headmistress, who had asked to be registered for his course, 'I am monarch of all I survey!' He loved to discover with his students the delights of the Greek papyri and early writings, based on such as

Milligan's texts, Theophrastus' *Characters*, *The Didaché*, Pseudo-Longinus' *On the Sublime*, Paul's Letter to the Philippians, and John's Apocalypse (Revelation). The inclusion of the last two is proper in this. The New Testament is insufficiently recognized as one of the glories of Hellenistic Greek literature *per se* – even if its Greek is at times poor – as Professor Peter Levi has been at pains to emphasize more recently. Willie's emphasis is somewhat different: he wanted to keep the Church's business at the world's centre, not at its periphery; he desired the unity of sacred and secular, not their polarization.

We must note his blind spots here, especially his ignorance of Aramaic, the language Jesus spoke, and his use of some questionable authorities for New Testament background, times and mores – such as David Smith's *The Days of his Flesh* and *Letters of St Paul*; or the works of Adolph Edersheim (all superb books in their own time). Both Matthew Black and C. C. Torrey had made major contributions in the former field, and the Dead Sea Scrolls were beginning to reinterpret the latter – to name but two. Expert in the knowledge of *koiné* Greek, Willie worked from an almost fixed point within it – the fault of giving out in disproportion to his taking in. But this could be misleading. Profundity is not the same as breadth. To labour long and deeply at the text of Scripture, which Willie did, is not less valuable than to read everything published on it – which he did not, although his reading was not excessively limited. He was not greatly interested to discover what *might* have lain behind his texts, or how translation from Aramaic to Greek may have influenced the transmission of such. Even his (much later) two-volume book The *Gospels and Acts*, while acknowledging the earliest Aramaic strata, scarcely comes to terms with their implications. Because of this gap, the Targums remained beyond his reach, as did the best reading of the Old Testament itself – and a whole range of New Testament background documents.

As far as New Testament times and mores are concerned, Willie was raised on the brilliantly descriptive, if dated, books of such writers as David Smith, Alfred Edersheim, W. M. Thomson and C. Tristram, as well as the even older authorities of Josephus and Philo (who remain critically important despite their age and ectopic Judaism). They had a profound effect on his expositions. But he did not marry that knowledge sufficiently to recent archaeological and related discoveries, which would have refined – even corrected – it. He virtually ignored Emile Schürer's multi-volumed *History of the Jewish People in the Time of Christ* (also old, but indispensable; now revised), as he did H. L. Strach's and P. Billerbeck's equally magisterial commentary on the New Testament, the Talmud and the Midrash, which began to appear in 1922. (His lack of German was also a limitation at this level.)

His ignoring of the Dead Sea Scrolls, among the most important finds of the century (discovered from 1947 onwards and translated, and still being expounded), is a concerning example of this reluctance to keep up with recent finds. These scrolls were written in Hebrew and Willie's mind appears to have been switched off by that fact, which allowed him to make some extraordinary statements – e.g. 'For a hundred years and more before the coming of Jesus Hebrew was a forgotten language ... The Jews no longer knew Hebrew. The scholars knew it, but not the ordinary people...' (*DBR, John*, volume I, p. 5f; reprinted in *DSB, John*, volume I, p. 5f). That comment was printed in July 1955 – six years after the discovery of the first scrolls. It has never been true that orthodox Jews forgot their Hebrew. Every boy learns certain portions of it before his bar mitzvah; in any case Hebrew and Aramaic are cognate languages, and mutually understandable. Willie nowhere shows a deep appreciation of the purely Hebraic tradition, which probably undid his hopes for a major position at a secular university. What he had of it – and it was very much – was filtered through Classical and Hellenistic Greek and Latin and English text traditions, sometimes, if rarely, French. It is an incomplete formation. It is not surprising that he quotes the Greek classical authors more than the Jewish; yet, with the exception of Luke–Acts and possibly Hebrews, the New Testament was written by Jews converted to Christianity, who were saturated in those Hebraic traditions. In the one area where his Hellenistic emphasis might have yielded more – the Septuagint versions – he wrote almost nothing.

The foregoing is offered to highlight his focuses, not to belittle his learning. Professor Alan Galloway speaks of Willie having an 'erudition of gargantuan proportions'. An Oxford Professor offered an example of it from his own experience. He could not find a Greek word in the Fathers that he knew existed and asked Willie, who was visiting his college at the time, if he could recall it. He could, and did, and then masterfully added four other places in the Fathers where it was found (of which the Professor was unaware), pointing out the subtle differences of usage – all from memory. In such matters his mind clicked on like a metronome. He was passionate in this love of Greek literature, and defended its development in principle and in practice. One of his students dared suggest that Greek was not necessary for him: he only wanted to be a pastor for his people; he had no linguistic gifts; there were plenty of translations to help him in his preaching. Willie razed the view savagely: 'You don't really know the New Testament unless you know it in Greek,' he retorted. A fellow minister whose son was studying under him asked how his son was doing. 'We're discovering first declension Greek nouns together,' Willie replied happily, referring to virtually the first lesson in Greek, which he himself had polished off at DHS nearly thirty years previously, aged sixteen; which he could still regard as discovery – wonderment assertive still.

This ever-fresh sensitivity to language may be construed as naive, but it is not that; in addition to the carefulness of the scholar he had the sensitivity of the poet. It was part of his genius, part of the crucial sense of wonder which so many have lost. With this, and undeterred by the 'clever' sort of philosophizing and pedantry that goes for wisdom in some quarters, he essayed a balanced theology, biblically grounded, centred on Jesus, and thorough – Paul *and* James; Peter *and* John; the Synoptic Gospels *and* the fourth; the Old Testament *and* the New. That done, he knew this was only half of his job. The Word had to be communicated; people needed to know; the prophet must tell. As Professor F. F. Bruce, another Highlander of greater scholarly acumen, who worked easily in more than ten languages, epitomized it at Willie's death, 'His concern for the careful scholarly study of the New Testament went alongside his concern to communicate its message.'

The focus of his erudition never changed, but we can define it more closely: it was a love for Christ the Word and a desire to share that knowledge which really identified and underpinned his work. Like Paul, unlike so many of his contemporaries, he was unashamed of it. Few theologians – and fewer church bureaucrats – speak as people *in touch, in love* with Jesus. Listen to them. Read their writings. When last did they refer to it, talk naturally of it, live as if they practised it? They are more likely to be found at a masonic meeting or a concert than a Bible study. They are ashamed of the gospel. It is almost beneath them. They make little embarrassed jokes about those who do take it seriously. The very idea is passé to them, sentimental, unmodern, even (they believe) unprofessional; which is why their speaking (can it be called preaching?) is so sterile, why their churches are empty, why those churches fail to pay their way, why they fail to influence people and society. These are the real resilers of the faith.

William Barclay achieved the opposite of all this: he was not ashamed of the gospel, or of Christ; his preaching sparkled and it filled the churches; his prayers moved thousands; his church achieved its economic goals, and helped to rescue Presbytery out of debt – as his writings later paid for many of his church's publications; he was successful through sheer spiritual power. Above all, he was in love with Jesus, in touch with him. As he said at the end of his life, by then Professor Emeritus of the University of Glasgow and Visiting Professor of the University of Strathclyde, 'The others we know about; Jesus we know. The others we remember; Jesus we experience.'

He knew what other ministers and teachers were up to: he was not prepared to sell the pass and follow suit, least of all to 'make an axe of the Torah' as the rabbis said (i.e. make money out of their work for it). He reacted sharply against such 'professionalism'. He did once essay it, as we saw earlier, mischievously describing his position in a letter to William Braidwood:

> In my spare time I am working on a book on New Testament Christology. It will be years before it emerges; my only object in writing such a book – which no one will ever read – is to prove that I too can write unintelligibly when I want to.

His mentors and colleagues then did not doubt that he could work and write 'academically', as their comments about his Bruce Lectures show; as their recommendations to other Chairs reveal. 'He has come to be regarded as one of the most vital forces in the famous Divinity Hall today,' the journalist Alexander Gammie wrote of him early in his university career, 'influencing the students alike by his sheer skill as a teacher and by the charm of his unobtrusive but warm-hearted personality.'

There was a downside to this. Alec Gilmore met him in Manchester in 1950 (Willie was lecturing at its Baptist College, part of the Faculty of Theology – the old stomping ground of A. S. Peake, C. H. Dodd and T. W. Manson – for which he himself applied, as we have noted). Gilmore was astonished to discover that Willie was only forty-three years of age. He had heard so much about him, yet, he commented, 'he looked like an old man'. It was true: photographs of that period sustain his judgement. But if Willie looked older than his years, he did not act it. He was still extremely vigorous, and loved playing football in the street with the local children on his return home in the evenings. (How many churchmen do that?) They referred to him as 'Daddy Barclay' and held him in great affection. His home was open to them and many crammed into it – friends of Barbara and Ronnie, and others who simply drifted in.

At such times he would tease and argue with them, as well as joke and sing; they loved his boisterous piano playing, were provoked by his outlandish comments which were designed to stir their minds and opinions – another part of his method, too often misunderstood. Kate aided him as ever in this, now somewhat recovered from the ravages of war but still painfully thin, as she would remain. Her husband's many activities and absences brought her especially close to Barbara. They frequently went about together like sisters – to the envy of other families and mothers. From time to time Kate would speak of her absent husband; sometimes he was actually *there*, hearing aid switched off, working, but not for her – to her great regret. She never opposed his work; she was proud of him, declaring him to be 'the greatest man I've ever met'. But it was the law of *costly* service that they were obeying; they paid the ultimate cost, and still served unstintingly. Kate did everything in the home for him. Of a highly practical disposition, she could rag him for his 'handless ways' – in good fun, usually.

He never did finish the 'unintelligible' book on Christology. But his comments show that he had now been afflicted by 'writer's itch'. As Ogden Nash remarked, 'When Ah itches, Ah scratches.' He itched and he scratched, with astonishing results. He had lost interest in the 'unintelligible'; his subject was too important to be continued at that level. Parts of this work (the less disturbing parts) saw the light of day in a series of articles for the *British Weekly* (as many of his books did), less some theorizing on the nature of Jesus, which went on to become his trilogy on Jesus: *The Mind of Jesus, Crucified and Crowned* and *Jesus as They Saw Him*, an excellent if untechnical work of 811 pages. That was the true focus of his faith, about which he was candid and unashamed.

Professor MacGregor, Willie reported to his friend Braidwood, was now being 'attacked by wanderlust in his old age'. This related to a lecture tour his chief was doing in the USA, leaving Willie to cope single-handed in the New Testament department. This was the man turned down for several professorships, the man to whom they offered but a temporary post; now the department depended on him. His labours were duly recognized by the authorities: his post was made permanent, after five years' gruelling work. There were now 140 students, at both ordinary and Honours levels, and Willie was hard pressed, preparing and delivering lectures and marking their assignments. (We may observe that Bruce was reading *koiné* Greek with just *two* students at Sheffield at about this time.) Secretarial help was virtually unknown. The students were his professional priority, of which I found not a single trace of criticism. By and large they were mesmerized by him. Outside college, in his *par erga*, as he delighted to call his secondary jobs, he was also at work in top gear; every weekend was taken up with appointments, as were most evenings.

This was not just locally. For example, he was now 'discovered' (as the *British Weekly* described it) by Edinburgh society, when he preached at Palmerston Place. He went thence to an Easter series at Morningside Church, also in Edinburgh, which gained 'rave' reviews; then to the Scots' Church in Crown Court, London. Next he was found at Perth for a Parent-Teachers' Association meeting; thence to a joint meeting of the leaders of the Lowlands BB; back down to Manchester; then to Victoria Tollcross – a link which continued on a regular basis for ten years. Thence to Strathaven where he preached a *ten-point* sermon regarding missionary support (i.e. financial). In all this there was another marked aspect of his professionalism, one his people at Renfrew had well known: his assiduous timekeeping. If he overran a service even by two minutes he was publicly contrite. One minister brushed aside one such apology, saying that no one would have noticed it. Willie pointed out that the ladies preparing the tea would have done so.

The Directors of the Western Committee of the National Bible Society for Scotland invited him to join its Board, which he did with pleasure – if not with the dedication they expected of him. Mere discussion was not for him, even at boardroom level, as Presbytery had discovered. It would be nearly five years before he made his second appearance at this Board, though he preached tirelessly around Scotland on its behalf. He behaved very differently in another appointment of this time, when he was nominated a member of the Senate of the University (in lieu of MacGregor again). This responsibility was welcomed alongside his position on the Faculty, and he never missed a meeting. He was also appointed External Examiner to the University of Edinburgh; and a year later to the same position at St Andrews. The Scottish Universities Missionary Association appointed him its Chairman.

All this was in addition to the continuing SSSU and RE syllabus work. It is not an exaggeration to say that he influenced virtually the entire youth population of Scotland in the late forties and early fifties. Most people would be delighted to be able to make that claim and nothing else. It was but part of his achievements. The preface to the Third Year volume of *A Syllabus of Religious Education*, signed by the two Joint Convenors (John Chambers and H. J. L. Robbie) and the two

Joint Secretaries (W. M. Wightman and A. J. Belford) – there is safety in numbers, especially where Barclay was concerned! – has this to say:

> To two persons, especially, must the major portion of the thanks of the Committee be given: to the Reverend D M G Stalker ... for the Notes on the Old Testament; and to the Reverend William Barclay ... for those on the New. Readers of the Notes will already recognize that these two gentlemen have made an outstanding contribution to Religious Education in Scotland.

To this we must add his specific church work, in pulpits and for ministers throughout the United Kingdom and beyond, not forgetting *The Expository Times* articles which catered for both: teachers and ministers. What Neville Cardus was to the cricketing public, what James Agate was to the theatre-going public, what Sir Mortimer Wheeler (whose writings he read with relish) was to archaeology, Willie was to the minister, the active lay person, the Sunday school and day school teacher, the BB leader, and so on – mammoth goodwill. Additionally, he made time to review books for other magazines: e.g. *The Scottish Sunday School Teacher*, *The Scottish Primary Quarterly*, the *British Weekly*, and *The Boys' Brigade Gazette*.

It is useful to look at his reviewing work in *The Expository Times* a little more closely. It meant at least one major new book to be read and written on every month (sometimes several, as he offered grouped reviews from time to time). Not a few have confessed that they would not have bought the journal were it not for his articles. Of fifty-four monthly articles printed in *The Expository Times*, selected at random, eleven concern biographical matters, ten theological, eight preaching, eight biblical introduction, seven poetry, six Church history, and four educational method. The books were usually the work of the best writers and activists in their fields. (We shall later see a marked change in the selection of his subjects; see p. 242)

Willie's style was sometimes uneven; he was now falling into the rushed habit of sending in uncorrected work to his editors. Thus we find repetition, tautology and an overuse of adjectives in his work, even a readiness to promote unproven opinions and exaggerations at times. Kathleen Downham, editor of SCM Press and a Barclay devotee, emphasized this particularly; his work was actually substandard at times. This has to be set alongside the immense success of his writings – not least for the SCM Press – and their superb clarity (once edited), in which he proceeded point by point, the points like telegraph poles marking the road along which he conducted his readers. For all that, he fastened on to other writers' fine phrasing like a gourmet – and could coin his own, to other gourmets' delight. For example, his reference to Father Andrew 'who saw loveliness in common things'; 'the echo of a great soul' in Pseudo-Longinus; his applause for the taut economy of T. S. Eliot; his immersion in 'a Tennysonian delight in words'. He praised the 'unselfconscious artistry' in an author, and admired the true scholar who offered 'a mastery of detail' in his work.

Rarely one to take the negative line if a positive could be found, he praised one author for his 'pleasant pugnaciousness' – a hint perhaps of the 'rare discussions' he had with his elders and managers in the fechtin' church. He enjoyed the mental romp for its own sake, but any such intellectual fisticuffs had to be played under his edition of the Marquess of Queensberry's rules – which included politeness, intellectual integrity and respect for one's opponent: goodwill prevailing. Few things earned his plaudits more than the use of uncommon words, despite his stress on the commonality of life. He believed that writers should educate as well as inform and entertain. It was not enough to supply mere facts; one had to *do* things with those facts, make them *work*. He disliked the use of loan words, whose use 'does not impress the scholar, which ruin the book for the man without the necessary linguistic equipment to understand it'. Notwithstanding that, he used them himself when necessary – antisyzygies proliferating. Non sequiturs were quickly shot down, sometimes as 'jesuitical comment' – a not too tactful description in that ecumenical age.

One had to be careful in claiming where truth lay. One author opined that 'an interpretation may be evangelically sound even though it is based on a doubtful exegesis'. The contradiction got its author a very sharp and public rap across the knuckles. Two things in particular Wille railed against, which he found 'irritating' and 'apt to repel' him: (1) 'the cult of unintelligibility', a stroke against some theological types who confused obscurity with profundity; (2) 'a distressing intellectual snobbery', which he designated the besetting sin of academics and Church leaders. Unintelligibility he judged a denial of a man's responsibility as teacher or minister – a sin against the light. Intellectual snobbery, its half-brother, was a denial of the law of love – the greatest commandment.

Nothing was so important as ministering to youth. Children and young people held the promise of the future, and very much of his energy to date had been spent on their behalf. In 1949 he wrote to Braidwood, '...besides these [some Bible Notes he was writing, see below] I am at work on a Bible Class handbook on Paul for the Church of Scotland, and three Boys' Brigade Bible Class Handbooks ... It will be 1950 before these things appear...' Hence his next book, *Ambassador for Christ*, a real book which has stood the test of time, got under way. What he had done inter-denominationally for the children of the SSSU, and secularly for those within the state educational framework, he was now called on to do for the young people of his own Church. It was geared to the needs of the Junior Bible Classes, its subject being developed over the then usual half-year syllabus of twenty-seven weeks. As was normal for such, he included a system of daily Bible readings for them to follow and so point up the week's lessons. It became one of his most successful books, all the more astonishing as it demonstrates the rare ability simultaneously to write for the twelve-year-old and lecture on Greek syntax to Honours-level students. The book was dedicated to his children, Ronnie and Barbara, 'and Kate, without whose patience it could never have been written'. Despite its low-level target readership, it is a rich source for his theology, ever Paulinist, ever evangelical – but never without the challenge of the real world and its responsibilities.

The next year *And Jesus Said: a handbook on the parables of Jesus* appeared, a longer book, also for the Youth Committee of the Church of Scotland. A novelist *manqué*, he loved stories, not least the stories of Jesus, and never tired of preaching and teaching them. He offered this material with a fourfold plea: it was not merely for the mind (having named twenty-six commentaries which lay behind his work), but required 'the necessity of prayer ... of quietness ... of devotion and of study' if its riches were truly to be appropriated. At the bottom of this is his careful linking of the sacred and the secular: the world viewed as 'the garment of God'. In this there is 'no mere analogy but an inward affinity between the natural and the spiritual order'. This is pukka Barclay. Similarly he commented of the sacrament as 'an ordinary thing which has in it a meaning far beyond itself'. The world, matter itself – at a time when its ferocious powers were beginning to be realized for destructive ends – cannot be denigrated; they are the theatre and the instrument of God's activities; the ordinary and the common cannot be intrinsically bad. It was one of the most important lessons arising out of the incarnation, that welding together of flesh and spirit, the human and the divine: 'what God has cleansed do not you reckon common or unclean', was how he later translated Acts

10:15. It underlay his ethic of social relationships, for which he cited Burns' condemnation of the *unco guid* mentality, the dangers of 'respectable' churchmen, 'the sin of exclusiveness and of contempt' as real evil; commonality had been obliterated; all was of God, and for God. These are repetitions, but he knew that such are an essential part of a successful teaching method.

The founder of the BB was a Caithness man, and Willie liked this association with his own origins, even as he loved its declared aim of promoting 'true Christian manliness'. Like the Youth Committee, it too had its handbooks. A national planning meeting was arranged at the Queen's Hotel in Birmingham, the site of many such endeavours (including, for example, the preparatory work for the Billy Graham campaigns that were shortly to commence). Willie was invited to join the Scottish contingent, and travelled with them from Glasgow. He jovially greeted his companions at Central Station – and announced that he would not be travelling with them. He would join them for lunch, but he would sit elswhere by himself and work. It caused a slightly unpleasant stir, but he insisted. Having found a comfortable corner seat, he opened his bag, unplugged his hearing aid, and got down to several hours' uninterrupted work.

His first book for the BB was entitled *God's Plan for Man*. It appeared for the session 1950/1, and took everyone by surprise by its popularity. It sold just under five thousand copies in record time (against the average sales of two thousand). The book centred on God's purpose for the world which was established in Jesus but required men – 'real men' – for its unfolding. That was the challenge he threw down. They were not necessarily the strongest or the fastest men – though he showed by apt detail how often such have committed themselves to God's purposes. But they were always courageous men; men who stood up for what is right. He developed this purpose from both Testaments, Old (ten chapters) and New (fourteen chapters), showing how history is subservient to 'the plan of God'. Interestingly, he did not have the same freedoms in writing this as he enjoyed for his earlier work. The Vice-President and Editor of the BB was Dr Martin Strang. He took a 'hands-on' view of editing, and not only cramped Willie's style but altered the order of his material, even remoulding some of his statements. Willie was unconcerned – goodwill demonstrated again. He was there to be useful.

It represents another facet of his 'service' concept: they may not take his time from work in inessential discussions, but they may shape his views in the way they believe will best serve boys' interests. That is, he will 'give them what they want'; he will 'write to order'. The Pauline ethic will hold for him: he will be 'all things to all men that some may be won'. Some scoff at this. They find in it a kind of weakness, of unprincipled behaviour – doubtless as did those who derided Paul. Willie ignored the insults and left them to it, content to let the evidence show whose work would prove to be the most useful. It did, and it was not that of his detractors.

This attitude covered both practical and doctrinal matters. The question of alcohol, or 'temperance' as they preferred to call it (pre-empting the debate by spelling it 'total abstinence') arose. Asked by the BB to write of something he now stoutly believed was wrong-headed, a conviction which he had won after hard battles with himself and his father's still pervasive influence, he did so – from *their* viewpoint, offering as good an argument for 'temperance' as can be found anywhere. George Mills, Secretary of the SSSU, had found him equally amenable in certain doctrinal matters which have not been explicitly recorded (one of them probably concerned the adoptionism of his 'unintelligible' book). That is another species of goodwill, in which someone lays aside personal convictions for the good of his weaker brethren. Let Willie have the last word on this Pauline principle, out of which grew his own:

> This is not a case of being hypocritically two-faced and of being one thing to one man and another to another. It is a case of being able to get alongside anyone. The man who can never see anything but his own point of view, who is completely intolerant, who totally lacks the gift of sympathy, who never makes any attempt to understand the mind and heart of others, will never make a pastor or evangelist or even a friend ... Paul, the master missionary ... saw how utterly essential it was to become 'all things to all men'.

Tens of thousands of young men around the world were touched by the lessons of these books. Many more were to follow. Out of the next thirty-two annual sessions in the BB – a worldwide movement – Willie's writings occupied no less than twenty-two, i.e. two out of every three. Not a few men would count that sufficient justification for a life's work; to Willie it was just another part, not even a major part, of his multi-faceted service for God. Thus came from his pen: *One Lord, One Faith, One Life* (1951/2); *God's Men, God's Church, God's Life* (1952/3); *The King and the Kingdom* (1953/4); and *God's Law, God's Servants and God's Men* (1954/5). All of these were recycled, some several times, and then made their way to an even wider constituency when the St Andrew Press republished them, as we shall see.

As if this were not enough, John McNaughton, the Convenor for the Glasgow Battalion, approached him privately. He had been thrilled at Willie's prayers – always reverent, never stilted, very practical and down-to-earth. Would he put some of them down for him, for use around the area? The result was *Camp Prayers and Services* (which also included a series of five-minute talks – unrequested by McNaughton – to accompany the prayers). The handbook circulated for a few years in a private edition, and then unsurprisingly found its way into print under that same title in 1958, continuing for many years after Willie's death.

He once described himself as 'a natural believer'. In this he is undoubtedly the product of his strict parental upbringing, his Church's catechetical method, a form of religious brainwashing. But he was not immune to serious searchings and doubt. And in this his 'middle period' we can witness some of these doubts surfacing boldly. The 'new note' in his preaching, which his father told him would follow his mother's agonized death, was not merely emotional. It was both philosophical and theological, and helped – as the war and especially the Holocaust had done – to restructure his beliefs. It had started to show itself in his undergraduate years, when he worked closely at the Greek Classics and came under the influence of that searing logic proper to their study. But it was then diffuse – overborne by credal constraint and paternal pressures, not least by the inertia of his own faith. As it developed it produced what we may call a sort of 'non-clinical schizoid' state in him, which he never truly threw off – perhaps there is such in all of us – in which his emotional life (i.e. religious devotion) was sometimes independent of his intellectual life (i.e. theological awareness). Not as an act of disintegrity or culpable dishonesty, but in the spirit of the distressed man who cries out, 'Lord, I believe; help my unbelief!' – the words of an honest man who knows his limitations, as well as the limitations of science, even 'the Queen of sciences'.

Willie believed in 'the possibility of the impossible' – his seventh published article as a minister (in February 1935) was about that idea exactly. It ever remained with him, surfacing again and again, for example in 1954, in his *Daily Bible Readings* (at Mark 9:24). He believed that it was axiomatic for a disciple to believe – a truism; it is what discipleship demands, the essence of faith. But paradoxes exist. He disliked them (an emotional point); he rejected them as an indefensible thought-form (an intellectual point); but he accepted that there was a point where intellect collides with faith, and knowledge with experience, in the big issues and mysteries of life. As Anselm phrased the experience, it was 'faith seeking reason'. His sometime denial of paradox (though he retained his antisyzygies) sometimes led to an undervaluing of problems and an oversimplification of arguments – never more so than when he found himself impaled on the horns of a personal dilemma of faith in a situation which required him to offer guidance and leadership to the public, to whose service he had committed his life. It was one thing to cry, 'Lord, I believe; help my unbelief!' but quite another to recommend it to those who, spiritually crippled, came for help – as he shows at this Mark 9:24, where he skirts the point and denounces the failure of the Church.

The issue was taken up by someone else, in a work which Willie reviewed in 1950. He quoted with autobiographical approval A. T. Cadoux's poem:

> I lived on borrowings of belief;
> Only the arguments were mine –
> An unremunerative brief,
> And hard, defending the divine.
>
> Then Jesus stood before my mind;
> I was arrested, held by Him;
> And in astonishment I found
> Belief in God no longer dim.

He had certainly lived on the borrowings of belief. He knew the battle and the hardship of the defence he was called to make; there can be no question that his experience of Christ was as compelling as the verse makes out. Nevertheless I seriously doubt that after his parish and wartime experiences he ever found belief in God – except in its most primary and naked form (the form of the distressed man, above) – 'no longer dim'. But that was enough, and it receives resounding affirmation in his autobiography, which he significantly offered as a *testament* of faith.

He was well aware that true faith must ever be 'faith seeking reason', and not vice versa. We believe, and commit ourselves; we learn, and we intellectualize. All of it based on the Word of God, constrained by that living Word, a double imperative: the personal Christ and the written word. Words were Willie's business. This found a neat expression 1952, in his first published comments on the challenge to Christianity of secularism. The book he was reviewing had been published in the USA and it cannot be ignored that Willie bore some sort of resentment against the USA at this time, as many did – perhaps akin to that of the elder brother in the parable of the prodigal son. Moreover, the book was by a woman, who had – unlike Willie – attained the rank of Professor. (It has to be said that he was a chauvinist who nevertheless loved the company of women.) He praised her for 'her absolute fairness of mind', her 'extraordinary power of lucid analysis', her 'unique gift for producing definitions which are helpful and stimulating' (she defined secularism as 'the ordering of life as if God did not exist', which he found 'adequate'). Of course, his eagle eye *had* to catch 'a shattering misprint' – immorality for immortality; *and* a Greek sentence 'wrongly spelled, wrongly accented, and wrongly printed': Women 1: Men 2 as the football commentator in him might have said. He gave its author full marks for her brilliant treatment of the subject: 'There are few better books on the modern situation than this.' Reason was satisfied; faith strengthened ... final score 2:2.

FOURTEEN

THE BATTERY-HEN YEARS

'Blessed is he who has found his work; let him
ask for no other blessedness.'

(Thomas Carlyle, *Past and Present*)

Mention has been made of Willie's *Daily Bible Readings*. They were
triggered by four things: his lessons for the SSSU, which informed
the Sunday School movement of Scotland for over five years – 'an
inestimable service' indeed; the very influential three-year *Syllabus
of RE for Use in Secondary Schools in Scotland* produced by the
joint Committee on Religious Education (hand-in-hand with the
Educational Institute of Scotland); and the two daily readings
schemes for the BB and Youth Committee handbooks of the Church of
Scotland – all of which had a similar, essentially devotional format, as
well as demonstrating his conspicuous didactic style.

In 1948 he was asked to provide a series of articles for the Church
of Scotland's magazine *Life and Work*. He did so under the title
'Beginning Again'. The Editor, Jack Stevenson, explained the objective
succinctly; it was to be 'a page for those who are wishing to find their
way into Bible Reading and relate it to their lives'. Willie's hallmark of
dual emphasis – Bible and life, faith and practice, pure and applied
knowledge – is again evident. Though written for members of the
Church of Scotland, the new series was advertised as an exposition of
Luke's Gospel 'for every man'. The magazine came out each month;
the series was also divided into weekly sections; they led eventually
to a *daily* segmentation which would soon be felt worldwide in over
thirty languages. Jack Stevenson's contribution to this has not been
adequately recognized.

The Church's Publications Committee, with long experience of this
type of reading material (Willie's father had taken part as a reader in
an earlier series, but it had existed as far back as Thomas Chalmers'
day in the mid-nineteenth century), had decided to resume 'nationally'
and with its own ministers and teachers what the International Bible

Reading Association had been doing on an international scale, under the title of *Daily Bible Studies*. It was the Scottish version of this publication which Stevenson was test-marketing in *Life and Work*. An arrangement was made for the IBRA to print and bind the Church of Scotland's edition of the books, in addition to handling their own, as Aubrey G. Smith its General Secretary explained:

> The IBRA received an approach from Reverend J W Stevenson ... to launch special editions of daily Bible reading notes for the Church of Scotland, carrying their name by Church of Scotland ministers ...One of the first was William Barclay. I remember visiting him in Glasgow ... We travelled, I recall, on top of a double-decker bus through the Glasgow streets, and sat in my hotel room considering a scheme I had drawn up.

Willie recalled it, too, but more personally. He did not then know it, but it was to have a massive effect on his life and work. 'It was just then that a chance to do something came to me out of the blue,' he explained somewhat airily to Braidwood. As if he were not already 'doing something'! As if it came out of nowhere! (Incidentally, the reference to their bus rides highlights Willie's courtesy towards his English colleague in collecting him from and returning him to the railway station, busy as he was.)

At the end of September 1948 a small (4 x 5in, i.e. 10.2 x 12.7cm) wire-stapled booklet of thirty pages appeared, at 8d per copy (3.5 new pence), under the title *Life and Work Daily Bible Studies*. Its subtitle was *The Foundations of Christian Faith: The Gospel according to Saint Luke*. Jack Stevenson contributed a Preface to the Scottish edition; Robert Denholm offered his usual one for the international edition (which was not called *Life and Work*, of course). To prepare the way for, and expand on, the booklet a three-part series on Luke was also written by Willie for *Life and Work* magazine. He entitled it 'The World's Most Beautiful Book'. The booklet had a spectacular response from the public. By the end of October the editor was reporting dramatic sales, and by early December it was out of stock. Willie commented laconically:

> Outside the college I have been busy with my pen. I have been doing daily bible readings with three hundred words of comment on each day's reading for the Church and for the IBRA. It does not sound difficult to turn out three hundred words per day, but it is a big task when you take it year by year [which, of course, he was not doing,

he worked on a quarterly cycle]. They have been selling up to 50,000 copies at a time.

G. J. Jeffrey and B. Burnet wrote the next quarter's notes, and J. A. Findlay, F. Greeves and Willie the quarter after that (on miscellaneous passages of Scripture). These latter were also printed in *Life and Work*. He wrote the notes for the third quarter (on Ephesians and Philippians) with G. W. Anderson, and they continued the process for the fourth, Willie writing on Corinthians.

At this point the Scottish edition was cancelled. Despite the numbers sold, a separate edition for Scotland was not, apparently, commercially viable, and the Committee swallowed its pride and once again merged its interests with those of the IBRA – temporarily. It may well have managed to keep going by itself had it accepted IBRA advice, but it sought to publish – in addition to the main booklet – one book for each age group, some of them also written by Willie. In so doing it undermined the economic foundation of the main booklet, for the IBRA had even agreed to subsidize the Church of Scotland scheme to the tune of 25 per cent of the costs – an undertaking from which the former was now forced to withdraw: the latter had neither the market nor the manpower for the enlarged scheme.

Yet the success of the main edition had made its point. So the Church, once it had regained its breath, decided on a new tack: to publish a series of readings, dated and geared to the needs of daily devotion, each centred on a single biblical book, but in book form. It was an idea come in its time. The new scheme was advertised, but then the Committee had to announce that it was having trouble finding writers able and willing to undertake the job. At the last minute an appeal was made to 87 Vardor Road, Clarkston, and Willie – now at this new address and up to his ears and beyond in commitments – again stepped into the breach. When the book eventually appeared – Acts had been selected for him, logically following the earlier Luke – he made this apology in the Foreword: 'The circumstances of the case demanded that it should have been written more quickly than it should have been ... the writing of this book has been a race against time in order that it should be ready for 1st January, 1953.' It was 213 pages long, and measured 4 x 6in (10 x 15cm).

He added a further point which is of great interest: 'The [entirely new] translation was made, not because it claims any special merit, but rather that in it ... the reader might be able to carry both the text of Acts and the comments on it wherever he or she went.' If the gender widening of his market is appropriate, the explanation is frankly unbelievable. The translation was not made to facilitate the text's reproduction in the book. There had never been a problem with reproducing the text of the *Authorized Version* in readings, booklets and commentaries, for a modest fee, and there are dozens of such to prove the point. Moreover, the New Testament part of the *American Standard Revised Version* (the USA edition of the *Revised Version*) had been published in 1946 to great acclaim, and was also available for such usage. (The whole *Revised Standard Version Bible* was published in 1952 to even greater acclaim, a singular breakthrough in biblical translation, to which Willie gave his own plaudits, referring to it in his later volumes.) The real point was that the Committee was strapped for cash. It could not, or would not, pay the royalty for this usage. A new translation would obviate the problem. Little wonder it had difficulty finding writers!

The IBRA confirmed the suspicion. And Willie confirmed it too. The memory of this embarrassment remained with him to the end of his life. As he wrote in his autobiography, 'Through no fault of the Association or of the writers, the series did not sell, and the Association ... was forced to discontinue them.' But the Association did *not* discontinue them! It was the extra series put on by the Church of Scotland (printed and bound by the IBRA) which were discontinued; and they all but wrecked a scheme proven in its usefulness. There would be no point (apart from a minor historical one) in dredging this up here were it not for the fact that the problem remained ongoing, and it sadly affected Barclay's and McCosh's relationship with the Publications Committee.

A brilliantly fruitful idea almost failed through its incompetence. Willie confirmed Richard Harkness's definition of a Committee – that it is 'a group of the unwilling, picked from the unfit, to do the unnecessary'. The Publications Committee – ever changing – never learned its lesson, and the work of many good men failed through this enduring fault. Happily, Willie's ability triumphed over its erratic manoeuvrings, to his public's spiritual if not his own financial advantage. Alongside the New Testament Readings a series on the Old Testament appeared. Despite having some first-rate men to write for it, there was no William Barclay among them. It disappeared and lay dormant until I resurrected the idea in 1978, when – based on the RSV – it moved to a very different style under Professor John Gibson's editorship.

So the little blue paperback *Daily Bible Readings – January to April 1953 – Acts of the Apostles* was published. Its author indicated his biggest debt in the significant dedication: 'In grateful memory of W D B and B L B from whose lips I first heard the name of Jesus and in whose lives I first saw him.' In this, it will be noted, his father had pride of place, his influence ever pervasive. It was 'partly in hope and partly in trepidation' that Willie sent it out. It had 'debts too many to mention'. We should note that he did not regard it as a commentary; it was not such in the fuller sense. It was not meant to be a technical aid to the text, though he did include brief comments on some of the technical problems from time to time (they cover less than twenty pages out of over five thousand in the series).

It was essentially a devotional aid. In this sense the later change of title from *DBR to DSB (Daily Study Bible)* is misleading; it was not for 'study' but for 'reflection'; not so much for the head as for the heart – for life rather than study. Had it been for study it would have been a very different book, and he may not have been interested in writing it, as we saw from his comments on 'soul-less things', his discarding of his 'unintelligible book'.

Hence it is prefaced by six prayers, three 'for use before reading the Bible' and three for use after it. This was to change. For as this one-off system of readings developed into a full series, as it became popular throughout the world, as students, ministers, lay preachers and Bible Class leaders discovered its high voltage for good, so the daily-use element was dropped, the dates were dropped, and the marketing of the series suggested more and more that it was a commentary. Even the prayers were dropped. Given its enormous success, it was an inevitable process. When I launched the slipcase edition in 1978 we found that its chief use was as an ordination gift, or one for students and ministers; it had reached its zenith, a pulpit *vade mecum*.

About the growth of the project Willie was typically lighthearted:

> The then Publications' Manager of the Church of Scotland came to me and said very bluntly, 'Would you be prepared to do us a volume of daily bible readings as a stop-gap until we can get someone useful to do them for us? I immediately agreed. When the first volume was coming to an end they still had not got 'anyone decent'. So I did a second, and so on and on until the whole New Testament had been covered.

We should treat this comment with the same carefulness as his 'bolt out of the blue'. Yet, five years and eighteen volumes later (the seventeen-volume division of the series took place in the sixties and was repeated in the 'revised' edition of the mid-seventies) his energy had produced a work totalling 4,812 pages. Such prolific activity reached its conclusion with the publication of the nineteenth volume, the third and final part of *The Revelation of John*. It was, on any reckoning, *a tour de force*: unrivalled in modern Bible translating and commentating, offering consummate scholarship expressed in modern terms, high theology encapsulated in easy language, the ethical imperative brought to bear on everyday issues, all brilliantly illustrated, with a devotional element that has inspired tens of thousands around the world for nearly half a century. The figures are spectacular. Each initial printing was for 10,000 units. With nineteen volumes of the first edition alone, something over 200,000 volumes cascaded around the world, at the rate of more than 34,000 a year – more than one for every linear mile of the planet's girth.

The work was immense, not least because, having embarked on his own translation for Acts, Willie was bound to continue it for the rest of the New Testament. There can be no doubting that it was highly congenial work to him, but it was exhausting, and took him outwith the New Testament for its execution – to the papyri, the history and the background books, as well as the Septuagint (LXX) and the translations. One hundred and nineteen commentaries were specifically named by him in it, in addition to lexicons, dictionaries, histories and a galaxy of books used for illustration. The commentaries he cited make a covert point that the superficial – i.e. stylistic – revisions of 1975–8 undertaken by James Martin failed to rectify: they remained dated (and worse, Martin sometimes altered the point Willie was making.)

Antiquity is no indication of quality in a commentary. The oldest cited by him – Luther on Galatians – dates from 1517, and is an all-time classic. But it is in the area of illustration and quotation that this datedness is most felt, though undoubtedly Willie would have wished for modern insights (such as Redaction Criticism) to be mentioned. At the time he reflected a wonderful array of literature, a mind replete with good things. Today such books are somewhat jaded, if not entirely forgotten, betokening an age long gone. No one reading his work can fail to be impressed by its range. 'Windows to let in light', as a great preacher once commented on this art of illustration, which Willie exhibited to a superb degree.

In no other sphere (except perhaps his ardent support on the terraces for the Motherwell Football Club) is his surging humanity so clearly seen. He has read everything and forgotten nothing. This adds to his writings a unique element – by virtue of sheer proliferation – and almost overshadows the text on which he is commenting: almost, but never completely. Light and lustre, interest and pointedness are added, but no more. When I was compiling the Index to the *DSB* series (now volume 18) it was this aspect which amazed me above others. I knew his ability to crystallize the main point(s) of a passage; his brilliance with Greek usage; his formidable background knowledge; his undeviating ethical and practical sense; his passionate and devotional applications. But I was breathtaken by the range of these quotations and anecdotes – from the Bible, the Classics, philosophy, science, the history of science, the world of business, poetry, art, warfare – the list is endless, as the names are profuse. They may be dated, but by and large they continue to make their point appositely; they are apposite because he knew men, their nature and their needs, which Scripture addresses with a 'Thus says the Lord'.

There are some oddities in his commenting, and a certain unevenness. He says what he wants to say about a passage, not necessarily what the whole passage is saying. Thus some of his expositions betray his own emphases and prejudices – his vendetta against 'the closed mind' is one such. There is no direct trace of John Calvin's exegesis in his work – especially strange considering the close relationship between Geneva and Scotland. (He found this legacy to be a harsh one, often foisted upon people by religious bigots from an age of bigotry, though he admired the courage of the reformers.) This is all the more surprising in that his Foreword to the volume on Ephesians refers to John Knox's love of Calvin's magnificent commentary on this 'Queen of the Epistles'; yet Willie ignored it in his own exposition. It reminds us that he never read Plato's *The Republic* straight through – though Arnot commented that he did study it from its index!

Even more strange is the lack of influence of some of the major recent movements in scholarship, such as the *Hermetica* or the Dead Sea Scrolls. We may put his datedness into perspective by the following reverse chronology of his sources: thirty-three of his commentaries date from the post-war period (which was burgeoning with commentaries); thirty-one date from between the wars; twenty-eight from the turn of the century; and twenty-two from the nineteenth century. As a guide to what was available to him, I note that one reference book at my elbow lists such works in English in their hundreds. It has to be said that his was a small, and sometimes puzzling selection.

We noted earlier how he ignored the Dead Sea Scrolls and the hermetic literature. This worried some of his most loyal admirers.

How could this man, who was ever calling for a bold move forwards to new opportunities, not grasp their implications? The outpouring – and it was just that – of detail on the Scrolls took place throughout his professional life as a teacher of biblical language and criticism. They were discovered in 1947, and since 1949 there has been an annual discharge of the new material and its interpretative comment which has considerably added to our knowledge of first-century Palestine. It is indispensable for our understanding of that period, as all are agreed – not least in the area of Jewish life and sects, on which Willie had much to say. Meetings and lectures, seminars and courses mushroomed all over the country following their discovery; some of his colleagues were hounded by the public for news and explanations. A mini-industry in their publications developed. Great claims for their implications were made – how they affected the Bible and early Christianity, how they were said to overturn historic doctrines, etc. These claims are still being made. Willie allowed them to pass him by.

British and American scholars were in the forefront of this development, and some were Scottish. One, Robin Watt, was even supervised by Willie for his PhD, on *Manual* III:13–IV:14, a disappointing experience Watt remarked. Not once does Willie refer to them, an astonishing omission for one whose key emphasis was the importance of language (but never Hebrew or Aramaic or their cognates) and its background for the study of the texts. Many years later in 1974, when tackled by his SCM editor, John Bowden, who was concerned at this omission in the text of his book on the Gospels and Acts (his particular focus was the parallel between the Dead Sea Scrolls and John – a particularly fruitful area of connection), Willie bluntly confessed, 'I am on ground I know very little about.' He cannot be excused for this omission. There is a sense in which it must be judged harshly: any work on the New Testament is incomplete without such inclusions. It is hard not to conclude that his mindset was complete by this time; that he knew what he knew and could not find time to be troubled by anything new; a blind spot had developed.

It was in 1953 that the pseudo-reformed journal *The Monthly Record*, an arbiter of negatively conservative opinion in Scotland, first indicted Willie for 'resiling the faith'. It was a charge with which the journal was to harass him until his death – and sully his reputation ever afterwards: goodwill repudiated. From now on he was to be a marked man in a different sense: by the antagonists of modernity, the obscurantists, who are ever afraid to step out boldly, think courageously, or seek to understand their fellow men sympathetically. Such were, henceforth, seeking to destroy his authority, his ministry, his witness, too often regardless of truth. He affected not to care, but he was a man who – bruised long ago by the incessantly negative attentions of WDB – needed acceptance and encouragement (one of his keywords), and who was vulnerable to being hurt by attacks on himself. Kate, brought up in sedate Dundonald, at the centre of the town's respect, was especially hurt by their venomous comments. It was not the acids of modernity which affected her, but the acids of unlove in *so-called Christian circles*, of those who could only snarl and sneer at the sacrifices they were making together for their work.

The *DBR* took off despite the problems, and showed its true mettle by a burgeoning influence. Willie has always stated that he embarked on the project not knowing that it was to be a series, well aware that he already had enough on his plate. He apologized repeatedly for the unseemly haste with which his work for it was done, emphasizing this point particularly in the second volume (when he returned to Luke): 'Again I am conscious that this book has been written with too much haste.' The spirit in which he embarked on it was one of pure service: he was willing to fill the gap, a motive that finds frequent expression in the forewords to the series' original volumes.

His attitude towards scholarship, in a scholarly position himself professionally, was critical for the series. Yet he was determined not to be technical. The 'soul-less' and 'inhuman things' were not going to preoccupy him here. He was in the business of making bread, not refining flour. He knew from his fourteen years at Renfrew that scholarly refinements *per se* left people undernourished. It was not enough to polish the cooker; one had to feed the people. Woe betide the cook who can only describe the ingredients!

His mood showed itself in two reviews from about this time in which he castigated two excellent scholars – H. F. D. Sparks and C. H. Dodd – whose brief books he deemed to be 'products of the study rather than the battlefield of life', a judgement that earned him a swingeing rebuff from Principal H. Cunliffe Jones. But Willie had made *his* point: a minister's primary role is to minister, to serve his people's entire need. In this series he was once again the minister – for a worldwide congregation. 'I have tried all through the book to make the life and words of Jesus live against their contemporary background and *above all* to make them *relevant* for today' (my italics).

Four emphases of Luke are enumerated by him: it is 'the Gospel of women', 'the Gospel for Gentiles', 'the Gospel of Prayer', 'and, despite its outstanding characteristic of universality, notably the Gospel of praise'. An aspect of this universality was demonstrated when he received a letter from His Honour Quashie Idun, the Chief Justice of the Supreme Court of Ghana, who had been overjoyed by it. It was a subject that was to develop, and evoke yet more criticism of his work. His local debts were again listed in the dedication, to 'The Kirk Session of Trinity Church, Renfrew ... in particular M[itchell] R[amsay] and J B K[idd]: men of God'. Such were the people he readily sought to serve.

He expressed one of his favourite aspects of Luke thus: 'There is a radiance in Luke's Gospel which is a lovely thing, as if the sheen of heaven had touched the things of earth.' 'Lovely' is another Barclay keyword. He was aware that the sheen could be spoiled by his translation of it: 'I would again stress the fact that the translation claims no special merit.' Yet in an age still unused to new translations – though they were beginning to appear – it is robust and clear. He was never entirely pleased with it, as the changes in his *New Translation of the New Testament* show. I have one of his copies of the original which he has carefully annotated, doubtless for a revision that never happened. It looks like one of the old study Bibles favoured by his father, with words being circled and lines crossing the page to spare areas of the margin in which his reconsiderations are placed. These come to a sudden stop at Luke 4:44 – when other pressures had undoubtedly caught up with him.

He was aware of the pressures he was putting on his readers. His volume on Luke is much longer than that on Acts (the Greek texts are nearly equal). The commentary on the former runs to 330 pages; that on Acts to 222. The idea of having long passages to comment on in three hundred words, one passage for each day over four months, concerned him: it was both artificial and superficial. He accordingly broke with it: 'I have made no attempt to make the passages or the comments of equal length for each day, for I do not believe that the words of the Bible can be measured out in equal portions as one might measure out yards of cloth.' He confessed to having made 'use of material which I have used in other forms in other books' – i.e. the 1948 *Daily Study Bible: the Foundations of the Christian Faith*, and the 1952 *And Jesus Said*, his exposition of the Parables which partly covered Luke.

In May 1954 the third volume of the series was published, and at 421 pages it was the largest so far. It dealt with the earliest letters of Paul: significantly with Galatians, Thessalonians and Corinthians, which had the very great advantage of tying together Paul's earliest thinking. This presupposed a chronological sequence that others strongly opposed. It has since been reordered, by which his original, fruitful emphasis has been destroyed. The subject of its dedication was George A. Mills, the General Secretary of the SSSU, and this is particularly interesting in the light of his willingness, at forty-seven years of age, to allow others to guide his work:

> ...to me a father in God who first gave me the opportunity to write a book [*New Testament Studies*], whose encouragement has often compelled me to go on when otherwise I would have given up, whose guidance has saved me from many a mistake, and whose wisdom has saved me from many a heresy; and to whom I owe more than I can ever repay.

He acknowledged the problems of understanding Paul's writings by emphasizing the hard objective behind his work: 'It is true to say of Paul's letters that they will not give the man who studies them a meal unless he is prepared to break mental sweat ... I wonder how many people ... are prepared to make the effort?' He ends his prefatory comments on a personal note: 'I can testify to what a glorious experience it has been for me to live with Paul for the months in which I have been writing these studies. It is one of the most enriching experiences of my life which has ever come to me...'

Once again he offered his own translation, this time acknowledging his use of the translations of the *ASRV* and J. B. Phillips. Some of the texts' technical matters find a brief airing: he espoused the 'South Galatian theory' as to the chronology of Paul's life (which places Galatians at the start of the Apostle's *corpus*) – a matter already adumbrated in the volume on Acts; he maintains the traditional view of the dating of the Thessalonian letters (many believe the second to have been written first; its primary place in the canon being based on the then usual method of placing the longest roll first in the collections); and he offers a brief outline of how the original four Corinthian letters developed into the two we have today. He offered little by way of comparative exposition – i.e. of the different emphases we can observe in Paul's developing thought, apart from the collocation of the early letters themselves. (He will offer more when he comes to Mark and Matthew.)

Mark was treated next. It appeared in September 1954, a mere four months after the foregoing volume. Its overall length was 420 pages – nearly one hundred pages longer than that on the longest Gospel (Luke); an appropriate length, he thought, for 'the most important book in the New Testament'. It is, he declared, 'the first life of Jesus ever to be written', and – less reliably – 'the life on which all other lives depend'. He stated that this Gospel 'is the essential Gospel', the preaching of Peter himself – in line with the ancient tradition of its origins. He does not offer a definition as to what constituted this 'essential' nature, but we should understand his emphasis on its 'plainness' as at least a clue. Luke, a far greater historian and a much more careful writer than Mark, having examined his Gospel and several other documents (see Luke 1:1–4), provides a more detailed account of 'the Foundation of the Christian faith' (as Willie subtitled his first exposition of it). What he most loved was not complexity, but directness, which he highlighted here.

From the essence of things he moved to the quintessence, by dealing with Paul's letter to the Romans, his next subject in the series, a slighter volume (of some 275 pages). This, he asserted, 'contains more of the quintessence of the mind of Paul' than any other document. He loved to remind his readers of the physical appearance of the great apostle as contained in the apocryphal book, The Acts of Paul and Thecla – 'of small stature, bald of head, with crooked limbs...' Dare we see something of Willie's own self-disregard in this, given his premature ageing, his deafness (which, he more than once commented, made people treat him as if he were stupid), his conspicuous hearing aid, his baldness and his corpulence? I think we may, as we must also observe what was said of the inward man: 'Paul, looking only at the goodness of God, did them no harm, but loved them greatly.' That could be Willie's epitaph. The book was dedicated to his departmental chief, G. H. C. MacGregor, whose eight years with this hyperactive assistant – if we can truly call Willie an assistant – would have been exhausting were it not for his tendency to go walkabout.

Willie observed that Romans had few technical problems. The main one concerned the length and the original use of the letter, which turns on the threefold doxologies of 14:23; 15:33 and 16:25–7. His view was that the main part of the text was an 'apostolic encyclical', which Paul had circulated around his churches, the different doxologies denoting the changed endings being necessary for this. The letter is of 'fundamental' importance – a word uncommonly found in Willie's writings, perhaps because of its misuse by some denigrators. 'Fundamental', the word-smith in him knew, dealt with roots. Here, however, he wishes to explore not the roots of Paul's teaching but its quintessence. He does not demonstrate how the teaching of this letter provided the bases for the great reformed doctrines; but merely to list some of his headings is to see how importantly he regarded them, how ongoing they were in his subconscious: God's Fidelity and Man's Infidelity; All is of Grace; The Exceeding Sinfulness of Sin; The Love from which Nothing can Separate Us, and so on. All of these he declared to be part of that quintessence of Paul – and of himself, by extension. His work as a middleman – an interpreter for the 'plain man' – caused him to paraphrase such leading words and phrases, not omit their essence, and concentrate on finding modern and relevant alternatives. It was a job full of dangers, from different quarters. Many failed to understand him in this; others simply refused to try. Mentally idle, historically frozen, religiously selfish, they reiterated the old phrases to increasingly smaller groups, bitterly denouncing those who had found a more excellent way: ever the story of theology.

If he ignored the existence of some technical problems, he admitted that he was perplexed by some Pauline concepts – e.g. human solidar-ity – though he accepted the social consequences of sin (an organic connection affecting all people, he affirmed, which is precisely what Paul was saying; he ignored its ethical paradox). His mind was grappling for concepts assimilable by modern men and women; he was not afraid to raise doubts over the shibboleths of yesteryear's theologies and disputes; nor was he afraid to admit – alongside the apostle Peter, no less! – that in Paul there are things 'hard to understand'. Willie prefers to slide away from such, and the sterile arguments that have gathered about them, to work in the area of certainties – two of which he now asserts with crystal clarity: 'Whatever else we may say about Paul's argument, it is completely true that man was ruined by sin and rescued by Christ.'

From the heights of Paul he soars yet higher – to those of John's Gospel. Here he is on especially congenial ground, not only because of the fine devotional pulse that throbs through it, but because of the Hellenistic background of its language and thought-forms (the actual background was still first-century Palestinian, of course). Once again we are forced to face his avoidance of matters Hebrew/Aramaic, his delight in matters Greek, a vein running throughout all his work which nevertheless recognized the high value of the Old Testament.

The sheer richness of John's recollections overcame him, and once again he was forced to alter his mode of treatment:

> I would like to point out one new feature of these Daily Bible Studies. [We should note this continuing daily emphasis.] None of the sections for each day has been allowed to become too long. In former volumes I put everything I wished to say about a passage into the reading for one day. In this volume, if there was a great deal to be said about any passage, I have asked the reader to spend two or even more days studying the passage with me.

The result was a book of two volumes: 646 pages of gripping meditation, exposition and application. Here, as usual, his statements are peppered with superlatives; they are signs both of his enthusiasm for his text and of his seriousness in applying it: Acts (and Mark!) are 'the most important book(s)', Luke 'the most beautiful', and so on. It would make an interesting study to put all these together. John, he now declares, 'is the most precious'. Its richness not only fed and energized him, it delayed him too, but even he cannot work incessantly: 'I would like to apologize to the readers of this series for the fact that the volumes are sometimes a little late in appearing ... the task of producing three or four per year, in addition to much other work, is no light one.' We should note that he is describing over a thousand printed pages per annum – in addition to the rest of his work, published and otherwise. There was a metronomic rhythm to it, week after week, month after month, quarter after quarter, year after year.

He added a word of thanks for the many letters he was receiving from readers – and offers another superlative: 'It is my prayer that one of the greatest books in the world will unfold for us even more of its treasures as we study it together.' 'Together' – the hallmark of William Barclay's teaching stance: he and his readers, he and his students, reading, learning, discovering together. It is the sign of the humble man, open-minded and open-hearted; the man of goodwill, serving his people.

It was the Gospel, he said, of the eagle's eye – the eagle being an old symbol for it (as man was for Mark, the lion for Matthew, the ox for Luke – but these symbols varied in the early Church). Of all living creatures it is only the eagle, he remarked, that can look directly into the sun without being blinded, '...and John, of all the NT writers, has the most penetrating gaze into the eternal mysteries and the eternal truths, and into the very mind of God ... there are many people who find themselves closer to God and Jesus Christ in John than in any other book in the world.' He lists some surprising omissions – 'iron-ration' omissions for which Willie himself, ironically, was often ruthlessly criticized and denigrated:

> It omits so many things ... no account of the Birth of Jesus, of his Baptism, of his Temptations; it tells us nothing of the Last Supper, nothing of Gethsemane, and nothing of the Ascension. It has no word of the healing of any people possessed by devils and evil spirits. And, perhaps most surprising of all, it has no parables ... so priceless a part of the other three Gospels.

The omissions – for the first-century, Gentile man – of such things fed his own ongoing concern for the modern. The subject of 'iron rations' was beginning to predominate. We all have our own intellectual baggage – the ideas and concepts and principles which furnish our minds and show themselves uppermost in our thinking and talking: 'out of the abundance of the heart [Hebrew/Aramaic for mind] the mouth speaks'. Willie spoke and wrote out of the abundance of his and it filled the churches, for he spoke and wrote of Christ and his work; as he himself had promised: 'If I be lifted up...'

While working on these Readings, he was also commenting on *A Draft Catechism for Use in Sunday Schools*, a series in the *Scottish Sunday School Teacher* which expounded formally the New Catechism of thirty-two articles that was being published throughout Scotland. But Willie was not mentally transfixed by creeds or confessions, which are not after all biblical concepts, but concepts deduced from biblical passages – a very different matter. He believed that they should be kept subordinate; that the Bible itself should predominate. Like John, he could omit some things.

He knew the need for prioritizing beliefs, the importance of having 'iron rations' – the things that matter most, the things to which people *in extremis*, whether of doubt or belief, of life or death, can cling. His mindset was formed by the biblical text – the whole text – not the creeds (despite his catechized youth). He knew his Bible too well to allow its truths to be imprisoned within the straitjacket of this or that Church, Council or Synod. Unlike the 'Wee Frees' and others, who had sold their spiritual birthright for a mess of seventeenth-century pottage, he hung on to his freedom – a genuinely *free* churchman, ever aware of the truth of John Robinson's statement, 'the Lord hath yet more light to shine forth from his holy word'. He was ever open to that possibility, that promise:

> John is not so much The Gospel according to Saint John; it is rather the Gospel according to the Holy Spirit. It was not John of Ephesus who wrote the Fourth Gospel; it is the Holy Spirit who wrote it through John ... Behind this Gospel there is the whole of the Church at Ephesus, the whole company of the saints, the last of the apostles, the Holy Spirit, the Risen Christ Himself.

It takes us back to his position on Acts:

> The Book of Acts has been called The Gospel of the Holy Spirit. If ever a doctrine needed to be re-discovered it is the doctrine of the Holy Spirit ... God is eternally Father, Son and Holy Spirit ... All the members of the early Church lived in the Spirit as they lived in the very air they breathed ... the measure of the Spirit which a man can possess is conditioned by the kind of man he is ... The early Church was a Spirit-filled Church and precisely therein lay its power.

This was stated before the explosion of 'pentecostal' and 'charismatic' church life in the sixties and subsequent decades; perhaps we should record that he was one of the harbingers of it. It was no new thing with him. In 1940, expounding the Church of Scotland's 1935 document *A Short Statement of the Church's Faith* (again to the readers of the *SSST*), he had affirmed that 'without the Holy Spirit Christian doctrine would be a dead body without a living soul ... The Day of Pentecost was the most important [another superlative] date in the history of Christianity.' If secret there be in William Barclay's life and ministry, that is it. Or, as the apostles themselves said on that historic day, the fulfilment of history: 'This is that...' (Acts 2:16).

He emphasizes the fact that the apostle John is not mentioned once throughout the whole Gospel. But 'the disciple whom Jesus loved' is. There was no question in Willie's mind that this was John, 'his favourite', as he declared somewhat controversially. It was this privileged one who bore witness to Jesus in his dual nature: for 'there is no Gospel which so uncompromisingly stresses the real manhood and the real humanity of Jesus ... On the other hand, there is no Gospel which sets before us such a view of the deity and the godhead of Jesus.'

One final word must be offered concerning the absence of the Lord's Supper in John. It is important for underlining the free-church, one-world theology of William Barclay, how the university lecturer made a uni-verse of his experience and learning, how the theologian in him theologized unitedly:

> There is no doubt what John is saying [apropos 6:50–9]. He is say-ing that for the true Christian every meal has become a sacrament ... every meal in the humblest home, in the richest palace, beneath the canopy of the sky with only the grass for carpet, is a sacrament. John refused to limit the presence of Christ to an ecclesiastical environment and a correctly liturgical service ... It is the wondrous thought of John that the communion table, and the dinner table, and the picnic on the seashore or the hillside are all alike in that at all of them we can taste and touch and handle the bread and the wine which bring us to Christ. Christianity would be a poor thing if Christ were confined to the Churches.

This view was not detached from reality, as some of his critics aver. For the first three hundred years of its existence, the Church did not have church buildings, and enjoyed an almost creedless state (by our much denser standards). The Bible was enough; the apostles' own confession was simply 'Jesus is Lord', the first and truest creed of all. William Barclay believed much and questioned much, but his iron rations – his minimum beliefs – are brilliantly and revolutionarily conveyed in this exposition of John. He was ever returning to this minimum, concentrating on the essence, leaving the peripheral for others; preaching the big themes, and emphasizing their logic.

The Epistle to the Hebrews followed, in March 1955, written specifically at the request of one of his readers, 'DA', to whom he dedicated his work. We do not know who this 'DA' was (David Anderson, of DHS?), but it is typical of our author that he should comply with such a request; 'giving them what they want', as Arnot said, though we shall see that it fitted perfectly with his development of the series. He was studying *with* his readers, but also – and essentially – *for* them.

Professor W. M. MacGregor, that sharp and twisted tutor of Willie's undergraduate days, made more than one impression on Willie. He had been a student of A. B. Bruce, of whom he said, 'he cut the cables and gave us a glimpse of the blue waters'. MacGregor was the first whom Willie heard lecture on Hebrews. He said, offering this dour man as fine a tribute as he made to anyone, 'These lectures I will never forget. To me they were the high-water mark of him who was the greatest interpreter of the New Testament I ever met. If this present book has anything of good in it, it remains due to the inspiration of W M MacGregor.'

His exposition of the treatise – Hebrews is that, though Willie called it a letter – ran to 251 pages. It had taken him, he said, seven hard years' graft to understand it (i.e. as the subject of one of his lecture courses at Trinity); its writing, of course, was done in a matter of a few weeks. The point required another superlative: it is, he said, 'the most difficult book in the whole New Testament' for the person of today. But, contrariwise, 'I believe that there is no book in the New Testament which is more worth the effort to understand.' He does not speculate as to whom the author was, content to agree with Origen and others that 'only God knows', though he had to be 'at least of the stature of a Barnabus or an Apollos' – two fruitful clues. He believed its recipients were probably an Italian colony or college of men destined to be teachers within the Church – 'written for a little group of scholars' (sic) – sometime around 65–85 AD; to whom Willie somewhat surprisingly does not impute Jewishness, as is usual, though he must have known the Old Testament thoroughly – especially one of the *Greek* versions of it.

If John gave him joy for its Hellenistic background (among other things), this document did so for its profound religious instinct. Willie commented that it had been his 'duty and privilege' for several years to lecture on it. In it the religious worlds of the Old Testament and nascent Judaism, of Greeks and Romans, turned his mind to the fundamental question, 'What is religion?' In its pages 'the very essence of religion' was unfolded. It is summarized in the writer's phrase, 'Let us draw near...' Access to God is therefore what religion is all about. That was ever Willie's view: his religion was *a genuine experience of God* – as was his preaching. It was never divorced from life or its responsibilities, and it centred on Jesus. Willie thus offered, without euphemism or platitude, a *relationship* with God. This was the secret of his prayers, his preaching, of all his many successes.

In addition to the lilting fluency of the document's Greek – 'the best Greek in the New Testament' – the Platonic world of perfect forms and patterns, of ideals and symbols, finds an appreciative expression in his pages. In such we come face to face with the best that ancient philosophy offered. And here we reach the apex and the reality of Jewish law and lore, of its revelation and its developments. The Chosen People's whole experience – their laws, precepts, judgements, sacrifices, priesthood, sanctity and religious routines – were *not* the final reality; they were but pointers to it. The fulfilment of those dreams and promises, prophecies and assurances, hopes and endeavours lay, Willie emphasized again and again, 'in the glorious picture of Jesus Christ, in all the splendour of His manhood and in all the majesty of His deity'. He describes him as perfect obedience, perfect man, perfect priest, perfect sacrifice – and perfect hope: God's answer to humankind's hopeless predicament, God's provision to our need: God himself, available to us.

Ephesians followed this exposition, and we see in his choice of it the logic Willie was applying in developing his series – it was now *his* series, unalterably stamped with his own personality, expertise and interests. In Ephesians the seventh – dare we say the perfect? – stage is reached. It offers, he roundly declares, 'the highest reach of New Testament thought'. Other volumes will follow, many of them, but we cannot question the fact that in March 1956, at the age of forty-nine, Willie had reached his expositional peak, his theological zenith. Significantly, it was at this time that his worldwide ministry really took off, establishing him with an apostleship unique in the twentieth century.

It is very regrettable that the exigencies of printing routines, and an inept editorial decision, later placed this, 'the Queen of the Epistles', 'the Supreme letter', 'the divinest composition of man', second to – of all documents – Galatians, to some modern eyes the least helpful. Thereby the Rolls-Royce was relegated below the workhorse; the queen obscured by her valet.

Willie dealt with 'the certainties' (another of his keywords) of Ephesians first: that it was by Paul and written towards the end of his life; that 'it is in fact in the last degree unlikely that it was written to the Church of Ephesus'. This is the sort of comment almost designed to send a shudder of fear (even anger) through the conservative ranks, who placed so much dependence on the unhistorical margin comments and headings of the *AV*. But there was much to be said for it, and when Willie was convinced of a matter he was nothing if not bold. So he argued the fact that 'in Ephesus' is not in the best manuscripts at the first verse of chapter 1; adding to this the quite impersonal nature of the relationship between writer and recipients; the stylistic differences, when compared with other letters; the unusual language it uses (over seventy words are unique to it compared with Paul's other writings); and certain differences of mental attitude, to which we shall return.

This was as it should be, but beneath this confident assertion went a fluctuating movement of thought – dare we call it a swithering?

– now conservative, now liberal. He knew where he stood, but he sought to keep an open mind on objections and problems. He *was* both conservative and liberal, searching and assertive, doubtful and forthright: antisyzygy man. And he can overleap the considered views of not a few scholars and advance a point of his own preference, as he does here when he announces that this letter is none other than the lost letter of Paul to the Laodiceans (see Colossians 4:16). A small but not inconsiderable blow for independence!

Content was always more important to him than peripheral details, to which he now turned zestfully. His sense of orderly development is contradicted by his enthusiasm for the sheer brilliance of his matter: 'The great central thought of Colossians [still to be dealt with] is the all-sufficiency of Jesus Christ; the thought of Ephesians is a development of that conception.' He expands on the latter thus:

> The key thought on Ephesians is the gathering together of all things in Christ. Christ is the centre in whom all things unite, and the bond who unites all things ... The central thought of Ephesians is the realisation of disunity in man, disunity in time, disunity in eternity, disunity between God and man, and the conviction that all that disunity can only become unity when all men and all powers are united in Christ.

Key thoughts, central thoughts – they were the acme of Paul's doctrine: 'all Paul's thinking and experience would lead him to precisely that'. He shows how Paul argues his case by use of his 'double thesis' – which, sadly, has also been obscured by the revising editor's uncareful work. In the first three chapters Paul deals with the conception of unity in Christ; in the latter three he deals with the position of the Church as the vehicle which brings it about. In this, 'Paul strikes one of his greatest phrases' (another superlative): the Church is *the body of Christ*, which Willie goes on to expound in typical style.

The next volume dealt with some of the practicalities of the Church, taking as its source-documents the so-called 'Pastoral Letters' – Timothy and Titus. Willie moved with equal ease from the theological heights to the practical plain, suggesting that 'no letters in the New Testament give such a vivid picture of the growing Church'. Perhaps we may even say that in reaching this *practical* point, a new zenith was achieved: the Gospel was now alive in flesh and blood; its second generation needs being set for all subsequent ones:

> In [these letters] we see a little island of Christianity in a sea of paganism; and in them we see as nowhere else the first beginnings of the ministry of the Church ... just because they are written when the Church was becoming an institution, they speak most directly to our situation and condition.

He cannot omit a major effect of these last letters on him: 'There are times when the Pastoral Epistles stress the word *all* in a most significant way' – in which we may trace the beginnings of his 'universalism' (but compare this element in Luke, above), which became a strong element of his thinking, one that requires careful elucidation. Its roots lay in the creation account of mankind, in the promise to Abraham through whose seed all people shall be blessed, in the prophets' *universalist* promises which were fulfilled in Jesus. His incarnation had implications which Willie understood but slowly, moving from face-value interpretations of texts (which incorporated vicarious atonement) to the doctrine of the cosmic Christ as unfolded in Ephesians and Colossians. At its heart stood the doctrine of the love of God: 'THE LOVE OF GOD FOR ALL MANKIND', as he put it. That, and that alone, predicated his theology. But he never 'developed' it; still less did he deal with it as part of 'the wider ecumenism'. He rested his case with it, content to state and restate it. He did develop alongside it other basics – the Lord's Prayer and the Beatitudes, a key part of his 'iron rations', the one welding the new relationship (by prayer), the other expressing it (in appropriate action). Only seldom do we see other aspects appear, and then but piecemeal.

The Pastorals are indeed a minefield of contentions. Willie wends his way through them assertively, defining the underlying issues: the developed organization of church leadership; its salaried officials; the order of widows; credal difficulties; 'the dangerous heresy' (i.e. incipient gnosticism – the overthrow of the simplicity of the gospel by superior 'knowledge'). He sees in the language of the letters one of the great problems – 36 per cent of it is unique, i.e. 306 out of its 848 words, 175 of which are not found anywhere else in the New Testament. Further, some of Paul's regular expressions – the turns of phrase and the grammatical elements that all writers use – are totally absent, no less than 112 out of a total 932; to which should be added that some of his missionary activities find no other collaboration in the New Testament (an unconvincing comment if they are among the last of the New Testament documents). Despite all this, 'we are still hearing the voice of Paul, and often hearing it speak with unique personal intimacy'. He leaves us to draw the conclusion that if Paul could leave them out in directing the ministries of Timothy and Titus at this crucial time in the life of the young Church, perhaps our own shibboleths are not so important after all...

FIFTEEN

'THE TRACE OF A GRIN'

'Courage is not simply one of the virtues but the form of every virtue at
the testing point, which means at the point of highest reality.'

(C. S. Lewis)

We are now halfway through *DBR*, this incredible undertaking: not
just a careful and imaginative translation of the New Testament that
brought its message home with lively force, but an exposition of it
which grappled with its major themes and problems, at the same time
offering devotional guidance of the highest order.

Willie had another life, however, several others in fact, all of which
he was managing to keep in good repair despite this four-page-a-day
diet of translating and expounding the New Testament. One of the
legacies of his wartime chaplaincy work continued long after the war:
the opportunity to participate in chaplaincy training and refresher
courses for the armed forces around the country and beyond. In
March 1956 he was found at one in the south, lecturing on the
Beatitudes to a score or so of officers – 'all Major-Generals and above'
as he described it to Charles Miller.

In the middle of this course he received some 'shattering news'
from Kate. He was perturbed at first by the time of her calling,
08.45 hours, which was most unusual. And then by its content.
The call, he commented, 'seemed to me to indicate either extreme
extravagance or extreme urgency ... I did not think that my wife
would be extravagant so I went to the telephone expecting death or
disaster...' To his joyful astonishment he heard that Edinburgh
University 'had had a rush of blood to its head and made me a
Doctor of Divinity, so DD will always stand for Death and Disaster to
me'. He continued, 'I did not in my wildest dreams think that I
would ever wear Edinburgh's scarlet and purple.'

Congratulations showered upon him – from Major-Generals down
to some very plain people, many of whom had never met him. Former
students and ministerial friends, college and university colleagues,

YMCA and SSSU officials, Presbytery folk and Bible Society workers, BB leaders and Youth Committee members, the editors and staffs of many journals and papers including *Life and Work, The Expository Times*, the *British Weekly, The Motherwell Times*, and *The Renfrew Gazette*, as well as readers from around the world: the list was endless; all were delighted, and all joined in the celebrations of 'their' man. One of his pleasantest surprises came from Trinity Church, Renfrew. They still regarded him as 'their minister' (to his successor's expressed chagrin). Appropriately, if not quite diplomatically, the presentation of his doctoral robes was made at his old church – at a social function which showed that they had not lost their flair for such things. Associated with them were Trinity College (in the person of Principal John Mauchline), the SSSU (represented by Mrs Murray, the new editor of the *SSST*), and the Publications Committee of his Church (Andrew McCosh). Charles Miller sent him a cartoon he had drawn of Willie atop a mountain. A. C. Dow, another old friend, greatly impressed, asked him how he should address him. 'I'll still be Willie to my friends,' the new DD growled.

It was not the only academic accolade he received. An invitation came from Duke University at Durham in North Carolina, to fill their New Testament Chair. It was a big temptation, he being still a mere Lecturer; but it was never a serious one. Too busy at home, with too many constraints, too much unfinished business: his family, friends, work, not least his Scottish interests. He said no, and pressed on. 'I don't think I'll ever be anywhere except Glasgow,' he told William Braidwood. Other accolades were to follow, but it is doubtful if any were so gladly received as the one from Edinburgh.

Halfway through the *DBR* series, amid terrific praise and gratitude, he returned to the beginning things, as expressed by Matthew's Gospel. This first volume appeared in September 1956, shortly after Kate and William Barclay's happy world had been shattered, when death and disaster did indeed visit and devastate them both: the irreparable loss through drowning of their daughter, Barbara, aged twenty-one; the delight of Willie's eye, the best friend his wife admitted she had ever had. They had been raised to the heights; they were now cast down to the depths. Their grievous loss was all the more painful in that it occurred while they were living in the full glare of publicity. Willie's diary was full, but his heart was suddenly made very empty.

At university reading English Literature, Willie's own favourite subject of long ago, Barbara had been doing well, 'going steady' with

Billy Regan, her Irish boyfriend. They had gone off on holiday together to Moville in Northern Ireland, to Billy's parents' home, prior to formally announcing their engagement. Billy's father had recently retired from service overseas, the family had bought a big house and, more excitingly, a sailing dinghy. It was the Bank Holiday weekend and there were pageants and displays at nearby Portrush in County Antrim – a familiar place to Willie, who had preached there on several occasions. Following a day of test-sailing, Billy's father pronounced their new boat safe for Billy and Barbara to use during the next day's regatta. During his testing of it they had been at the swimming gala, where they did well in the races, being good swimmers both. But the weather had got up overnight, a storm warning was issued, and the regatta was cancelled. They were very disappointed, as was young Nicholas Wakelin, aged twelve, who was staying with the Regans, his own parents working for the British Council in Pakistan (as it was then called).

Billy was already a good sailor. Despite the weather warnings, they set off for their own test-sail and tacked west, watched by the family – the last time anyone saw them alive.

The telephone call came through to Willie on Saturday 10 August – a call he would never forget. He was just about to leave for Edinburgh, where he was due to preach the next day at Palmerston Place. 'Missing. Searches. Lifeboats out. Sea-rescue under way.' The words invaded his mind as if unreal. Nothing was sure. Nothing made sense. More telephone calls. The bleak news hardened with the deteriorating weather. Kate became distraught, then hysterical. A telegram was sent to Ronnie, who was teaching near Orléans in France. It read, 'Barbara lost in boating accident. Come home soonest. Dad.' It did not make sense to Ronnie either, meriting a long-distance call to the UK, when the awful truth took possession of him. Willie, on tenterhooks, refusing to let down the waiting church people, preached at Palmerston Place, Edinburgh, with a breaking heart, scarcely aware of what he was doing. He emerged from the church to find banner headlines on the streets and in *The Sunday Post*, declaring his loss, her death. He clung to wisps of hope, and flew – despite his fear of flying – to Belfast the next day, in atrocious weather. The Regans never forgot the way he comforted them in *their* sorrow; nor did the Wakelins senior on their arrival from Pakistan.

There was no news of the missing trio, but the boat was eventually found – empty, and curiously its interior was dry. Even its cushions were intact, and there was not a trace of water in it; the boat had not capsized. The mystery deepened. How could all three have fallen in? Had one, then two, gone overboard voluntarily, perhaps to rescue one of their number – the twelve-year-old perhaps? Could foul play be ruled out? This was IRA country, and Willie was no friend of the republicans – or of the hard men of the Orange Order for that matter. His preaching against bigotry and violence cut both ways. There was nothing for them to do but wait, painfully – and for Willie to make even more painful telephone calls to Kate and Ronnie at home, who were now joined by one of Kate's sisters.

Evidence of the weather made the situation worse. Actual gale conditions had been declared; it had rained incessantly; the wind had wreaked havoc in the area – trees were down, a bread van was blown into the sea, electricity cables and telephone wires were also wrecked. Cruelly, the naval vessel *Empire Demon* had been diverted from searching for them when another boat went aground – a Russian tug. It was towed into Moville Bay, the sea being too rough to bring it into Loch Foyle. The cruel suspense went on and on. What had they been thinking about, to go out in such conditions, not to come in as the weather got worse? Why did they ignore the warnings, the ban?

For three whole weeks nothing was heard. Kate was inconsolable. Willie worked as never before. 'If I'd stopped [working],' he confided to a friend later, 'I would never have begun again.' To another he admitted that his daughter's loss 'would either kill me or drive me to work twice as hard'. He had no choice. His work was his diversion from the hell he was living through – from the question marks that were stabbing his dearest doctrines through the heart. Kate had no such escape. She descended into an abyss of grief and loneliness. Where was her little girl, her best friend? Why had they sailed in such conditions? Why were they not in the boat? Where was God when she was so desperate? She found she could not call upon him, let alone pray. These were depths beyond belief.

It was not only at his desk that Willie sought to work through this agony. He continued to fulfil his many preaching engagements, astonishing people by his apparent fortitude – a strength he did not feel. 'No news yet?' became a question which harrowed his soul. He did cancel one engagement, at Bristol, against his own wishes. He did so for Kate, who now could not be left alone. A total collapse was feared. Together they hoped, and together they feared: every parent's nightmare. Could there be a miracle? Would they be found?

We should not mistake the roots of his fortitude. 'Cyril,' Willie commented to one friend who expressed surprise that he could still preach under such conditions, 'if we who call ourselves Christians cannot keep going through times like these, who can?' Years earlier, when editor of the *SSST*, he had published an article which contended that 'it is in adversity that men often show their real greatness'. He was proving the point just now. The adversity was very nearly killing him and his wife. He merely kept going, haunted by his own words, stretched by his own resolution as never before – not even the harrowing death of his mother had cost him this much. In *Ambassador for Christ* he had written, 'There are basically two types of people: those who are mastered by circumstances, and those who are masters of their circumstances.' His own words were impaling him. He too fought against being enslaved by grief. W. E. Sangster, he often recalled, spoke of visiting a gravely distressed girl whose eyesight had been terminally damaged. 'Give it to God,' the minister gently urged. Willie was learning to give Barbara back; but the pain was beyond belief, the reason unmeaning.

At the end of the third long week, Nicholas' body was found at Culdaff, twelve miles away, on the bleak coast of County Donegal. Their worst fears were coming true. The death certificate tersely read, 'Asphyxia, due to drowning' and a verdict of 'Death by misadventure' was later recorded. Willie, the master wordsmith, turned the words over in his mind: cold, bleak, uncomforting words; harbingers of a yet more terrible sorrow. A week later, at 15.30 hours on Friday 31 August, Billy's body was found off the Benone beach, on the opposite side of Loch Foyle at Magilligan Point, an isolated, melancholy spot even in summer. More telephone calls. More fear. Less hope. Why had they not found Barbara? Why was she the one still missing? More wild ideas. More pain. An unkind fate had stricken the one to whom kindness was a cardinal virtue. Then, four hours later, Barbara's body was found, half a mile from where Billy's had been recovered. The sea had dealt its final blow. More telephone calls; shafts of unspeakable pain; the death of hope.

The bodies were taken to Roe Valley Hospital, near Limavady in County Derry, where Billy's father and Willie – who had once more flown to Ireland – had the horrible task of identifying their defaced remains. Broken, he returned with her body to Glasgow, hope extinguished, without answers for the burning questions, his only salve to let go – which he could not do. Barbara was cremated at Woodside, Paisley. The family, riven by distress, were desperate for the privacy they knew they could not have. Many were the consolations they received, but what use was consolation? Willie put on a brave if tear-stained face. Kate tried, determined to express the Christian hope in which she had been raised;

but doctrine, words, hymns can be taunts as well as props. She found them such just now. It was too much. Too much for the woman who had loved beyond telling; to the woman who had worked herself to a standstill; too much even to cry, 'Help thou my unbelief!'

'This is only the end of one chapter,' Willie bravely explained to a former parishioner, 'it is *not* the end of the book.' His faith was barely intact, his heart was broken. As Burns explained:

> You think I'm glad; oh, I pay weel
> For a' the joy I borrow,
> In solitude – then, then I feel
> I canna to mysel' conceal
> My deeply ranklin' sorrow.

It was the solitary hours that were the worst – infinitely worse for Kate who had little work in which to bury herself. It takes a great man to withstand this sort of pressure – made worse by his wife's inability to cope, courageously as she might try. Not that she did not cope, outwardly and publicly. But the inward reality was very different: grief, questions, the feeling of being ignored by the One whom they had served for over twenty years, feelings of rejection, of being attacked at the very fibres of her being – the stuff of nervous breakdown. Willie now had two victims on his mind – his darling daughter and his much-loved wife. How could it happen? What now of providence? What of God's love? What of his promise to protect and keep? Why them, when they had given so much to the sacred cause? They had given their time and their talents, their all; could more be expected of them? The questions coursed his mind as the scalding tears coursed his cheeks; they would not stop. It was very difficult – impossible – to go on. He went on, heart-scalded, still questioning.

> They on the heights are not the souls
> Who never erred nor went astray;
> Who trod unswerving towards their goal
> Along a smooth, rose-petalled way.
> No. Those who stand when first comes dawn,
> Are those who stumbled – but went on.
>   (John Oxenham)

'Oh the bliss of the broken-hearted!' was how Willie translated Matthew 5:4, 'for they shall be comforted': words he learned at his mother's knee and on which he leant when she died; words that he was once more forced to make his own now that his world had fallen apart and his peace of mind had been shattered through savage and unexpected death, by nature in the raw. It was a message he had to relearn, not for old age when one can look back and enjoy long memories, but for the start of a young gifted life, prematurely destroyed. He drove the point home by calling attention to the fact that the word translated 'mourn' was 'the strongest word in the Greek language' – a superlative that he would gladly have done without. It is doubtful if he ever found the comfort (a keyword) he needed; and Kate certainly did not. There was not now 'a new note in his preaching', but the old one reshaped in the fire of deepest suffering. The comment about his DD was no longer funny; a joke he could not forget.

The length of Matthew did not really require three volumes – Luke is longer, by 4,800 Greek syllables as he once pointed out, ever the careful scholar. But he had divided the first Gospel into three unequal parts: 1–7; 8–13; 14–28. (We may surmise that he intended a fourth, thus giving each part seven chapters, but the last two parts were put out together under this great strain.)

He suggested that Matthew was based on 'two great characteristics'. First, that of the teacher, for 'in no other Gospel is the teaching so systematically assembled and gathered together'. Second, that of the Kingship of Jesus, for 'it is pre-eminently the Gospel which is concerned to show us Jesus ... the man born to be King'. The two concepts are fused in the 'Sermon on the Mount', whose three chapters account for a full quarter of his total exposition of the Gospel – another inequality. He called them, paradoxically, 'the new law'. It was obviously an unbalanced division of the text, but one that expresses his sense of its importance.

Soar as he might with Paul's cosmic Christ, with his universalist message, with John's mystical teaching and his sacramental world-views, with Hebrews' vision of the other world, Willie's feet were ever firmly on the ground; ever mindful that the point of it all was discipleship, whose precepts he expressed in a triple epithet: 'All are agreed that in the Sermon on the Mount we have *the core and the essence and the distillation* of the teaching of Jesus to the inner circle of His chosen men.' (Not all are agreed about this last point regarding the 'inner circle', as 7:28 suggests, though Willie dissented.) The 'new law' as core, essence and distillation of the Gospel, was an impossible ethic. Yet this core, essence and distillation was central to the teaching of William Barclay.

The volume on Philippians, Colossians and Philemon followed, the former known as 'the epistle of joy' by the commentators. Willie expounded it, as he said, out of a 'well-nigh broken heart and spirit', but this did not affect the buoyancy of his treatment. Many have used and profited from it without being aware of the ordeal its commentator had just gone through.

He found in Philippians a key principle. Something of the Church Universal is recalled in its verses: class, condition and status are irrelevant to it – 'the whole Empire was being gathered together into the Christian Church'. The egalitarianism which was an intrinsic element in his mind and in his treatment of others he found here in theological and ecclesiastical expression. He was at pains to make the point, as he knew others were at pains to destroy it. Turning to lesser things, he noted the 'extraordinary break' at 3:2, suggesting (among other things) that we probably have two letters of Paul here, cemented together editorially when the Pauline *corpus* was put together (a matter Polycarp alluded to when he spoke of the letters his hearers had received from Paul). Willie admits, however, that it was not the only explanation.

Out of 'the unimportant town' of Colossae came a letter that sets the scene for the crucial views Willie expressed in commenting on Ephesians. He now makes good his chronological inversion. Behind the letter lies 'one of the great problems of New Testament scholarship', one that threatened to turn Christianity from a vital, personal faith in the Son of God into a philosophy – and worse, a theosophy. We know it by the name 'gnosticism', from *gnosis*: to know – and we have already come across it in the brief review of his treatment of the Pastoral Letters. It would not be his last word on the subject, but he was never more certain that it was Paul's: Jesus is enough! He contadicts his earlier view and suggests that *this* letter is the acme of Paul's vision: 'No Pauline letter has such a lofty view of Jesus Christ, and such an insistence on his completeness and finality.' He added Coleridge's comment – 'Colossians is the over-flow of Ephesians' – to make the point, emphasizing that it was not a new concept hatched up by Paul, but one which had its roots as far back as I Corinthians 8:6.

In stating that Philemon is 'the only private letter of Paul that we possess' he overreaches the evidence – the Pastorals were such, too. But its effects were private in a way the others were not, so perhaps we should not be too critical.

Willie loved to quote the words of the great commentator J. B. Lightfoot, who said of Paul's attitude towards slavery (which some find a problem) that the word emancipation 'seems to tremble on Paul's lips, but he never utters it'. It is not the whole truth; it trembled there meaningfully at times: 'Where the spirit is, there is freedom.' But there were legal as well as economic reasons why Paul should not have said more, working with an eye over his shoulder in view of the Jewish leaders' attempts to prosecute him for allegedly undermining the State. Few can mistake the practical force of such texts as 'in Christ there is neither slave nor freeman', etc., a principle Willie seizes to press once more the dangers to the Church of its besetting sin in sustaining class, privilege and elitism. (It is a curious fact that so much class-related and elitist baggage has been allowed by those who question Paul's 'compliance' with slavery; the subjects are at best matters of degree, not absolute status.) The principle was thoroughly Willie's own, a Pauline trait in him: 'When a relationship like that enters into life, social grades and caste cease to matter. The very names master and slave become irrelevant.'

His work for the series was almost done. The two volumes dealing with the letters of James and Peter, John and Jude, came out quickly, within two months of each other. Taken together they comprise nearly seven hundred pages of exposition. The demon of grief was driving him hard.

Willie has often admitted that it was this concentration on his work – greatly to Kate's loss – which stopped him from breaking up over Barbara's death. Imagined sounds of her despairing cries and pictures of her fighting against the turbulent waves were barely kept at bay by this gigantic effort. He spoke of it to such as Professor G. W. Anderson and James Little. They were moved to hear him say that he had almost lost his faith in the ordeal, so great was the impact upon him.

I am not sure that he did *not* lose his faith in it; certainly it changed. However this may be judged, he did at least regain it; but it was never quite the same thing. James Little agreed and, replying to my question on whether he had really dealt with the loss or merely shielded himself from it through increased effort, he said, 'I sensed that in Willie myself ... It was as if he was papering over the cracks that might be there underneath, as if by repetition and enthusiasm he could avoid facing doubts that were to be resolved.' Only parents who have known this devastation can understand its torments; no one who has not been there has the right to cast an opinion, still less to judge. We merely observe the effects, standing on ground hallowed by anguish. Unable to resolve it, or to make sense of it, weighed down by his inconsolable wife, Willie worked on, feverishly.

He loved James, that superbly practical letter, which warns against doubting (1:6); which demands to know 'What is your life?' (4:14); which asks, 'Does anyone suffer?' (5:13). He quoted the French expositor J. Marty with approbation: 'The epistle is a masterpiece of virile and reverend simplicity.' The simplicity he loved was there by instinct; it was even emphasized in the Greek meaning of his wife's name, Katherine ('unmixed' or 'pure'). He was careful not to make it simplistic – as if he could with all that pain.

Such simplicity was abundantly true of 'Camel Knees' as the early Church called James, the brother of Jesus, whose letter, commented Willie, was 'a new discovery to me'. He disagreed with Luther, who famously dubbed it as 'a right strawy epistle' – not out of a denial of those evangelical impulses which characterized the great reformer, but out of the realization that right behaviour is the true insignia of the Christian; that faith and life cannot be divorced. It did not embarrass him to speak of the good life – he loved it – the pleasures of life, its goodness; but he never clung to them. He could live simply as well as preach child-like simplicity. He could not see how any other life could manifest itself, given the generosity of God – given his goodwill, which Christianity hailed and asserted. Willie taught that goodwill as part of Christianity's furniture: its social ethic; his victorious answer to Death and Disaster.

In dealing with Peter he accepted without hesitation that it was the work of the impulsive apostle, that more than human figure who bounds through the stories in the Gospel of Mark, ever willing to risk putting his foot in it, ever the enthusiast – a man after Willie's own heart. Resorting to another contradictory (and treble) superlative, he regarded this letter as 'the best known and loved, and the most read' of all the New Testament writings. It was written 'out of the love of the pastor's heart to help people who were going through it and on whom worse things were still to come'. He had been going through it himself of late, but he was even more moved at other people's grief and loss. He noted the warmth of the apostle's personal attitudes; and he denigrated the churchmen who spoke 'with the east wind in their voices' – so typical of him who passionately loved the camaraderie of Glasgow, its easy social structures, its warm westerly airs.

He noted the concurrence between the teaching of this epistle and the *kerygma* (preaching) of Acts, defined as 'the fundamental ideas which the Church ... heralded forth'. They constituted 'the five main planks in the edifice of early Christian preaching', as well as revealing the relationship between it and 'the Queen of the epistles' (see p. 165). He thought it not impossible that Paul's 'encyclical' may have been used by Peter, thus reversing the 'stream of tradition' – a not improbable point given the proximity of the epistles' recipients (see I Peter 1:1) and Peter's grumbling about 'the things hard to understand' in Paul.

The letters of John and Jude (Willie stated that John's was a homily rather than a letter) were too often ignored, he argued. They are of 'the greatest importance' – another superlative – 'for the light they shed on the thought and the theology of the New Testament, and for the information they supply on the administration of the growing church'.

As with I Peter, he believed that John's letter was written near to Ephesus, perhaps about AD 100, when the Church had lost its initial glow. (We should beware of making this declension an argument for the dating of the letters. There is enough proof of it in the known early documents to undermine it as such – e.g. Peter's, and that of Demas.) John had written to counteract that decline of the soul to which all are prone, as well as to refute the gnostic teaching that was a growing influence in the area. This danger, albeit from another source, was also observed in Jude, specified as 'false doctrine and misguided ethical teaching'. They were the twin dangers that ever confronted the Church, mutually dependent.

As if to celebrate his fifty-first birthday – there was little else to celebrate – the first of Willie's three volumes on The Revelation of John appeared in 1958. He dedicated it 'To all those Readers who began with me at the beginning of this series and who have persevered with me to this the end'. His Foreword is heavy with gratitude – to the Publications Committee, its Convener (W. M. Campbell) and its Publications Manager (Andrew McCosh). Referring to *Acts*, he commented, 'I never meant to go beyond that volume.' He acknowledged that the whole work had been 'a heavy task', yet 'I have nothing but regret now that I have come to the end of it.'

He slips into a whole series of superlatives as he conducts his readers towards the end of his work, for 'the *Revelation* is notoriously the most difficult book in the New Testament'. It is unique, and it is his hope and prayer 'that this volume of studies will do something to unlock the wealth of what is one of the greatest and most dramatic books of the New Testament'. A total of 560 pages of exposition formed these studies. He lists the rich array of commentaries on which he had been able to call, and the books about apocalyptic literature which bear on its themes. This latter, he emphasizes, is critical for the 'decoding programme' which has to take place if Revelation is to be understood. Twenty years previously, in one of his threshold evangelism pieces in *The Renfrew Press*, he had used Edgar A. Guest's lines:

> Somebody said that it couldn't be done,
>   But he with a chuckle replied,
> That maybe it couldn't, but he would be one
>   Who wouldn't say so till he tried.
>
> So he buckled right in with the trace of a grin
>   On his face. If he worried he hid it.
> He started to sing as he tackled the thing
>   That couldn't be done – and he did it!

'Remember these lines,' he had exhorted the people of Renfrew. He did – and he did it, the thing that couldn't be done, just as countless thousands around the world have done, in many languages and denominations, whatever their creed, class or colour. He did it. He did it for God; and he did it for them, *his* people – this man of unsurpassed goodwill; this man of the broken heart; this man with the trace of a grin on his face.

'His' people were not slow to respond. *Life and Work* acknowledged the brilliance of the expositions in providing 'a more vivid sense of what Christian faith really is' in their display of 'the extraordinary drama and poetry and sheer knowledge of life which is wrapped up in the Old and New Testaments'. The *British Weekly* called them 'the best Bible Readings in print'. *The Motherwell Times* fastened on to 'the simplicity of the exposition', the 'easy, acceptable style of the writing', adding that total sales had now reached 320,000 copies and that a special edition for the USA was under way, which would more than double their production. A deluge of letters from individuals came into his editors' offices and those of the Publications Committee; many more came to Willie directly.

By and large these were all 'popular' acclaims. Another vital facet must be mentioned. It concerns Willie's penetrating understanding of his text, the integrity and translucence of his translation. These qualities should not be overlooked. We need to emphasize the particular aims of the *DBR* (the title is itself an important emphasis), best focused perhaps by the six prayers which preface the first volume – a very Barclayan mode of Bible study – one each from Bishop Westcott, Principal George Adam Smith and *The Book of Common Prayer*; three from Willie himself, which are prayers for clarity, understanding and application.

He was at pains to disown a scholarly objective *per se* – we may call this 'commentary status'. Yet, despite his disowning of that term, his work was characterized by a tireless search for what the text is actually saying, its meaning for its original readers as well as for us today. It often reveals a mind more alert and better informed than those who publish full commentaries, who skip or obfuscate difficult or 'meaningless' phrases. Willie may skate over a point too quickly, he may even omit some among more general observations, but his eye frequently catches a phrase which others have missed and which he will seize on and expound decisively: garnishes for his iron rations.

Take one example. In his provoking book *Christ and the Cosmos*, Dr Gordon Strachan draws attention to 'the anti-cosmic prejudice in most commentators', in particular to the 'gate-portal' connection at Revelation 21:21 (an area which excited Willie, although he did not advance his thinking on it). This is admittedly abstruse stuff. But listen to Strachan's frustration over the commentators' omissions: 'Alas, there is no lateral thinking in [R. H.] Charles or his disciples. The only scholar who, in my knowledge, accepts this link is William Barclay in *The Daily Study Bible*...' I remember Strachan telling me of his amazement at discovering this, surrounded as he was by over thirty commentaries – and finding the clue for it in this mini-commentary for popular usage. The term 'lateral thinking' had not then been conceived; it cannot be understood technically here. But it says a lot for Willie's careful persistence to winkle out uniquely such an item for his readers, and that at the weary end of so large a venture.

His volumes were created in a period of mass evangelism. They were very often the most-used single tool of those who found faith through them. Further, hundreds of ministers and lay preachers found their understanding of the text of the New Testament greatly improved by Willie's ability to latch on to the salient points – and very many found their pulpit preparation vastly easier. And it must be said that thousands of church-going people became aware of identical quotations and illustrations appearing in different contexts, whose source was obvious to the knowing. Even when some could not abide his theology, they still used his work – without acknowledgement.

Of course there were critics. Liberals said he had not gone far enough; conservatives said he had gone too far; some complained of his ill-disciplined biblicism, others that he had watered down the biblical message. Like Jesus, he piped for some, and they did not dance; he wailed for some, and they did not mourn; he ate with some, and they called him a glutton; he drank with some, and they called him a drunkard. It has an oddly familiar ring to it. Once again wisdom is justified by its children, now spread around the world.

'DR WILLIAM BARCLAY HONOURED' ran the headline in the *British Weekly* at the end of December 1959. It reported a banquet marking the completion of the series, and its conversion into a seventeen-volume set. These famous 'little red books' (the original *DBR* had appeared in a variety of colours: green, blue, red, brown, orange and purple) were to last for nearly twenty years. It became news throughout the Christian world and well beyond. Many local papers acknowledged the occasion, including *The Glasgow Herald* which was thereafter to record many events in Willie's life, usually fastening on to the more contentious.

It cannot be said that the celebrations outranked those earlier ones at Trinity Renfrew. There was no choir, nor were there any solos; Kate was given a set of the *DSB* (as we must now call it); Andrew McCosh toasted Willie's health, which was followed by speeches from the Moderator (on behalf of the Church of Scotland), Professor James Stewart (on behalf of preachers and ministers), Frank Doubleday (on behalf of the Epworth [Methodist] Press, booksellers and the ecumenical community), and others. It was a time for joy, but for Kate and Willie their sense of accomplishment was tainted. Their hearts were still sore; unanswered questions still loomed in their minds: their hope disfigured by pain. Others celebrated for them.

The twenty-seven books of the New Testament had each been translated, introduced and expounded – not word by word, but theme by theme, as they appealed to their expositor – with a host of detail, religious, historical, cultural, literary and so forth. Quite apart from his own well-stocked library, Willie had borrowed 243 books from Trinity College. 'If it's not there, ask Willie,' was a phrase often heard during those 'battery-hen years' – an epithet the *Methodist Recorder* coined for them. The whole series now ran to 5,676 pages – averaging over two and a half pages of writing a day for six years (in addition to other writing, lecturing and preaching). It contained 8,557 biblical references – over 2,500 to the Old Testament, nearly 6,000 to the New; there were references to 7,509 personal names; 488 allusions to the Classics; 11,188 subjects were dealt with; and 1,909 Greek and other foreign words defined. When my Index to the *DSB* was compiled in 1978 it ran to 213 double-column pages with tens of thousands of references.

Let our marvellously gifted author have the last word for now (from the last page of the final volume): 'It is surely symbolic, and it is surely fitting, that the last word of the Bible should be GRACE.' He once referred to 'grace' as 'a lovely word; the basic ideas in it are joy and pleasure, brightness and beauty; it is, in fact, connected with the English word *charm*'.

SIXTEEN

PRESSING ON

What fortitude the Soul contains
That it can so endure
The accent of a coming Foot –
The opening of a Door

(Emily Dickinson, 'Elysium is as far to')

'He will never glory in any of his achievements,' Willie wrote in explanation of the heading, quoted in our chapter title, given at Philippians 3:12 (which, he emphasized, deals with one's character, not one's work). It explains that negative *frisson* that Willie often encountered in his professional colleagues: 'There is no room for a person or a Church which desires to rest upon its laurels ... [Paul] is *reaching out* for the things which are in front ... It describes him with eyes for nothing but the goal.' It was ever so with William Barclay.

When Robin Sterling of the *Motherwell Times* approached him for an autobiographical article, Willie agreed, saying, 'After all, I'm a member of the National Institute of Journalists myself.' It was an association of which he was particularly proud. Arts and theological degrees, political economy diploma, ordination certificate, even a doctorate, were just part of his baggage as a minister and teacher, a requirement of his Church; this membership put him among working people, and was effected on the basis of his ability as a wordsmith in their domain, which he confirmed over many years, in many papers and journals. He had a rabbinic attitude towards the sanctity of ordinary work.

He had made his reputation long ago in *The Renfrew Press* and other publications, not just as a journalist, but as a *journaliste* in the French sense: one who works on a daily basis. W. H. Auden quotes Karl Kraus' comment on those 'who write because they have nothing to say; they have nothing to say because they write'. Willie was not that sort. His head and his heart were full; he could not but write – and speak – of what he had experienced, of what he *knew*. He was especially glad to do so in the journalistic manner. His original *Bible Readings* particularly were for daily use, on a specific, dated basis – only afterwards being extended to general usage, for the Church of Scotland; like those of its Youth Committee and the BB.

In reviewing the work of a journalist for *The Expository Times*, under the title 'Mr Poritt, Journalist', he wrote: 'The first thing that a journalist must learn is to be interesting.' It was a lesson which Willie learned at his father's knee, then as a young speaker in the YMCA and local churches, and well before he published his first journalistic piece in 1933, the piece that launched him into 'threshold evangelism', which went on to achieve so much. Indeed, his published pieces in *The Dalzielian* in the early twenties were whacky contributions to it, not least the entertaining description of his mother's society and mores. 'Interest' was a particular WDB trait. As was said of his 1908 lecture on Browning's *Paracelsus*, 'we listened with great attention'.

In *The Motherwell Times*, Mr Sterling lionized a man in his thirty-fourth writing year. His brain had not been distempered by writing (as Juvenal warned of its practitioners), but he had been well and truly infected with writer's itch – *scribendi cacoethes*. He was given his first full page by the Editor of the *British Weekly*, Shaun Herron, in 1955 – five years after *The Expository Times* had given him one in its pages. His work on the *DBR* had begun before these other exploits, in 1948.

In writing his books Willie was on a more flexible schedule than that for his journalistic pieces – which very frequently saw him driving into Glasgow to catch the midnight post to meet his deadline. If he chose to take Kate to hear the Scottish National Orchestra (its Saturday evening concerts were one of their favourite outings, as were the operas of Gilbert and Sullivan) he simply had to ratchet up his writing speed for a day or two in order to stay on schedule. The work he did for the *British Weekly* in particular was a formidable labour, part of which ran hand-in-hand with his *DBR* commitments, and which he sustained for eleven gruelling years. By contrast, that for the *DBR* was relatively short-lived, running for five years – 'his battery-hen years', as the *Methodist Recorder* named them. 'What an inspiration William Barclay's page is,' wrote one delighted reader; a comment that could be multiplied very many times over.

He was interesting; he was informative; he was challenging; he was inspiring. His readers loved him – though not without exception. S. W. Murray, an Irishman of a different vintage from Shaun Herron, complained about Willie's criticisms of E. J. Simpson's book on the Pastoral Epistles. Those who read the Foreword to his *DSB* volume will find a very different – and complimentary – appreciation of the evangelical commentator. Some failed to understand him – others did not bother to try, preferring Bishop Barnes' state of mind. (Barnes was Bishop of Birmingham; historically agnostic of Christian origins, his book inspired several rebuttals in the forties, from such as C. H. Dodd and F. F. Bruce.) Some loved to take him out of context, contenting themselves with small-minded views of his work. John Tait of Inverness was one such: Willie was faulted by him for his definition of 'sadistic', a pedantic point. T. J. Foinette of Plymouth complained because he described a book as 'inhuman' – only people can be so described, he argued.

Usually the letters he received were complimentary, sometimes not. He carried on regardless, feeding hungry hearts, goading sleepy minds, stimulating and facilitating the work of teachers and leaders, pastors and preachers everywhere, adding lustre to thousands of lives by his lessons and expositions. 'Such a prince of expositors,' declared the venerable James S. Stewart, a prince of the pulpit himself, following up this remark with a cluster of epithets which rank among the most admiring Willie ever received: '...a man possessed by the Gospel and passionately eager to share it. Everything from his pen is characterized by freshness and lucidity, vivid illustration and telling phrase, accurate scholarship and spiritual insight ... this distinguished and well-loved scholar-evangelist...' One of the curious aspects of the reactions Willie engendered was this sort of admiration from highly respected leaders, which was not always followed by their adoring public. Charles Duthie, the Principal of the Scottish Congregational College, exclaimed, 'What insight, what diversity, what maturity, what devotion, above all, what *labour* goes into this page!'

Let us take one year as an example of what Willie's labours achieved. In 1955 he offered four *DBR* volumes (two on John, one each on Romans and Hebrews – a very rich selection); a book on the miracles of the Bible; his *New Testament Wordbook*; and six booklets for evangelism (*The Christian Way*, which I later included in *Turning to God* – his book on religious conversion – in 1979). He also continued his exposition of *The Draft Catechism* in the *Scottish Sunday School Teacher*, made twelve full-page contributions to *The Expository Times*, and fifty-two pages to the *British Weekly*. A battery hen indeed, laying golden eggs which benefited literally tens of thousands around the world. But this was not all. Priority was *always* given to his students at Trinity College. It was a principle with him that his 'day job' came first, and his *par erga* second.

Moreover, most weekends and often during the week, he made himself available to preach and address congregations and groups of various kinds all over the country, in some of the most prestigious pulpits to some of the most discerning congregations – in Glasgow, Edinburgh, Newcastle, Manchester, London, Bagshot, Limpsfield, Reigate, Eastbourne, Bournemouth and so on. At Manchester Central Hall, one of the pulpits made great by A. S. Peake, WDB's admired model, he preached fifteen times. (I attended one of these myself. In addition to a packed hall it was impressive to see students from nine theological colleges, as well as their tutors, and at least three college principals.) At some such pulpits he had a regular 'slot' which continued for ten and more years. Other places were not so lucky; his diary was already full. He preferred to return to the old haunts, being a man of regular habit – to the Newcastle Y, to the Central Baptist Church, Holborn, Manchester Central Hall, etc.; sacrificially pressing on. Some of his journeys were done by train; many were by car, and he refreshed himself on the way by stopping to view the historic sites – at York, Manchester, Birmingham, Lincoln, Peterborough, Oxford, Cambridge, London.

He also found time to move house again, to Berridale Avenue, Clarkston, where a semi-detached dwelling (Jack House wrongly described it as a villa) took over from the terraced one that had sufficed until now. After all, his library was swelling – not only with books, which were everywhere, but with model railway engines and carriages and other models. (At the end of his life three shelves of his library were occupied by railway books. He was a notable expert on all such matters, not excluding the technical.)

He was a walking, personalized ecumenical movement, unconcerned at the pedantries of the religiously frigid, ever ready to offer an outstretched hand to a fellow believer, whether Anglican, Baptist, Congregationalist, Methodist, Salvationist, Quaker or whatever, even 'free thinkers'; he was available to all – so long as he was *useful*. Once, at Bagshot, the Chaplains' centre at which he loved to lecture from time to time – 'to Major-Generals and below' – denominational matters obtruded and arguments bedevilled the atmosphere of retreat. The Anglicans were in the majority and stood on their 'established' dignity; the non-conformists – i.e. the folk who refused to conform to Anglican ways but who were only too ready to conform in ways different from the Anglicans – claimed their spiritual birthright of personal freedom. As matters threatened to get out of hand (these were days when such still took their convictions seriously) Willie was asked to intervene. He did so, with dramatic results, not by bullying or laying down the law, but by the simple invitation to share Christ together in a Quiet Day. It had a powerful, sobering effect.

'His was the aura of saintliness in those days,' remarked one of those present, a description that will surprise Willie's detractors. It was this which turned antipathy into unity (not uniformity, in which he did not believe). At another residential conference he heard that some of his hearers refused to accept his baptism as legitimate. So, as guest speaker no less, he refused to share their Communion! They took the point, and worshipped together, duly contrite; these matters were not to be prejudiced by such unthoughtfulness. His own Church had recently changed its regulations about inter-denominational Communion, widening it, and he had a point he was glad to make. He ever asserted the reality of the Church as a *family*, which many found simplistic, even embarrassing. They preferred their worldly pageant, their position, their dignity. Willie loved to remind folk of the late Bishop Newbigin's response when squabbles threatened to break out in the Church of North India. The Bishop simply took out his Bible and suggested they review the situation in its light.

When the rock'n'roll craze hit Britain in the mid-fifties, alarm bells rang throughout the churches and the homes of the devout. It was characterized as 'jungle music', lewdness, degrading behaviour. Willie judged it for what it was: a musical form with something to say, expressive of the age. He was ever open to what was being said. How could one preach effectively without *listening*, he – the deaf man – would challenge? Was it not necessary to preach, the Bible in one hand, the newspaper in the other, i.e. relevantly? He enjoyed such music. He perceived what many could not, even when it was described for them: a reflection of their humanity, needs and aspirations, their vision and spiritual impairment, their cry for a reality that satisfies – as all works of art suggest; as David had done when he danced before the ark – 'lewdly', according to the *unco guid* of his day (see 2 Samuel 6:16, 20). Willie did not forget that David's critic was a spokeswoman for the status quo, who wanted to keep up the traditional postures, even if religious meaning was stifled by them. The dominical call, 'If *any* man will, let him come...' resounded in Willie's ears. He refused to alienate people from Christ by criticism or prejudice. He hated those voices which had the east wind in them – cold, drying voices. In any case, he knew that 'to the pure all things are pure'.

Another vogue hit Britain, less overtly and not least within the churches: busyness. Here was a man who filled every unforgiving minute, but still always had time for people. He never appeared to be in a hurry; he could do what others with far more time on their hands could not do. He was surrounded by non-stop clergymen who were hounded by ever-growing lists of meetings annd committees, attending to every activity open to them, unable to discriminate, unable to delegate – whose churches were visibly emptying before their eyes. Like Martha, they had forgotten 'the one thing necessary'. Busy about many things, they ignored the important. For all his busyness – and it was to some frankly alarming – William Barclay never did that. The one thing necessary, attention to Jesus, was still dominant, the fulcrum of his life.

Some of his clerical friends had a centrifugal attitude towards their ministries; Willie's was centripetal. That was the secret of his success. It kept him motivated; it kept him balanced; it kept him focused. Alive to the new and the novel, he regretted the *quest* for novelty – which included everything except prayer and Bible study. All over the country Bible groups were closing and prayer meetings (what an old-fashioned concept!) were closing down. Ministers' trousers were no longer baggy: they had forgotten how to pray, and had learned to dress well instead.

I remember Willie appearing before a large audience of no-nonsense northerners at about this time, one of several in a series of lunchtime meetings. Other preachers had started by thanking the committee for inviting them and saying how good it was to be back in their famed city, how nice it was to meet old friends again: bonhomie all round, jovial backscratching. Not so Willie. He stood up. His voice rasped out, and we suddenly realized he was praying: hard-core prayer, about ourselves and our need of God; expressing joy at his goodness and provision; asking for forgiveness for our selfishness. They were short prayers and very direct, prayers that sanctified but which were not sanctimonious: of the workplace, the kitchen sink, the football field. He read a short passage from Matthew – the Sermon on the Mount, as ever – and then he laid its challenge on the line. *This* is what Jesus expects, *this* is what we must do, *these* are our marching orders. We sang a short hymn – why was it that everything about his services seemed short, yet he had the same time as everyone else? Another short prayer followed, a blessing – and he was gone. But the challenge remained, and the aura and memories of the man.

In his autobiography Willie speaks of one of Gossip's stories about Principal Rainy and a fine, scholarly sermon he had delivered. 'But will the simple people follow him?' queried someone. 'Oh, well,' said

Rainy, with that hauteur that has emptied too many churches, 'they will have the comfortable feeling that something very fine is going on.' One never gained that feeling from William Barclay – neither from his books, nor his preaching. It is not too much to say that he despised it, and it made him immensely sad. He took his commission more seriously. In listening to him one is confronted with truth – about oneself, the world and God. It is a confrontation that can only lead to acceptance or rejection. He preached, as good advocates argue, for a verdict.

At home fibrositis had settled on Kate. Willie's 'real gem' – a telling description of her, given by their garage mechanic – was in difficulties again. And he, who prided himself on being 'indestructible', admitted that her physical state was 'very crippling'; she was 'pretty well helpless'; she had 'insuperable problems'. Electric treatments and massage were prescribed, but to little avail. The physical merely reflected the psychological: it was getting worse. Shock and loss had developed into depression and anger, thence disillusionment and scepticism. A range of nervous disorders followed one after the other: neurasthenia, neuralgia, eczema, persistent insomnia. Today her condition would be recognized as Post-traumatic Stress Disorder; then it had no such name, not even a reality, clinically speaking. She endured a proliferation of 'accidents' – cries for help and self-punishments which few heard, and fewer responded to, not excluding the indomitable, busy-busy Willie himself. The very qualities which had made Kate such a superb minister's wife – of sensitivity and efficiency – now worked against her pathologically, remorselessly. Willie could not handle this. He was all sympathy, but his way out of problems was different. He escaped, by working, by forgetting – though he never forgot; he simply shrugged off the unpleasant. Kate meanwhile all but drowned in the ravages of her grief. No one offered her an escape, and only bland words and gestures of sympathy came her way.

She needed to talk, but there were none qualified to listen. Some were ignorant of her struggles; some simply could not cope with them; some were put off by her former competence. Marie Campbell, a former parishioner (how often she had rallied round in aid of her minister and his wife!), telephoned, but too late. 'I would have given my right arm to talk to you,' Kate commented. But talking was not enough. The Reverend Sinclair Armstrong, a former student, visited them. On seeing him Kate simply collapsed into his arms. He found Willie at his typewriter, his face wet with tears. Kate's sister visited. 'My wee Barbara,' Kate repeated, desperately. She could not let go. Her sister recalled the early days at their father's manse, when they were little girls: when ill, Kate would simply turn her back on everyone and face the wall. She did so now, in full public view.

They no longer went to church together. Willie went to Williamwood, Kate to Clarkston. The division was symbolic. It was an empty routine for her, just habit and duty prevailing. She confessed that she had lost her faith. She was utterly alone, apart, even from her husband. Cynicism grew yet stronger. 'There remains nothing now but to go on,' Willie had said to Rita Snowden, replying to a late letter of consolation. Pressing on was never harder. He pressed on, nonetheless. The next article had to be written, whole volumes remained to be prepared. This is what he wrote when the storm on their private lake broke over them, in which he confessed to his own problem:

> In this story there is something very much more than the story of a calming of a storm at sea. Suppose that Jesus did in actual fact still a raging storm on the Sea of Galilee ... that would in truth be a very wonderful thing; but it would have very little to do with us ... If that is all the story means, we may well ask, 'Why does he not do it *now*? Why does he allow those who love him nowadays to be drowned in the raging sea without intervening to save them?' *If we take the story simply as the stilling of a weather storm, it actually produces problems which for some of us break the heart* [my italics].

He did not actually deny the story's literal interpretation, as some of his critics have claimed. What he did say was this, 'There is something very much more than the ... calming of a storm at sea ... the meaning of the story is far greater than that – the meaning of the story is not that Jesus stopped a storm in Galilee; the meaning is that *wherever Jesus is, the storms of life can be calmed.*' This is existential faith, faith that hangs on, whatever the circumstances – faith that produces, if not a laugh, at least the trace of a grin. That was his message, now burnished through fire.

David Winter interviewed him at this time for the BBC programme *Lift up Your Hearts.* He asked Willie about the tragedy. How had he been able to get through it? The calming message of Jesus was Willie's reply. In response to that broadcast he received over 600 letters – having given a personal testimony to faith, which electrified the thousands listening to it. He had spoken openly of death and bereavement, of faith's conquest, of Jesus' presence in adversity. Not everyone reacted positively. One letter came from, of all places, Northern Ireland, the seat of their disaster. Having replied by circular letter to them all,

Willie destroyed the letters he had been sent. But this one he could not destroy. He kept it for the rest of his life – as if mesmerized by it, the frozen posture of the rabbit before the python. Kate, mortified, found it among his papers after his death. It simply read:

> Dear Dr Barclay,
> I know now why God killed your daughter; it was to save her from being corrupted by your heresies...

It pierced his soul. He died with it on his heart twenty years later, still aghast that any human being, let alone a Christian, could write such evil. Goodwill was never more undermined, never more ravaged. Such is the measure of some people's religion – Willie could not call it faith; such the shallowness of their understanding of God – if the capital dare be used in this context.

Goodwill recovering, he rearmed himself to continue to work for good, 'from faith to faith'; for people, not deathly belief; for Jesus, not those who defied him by their sick hatreds, their mindless and unrecognized fears.

Ironically, an offer now came to him from the Presbyterian College in Belfast (now the United Theological College). The Chair of New Testament Studies was vacant, would he like it? Had the tragedy not happened, he may well have accepted it. Ronnie had become engaged to a young lady from nearby Colraine; Barbara had been virtually engaged to Billy, a local boy; it would have been a perfect opportunity. He said no. Life went on.

The *DSB* was placed in the hands of a London representative, C. Vernon & Sons Ltd, to maximize its sales. Willie's publishing interests were shifting from Edinburgh and Glasgow to the capital. Wm Collins Ltd, the SCM Press and Epworth Press, as well as the *British Weekly*, were now his chief supporters, all in the south. He had also become a member of the Scottish Advisory Group of the Guildford firm, the Lutterworth Press (now of Cambridge). A transatlantic dimension to his work was developing too and would soon lead to influences on every continent, in many languages.

A new Professor of Divinity was appointed at Glasgow, Ronald Gregor Smith, who had a powerful and liberalizing effect on Willie, as did Ian Henderson. The changes in him were not all subjective and emotional. The world was changing faster than ever before. As he once recollected:

I remember the time when an aeroplane was an incredible sight

I remember when motor cars were rarities

I remember the first wireless sets

I remember when people could not have proper medical attention,
  because they could not pay for it

I remember children with rickets and diptheria

Continental theology and philosophy were again relevant, rampant
even; teachers and preachers had a duty to come to terms with the
many new approaches being suggested; new challenges were being
thrown down, by believers as well as the agnostic or frankly atheistic.
'Agnostic', Thomas Huxley's clever word, had recently been coined
anew by Leslie Weatherhead. In his own field Willie came under greater
pressure as the writings of such as Rudolf Bultmann – merely one of
a long line of powerful writers on the New Testament – now made their
extraordinary impact. Willie responded to his old tutor; his book *The
Three Gospels* came out in 1966, a revision of a series of *British Weekly*
articles from 1961–3, now made into a quasi-academic book.

Willie embarked on his Kerr and Croall Lectures. The former were
given at Glasgow University, and dealt with 'Educational Ideals in the
Ancient World'; the latter, on 'the Religious Vocabulary of St Paul',
were delivered at Edinburgh University. The Kerr Lectures grew out of
his little publicized work as Head of the Hellenistic Greek Department,
and the material was published in 1959, both in the UK and in the
USA (in the latter under the title *Train up a Child*). We should not
underestimate the work he put into this – nor its underlying motives.
It is a *tour de force* of careful scholarship, which only its narrow spe-
cialization prevented from wider acclaim. It covered the education of
children in Israel, at Sparta and Athens, and under the Romans, with
extra chapters on the Christian response to paganism in the early
Church, and its general attitude towards children.

A year later he published a series of fourteen articles on 'Hellenistic
Thought in New Testament Times' in *The Expository Times* (1960/1),
offering more extensive Greek studies to its constituency of teachers
and ministers. This was also secular in tone, dealing with the main
movements of thought and the philosophies: Stoics, Cynics,
Epicureans, etc. If we may say that his faith was shaken to its core by
his greatest tragedy, we may not go beyond that and say it was shaken
from its core. To some extent it reoriented his faith: it opened it up to
the wider world. With providence, as so many people did, he had

genuine difficulties; he was never afraid of claiming that God did indeed move in mysterious ways. But with Jesus and his message he was satisfied to hang on – and to press on.

His work continued. It found ready fulfilment now in work for one of the translation panels of the British and Foreign Bible Society – the Greek–English New Testament Committee – for which he did much unpublicized service. If it was quietly done, he was not known as the Committee's quietest member. His hearing aid whistled and screeched, he was constantly moving his feet, his papers and chair, and his interjections could be brusque. They were also very quick off the mark. While some members riffled through their papers, looking for the errant note, Willie, with his phenomenal memory, supplied it in a trice. When the panel could not agree on a reading or rendering, special Notes were required to set out the arguments for the variants. He did more than his fair share, delighted to be burying himself, practically, in the 'inhuman things' of Greek grammar and lexicography, wallowing joyfully in 'the empirical ditch'. This work developed into an invitation to join the society's Translators' New Testament Panel, which was working on the *Diglot*, preparing the Greek part of the text specifically for the use of Bible translators around the world; a most valuable service for missionaries and ethnic churches.

When attending such meetings he stayed by himself, as usual – in local hotels, not at the guestrooms provided by the Society. He could now well afford to do so, and he thoroughly enjoyed the lifestyle offered, as well as the opportunity to observe a wide assortment of professional people. He hated the second-rate – in restaurants or hotels, as in other spheres; and he needed his privacy. One of his favourite hotels was the Randolph at Oxford, the haunt of many academic and publishing types among the gleaming spires. He and Professor William McHardy, an old friend from Glasgow days, delighted in its comfort, *haute cuisine* and its splendid cellar. A certain youthful exuberance marked their enjoyments. On one occasion, McHardy asked if Willie would like a glass of wine with his food. 'A *glass* of wine?' his fellow translator queried. 'Well, then, a bottle...?' 'Now you're talking!' They developed a discerning palate for claret, but on the whole it was the national tipple which commanded their more serious allegiance. The BFBS paid expenses, but no fees. These were 'capped' after a few months – their tastes were too much for the charity. It made no difference; they footed the bills themselves henceforth.

There is no doubt that major changes had taken place in Willie. He was now less cautious about expressing controversial views – indeed, he had begun to *enjoy* the provocations to which some of his statements led. He was saddened by the Pavlovian reaction from some theological bullyboys, mainly from conservative ranks, such as Ian Paisley of Belfast or Jack Glass of Glasgow, aided ever by the sour eructations of *The Monthly Record*. Even such as Martyn Lloyd-Jones was wont to throw the baby out with the bathwater. But this did not stop Willie airing his convictions.

His opponents were already beginning to sound off their one-sided, one-eyed views and single-dimensional grasp of Scripture, the Church, ecumenism – even the Pope. Willie rose to their challenge; goodwill asserting. His 'weaknesses' were often remarked on, to which he would retort that Spurgeon smoked, Calvin played bowls on Sunday, Luther's language was far from decorous, and alcohol had never been condemned by the Church's councils – still less by Jesus. Goodwill, he urged, must not be defeated by ignorance or obscurantism, nor God's truth by man's incapacities or idleness of thought. He offered his own perceptions in clear statements – a broader, more informed view, in which he attempted to combine old knowledge with new, providing insights for the present day, not the reheated pottage of yesteryear. He was not a party man; he practiced the truth of 1 Corinthians 3:3ff (which warns against party spirit) as well as the exhortations of Philippians 4:8f (see p. 60), and sought to disseminate them.

One major change in Willie was his use of alcohol, now much more pronounced, as we have seen. He had long rejected his father's teetotalism and accepted its basic propriety, based on a careful and open-minded biblical study. With the pressures of his work – and the recent high emotional stress – he needed to switch off quickly and alcohol was undoubtedly a beneficial agent in this. Like tobacco, it relaxed him (we should not forget that this was well before medical science had discovered its dangers). It became a solace. His love for it, and ultimately his reliance upon it – at a much later point – was to give him and his family and friends much heartache. Here we merely observe his need of it and its resultant mechanisms in his highly stressed life.

He was once taken to task by a hotel manager for making too much noise in his room. Without realizing, he had been pacing back and forth, as he was wont to do when thinking. There was a loose board which creaked every time he passed over it, which, of course, he could not hear. But the guest below him could, and eventually could bear it no longer and called the manager. Willie was suitably contrite.

He was not contrite over another faux pas. He attended a dinner at which many distinguished folk were present. 'The Reverend So-and-So will say grace,' declared the chairman. At which point Willie, not hearing the Reverend's name, jumped up and said grace himself. 'The hands are Esau's hands,' commented one minister, 'but the voice is the voice of Jacob!' He was not contrite because he was never told what had happened: he was too much loved for it to matter. On another occasion, he turned up without having completed his preparation, a rare happening. They were due to meet in the bar before the start of the meeting. Willie excused himself, went to a corner table of the heavily crowded and smoky room, unplugged his hearing aid, and worked without interruption. His contributions to the study group that day were faultless.

Drip-dry shirts were introduced and Willie, 'handless' creature that he was and ever ready to discover something new, was in his element with them. It meant less clothing to carry about and more room for books – and reduced living costs. The chambermaids were surprised to see this reverend gentleman's bathroom festooned with his dripping shirts. But Willie was gleeful. His strong principles of economy – of money and time (we might add labour, for he believed in shortcuts whenever possible) – were upheld.

He was especially glad to be offered dining rights at Christ Church College, Oxford, and with it the opportunity to say prayers. For all his genuine concern for the 'common man', there was something essentially bourgeois in his appreciations. He loved the high life of hotels, first-class service, high-quality cuisine, comfort and stimulating talk. He loved the lifestyle of the Fellows, their life in college, its behavioural patterns, not least the male ambience.

With all this developed a growing enjoyment of their salty, sometimes Rabelaisian conviviality – a reminder of the music halls of long ago. Ministers should develop 'unshockability'; they should be able to sit with the outcasts of polite society and win them. Willie did so to a high degree. Asceticism for its own sake had never been part of his world-view, quite the opposite in fact. He believed that it was a denial of the world, a rejection of the natural, of God's ordering. To deny himself as he did in wartime conditions, for good reasons, was one thing; to do so for a weak-minded shibboleth was another. It was a meaningless stance, an affront to the good things of God, even if the end was ostensibly 'religious'. He had grave doubts as to the reality of such 'religion', being as it was a flat contradiction of Jesus' lifestyle. It was on a level with eating fish on Friday: a hangover from man's childhood. The new man, man 'come of age', thought Willie, should enjoy his freedoms and his world. We may not take this too far. Willie imposed limits of enjoyment upon himself out of principle. As he said in his autobiography, he would 'rather have a week's holiday in real comfort than a month in more primitive conditions'. A week, or maybe two...

An example of this sensitivity to the need for limits came when his publisher, Sir William Collins, expressed concern at his staying at the central Y in London, in which he had a monk-like cell formerly available for married students. Willie loved it. He took it in the vacations – at Christmas, Easter and in the summer – when many students were away. When in London over the weekend he often supplied pulpit for Howard Williams, minister of the Central Baptist Church, Holborn, a spiritual home-from-home for him.

Sir William offered to put him up at his own expense at the London Hilton: an open invitation, a blank cheque. Willie would have loved it, but he declined the offer. It would have meant death to his contacts with ordinary people, to his ministry for the plain man, and he knew it. The directors of the Y came to his aid and gave him a (very modest) penthouse flat – Room 200 – which henceforth was known as 'the prophet's chamber'. It was a simple suite, but ideal for his purposes, offering that privacy and quiet that he needed, yet surrounded by the young men of the Y, and in the heart of London to boot.

Harry Stevenson, the General Secretary at the Y, often found him deep in conversation with its young men after midnight, arguing hotly, Willie goading them on by startling suggestions and outrageous claims. From time to time he took prayers there, which were always popular. It was an example of the incongruous claiming the unlikely: this short, fat, balding, toothless individual (he wore dentures but post-war fittings were not well done), with an old-fashioned hearing aid laced to his head, was the centre of attention, idolized by the young men from all around the world. Sometimes Stevenson went to his room, usually to find Willie in his shirt sleeves, or less, bent over his typewriter, a neat pile of paper on his desk, the pages spotted with crossouts or overtyping. He worked here with little to refer to on his small table, usually only his Greek New Testament – and his prodigious memory. Every day that he was away from home he had one crucial telephone call to make: at 20.00 hours sharp he spoke to Kate, catching up on her news, assuring her that he was well, that he would soon be home – traces of his concern for his aged father in the early days at Renfrew, if no longer concerned at the cost of his nightly phone calls.

Part of his joy in the early days in London were the Lyons Tea Houses, where he could get a cheap but reasonable meal (we are not talking *cuisine*, of course) and listen to a six-piece orchestra – a genuine treat for this music-loving man. As they were swept away by the sixties he had to find alternatives, but the choices were not always good. His searches took him into some curious places, not least in nearby Soho. The area certainly augmented his education somewhat – a throwback to his driving to the central Glasgow post office and catching the midnight collection to meet a deadline. The area was frequented by prostitutes, with whom Willie talked, often giving them cigarettes and even money for tea at a late-night cafe nearby, seeking to offer them a higher life. They were astonished that a man wearing a clerical collar should be willing to be seen with them, and friendships of a sort did develop. He was affected by these girls; concerned at the degraded and degrading lives they lived; ready to suggest help for them through statutory and church bodies.

Sometimes he stayed out talking to them until 04.00 – to return for his short night's sleep, and to rise for another packed day following it. In London, near to Soho as the Y was, he had the chance to see such life on a capital scale, and was shocked by its flagrant commercialism, its seedy violation of human norms. That, too, added a new note to his preaching. We may see something of this in his treatment of the story of the woman at Sychar's well: 'There are few stories in the Gospel record which show us so much about the character of Jesus as this story does,' he stated about John 4:1–9. 'Here is the beginning of the universality of the Gospel; here is God so loving the world, not in theory but in action.' This was a lesson he had first learned when carrying drunken soldiers back to their barracks in Renfrew during the war.

From time to time he preached at the Salvation Army centre in Oxford Street, ever supportive of its valiant rescue work. Once he was so moved by a down-and-out's contrition at the penitence rail that he had to retire to a side room to dry his own tears. He was an emotional man, whose reasoning could be swayed by subjective feelings as well as moved by the sufferings of others; and by literature (poetry especially) and music, as many of his students testified, frequently seeing him reduced to tears while conducting them.

He was always available for the work of the BFBS, even as his father had been for the Scottish Bible Society. Once he drove the Translations' Secretary to a local meeting, passing through Renfrew. 'It was here that I learned what the Gospel was all about,' he commented of his 'cloth-capped' congregation. Dr Wilfred Bradnock is one of the few men to have called attention to 'the keen nationalism' that was part of Willie's make-up – usually kept under close restraint. He was indeed against asserting it when more important things were at stake, and it is noticeable how few Scotticisms appear in his published work – unlike his lectures or sermons.

In the late fifties Willie was invited to join the Apocrypha Panel for the *New English Bible*, under Professor McHardy's chairmanship, which enhanced their friendship: another largely unrecognized service. It was during the Panel's work that Willie's friend became uncomfortably aware of one of his blind spots – his lack of Hebrew and its cognate languages; his readiness to speak on matters concerning them in ways which were no longer acceptable to informed opinion. It was a major hurdle to full authority in his work. For example, on one occasion he startled everyone in the group by announcing a trinitarian explanation for the more correct 'plural of majesty' (the 'Let *us*...' at Genesis 1:26, etc.), which has long been recognized by scholars and informed laity – a simple throwback to his conservative days in Motherwell.

Neil Alexander comments of his visits to Oxford that 'he overvalued the attainment and experience that he did *not* have, and the type of man they might have made him, and was too impressed by others'. But this came not from the early days, when he was lauded and fêted for his own astonishing contributions to Christian work and literature; when invitations poured in. Tensions did arise later, however, as new and thrusting young men came on the scene, fortified by their penetrating specialist studies. The *odium theologicum* all too easily exists alongside the *odium scholasticum* – its pretences and its jealousies. It is not easy to sit under the chairmanship of such as C. H. Dodd and his brilliant team, men with multiple doctorates, with publications which have changed the direction or altered the weight of international scholarship; men who have negated the force of unbalanced learning, great as it was, from such towering figures as Baur, Bultmann or Barth. Willie was always glad to give 'honour where honour was due'; he knew in the early days that he was admired for his own erudition and powers, and invited to share it with them; but he felt keenly the later movement away from him as younger scholars took over.

Bradnock asked if he could be of assistance to him in some practical way. He was astonished at the reply. Willie asked him, not for a writing case or a new typewriter, as had been expected, but for the Nestle-Schmöller *Novum Testamentum Graece* to be bound together with the *Hand-Konkordanz*, which would facilitate his use of them. It involved more work than Bradnock had anticipated – an involved correspondence with the Stuttgart publishers, who were equally surprised at the odd request. A huge, cumbersome volume resulted. Willie travelled light when on tour for these meetings. That is to say, his personal effects – of which he very often left a trail behind him – were carried in a small attaché case. (On more than one occasion he returned to a hotel to find his long-lost articles neatly laundered and waiting for him, to his delight – with a large bill, which was not so pleasing.) His professional effects – the several books, his typewriter, his stationery supplies, any number of papers, essays and examination papers, uncorrected proofs etc. – were a different matter.

The *Daily Scottish Express* spoke of his 'marathon speaking spree' in January 1957. It was *the* annual event, when Burns was in spate, a time of increasing importance to Willie as he became known to the societies south of the border as well as those in central Scotland. High praise for his Burns' addresses was never likely to endear him to the more conservative elements, but they were important to him. In them he touched a vein which concerns all Scots, honouring one of the institutions he believed should be immortal. In them he celebrated the work of a man whose voice was nothing if not prophetic, despite his personal behaviour. It was not unusual for him to address the same men on a Saturday night 'secularly' and on a Sunday morning 'religiously' – an often unholy supper prefacing holy Communion – but Willie refused to express such artificial distinctions.

Willie was now getting by through work and travel and brilliant successes. Kate had no such outlets, and continued to fall victim to grief and depression – a lethal cocktail. Their answer to it was surprising to many of their friends and aquaints: they increased the size of their family. They adopted a little girl from the Quarrier Children's Home, Jane, who was six years of age. Somewhat alarmingly perhaps, Willie wrote that her coming would give his wife 'something to do'. He conceded that in the circumstances 'there might have been trouble', but the matter worked out well and he later judged it 'a complete success'. Whatever the experts might say about the motivation of her adoptive parents, Jane stole their hearts, took them out of themselves, and gave Kate a new reason for living. 'She is very pretty and charming,' Willie proudly wrote on one occasion. She was aware of her adoption, so they did not feel that later upsets about it would occur.

Almost on arrival, Jane went down with tonsillitis, and had to be taken into hospital for a tonsillectomy. The mini-crisis – of great strain to Kate at this time – did the trick, and the bonding was effected. Kate immediately improved; she began to put on some weight and was able to dispense with her sleeping tablets. 'It may seem reckless to start all over again at fifty,' Willie confided to Leslie Mitton, his editor at the *Expository Times,* 'but it has worked.'

British Weekly readers, who had long been kept informed of the goings-on of the Barclay household (its members were used as subjects for Willie's 'parables from life' approach) were now introduced to another member: 'Dumpling', Willie's name for the vivacious little girl who was transforming their home from heartbreak to happiness. It is a moot question as to who was more popular, Jane or Rusty (the latter a Staffordshire bull mastiff that dragged its owner around the streets at night on walkies; the dog he once described as 'overweight, decidedly overpetted, and near human'). Rusty was a character. He had 'an unlimited capacity for doing the forbidden thing' and Willie's page now sparkled afresh with stories about him, all turned into parables. He was 'the perfect example of unreformed man', Willie commented: wagging tail at one end, snarling mouth at the other. 'Which end am I to believe?' enquired his master pointedly.

Dog

Sammy the Siamese soon joined Rusty – another 'reckless' decision that worked out well. And he, too, soon found literary fame. Unfortunately, he did not last long. Not because of Rusty, who behaved like a gentleman towards him, but simply because he died – without warning. 'The best medical attention in the area could not save him,' Willie confided to his large public. The gloom did not last for long. Tiptoes, another kitten, entered their life, aged three weeks, and was soon taken in hand by Jane and Rusty – to the renewed delight of his readers.

A great weight had been lifted from Willie's shoulders; his home life had changed dramatically. He was now the overprotective father, taking time off (a thing unheard of previously) to take Kate and Jane to restaurants and the airport – one of *his* favourite tea-places, to be sure; on outings to local beauty spots such as Bonnyton Moor or Crow Wood; and on away trips to England and Wales (Llandudno was a particularly favourite location). They also took in music concerts, art galleries, cinemas and theatres – and Gilbert and Sullivan, which Willie considered the best introduction to culture for a young person (next to books). Jane did not agree. She burst into tears at the first performance and refused to return.

SEVENTEEN

PREOCCUPIED WITH THE PLAIN MAN

I ... am convinced of the moral and academic necessity of sharing scientific work to the fullest possible extent with the man in the street and in the field.

(Sir Mortimer Wheeler, *Still Digging*)

It was not just family responsibilities, lecturing, preaching, translation panels, journalism and books that were claiming Willie's time. 'Radio religion' was on the increase, opposed by some, feared by others – even by the churches, ever anxious for their collections and the control they had over people's lives. Broadcasting had become a key feature of society – an unlikely feature for Willie at this time, given his gruff voice, yet one that deeply challenged his interests.

Stanley Pritchard, an Assistant Producer of the BBC and known well to Willie – he had supplied pulpit for him at Renfrew – found his 'Glaswegian' accent, guttural voice and fast delivery almost impossible to deal with. They broke every rule in the book. Macaulay's prediction was coming true at least in this field (see p. 31). But, when he did essay an entrance to this new, exciting world, his voice and delivery were not his real problem. The difficulty came from his lack of 'feel' for his audience; his inability to gain a rapport with them from within the studio. Secluded there, he could not see his listeners, let alone judge their mood or their reception of his material. In the pulpit he put great store on this interplay between himself and his congregation; it was a part of 'giving them what they want'. He 'played' his listeners like the old music-hall stars whom he venerated, such as Harry Lauder, Jimmy Edwards and Arthur Askey. Willie admitted that he needed such rapport before he himself could catch fire.

So Pritchard instructed him: 'There's a man in his house reading the Sunday paper. Stop him!' It worked. The mental pictures formed, and he improved. Willie confessed to being terrified of the microphone,

of the sound of his own voice on tape. The need to be interesting intensified; it accounts for some of his wilder, more provocative statements:
he was stopping them in their tracks! But he managed to establish that
personal link between speaker and listener. His old habit of preaching
as if to one member of the congregation (though not *at* them), rather
than to a sea of faces, was thus reworked for this new medium; another learning process. His first broadcast was made in 1949, his second
in 1954. His activity in this arena reached a peak in 1956, in the David
Winter series *Lift up Your Hearts* referred to in the previous chapter. It
developed, and he became truly famous in 1962 – now in television,
not radio.

The day was not far off when, out of this rich experience, he would
make perhaps his most important suggestion, certainly his most novel:
for a Church of the Air. It was left for others to make good the idea. We
still have not fulfilled it. The claims of the establishment, the high cost
of buildings and their maintenance, a desire to control people – not
just shepherd them – all make it less possible. Leaders refuse to give
such a lead, content in their apathy. Meanwhile the University of the
Air – the Open University – became a stunning success.

Willie's third experience in broadcasting – a short series on the
Beatitudes – took place in 1955. His apprenticeship was long in fulfilment. This needs to be emphasized, for James Martin and others have
described a picture of early success which is wholly at odds with the
facts. He had to unlearn much before he could learn this new technique, and he admitted to finding it difficult. This should not surprise
us. He was now a man of almost fifty, whose father had been born
nearly a century before. His world had been old – Edwardian, thoroughly literary, only partly rescued by the appearance of 'magic
lantern slides'. Willie remembered clearly the day they bought their
first radio set: a thrilling day.

The wife of his old friend William Braidwood, living in Sussex,
heard one of these broadcasts on the Beatitudes and recognized the
gravelly voice immediately. She wrote to say how much she had
enjoyed hearing him again. The Braidwoods had kept in touch and
used to travel to London to hear Willie when he preached there, as
many did. But Willie, unusually, was late in replying. Between the end
of this broadcast (26 January) and the date of his letter to her (15
February) he had written 'rather more than seven hundred letters' to
those who wrote in to him in response. That means he had written
about 240 letters a week, in addition to his other work, and without
a secretary.

He may not have been able to see his listeners, but they were now as real to him as if he could. He was there for them. He confessed to Mrs Braidwood that he was 'terrified of the microphone'. The BBC had informed him that twelve million people would listen to his broadcasts. He found that responsibility not merely an ordeal but an overwhelming burden. He tried to picture twelve million people, recalling the crowds at Motherwell FC and other places. There was no comparison. But he did it, and it exhausted him. 'To call a man a martyr did not necessarily mean to say that he had died for the faith; it could mean that he had lived for it,' he once remarked. That was Willie's way; this man of the silent world, this man of the broken heart; withal, a man of triumphant faith.

The world was changing, and it demanded changes. Youth groups were emptying, churches were dying; how could people be contacted, be fed? Kenneth Galbraith dubbed the period the 'Age of Uncertainty'. Bernard Levin, one of the most perceptive journalists of our time, wrote this in his book *The Pendulum Years* (1962):

> Fashions changed and changed again, changed faster and still faster: fashion in politics, in political style, in causes, in music, in pop culture, in education, in beauty, in heroes and idols, in attitudes, in responses, in work, in love, in friendships, in food, in newspapers, in entertainment ... What had once lasted a generation now lasted a year, what had lasted a year now lasted a month, a week, a day. There was a restlessness in the time that communicated itself everywhere and to everyone, that communicated itself to the very sounds in Britain's air, the stones beneath Britain's feet.

Willie's motto was 'forward, not backward'. This meant change, and work – arduous work – for which he was abused and misunderstood, slandered and libelled. Some wanted to change the foundations of faith; others opposed change in every form – even the *King James' Version* of the Bible (now 250 years old) was declared immutable by some. Willie recognized the need to change the way we understand and express the old truths; to find new language for yesteryear's truths. This was a duty as well as a need: today's children cannot be fed in yesterday's style. The comprehension gap in British Christianity – in American still more – was widening. Intellectually pressured and embattled, the conservatives engaged in a defensive war. There were exceptions, and not a little careful scholarship and apologetics, but the noise value of the less enlightened members, the unknowing and the fearful, undid much of this good work.

The progressives, i.e. they who pressed on, had to tread warily; some lost their livelihoods for their honest thinking and plain speaking. The admirers of former heroes of religious persecution had themselves become persecutors, often blindly so. Willie was not of this coinage. Goodwill to all men required honesty to all as well as love and forbearance. His endeavours against the 'closed mind' accelerated, and more enemies were gained. It led to their casting taunts and aspersions; he countered by explaining contexts, declaring more vividly the iron rations, stimulating the life of prayer. Articles and books on 'fundamentalism' appeared, but the one fundamental thing about the fundamentalists was that they could not agree even with each other: 'Every man did that which was right in his own eyes', again.

In more than one sense this is too stark a picture. Mass evangelism had made an extraordinary impact (not least through the radio); Christian publishing had never been more virile; church unity had taken great steps forward; intellectual challenges were being met; lay people were being mobilized; the ethical outreach of the churches – towards the poor, the Third World, the underprivileged – was increasing; real advances were being made; people's perception of the faith was 'maturing', becoming more historically and culturally aware. The milk of the Word was being replaced by the meat of meaning, implication and application. Generalizations are always misleading. It is wrong to believe that Willie was not acceptable to many evangelicals – he was often less acceptable to the liberals, who found his biblicism too demanding, his prayers too shaming. He got on extremely well with not a few of the former who, if not exactly enamoured with the name 'conservative' being thrust upon them, were sufficiently identified with its interests not to complain.

F. F. Bruce, the Editor of *The Evangelical Quarterly*, became coeditor with him in a series of twenty-two Bible Guides from Lutterworth Press, dealing with all the biblical books, from Genesis to Revelation. The series was another sign of the times. It was free from technicalities, based on generally accepted conclusions, written in a clear and easy English idiom – a field in which both editors had already conspicuously succeeded. The series included some of the best known names in contemporary scholarship on both sides of the Atlantic.

Willie's volume appeared first, unsurprisingly. While others were clearing their desks, sharpening their pencils, readying themselves, he started straight in with the writing. *Making the Bible* was a general introduction to its origins. He later followed it up with a second, on Hebrews. In addition to their own volumes, the editors – having decided with the publisher who should make the contributions – had to read the scripts, assess them, call for any reconsiderations they thought necessary, and pass them for publication. It involved a lot of work. There was opposition to Bruce and Barclay working together – not quite as the wolf and the lamb, but nearly so to some minds. The theological fur flew. Even the *British Weekly* characterized it as 'a bold move'. Harold Lindsell was less charitable in his reviews, as is often the case with 'reformed' Christian spokesmen. He denounced one of the authors (who had dared deny Pauline authorship to the Pastoral Epistles) as producing 'deception, fraud and plain lying ... pseudo scholarship'. If the most outspoken, he was not alone. Those who thought they understood Barclay denigrated Bruce; those who thought they understood Bruce complained of Barclay: judgement by prejudice, and by minds in every sense inferior to the two Highlanders, both First Class classicists, both with theological doctorates, both tireless church workers.

Scott Latourette has described Church history as an incoming tide. All around the world there were signs of that steadily increasing, inward impulse. Unhappily, too many were fixated upon its backwash, unable to see the clear beach-marks before them, unable to judge the movements aright. Many congregations were declining, many churches were being closed. It is a moot question whether less or more were being touched by the gospel, given the extraordinary statistics of radio, the increasingly important television viewing figures and the rise in charitable giving. The way Christianity itself was expressed, especially its western church style, was changing. Despite the conservatives, it was becoming more open, more flexible, less hidebound by tradition. Willie saw great opportunities in it.

He, who had never been a convinced churchman (i.e. an upholder of the body ecclesiastic for its own sake – though he believed strongly in the Church, the centrality of its worship, its mission to the world, its work for society), began to think of Christianity in subtly different ways: a bold extension to his work at Renfrew and around the country. Had he been given the Practical Chair that he desired, it is beyond question that he would have developed such things much further and more systematically. He got on with what came to him, never refusing. He was influenced by the changes to which we have referred; he refused to put them down to people's rejection of Christianity *per se*, as many did. He often quoted G. K. Chesterton, the Roman Catholic writer, who said: 'Christianity has not been tried and found wanting.

It has not been tried.' In this the inability of ministers and lay leaders to think and work creatively played its part, as did the apathy of their congregations. He was disturbed by their unwillingness to be flexible, to experiment; by their worldliness, their prayerless lives, their unfocused religion – which denied both Christ and Bible the highest place in their cosy religious schemes.

He was thinking differently, but always of the individual's response to God; less church-oriented, less institutionalized, less entrammelled by regulation, church law, due order and so on. 'Where the spirit of Jesus is there is freedom,' Paul had declared, and worked accordingly. Willie, now celebrating the semi-jubilee of his ordination in the Presbytery of Glasgow – at the sort of 'do' that he enjoyed – wondered what it *meant*. He could see as never before that spiritual freedoms were restricted by the surfeit of organization; spontaneous responses were suffocated by law and precedent; people were shackled by tradition and form. He had no time for what C. S. Lewis termed 'liturgical fidgets'. The essence of things was at stake, not its appearance. He was again seeking to answer questions. He knew that God could be encountered anywhere, worshipped everwhere. No one may dare call common what God has ordained. As General Pitt Rivers once remarked, 'Common things are of more importance than particular things, because they are more prevalent.' Willie deeply believed that: 'The daily round, the common task' really do 'furnish all we need to ask'.

The Expository Times hailed enthusiastically the first volume of his trilogy, *The Mind of Jesus* (1960) – it was the intelligible expression of his ironically labelled 'unintelligible' essay of the mid-forties, 'theology presented in personal and preachable form'. Willie was content with that. For him Christianity was in essence a one-to-one relationship – the individual with God, with Jesus – but he also insisted, contrariwise, that there had to be a corporate expression; the Church was 'the body of Christ'. Even the creeds had taken on new meaning for him, thanks to Bishop Barry's emphasis that they were a corporate, not a personal, confession of faith.

Hand in hand with all this was still his primary work: his involvement with his students. He fully undertook the necessary assignments of the Faculty, now a member of its timetable subcommittee, a College representative on the Bruce Lectureship Trust, conductor of the College choir, go-between for College and University, and an indefatigable lecturer. In addition, he delivered a refresher course for former students. He also ran an Adult Education course, a three-year programme. Local schools were claiming his time for short talks, too, among them Hillside Academy, and then DHS – a special occasion, when he returned to his old school after thirty-three years, 'duly clad in full panoply' (the scarlet robes of his Edinburgh doctorate). He was enrolled as a member of the Scottish Cricket Union, and contributed a piece to its journal under the title 'I remember', recalling old times and principles, and emphasizing anew the changes he saw taking place.

A burst blood vessel in the spring of 1959 had slowed his pace of working. He changed, not by doing less, but by taking on a secretary, which enabled him to do more! His weekly correspondence never fell below an average of forty letters, often more. He changed his diet – his obesity was his doctor's chief anxiety. Large meals supplemented by frequent snacks were forbidden. His love of chocolate and biscuits, and gargantuan portions of cheese, were banned. Gone, too, was the alcohol; and his regime of eighty cigarettes a day was drastically amended. (He had justified such high consumption, and his other appetites, by his workload. 'Doing the work of three men,' as Kate used to say.) In place of richer preferences came chicken and sole – which he liked; black grapes and custards – which were 'bearable'. Jane smuggled in one of his favourite snacks when the coast was clear: fresh bread generously coated with butter and raspberry jam. It moved him to write on gluttony; to which was added the Delphic lesson on moderation in all things: *mēdēn agan*. He found that fasting was good for him: it improved his appreciations of the things he most enjoyed!

His diet did not survive the six-month lay-off ordered by his doctor. By August he was feeling indestructible again; the new academic year opened with gusto; good resolutions were forgotten. His College regime soon got up to speed: the weekly pressures, special lectures, conferences all over, committee meetings galore – and then a trip to Andover, where he lectured three times to RAF chaplains.

The subject of ethics was now taking over from biblical studies, not by replacing them, but by becoming their focal point: the Fatherhood of God *and* the Brotherhood of Man – old terms and emphases with new phrasing and applications. He was still seeking to offer 'decided answers'. So *Flesh and Spirit*, a study of Galatians 5, appeared (1962); then *Turning to God: a study of Conversion in the Book of Acts and Today* (1963). These were followed by *The Plain Man Looks at the Beatitudes* (1963), his first Plain Man book. Then came *Christian Discipline in Society Today* (1963); *The Old Law and the New Law* (1966); *Thou shalt not Kill* (his latest contribution to pacifism, 1967) and *Ethics in a*

Permissive Society (1971). *Ethics in a Permissive Society* was his first book to obtrude a contemporary note into its title; it was his eighty-third. (He wrote eighty-six in all; plus twenty-three edited volumes of others' work – see the abridged bibliography – plus his stint as editor of SSST.) *The Plain Man's Guide to Ethics* followed in 1973.

In August 1960 he undertook a Lectureship – the Joseph Smith Memorial Lecture – at the Selly Oak Colleges, Birmingham. A former lecturer there was now his colleague at Glasgow – John Foster, who had replaced W. D. Niven as Professor of Church History. The lecture was printed that year under the title 'Fishers of Men', and enlarged into book form in 1966 with the same title. It is yet more evidence of his concentration on practical matters. Here, in Britain's second largest city, once 'the workshop of the world', the plain man's needs were impressed upon him yet again. As Paul was moved before the Areopagus, Willie found this place – as he had found it ten years earlier when he had first visited the city – a tremendous challenge.

He made the point candidly in an interview with Stanley Pritchard: 'I began to see that I never could be a great technical scholar ... I began to be more and more conscious of the wide gap between ... the work of theological experts and the man in the street ... The problem of communication began to be the problem which came first in my thoughts.' It is not the whole truth. But 'soul-less things' were not for him – still less the rivalry that earmarks so many of them, as Auden portrayed it in hymnic style:

> Lone scholars sniping from the walls
> Of learned periodicals
> Our faith defend;
> Our intellectual marines
> Landing in little magazines
> Capture a trend.

His aims were not new. There has always been a need to popularize learning, to spread the Good News in vital ways. Wesley said he wanted 'plain truth for plain people'; the Highland Scot, W. R. Nicoll, a genius in the ranks of journalists and editors, commented, 'The fact is that the Spurgeonic type of preaching is the only kind that moves democracy.' The lowlander, D. S. Cairns, prescribed that the theologian should preach in relation to 'plain human needs, if he is to be a good theologian at all'.

Willie was voicing his own ideals at the same time as the Swiss protestant theologian Karl Barth – claimed by Roman Catholics as the greatest theologian since Aquinas – was offering the popularization of his views in his *Evangelical Theology*. Samuel Mucklebacket (pseudonym for the journalist James Lumsden), a Lothian journalist, expressed it thus: 'Mind, I want nane o' yer lang interminable, wearisome yarns. Brek the shell o' yer tale affhand, and hand me the kernel precise an' concise as the yowk o' an hen's egg.' In our own day, Lottmann commented in his brilliant biography of Albert Camus, 'It is sometimes advantageous to art to descend from its ivory tower, and believe that the sense of beauty is inseparable from a certain sense of humanity.' Many were doing just that in different fields at this time: the Radio Doctor, C. S. Lewis, Mortimer Wheeler (who named the technique the '*vulgarization* of scholarship'), Alan Gemmell, Patrick Moore and so on; as Willie was also doing, and determined to do more so.

To popularize is to simplify, to opt for the plain. It has an honourable lineage. Long ago Cicero took up Theophrastus' emphasis in determining three styles of literature: grand, intermediate and plain. The Jews went before him, with their practical wisdom literature (their Syriac translation of the Scriptures was called the *Peshitta*, i.e. the Plain Version). 'Follow me then to plainer ground,' exhorted Shakespeare. Wycherley's comedy *The Plain Dealer* was published in 1676, the idea being perpetrated under a publication of that name by Aaron Hill (Pope's correspondent) fifty years later. It has its followings elsewhere, for example, in the Italian literature called *Elementiro* (brevity, notably). In 1919 Mowbrays of Oxford had published the first religious book with this theme: *The Plain Man's Book of Religion*. Its author was a high churchman, former Canon of Ely – he had a very different conception of plainness from his successor of Glasgow. In 1931 A. S. Peake's posthumous book *Plain Thoughts on Great Subjects* appeared, an appropriate title, for few men had secured the influence Peake had across denominational barriers, north and south, from the largely 'working-class' constituency of the Primitive Methodists to the high Anglicans. There is a direct line between Barclay and Peake.

Alec Vidler published his influential *Plain Man's Guide to Christianity* in 1936. I suspect that Willie knew this book, though I have not found any specific reference to it in his work. He specifically owned that it was from Vidler that he obtained the idea of becoming 'a theological midwife'; but there was more in it for Willie. Vidler was a liberated thinker, unafraid to ask hard questions, to take bold risks. In 1941 Lindsay Martin had written *A Plain Man's Life of Christ*, and this was followed by Leslie Weatherhead's *A Plain Man Looks at the Cross* (1945), to which Willie often referred. In 1953 Willie reviewed Williams' *A New Testament in Plain English* enthusiastically, specifically calling attention to its 'refreshing plainness'. The translation rested on the *Interim Report on Vocabulary Selection* of 1936, an important document in the history of biblical translation. In 1956 William Neil published his *The Plain Man Looks at the Bible*, which again brought the importance of the concept to the attention of the public and – more importantly for Willie – to Sir William Collins, who now involved him with it, specifically.

Let us be clear about one thing: plainness in this context does not mean superficiality, still less dullness; his work was very far from being 'a plain Jane'. It bursts with life and vitality, with *bios*. Stevenson's use of the word (see the prefatory quotation to Chapter 2) exactly explains it, unsurprisingly for a man of Willie's Eng. Lit. tastes – especially when they are Scot. Lit. It is daring, adventurous, and above all, true to life. It excited the public who bought his books in huge quantities; and it excited some theological types who felt demeaned at the exposure of their mystique to plain language and everyday illustration.

It was now the era of pop art. In a reverent, disciplined and careful way Willie was offering 'pop theology' – the word of the gospel – that which St Paul admitted was 'foolishness to the wise'. Willie was never ashamed of 'the folly of what we preach' – a rejected, shamed, crucified man who would not save himself from the indignity of a felon's lot; who delighted to be called the friend of outcasts and sinners. *That* was true goodwill; the sort Willie sought to emulate and preach. To do this he dared to listen to what people were saying, long before the others (save the comedians and actors) woke up to its importance – in pop music, pop poetry, pop art. By this time the 'pop' concept was over ten years old. It grew out of his work for young people particularly – what they were saying, thinking, doing; their thought-forms and aspirations. Reviewing a biography about Ernest Renan in 1964, he commented, 'He who wants to serve [mankind] must get down to its level, speak its language.' He agreed with the Frenchman's criticism of those who fail to do this, of those who 'stagnate indulgently in their warm environment'.

We may recall Willie's interest in the jazz of the thirties, one of the key sources for pop culture – the people's culture. It was not confined, however, to the Anglo-American scene. The vogue of *nouveau realisme* on the Continent was widespread, often linked to existentialist philosophy and its concepts. But as that social commentator-cum-jazzman

George Melly has characterized it, it was a revolt *into* a certain style, not a substantive rewriting of the human condition from the outside. For Willie it was the simple reassertion of the gospel and of the duties of discipleship in modern terms; of a faith that claimed the best for God – a procedure which began when the great Hellenist writer of the first century portrayed Jesus scintillatingly as the Logos; when Paul brilliantly projected him as the *plērōma* ('the fullness') of God; when the writer of Hebrews colourfully described him as the Great High Priest; all concepts with which their people were on easy terms.

So the Plain Man books were born, out of Willie's journalism, but on a much wider scale and in a more enduring form. The first, *The Plain Man's Book of Prayers*, appeared in 1959, his forty-fourth book. It was by no means his first attempt at printed prayers – that goes back to his work for the *SSST*, and even before that, to his church magazine at Renfrew. (*Camp Prayers and Services* was his first book on prayer, in 1952.)

There is one aspect of Willie's published prayers that has been ignored by his observers: it is a species of poetry in free verse. Throughout his life he evinced a love, and a fine knowledge, of poetry. His first three pieces of published work (in *The Dalzelian*) were all poetic; his love of song (which must include hymns) lay partly in its poetic form; his last work, unfinished and posthumously published, was on the Psalms. He was well aware that much of his beloved Greek literature was in poetic form – as was the Old Testament itself, as modern translations now demonstrate; as was much in the teaching of Jesus, once translated back into his native Aramaic.

It is appropriate that his first Plain Man books should be in this mode, for it was the most influential until the modern era, when printing made prose works available. Above everything else, poetry is memorable. It is another reminder that there is more to William Barclay than his outward forms reveal; in these prayers we may see not just the soul alive to and dependent on God, but the poet *manqué*. Many poets are guilty of employing 'poetic diction' – a pseudo type and use of language. Thomas Gray specifically declared that 'the language of the age is never the language of poetry', a view which Wordsworth strongly combatted. Willie also freed himself from this view and became a dynamic witness to modernity as God's present theatre of action.

He laid down seven 'laws of prayer':

1. We must be honest.
2. We must be very definite.

3. No real prayer is without self-examination.
4. God cannot grant a selfish request.
5. God always knows best.
6. God will not do for us what we can do for ourselves.
7. Prayers move within the natural laws which govern life.

There is much of his theology in these simple rules, ground out of personal experience and won hardly. They represent one of the new emphases mentioned above, which were now finding more and more clarification in his writings. 'There is no special language in which to pray,' he asserted. 'All that God wants is that we should speak to him.' He emphasized prayer as a *natural* activity, with five aspects: invocation, confession, thanksgiving, petition, intercession. As with Brother Lawrence (whose writing he loved), simplicity was the key, form was secondary. James Martin could not be more wrong to assert, 'Willie Barclay never used the traditional "thee" and "thou" when addressing the Almighty in prayer.' He did so throughout his ministry at Renfrew, and for many years after it. He was still doing so in his first Plain Man book, and continued for some time after that. The majority of church people, then and for many years afterwards, still used 'thee' and 'thou'. Prayer was never mere talk with Willie, a matter of outward form. 'Prayer is not a monologue in which we do all the talking ... The highest form of prayer is silence ... We linger in his presence ... we lean back in His everlasting arms.' *The Plain Man's Book of Prayers* became his all-time best-seller, going through eleven reprints in ten years. It is still going strong today.

In 1962 his second Plain Man book appeared: *More Prayers for the Plain Man*, continuing the work of the former volume, though the prayers are somewhat longer and include prayers for special days and subjects, particular moods and feelings, even 'A Prayer for Animals'. The use of 'thee' and 'thou' is now abandoned. There are to be no false dichotomies: 'Life would be very different if each of us could take the whole of life to God,' he said, asserting his dual conviction of the compatibility of the sacred and the secular. Alongside this was published *Prayers for Young People*.

The series was now in full swing. *The Plain Man Looks at the Beatitudes* followed in 1963, a reprint of articles first published in *The Preachers' Quarterly*. Focusing on the Sermon on the Mount (Matthew 5–7), it is the most thorough of his treatments of this cardinal passage since the *DBR* commentary of 1956, and was here applied more extensively.

The following year *The Plain Man Looks at the Lord's Prayer* was published. These two texts, the Beatitudes and the Lord's Prayer, were now the most frequent locations of his preaching and teaching around the country – his iron rations. One can go for many days on such fare. They suggest that other, allied mindset of his: an occupation with the practical simplicities, the basics, of the teaching of Jesus. We should not ignore the cultural conditioning that is imposed by this selection. Jesus spoke in these passages to the 'largely uncultured crowds of Galilee' (which description is often taken too far – they were the hellenized element in Palestine). His message was that the Kingdom of God has come; that it centres on himself; therefore, its demands and privileges are theirs. It is not the whole truth of the gospel, but it is its *essential* Good News, whose tenets were sufficient for William Barclay.

It cannot be the whole truth. The whole truth is unattainable, but it is the starting point, and Willie's mind was focused on those 'unchurched masses' – and the churched ones – who needed that first step. His huge successes showed how ready people were for it. It was not offered as the *haute cuisine* of theology; he was merely 'one hungry man telling another hungry man from where to get bread'. More had to follow, he was the first to admit, and they did – in 1966, when *The Plain Man Looks at the Apostles' Creed* was published, based on articles which had first appeared in the *British Weekly*, in which he set a dogmatic fire among the heathers and havers. Nevertheless, there was an undeviating loyalty to the central truth of the gospel running throughout the book's long length (of 384 pages). It may be summed up in his own words:

> The Church had a creed long before it had the Apostles' Creed. It was very short and very sufficient. It was the uncompromising statement JESUS CHRIST IS LORD [his emphasis] (*Romans* 10:9; *Philippians* 2:11). It is in the light of this prior statement that all subsequent creeds have to be read.

We should remember that he was writing in stirring times, speaking to them – the seething sixties, when some chose to seethe over the wrong things or for the wrong reasons. Bishop John Robinson's book *Honest to God* was published in 1962; Willie was well aware of the ferment it was causing. Robinson followed it up with another, in 1964, nearer to Willie's intention, called *The New Reformation?* As the saintly Thomas Merton perceived, 'There is something stirring here.' Robinson's book was a popularization – we should not forget that he was a very fine New Testament scholar, whose *Redating the New Testament* ought to be read by every student. He was seeking to reduce the profundities of philosophers and theologians and the accretions of an unminding tradition to more reasoned form for ordinary people, perhaps overreaching himself in the process. Willie's publisher at SCM Press, David Edwards, with whom he enjoyed many a meal and fine claret, gave him an advance copy of *Honest to God*. Willie said that he agreed with much of it, noting that much of it was not new. But he also said that he could *never* have written such things himself. It was too destructive, too complicated, too *unplain*. As Pascal had discovered centuries before, the God of the philosophers is not the God of the Bible, not the one to whom men and women turn in their need. The one who mattered to Willie was 'the God and Father of our Lord Jesus Christ', to quote Paul, whom Jesus defined definitively when he called him *Abba*: the basic affirmation of theology, as well as prayer and ethics.

The Plain Man's Book of Ethics appeared in 1973. In a sense, this was even more basic than that dealing with the Beatitudes, for it dealt with the Ten Commandments. This had also appeared as a series in the *BW* (happy the magazine readers of those days, who were fed on such good things!). It preceeded his much more radical *Ethics in a Permissive Society* – his Baird Lectures for 1971 (published in 1973) – which was the last Plain Man book, or at least of *his* Plain Man books, we should say, for others have jumped on the bandwagon since. But it was not his last book of that type. Willie had developed the theme, made it truly his own by great learning, vision and dexterity, explored its possibilities in a succession of books – and been praised and abused for them according to the reviewers' wont. As his beloved bard of Stratford-upon-Avon ruefully commented:

> Cannot a plain man live and think no harm
> But thus his simple truth must be abus'd
> With silken, sly, insinuating Jacks?

EIGHTEEN

CRESTING THE WAVE

Never let success hide its emptiness from you ... Keep
alive the incentive to push on further – that pain in
the soul which drives us.

(Dag Hammarskjöld, *Markings*)

Willie's fifty-seventh year, 1964, was a telling one for him. Had his
father lived, they would now be celebrating the centenary of his birth.
As it was, he heard from his parents' old maid, Rebecca, with whom
he had kept in loyal touch for many years – the elder sister he never
had. She was on the verge of retiring from her post as Head of
Domestic Affairs at a large Glasgow Hospital. The old life was being
inexorably closed down; new life was emerging. Yet there were no new
exploits for Willie outside his work. Work dominated his life: he lived to
work. He was by now very well off, if not rich (his generous lifestyle
forbade that). Kate was happier than she had been for some years; his
family was prospering, and his first grandchild was awaited with keen
anticipation; he was widely fêted by most, if despised by some.

Karl Barth described the then current condition as 'a theological
Vanity Fayre'; Paul Tillich had referred to it as 'a shaking of the foundations'. Willie, looking older than his age and stone-deaf (he had a
flashing light fitted to his telephone to warn him of incoming calls),
was enjoying life as never before, stirred by the changes but not
shaken. 'I can sleep anywhere, work anywhere, and shut myself off in
boring committee meetings,' he declared to his *British Weekly* readers
on the advantages of his hearing aid, a new type which released him
from the hardships of the previous ones. He did all three more frequently, having honed to a fine art his ability to cat-nap. He even
attempted house-painting, having discovered non-drip paint, which
inspired him to say that 'technique is everything' – evidence of his
making a point by overmaking it, by exaggeration: the art of the story-
teller not the scholar, and something which was to grow as part of his
style.

In Glasgow he took part in an event which was meant to stir the politicians as well as the people: an anti-nuclear campaign at which he gladly preached on 'The Church's Choice: Faith or Obliteration?' This antagonism between Church and faith was not new – it lay at the heart of his Free Churchman convictions. He applied faith as essentially conjoint with ethics, even when others called for their denial in practice, hamstrung as they were by their societal entrapments. 'You can't defend a Christian civilization by war,' he insisted, an insistence that went around the country as the *British Weekly* picked up his message and relayed it to its readers. But this was not an age for ecclesiastical revolution.

It stirred some in a different way to that intended, provoking more people to disown him, to aver that he was 'interfering' in politics, speaking of issues he did not understand. He had been there before. He remembered being condemned by his ministerial colleagues in 1938 for his pacifism; some had even denied that he was a Christian in their attempts to silence him. He knew they would do it again, but he was unshaken by their antagonism: he would never be a panderer to their establishment-mindedness. He was appalled by their easy, materialistic renunciation of the cardinal ethic, 'Do not kill'; by their sneering renunciation of the message of Jesus, 'Turn the other cheek'. He challenged them: 'Can you imagine Jesus pulling the switch that will set off the Bomb?' adding, 'Great Britain showed the way to Democracy, perhaps now she should show the way to Theocracy.' The resultant silence was deafening.

His admiration and work for the YMCA had continued. In 1961 he spoke at their annual conference, a major international event. Such was the reaction of its General Secretaries that he was invited to do so again. In 1974 they repeated the invitation yet again, thereby creating a precedent: no one had ever spoken at their conference three times. No one has since. As if to make the point, Willie returned for a fourth time in 1975, once more doing the thing that couldn't be done, the grin still there, though now more of a broad smile.

The Baptists invited him to speak at their Lay Preachers' and Lay Pastors' Conference at Oxford, well aware of his long association with their cause. He dealt with the different emphases in the writings of John, Paul and Hebrews with aplomb, following up the lectures with question-and-answer sessions that some listeners found astonishing: the breadth of his knowledge and his instant recall astounded them. In such company he was in his element – drawing on his enormous erudition, illuminating it to stunning effect, provoking them to debate, teasing them with paradox, at once humble and audacious. The Secretary of the conference, John Hough, interrupted him in his room one afternoon. He did so cautiously, expecting to find him resting. Willie was sitting in his vest at the table, without socks or shoes, surrounded by books, typing furiously. 'Can I do anything for you?' Hough asked. Willie thought for a moment. Apart from the colleges and the Randolph Hotel, Oxford meant only one thing to him: Basil Blackwells, the international booksellers. He asked Hough to take him there. His host could not believe the number of books that he bought, shuddering at the invoice submitted for payment.

A month later Willie was back in the south, this time at Cambridge, doing for the Presbyterian Church of England (now the United Reformed Church) what he had done for the Baptists. Within a month he had made his mark on the two oldest university towns in England, and on two of its oldest Free Church denominations. Here he dealt with a similar theme to that offered to the Baptists, 'The Gospel and the New Testament: Many Ways to God', now a regular emphasis of his. Back at Trinity College, and after a holiday at Broadstairs with his family, he commenced a new course for lay preachers. 'All Roads lead to Trinity,' the *British Weekly* reported, such was the course's popularity.

At the end of 1962 Willie had returned to the radio studio to deliver a series of five talks on the Bible and how we should use it today: (1) Why read the Bible? (2) What do we mean when we say that the Bible is the Word of God? (3) Bringing the Dictionary to the Bible; (4) Bringing History to the Bible; and (5) Finding the Faith in the Bible. It had an unexpected outcome. It was this series that confirmed to Ronnie Falconer, Head of Religious Television in Scotland, that Willie was a natural communicator; that he *must* give him his own television series. The idea had already been put to Willie, and had been abruptly turned down by him. He was no publicity seeker – well, only for the right reasons! He knew he was no film star, and had no intention of competing with such. He gloried in being the plain man. It was one of the very few occasions when he refused to move forward, when he took fright at the responsibilities offered to him. Falconer was not a man to be put off. He turned to Kate. Would she help? Clever man, Falconer. He knew them both, and knew that Kate had her ways. She did. She called her husband a coward! Stirred to the depths of his manliness, Christian and otherwise, Willie relented. He asked but one favour: that his students be with him, to give him 'atmosphere'.

They gathered in the buildings of the former Black Cat Cinema in Springfield Road, Glasgow. Willie was not at all superstitious, though he did once write, 'Many a person will have a pleasant feeling when a black cat crosses his path.' Perhaps this was a good omen? The televised lecture went ahead, his students asking 'planted' questions to make it look less artificial, but which, of course, had the opposite effect. The result was not an unqualified success. Willie himself went down well with the viewers, but his self-conscious students irritated them. Their presence was unnecessary; their questions were false – untrue to the life of the viewers. As Falconer expressed it, 'The viewers demanded Barclay on his own, with a free rein to get on with his job.' And so in the end they got him: vintage Barclay, plain, without frills, preaching from the heart, preaching Jesus.

The format was changed; the venue was changed; he got on with his job. Now situated in his own lecture room at Trinity College, at his own blackboard, clad in his usual chalky gown, he *lectured*, a sportsman's stopwatch on the table to ensure accurate timing. And he did, once again, the thing they said couldn't be done. He did it his way. It was not exactly a 'talking head', which broadcasters fear. He walked up and down, he turned over his notes, he turned his back on the viewers, he wrote on the board – all with resounding success. He defied all the rules – fast monologue, harsh voice, thick accent, a hearing aid wire sticking out incongruously, an unshapely figure. He did at zero cost what Bronowsky and Clark and others were to do later at enormous cost, with researchers, multiple scripts, journeys around the world, royalties for use of copyright and private material, etc. Falconer and he did it on the cheap, with total success. Falconer's judgement says it all: Willie was 'the great master of his art'. But there was more than art involved. His art was one thing, his integrity was another; his message was all. Here was a man who thought, lived and taught his message with total abandon; a genuine man, without artifice or pretension, goodwill personified.

It was not the theologians that he reached, still less the philosophers, and not even the ministers (many of whom said they had not found time to watch him). It was the ordinary people who watched him – and came back, repeatedly, for more. 'The viewers loved Barclay,' his producer commented. Did they love Bronowski? Clarke? Moore? Did they love any of the TV pundits? Willie was himself, and he *gave* himself. 'Never underrate your audience,' he advised. He never did so. He respected his hearers and viewers. If anything, he overrated them. He stretched them. He used long words. He emphasized

Greek usage. He transliterated. He preached. They loved him for it: in Scotland, America, Australia, New Zealand – wherever he was broadcast. He explained his manner:

> Nothing less than the best will do. The person who is going to listen does not want pleasant little talks or souped-up children's sermons. He wants to know what the Bible is saying, and what religion is all about. The broadcaster must speak as a thinking man to thinking men.

In that we have his broadcasting philosophy, the main point of which is that it is not a philosophy of broadcasting but a confession of solidarity: patronizing tidbits are eschewed. He lived and thought as other men – ordinary, plain men. He listened to them; learned from them; and thus could speak to them. 'A broadcaster ... must always work hard to hold their attention ... He should always remember that he is at the mercy of a switch. It is his job to ensure that the viewer or listener does not use it.' As a result, and for the next eight years, as Falconer has recorded, Willie dominated Scottish, Australian and New Zealand religious television. (The English were denied him, thanks to the pretentious 'experts' who disliked his accent, his style, his directness, his theology; 'not one of us,' they said. They did condescend to put out a few of his telecasts: on Tuesdays after 23.00!)

Every one of his broadcasts dealt with a New Testament theme, boldly and candidly. By public demand, his series on the Beatitudes was shown no less than three times in every state of Australia. The Supervisor of Broadcasts there said that 'it was the best thing we had ever put on'. The English largely turned their backs on him and his techniques, yet again. They opted for the novelty approach – a doubting bishop, a gay minister, a renegade nun; anything that would tickle the imagination, or appeal to the lowest common denominator. Straight biblical teaching was dismissed as irrelevant. Entertainment was more important than education: 'It couldn't be done,' they cried – there was no one willing to try – the viewers and listeners switched them off, permanently.

Let us run a few years ahead, and listen to Willie at the close of his life, not reminiscing emptily but reflecting on his work and projecting his thoughts towards the future which he knew would not be his. 'The future of religion,' he urged, 'lies with broadcasting ... A Church of the Air is not an impossible dream.' Two years before this the Open University – the 'University of the Air' – had been launched, to terrific opposition from certain sectors (often the same sectors as refused Willie's ideas), who judged it an impossible dream, a waste of public money, educational foolishness. Today it is a worldwide success with a growing reputation, emulated by many. From its earliest days Willie had seen broadcasting's immense potential for good, and welcomed it. He also saw its potential to weaken Church structures and attendant paraphernalia – and ignored it. The Church, he believed, should make and remake its own structures.

The message *is* more important than the means – despite Marshall McLuhan's observations to the contrary. Society is changing; people are changing; *ergo*, the Church must change: the simple, syllogistic logic of William Barclay. He was ignored. Since then Church statistics have continued to show plummeting numbers; churches by the dozen have been forced to close; ministerial training has declined: people continue to vote with their feet. Many good people have left, not a few have been forced out; programmes and departments have been reduced; retraction has become a creed.

Falconer vividly recalled that fellow ministers 'on the whole were hostile' to Willie's broadcasts. His views were attacked, his personal lifestyle was attacked, his techniques were attacked. All that in the face of his obvious, soaring success. Falconer commented sadly,

> It was ever thus ... His brethren were ungenerous and derogatory. Call it professional jealousy or what you will, this was one of the hardest facts I had to stomach in my work ... It took five years of brilliant communication before parish ministers at last recognized that he was an immense ally to their cause.

What they scarcely learned in five years took them five minutes to forget, hog-tied as they were to tradition and inertia, doubting the ability of the gospel to make its own way. Willie himself acknowledged that he had frequently suffered from 'the envy which provides the mud that failure throws at success'. He said, 'I never knew what hatred was until I began to teach.' This came not just from the obvious sources inimical to a broader view of God's world – a truly reformed theology, an enlightened biblicism – but from those who actually shared his viewpoints in theory: fellow academics and contemporary church leaders who resented his success and his wealth.

Kate found this animosity soul destroying. She saw her man wounded for giving his all, ridiculed for being candid, ignored for offering his convictions – for which she and her family had sacrificed not a little. She, too, saw that it was largely out of envy that many spoke against him, and out of guilt at his sacrificial commitments and their own self-servings. Her dismay turned to anger, then rejection. It was exacerbated by the heavy demands made by Jane at this time, who was proving a handful as she discovered herself in 'the age of flower power'. Outwardly Willie remained solid and defiant, though inwardly the attacks took their toll. The effects on Kate were not so easily managed; her friends were alarmed, her sisters more so; it became at times an intolerable pressure on him. Cresting the wave as he was, there were times when he all but went under: the hand of his brother was against him.

We have moved from the particular issue of broadcasting, from his vision of a universal Church of the Air, to less pleasant, more mundane things. But that was how it was. The old criticisms had turned into hatred or worse – sometimes into a patronizing acceptance that was insincere, because unfollowed. They resurfaced with every new-found success, and continued to gather pace. Beyond it all he saw the people that mattered – anxious men and women searching for clear guidance, distraught widows hoping for solace, rudderless youths lost in their self-confidence, children growing up in an increasingly promising world yet unarmed for its dangers. He pressed on. He enlarged his interests. He taught more roundly, his work becoming more secular, more practical. For example, together with Allan Young of Troon, a League of Volunteers of Comfort was launched – a sort of Alcoholics Anonymous for the bereft and sorrowing. Unfortunately it died for lack of volunteers, not for lack of sufferers.

Where, actually, was he going? Having completed a series of popular commentaries on the New Testament, lectured endlessly on its technical matters, and defined its essence in terms of lifestyle, ethics and the prayer life that should go with these, Willie was facing a quandary. He faced, he said, two possible directions: one being 'too detailed, too academic, too arid', the other 'painting ... with too big a brush'. He had sought to find 'the happy medium between too much and too little', but the real problem was that he was trying to do two very different jobs. He was now both a practical and an academic lecturer, yet he was increasingly ignored by both sets of colleagues. He was haunted by the need to communicate to people on the widest possible scale, and to fulfil his responsibilities to those people in training – an equal joy to him.

The problem was exacerbated by his Head of Department's health failure. In late 1962 MacGregor was again taken ill, so Willie again ran the Department single-handed – as well as the Department of Hellenistic Greek – now enlarged by a new qualification for less academic students, the Licentiates in Theology. Thus started his 'worst year to date', in which he was lecturing for sixteen hours a week, five of which entailed the provision of new material. This was his main work, the area of his professional appointment. We mistake him if we underestimate his feelings about it. It was repetitive, schedule-grinding work, but to him it was a special responsibility: training men for the ministry and for educational posts (for trainee secular teachers were now a conspicuous part of his lecture room). Professor MacGregor went down with bronchitis, then heart failure; it was clear that his chances of returning were virtually zero. Talk of his replacement became rife, but Willie – to his great hurt – could see that he was not regarded as the obvious successor. Despite his seventeen years in the Department, in many of which he had virtually run the whole thing himself; they refused to recognize his qualities, his input.

They doubted him, a doubting which became public. To quote his own words of 1946, in their minds he was 'not a real Professor'. His doctorate had not been 'earned' at a research level; his books were not academically oriented; there were gaps in his overall knowledge; datedness was visible. Worst of all, his attitude, his 'tone', was not professorial; he could be 'a loose cannon'. It was not just his thick accent and harsh voice which worried people, but his uncareful statements, his politicized views. This was the era of the clean-shaven, JFK type; Willie's projection was wholly different – he was more of a nineteenth-century type. He was wounded by this doubting of him, by this lack of recognition of the way he had given himself to his students and their interests: goodwill unrecognized, thwarted indeed.

It was these pressures which stiffened his resolve and made of him something different, as those who really knew him from the thirties, forties and fifties have been careful to emphasize. The changes seen then continued, only more so. He was now successful, wealthy, a man of influence and prestige – notably outside the University; it all helped to alter him. He was a hugely human man, appreciative of and affected by the needs and foibles of others. He gave generously to whatever cause presented itself to him, sometimes unwisely, as Kate – 'who would never do anything extravagant' – saw. She criticized him for it, as did other family members and friends. He entertained, at home and at College; students – past and present – were not the least of those helped by him, with money, show tickets, gifts for their families, even complete holidays. He took a regular table at the Royal Automobile

Club in Glasgow; he spent lavishly at hotels – star-rated hotels – and he waived his travel expenses from the organizations for which he freely worked around the country. At óne stage he had £50,000 in his current account, which even upset his bank manager, who suggested that he should invest it. Why? Willie demanded. Why invest, when most of its returns would be taken in tax? He preferred to invest it differently: in people, for people.

His diary was stuffed with appointments and demands, at College and elsewhere. He still continued to write each week for the *British Weekly*; he became more active in the peace movement as the Cold War intensified and the horrors of Vietnam were revealed – not least for the Fellowship of Reconciliation. He travelled up and down the country teaching and preaching; he attended the committees of the Bible Society – on the Apocrypha Panel, and the Translators' New Testament Panel. The list is endless, and threatens to be repetitive. His thirtieth year in the ministry was celebrated, amid great correspondence demands, now alleviated by a dictating machine and part-time secretarial help, though he still insisted on typing all the personal letters himself. He managed to keep up his footballing interests, especially overjoyed when Scotland beat the old enemy.

Professor MacGregor died, after thirty years in his Chair. Willie's 'protracted ordeal' as he called it – the selection process for the new Professor – wore on, and wore him down. Neil Alexander described it as 'agonizingly slow and incredibly painful' to him. He needed three references; he provided four. It was a defining moment in his life, not just his career. The references came from some of the most prominent names of the time: Professors W. D. McHardy, M. Black, A. M. Hunter and G. D. Kilpatrick. The ordeal was painful because MacGregor himself had refused to recommend the man who had aided him loyally for seventeen years; who had kept the Department going when his own ill-health obtained, which was often; who had placed the University at the centre of the world map religiously speaking. It was all the more galling that he should have done so given that MacGregor's own level of scholarship, which cannot be ranked higher than Willie's, was more restricted and certainly less influential, and his published work was small – workmanlike, but unremarkable – despite Willie's effusive comments about it in his *DBR*. The level of postgraduate work MacGregor had gained for the Department was poor compared with other universities.

There is, of course, a tradition whereby outgoing leaders have no say in their successors. Their retirement is seen as a chance for change, for new thinking and direction, and quite properly so. The new appointment was a Senate decision, not a departmental one. But it was obvious that Garth MacGregor's lack of support had another motivation, which contrasted with his effusive comments over Willie's Bruce Lectures and his recommendations of him for the Aberdeen Chair. He was registering his disappointment in Willie. He did not believe that Willie should have the post, and said so plainly according to Ronnie Falconer, Willie's confidant of this time. We may never have the full picture; we shall certainly never know his pain.

It was nothing personal, insofar as one can say that, given the nature of the rejection. Perhaps MacGregor was offended at the lack of academic publications (only *Educational Ideals in the Ancient World* – Willie's Kerr Lectures – could claim to be such at this time, and that was not a New Testament matter); perhaps he was offended that the Bruce Lectures had not been published; perhaps Willie's more recent, more politicized views had concerned him; perhaps his increasingly 'eccentric' lifestyle, his socializing, his advancement of contentious views, worried him; perhaps it was his churchmanship, his relegation of form and order as of lesser importance; or his personal appearance – we might remember the epithet 'old man Barclay', to which a certain unselfconsciousness in dress was now attached. He was not an untidy person – quite the opposite; but his students held that he looked as if he had been dressed by a committee. This was not always the affectionate exaggeration it was meant to be; the grain of truth in the description irritated some.

Willie commented of MacGregor, 'I went to see him in his last illness, to tell him not to worry, that all was well with the Department ... He put his hand on mine and said, "Willie, when I die they'll find your name written on my heart."' But not on a letter of reference. A Judas touch? There is no trace of resentment in Willie's account, none of the immense hurt he felt. William Barclay was that sort of man. He lauded his chief and his work – in his *DSB*, in the *festschrift* volume he and Hugh Anderson edited in his honour (which became his memorial volume). In his autobiography he only offered praise and affection for the man he had known for thirty years. But at the time he agonized. As Alexander commented, 'What rankled, I am sure, was the discounting of his universally acclaimed seventeen-year teaching record in the department as the Professor's right-hand man.' Alexander specified that the University Court had five misgivings about appointing Willie: his controversial views, his questionable academic fitness, a belittling of his books, a lack of philosophical acumen, a failure to grow mentally. I cannot comment on these, not having access to the discussions, though the Faculty Secretary kindly made available to me its main records – which do not substantiate them. But nods and winks are not conducive to minuting. Others have alleged that Alexander's comments are not free from some subjectivism, but the central point is clear enough.

Willie's application form makes impressive reading: his excellent results at DHS; his First in the Classics; his prizes and his accomplishments in PE; his Distinction in Divinity; his record at Trinity Renfrew; his external Lectureships – at Edinburgh, St Andrews, Aberdeen and Leeds (the Bruce, Kerr and Croall Lectureships); many other occasional Lectureships and Examinerships around the country; his work in two departments of the University, one as its long-serving Head; his 'twenty-nine' (sic) listed books (the actual figure was much higher; he excluded the more popular ones, as he did his secular RE involvements); his journalism. It took them a further three months' deliberation to decide; an agony of waiting.

On 28 May 1963 *The Scotsman* and *The Glasgow Herald* had announced the verdict. It appeared in the week Willie wrote an unusually disheartened piece for the *British Weekly*: 'The Truth about Ourselves'. The pressures were telling. He who had soldiered on against withering public criticism in the past, who had ignored much ill-will and pressed on dauntless, ceded: 'I believe that everyone requires a compliment now and again.' W. R. Nicoll had said of Ian MacLaren (a.k.a. John Watson), 'He could face contradiction and opposition, but not the steady environment of antagonism.'

It was announced that Willie had got the job. By now much of the joy had gone from him; he had been drained by the open doubting of his abilities. It is very uncertain whether he ever recovered from this. It did not make him bitter, but it did make him more than a little rueful, perhaps even sceptical, of his colleagues.

Close colleagues such as Alexander have spoken of Willie's sense of 'inferiority' being present in some of his statements of this time, especially in relation to colleagues from the south. My own view of this is that it did not stem from any sense of academic inferiority – with his credentials and record he had already proved his mettle – but from politico-social factors, at the back of which was the destructive effect of his overbearing father, which now resurfaced under the strain. Again, many have stressed his great politeness, his self-effacement, his reserve, his shyness, his contentment in taking the second place, his exaggerated acclaim of others. All of this accelerated once the belligerency of youth was eroded; even more so when, having given his all, he found it was insufficient to carry the day easily. His natural magnanimity – his goodwill – operated here. But there was a negative side. He needed compliments, he needed applause. One of his key-words was 'encouragement'; another was 'comfort'. He pretended not to need them; he deflected them when offered; but they were important to him.

Much of this sprang from a harsh and dominating father who, less worthy and gifted than his wife but infinitely more ambitious, charged through life, awesome in his determination to succeed, a determination fired by religious certitude – a lethal cocktail, as general Church history shows. It was WDB who was the possessor of the true inferior-ity complex; his overcompensations are written large throughout his life, as are his bombastic and external certainties. He was not the man to speak of life at Low Street, Fort William – unlike his son who gloried in his humble antecedents and his 'village joiner grandfather'. Less visible is the record of WDB's explosive temper, his intolerances, his certainty of himself at the expense of other people. 'When did you first realize that your father was not infallible?' a psychiatrist once asked Willie. He thereby put his finger on Willie's Achilles' heel. Willie, the inheritor of his mother's temperament rather than his father's, had been deeply marked by it, caught up in its duality. It accounts for that antisyzygy – that clash of opposites – which we see in his life and work.

There was some gladness at the appointment. He was not a man unable to make light of an opposing situation however hard his heart ached; and a large group of friends celebrated it with him. One of the first letters he received in congratulation came from Jimmy 'Monkey-Brand' Paterson, his Greek teacher at DHS of forty years ago. 'You lit the fire,' Willie replied generously. To an old schoolfriend, Walter Henderson, he wrote of this letter from Paterson, 'I felt that it should have been *I* who was writing to thank *him*. We owe him a lot...' This hyperawareness of others, this willingness to give more than due hon-our, is not a mere sign of his good manners, but of some self-doubt, of his unwillingness, his inability, to take himself with absolute serious-ness. WDB would simply have said, 'Thank you very much', as we know he did say it, often; as did his wife – with more realistic grace.

The day following the news of his appointment found Willie at his desk, his professorial desk, a little earlier than usual, reforming what he knew had long needed reform: the Department of which he had been Number Two for seventeen years. There is a massive difference between the introduction to the Department's courses in the *University Calendar* for 1964/5 and its predecessors. It bears all the hallmarks of the new Professor's hand: greater lucidity in stating the aims and objects of the courses; shorter paragraphs; a more direct style; better organization of the material (subsectioning was always one of his great abilities); broader views of the subjects offered; and – at fifty-six – a definitely more modern approach.

This was vintage Barclay: clear thinking and positive writing, the dual indicators of his serious commitment. The 'new' subjects included Form Criticism and Gnosticism (they did not appear in his *The First Three Gospels*, cf. p. 285); the recommended textbooks are more recent – over twenty new ones were listed. They included 'conservative' as well as 'liberal' names (these labels are foolish in an academic context, but have sadly become current; the point is made here to demonstrate his open-mindedness: 'all truth is God's truth'). He turned on the heat *practically* by revising the 'Exegetical Exercise', revising it for the first time in forty years and gearing it properly to modern needs. From now on, despite his ongoing *par erga*, his Department would come first, although, of course, it always had.

Throughout his life Willie remained a most generous man, with his time, his gifts, his books and his money. Fellow ministers were not the least beneficiaries of this kindness, but they were also the objects of his criticism. He had little sympathy with those who did not give themselves unreservedly to their people, especially with the careerists in the Church who looked to station and status rather than service as their fulfilment. He served his people, of all ages, wondrously. He said he wished to be their friend – and he became such to vast numbers of them the world over.

But he refused to dilute the challenge of Christianity, of discipleship. They were rigorously informed of their bounden duties, in the home, at work, wherever. His was not a church-laden view of the Christian life. He believed in the Church, its sacraments and ordinances, but only as far as they *served* the interests of the gospel and the people it served, of God himself and devotion to him. He was ruthless in his criticism of practices and traditions which got in the way; of people whose 'selfishness' made of the Church a less useful thing.

Was formal dress a barrier to true worship? Change it! Were pew rents an impediment to people attending church? Get rid of them! Were long prayers and old-fashioned language unuseful? Shorten and

modify them! Was the language of the *Authorized Version* unhelpful?
Modernize it! Were hymns old-fashioned and untheological? Jettison
them! And so on. He had little time for those who would not move with
the spirit of the times, the ecclesiastical dogs-in-mangers (of whom
Paul issued his own warning, in Philippians 3:2, suggesting they were
best avoided).

He was a man of reformed faith, who believed that reform and
adaptation were the *duties* of every disciple, at all times and for all conditions. His main sympathies were for 'the unchurched masses' with
whom he delighted to brush shoulders – men and women of every
walk of life, not least those whose lives had been wrecked by circumstance and tragedy. Most moving of all the compliments paid to him
were those that came not from fellow academics, ministers or church
people, but 'outsiders': his garage mechanic, the doorman-cum-
porter, those who shared the football stand with him, the unnamed
man in the pub who shouted across the smoky bar, 'Och, 'tis yon fella
Barclay!' (when he had been awared the CBE). He appreciated that
friendliness; he had no 'side'.

It was for this reason that much of his energy was given to
groups and organizations outwith the churches, why he had little
patience with church committees. He loved involvement with 'non-
denominational' organizations such as the BB, the Bible Societies and
Associations, the YMCA, the Salvation Army, the Fellowship of
Reconciliation, and a score of 'secular' bodies (social, housing, literary, philosophical, peace groups, etc.). Quasi-church bodies, such as
the Sunday School movement and the HM Forces chaplaincy groups
were similarly aided by him.

NINETEEN

PROFESSOR – AT LAST

The reward of a thing well done – is to have done it.
(Ralph Waldo Emerson)

In the previous year, 1963, John F. Kennedy had been assassinated, which had sent a *frisson* around the world, contributing to its uncertainties. Willie's mental and cultural furniture was changing with the removal of familiar figures: MacGregor and Professor Pitt-Watson through death; and Andrew McCosh through his resignation from the St Andrew Press. One of McCosh's innovations was the Goodwill Scheme, by which churches of the Third World were enabled to buy the *DSB* at cost – a deliberate sacrifice by the Church of Scotland, and by the *DSB*'s author. (It was later amended in favour of Church finances without Willie's knowledge and to his great annoyance.) The editorship of *The Expository Times* changed, the honoured name of the Hastings being succeeded by that of C. L. Mitton, Principal of Handsworth Theological College.

In agreeing to stay with that journal, Willie made one of his own major changes known – to the Editor's expressed surprise – in the highly significant request that he review only 'secular' books from now on. He wanted to *listen* freshly to people's questionings, the better to offer 'decided answers' and to pass such on to his teaching and ministerial colleagues. It was his answer to the changes which were taking place, foremost in which (religiously) was now the 'debate about God', precipitated by the ideas of Friedrich Nietzsche, illumined by the self-authenticating Martin Heidegger, developed by the ever-anxious Paul Tillich, and popularized mystifyingly by John Robinson. Willie doubted that the Bishop's questions were those understood, let alone raised, by the plain people of Woolwich – or anywhere else. He needed to sound afresh these waters of doubt, uncertainty and unbelief – and secure decided answers.

He was haunted by the confession of one of his father's favourites, the evangelist Gypsy Smith:

Lord, we are so busy studying deep theological questions, arguing
about the validity of critical enquiries as to the dates of the books of
the Bible, preaching and hearing eloquent discourses, comforting
and edifying each other, that we had to leave the Christless masses
alone...

Willie had always been deeply concerned by their plight. Through the
boisterous behaviour of the Clydeside folk out enjoying themselves he
had discerned emptiness and fear. At Renfrew he had made a magnificent effort to meet their needs, to open the gospel to them – and not
just to the people of Renfrew, but to the servicemen and women from
all over the UK and further who had attended his meetings. His *par
erga* – his night job – had of late intensified this approach, in journalism, radio, television and the Plain Man books. Even now that he was
a Professor he could not ignore the 'Christless masses': he would be
that practical Professor...

He went on pilgrimage (the word he used in *The Expository Times*,
gadflying as ever) to hear the Beatles with Jane. Her sympathies with
the hippies were causing Kate headaches. Willie was laid back, learning, even enjoying the times. He remembered his own youthful exuberance; he was committed to discovering what this new vogue was
really about. Radical-chic was in, and Willie needed to answer it, not
by offering gospel-chic, but by understanding the new generation –
their music, songs, films, drama, poetry, dance – and their disappoint-
ments with, and anger against, society. Wise doctor that he was, he
knew that one cannot prescribe unless one has first diagnosed; that
one cannot diagnose unless one has first examined – though many try
to do so with worn-out instruments, outdated techniques and lethar-
gic minds. He was not only observing them closely, he was also reading
their literature, their newspapers, hearing their calls for change,
studying their hopes. Students especially came under his examination.
While others bemoaned them, castigated them, concentrated on the
symptoms rather than the realities of a decadent if ebullient society,
Willie looked deeper, perceived their cries for justice, their pleas for fairness, their spiritual depression. He found himself on their side very
often – which got him into further trouble. *He* was now berated with
the dissidents and the loonie left. He was not interested in the status
quo; he was committed to the future, to the Kingdom of God and its
righteousness – the childlike faith which makes its coming possible.

In all this, his work for the Department was by common consent
faultless, both in administration and in student formation and care. If

there was an area in which he could be judged wanting, it was that of postgraduate study. Glasgow was in danger of being left behind, in contrast to such Faculties as F. F. Bruce's at Manchester. We should remember, however, that Scottish Professors regarded first-year men as their special responsibility – as Willie emphasizes in his autobiography.

He was lecturing for too many hours – no less than fifteen per week, of which five covered the new subjects he had introduced. He worked his post as if it were a church appointment, which it had been: to teach New Testament was to teach God, though the academic aspects obtained. His aim was to prepare men for the ministry – of preaching, teaching and pastoral caring. *Pure* scholarship – 'soul-less things' – was not his forte, and he never claimed that it was, though he did it brilliantly. Some of those who went to Glasgow were disappointed. They failed to understand the particular ethos in and for which he worked.

The sixties were now seething uproariously. William Barclay was not the sort of man to hold back in such a time. Some local issues provoked him to express himself. He again expressed his revulsion for the Orange Marches which were stirring up religious strife in Glasgow and Northern Ireland, the two places nearest to his heart – a strife which led to that hatred which was to have dire consequences in the UK over the next thirty years. Ironically, it was a time of accelerating goodwill among the churches. The Orange Order was seeking to wreck this by its factionalism and small-mindedness, denying to others the freedom it demanded for itself. Commented Willie of the true leader, 'The main thing which clearly matters is not theology but personality' – character not doctrine. The opposite was the Orange Order's line, and they practised it vehemently, with a worn-out theology, a myopic vision and ill-will.

Willie had long been their bogeyman; now he became their sworn enemy. To them his social sense, his *practical* view of faith and its application, was anathema; to him it was taking the story of the good Samaritan and the teaching of the Sermon on the Mount seriously – reading the New Testament without credally tinted spectacles. The reality of their faith, on the other hand, he found well expressed in Stephen Colwell's dictum: 'a creed without charity, theology without humanity, protestantism without Christianity'. Willie's own concern with 'the social gospel' – a misnomer for his views – has already been seen; now it continued and developed: forwards, not backwards.

He became involved in a number of housing schemes, contributing generously to them. This was one of the great needs of the sixties, as organizations such as Shelter were demonstrating. He was particularly active for Tenovus, a Glasgow scheme. He was careful to sustain a balanced view, as may be seen by his strong welcome of a biography of Billy Graham. He said of the evangelist's message, 'It would be difficult to find a better summary of salvation.'

One incident concerned the law of the land. It arose out of that species of blasphemy he felt was perpetrated in declaring natural disasters 'acts of God' – a matter which churchmen and theologians have long ignored, in which they fail to witness for or defend their faith. Why should natural and – even worse – human-caused disasters be blamed on God? Why was Aberfan attributed to him, for example? Behind his principle of utter honesty and correctness we may see the conscientious *defender* of the divine. Further, we may feel in it his continued pain under the impact of that hateful letter, 'I know now why God killed your daughter'. He is often judged for being superficial theologically. In statements like these he shows that the heart of the matter is his; that mere sophistries – whether legal or theological, ecclesiastical or juridical – need to be reformed as much as church order, public prayer, hymns, etc., if truth is to obtain. He could not understand why they happily engaged in 'the death of God' debate, when the actuality was the death of language about God; its underlying thought-forms, not the reality – an ongoing activity from the beginning, as his NT work demonstrated. He regretted his colleagues' obtuseness in such matters; they derided his naivety. He knew that to change it, to reorient one's understanding of it, is to recreate theology, to write it anew; to think of God and his world in a different light. He was not afraid to do so, to ask difficult questions, or to offer unpopular answers.

His third televised lecture series now took place (1964), his subject being 'A People's Jesus'. That was ever the thrust of his work, the core truth of his message, and it did not change. It was an extremely busy time for him, so he delivered two lectures per evening. At one of them a technical fault developed, which required him to give the same lecture twice. He cheerfully went back to his rostrum and did the whole thing all over again. He was nothing if not flexible, fluent and willing – goodwilling. 'The Barclay style' was now there for millions to see, and see it they did. The unlikely figure he projected was forgotten in an instant; the voice grated on, the arms waved, the gown flapped; never mind all this: he held them spellbound.

His son Ronnie was invited to sit in the control room for one of these lectures. Willie always offered a full script before the lecture to enable the producer and his engineers to plan their shots, lighting, illustrations and so on. The trouble was that the lecturer did not follow his script. The first few sentences were word perfect. Then he soared, animated by his subject, geared to the obvious response of his entranced audience: this nuance, that fact, this application, that illustration. 'He's on page x,' the perspiring engineer would mutter, only to find that he no longer was; a new tangent had been engaged, a new vector taken; he was somewhere else, soaring still. 'Back to page y!' another would cry, but already it was too late; he was off again. They improvised as he verbalized, mobilizing his fecund imagination and well-stocked mind to drive home his points. They eyed the clock anxiously – and lo! the soaring was diminishing; he returned to his script, word perfect; he reached its promised goal, point z in view. He closed his lecture on its sixtieth minute. They mopped their brows and congratulated him – and themselves.

Similar feats occurred even without his being warned in advance. One producer asked him, recording equipment in hand, for an instant three-minute radio broadcast. There was no question of his refusing the request; the need was evident. Willie thought for a few moments, wrote a few points on a piece of paper, adjusted his hearing aid, addressed the microphone and began. Two minutes and fifty-seven seconds later he stopped: a perfect provision.

This year he had three books published, by three different publishers – William Collins & Sons, SCM Press and Westminster Press. Three other books were on course, and he was working at his 'biggest' project to date – a fresh translation of the New Testament. Copyright prevented him from offering the translation he had rushed through for the *DBR*, but he needed to move on in any case. He had fresh things to offer, thanks to ten years and more of 'discovering' Hellenistic Greek with his students. The new translation would be a paraphrase, in fact, in order to elucidate the nuances of the Greek. It was an age for paraphrase, as J. B. Phillips, F. F. Bruce and others had made clear, not least the very successful (if overzealous) *Paraphrase Bible*.

William Barclay was of the old school of translators, for whom the completest accuracy was obligatory. When he had all but completed his work, the United Bible Societies' Greek text was published. Willie went back to the beginning and thoroughly revised his translation in its light. Others were not so meticulous. What he would have made of such monstrosities as Robert Walker's *Correct Parables* we can only guess. What is certain is that its 'political correctness' – a societal-establishment ideology – would have been anathema to him. To substitute 'cerebrally challenged bridespersons' for 'foolish virgins', or a 'negative-attention-getting son' for the 'prodigal son', would have caused him to shake his head with sorrow at its absurdities – and increase his sympathies for the plain man.

A new opportunity arose through a meeting (at the Y) with Douglas Millard of James Clarke & Co. of Cambridge. Willie could not resist a new challenge, could not say no, and this relationship throws a peculiar light on him. Of all his publishers, it was Millard who pressed him most, remorselessly so. He wanted anything from Willie, and everything. In addition to discussing general matters with him, he used him as an (unpaid) editorial consultant, even a bibliographical advisor. An ignorant man, he asked Willie to become his editor on a series of foreign theology. Willie agreed, whose knowledge of German was negligible, who had largely ignored untranslated German works until now. He gave one such manuscript to his son Ronnie to read for him – Manton's *German Grammar for Theological Students* – and then urged Millard to reject it. He did so. Another publisher took it up and did very well with it. Millard was not amused. On another occasion Willie recommended Dibelius' great work on form criticism for translation, which Millard expedited – only to find that the Americans had already done it, that it was currently available in the UK, their investment was totally wasted. Millard was even less amused, though he could have consulted the bibliographies himself.

There are more than three dozen letters encapsulating their relationship, many of them couched in apologetic terms, both men realizing that they are pressing the other unfairly. One suspects that the constraining interest was the entrée it gave Willie to the National Liberal Club in Whitehall, an old ambition: to work like W. R. Nicoll worked, to sit where he sat. But the labour was costly. Professor G. B. Caird remembers Willie's playful comment at this time, 'I'd be worn out if I had more than five hours' sleep!' He rarely got it. Merricks Arnot once needed him urgently. 'Phone at 2 a.m.,' suggested Kate, 'he's usually available then.' It worked. Consultancy work of the sort Millard needed was simply not Willie's metier, and after eleven uneven and unproductive years their relationship ground to a long-overdue halt.

It was so different elsewhere. David L. Edwards of SCM Press offered his own comment when prefacing *Testament of Faith*. Having spoken of Willie's 'astounding industry', he says:

For some years I was one of William Barclay's publishers and his name stood at the top of our authors' royalties. During those years I never discussed with him either publicity or money. He would sign any contract sent to him without a quibble over its financial terms, *provided only that the book proposed might be useful* [my italics].

He was at the top of the royalties list because his books were useful. To Paul Meacham of the Westminster Press (who was handling the American edition of his *DSB* and other books) he acted similarly, writing when he sent one manuscript:

Here, then, is the book [*The All-sufficient Christ: studies in Paul's letter to the Colossians*]. You need not refer to me about the adjusting of any words or phrases necessary for American purposes. I give you *carte blanche* to adjust as you like.

Accuracy was important, as many authors found to their cost when he reviewed them, but communication was even more so; the right idiom had to be used, whether in Newtonmore, Newcastle or New York. As Edwards observed, 'he had an extraordinary appetite for words' – for right action, too. It was the same when he authorized foreign translations of his books; translators had to select the most appropriate expression – as he sought to do when translating himself. The central point was the meaning, the message.

The monetary aspect he left to take care of itself, trusting in the goodwill of his editors, which was not always to his advantage. Sometimes he gave away his rights; sometimes he transferred the royalties to the benefit of others (e.g. the Youth Committee of his Church); sometimes he insisted on reduced royalties (e.g. for the Japanese edition of the *DSB*: 'it will not be a big royalty, nor would anyone wish to make money out of the Japanese Church'). He even overlooked the breach of contract with the Church of Scotland in its failure to keep to the agreement under the Goodwill Scheme when the second edition of the *DSB* was published. And he accepted without demur the miserly 4 per cent offered by it for the overseas sales of his books, turning a blind eye to the fatuous excuse that they had lost the contracts.

Sometimes he did put his foot down – for the sake of others. The Saint Andrew Press sought permission from the BB to reprint *The King and the Kingdom*. Willie gladly agreed. It offered 2.5 per cent on sales to 10,000, and 3 per cent thereafter. The BB leaders were not amused, and complained of their ill-treatment. The Secretary wrote a sarcastic '£106!' (for *total* projected revenue) in the margin, and asked Willie — who knew nothing of the fiddle — if he agreed. He replied:

> The Saint Andrew Press proposes to take 50% of these royalties ... and this will mean that the SAP, who have done nothing whatever to earn the money, will receive more than me, the author, and you, the owners of the copyright; which, as Euclid says, is ridiculous.

A new, fairer agreement was forced on them, which went through. On receiving the first cheque, the BB Secretary found that the SAP had made yet another mistake: it had been given both its own and Willie's share of the royalties. The Secretary offered to send it to him. Willie replied, 'Just do as you wish about the cheque.' Euclid was satisfied; the money was irrelevant.

Deeply satisfying to him was his ongoing work for the College Choir — he saw it as outreach, not entertainment: an outreach that must interest and entertain. It raised money for the College, and brought to young men and women the challenges of the ministry, key motives for him. It involved a lot of time and effort — in choosing appropriate songs and hymns, rehearsing, arranging venues and travelling around Scotland. In 1964, amid all his busyness, five places were thus served: Forres, Elgin, Abelour, Lossiemouth and Hopeman. While in the area the students visited the parishes — schools, workshops, etc. — and supplied pulpit. In Elgin they recorded a broadcast service from High Street Church and held a Youth Rally. While the students were thus busy, Willie occupied himself at his typewriter at the Station Hotel, Inverness.

This over, he was off south again — to Bagshot for another chaplains' conference; thence to London for the BFBS translation meetings, back to Glasgow for a month, and then back south to Oxford, for work on the NEB Apocrypha. He returned via Newcastle for a meetimg at the Y, then went south again to Scarborough for a Baptist conference, following which Bloomsbury Central Baptist Church claimed his energies. 'Delegate that work,' he wrote in the *British Weekly*, but there is little evidence that he did so himself, save in his domestic arrangements, where Kate was ever ready to comply. She rebuked him for pride at this time, when he refused to stop for a torn muscle in his shoulder, which he got from playing 'a lot of golf' on his holiday. His doctor disagreed. It was not pride but conceit, he suggested; why should a wealthy man nearing sixty work so hard?

One of the answers was that work was a principle of life to him – in its intensity, not just its general necessity. He lived to work. Ten years on we will find him averring this as *an article of belief*: 'I believe in work.' In addition to working hard himself, he provided much work for others: his writing created many jobs, and made many more bearable. Raymond, a young Methodist minister, asked him how he did it. He offered his rules:

1. He began each day early, leaving home at 08.00, beginning work at 08.30.
2. He kept going, seizing every opportunity.
3. He kept to his schedule, regardless of feeling 'inspired' or not.
4. He did the work he was paid to do – which sometimes meant saying no.
5. He employed every labour-saving device he could: e.g. a dictating machine, and a secretary, which enabled him to do his forty or fifty letters a week.
6. He tolerated no distractions; his deafness was the perfect answer.
7. He kept going on five hours' sleep a night.
8. He practised the art of cat-napping.
9. He was blessed with a good wife.

He was often at his desk before 08.30, which was not a problem, Kate being busy with Jane. This was after he had breakfasted and taken Rusty (now a pudgy ten-year-old) for a walk – if being dragged round the block by an overexuberant bull mastiff can be called walking. Willie was almost constitutionally incapable of saying no, nor was he concerned about repeating himself. Many of his books repeat both content and illustration. No matter. He was writing for different organizations, different readers, and different needs: the *SSST*, the Y, the BB, the Youth Committee, *DSB* readers, the *BW*, *ET*, and so on.

He tolerated every distraction. He regarded Kate as his greatest blessing; yet he confessed to believing the old proverb that a doting wife makes a bad husband; he demonstrated the fact continuously, and admitted it. 'There is no surgery like the gentle surgery of love,' he opined, who had often winced under his father's rages, while being strengthened by his saintly mother's quiet fortitude. Kate's unstinting care – her criticisms as well as her support – strengthened him likewise. He hated doctoring, dentistry, hospitals and every such physical intervention, but he was impressed by their healing arts. The blunter instruments of criticism had often been applied to him. The attacks got worse: the bludgeoning techniques of half-educated clergy and their lay supporters now frequently berated him. They had little outward effect; he knew that no one erects monuments to critics. He commented, 'I have all my life been grieved that the word "evangelical" should have been annnexed as their private property by people who think in a certain way. An evangelical is a man of the Gospel.'

He was such a man, unstoppable in its cause. They would not stop him now, whether their attacks be professional or personal. 'The greatest heroism of all is to keep going,' he said. Those who boasted of preaching the gospel of love often bared their teeth in response to his preaching, unable to see themselves truly. His openness offered some curious opportunities. One of them was to address a meeting of the Glasgow Rangers football team and their friends. Fifty-five people turned up to hear him preach, which he did using illustrations drawn from his staggering memory of players, teams and cup-finals over the last century: threshold evangelism which won deep appreciation from his hearers.

The second half of the summer of 1964 was like its first half – lecturing at a summer school, travelling to Blackpool, down to London, on to Oxford, thence to Skegness, back south for a triennial international conference, north to Motherwell. The year was to finish on a high note. 'The astonishing Dr Barclay', exclaimed the *British Weekly* headline for 2 December. The headline referred to the millionth copy of the *DSB* (UK edition) – which was presented to Kate. In the States, which came late to the scene, they were already past the half-million mark and growing stronger by the week. In addition, its translations into Mandarin Chinese, Norwegian and Spanish were announced. Denis Duncan, the new *BW* editor, commented, 'his is the most outstanding personal ministry of print the world has ever seen'. Willie slipped away to his London hideout at the Y, to continue his work undistracted. In a later poll taken by the paper, he was pronounced seventh in a list of the ten most important people of his day. Some scoffed at this, not excluding those ministers who used his material. I once heard him criticized by the chairman of a well-known evangelical publishing firm, who was anxious to tell me how 'unsound' were his views, how uneven his commentaries. (Willie had sent me a brilliant sales puff to launch a Bible commentary campaign for the company. I was berated for my 'error of judgement' – despite the success of the campaign!) But I spotted a set of the *DSB* on the chairman's bottom shelf, and referred to it. A rueful, if hypocritical, grin followed – and a change of subject. They might make of him an 'Aunt Sally' target, but very many found his work indispensable.

In early 1965 he was made Dean of Faculty, and his workload increased yet again. It was to increase yet more, to an unbearabe level, and would ultimately shorten his life.

Former colleagues of his have been anxious to say how businesslike was Willie's deanship, how attentive he was to detail, how prompt were his answers to questions and problems, how smoothly he cared for his students, and how thoughtful were his plans for developing the courses and making them more relevant. 'They completely underrated his powers as manager of departmental affairs,' Neil Alexander stated – including in this teaching and examining as well as managing. Principal Galloway commented, 'He ran a tidy and happy University department. He did his tour of duty as dean ... with flair, *panache* and evident enjoyment.'

His *par erga* continued as before; but he kept to the golden rule as he had always done: his main job was at the University; it never came second to his other work, no matter how pressing the deadline. He never accepted any invitations that clashed with this primary responsibility. As Dr Galloway said, 'This massive public involvement never tempted him to give short measure to the affairs of scholarship ... He never stinted his availability to his students.'

Chief among his *par erga* was the New Testament paraphrase, which Collins published in 1968. It had taken him six years to complete – proof of the intense care with which he discharged his task, his most important to date, and so different from the hasty gallop of the translation for the *DSB* series. It is a work of consummate scholarship, made to look easy by his method of typing directly from Greek text to paper. Behind this, however, rested avid reading and study, careful preparation, much thoughtful work and that phenomenal memory which awed so many – from first-year students to Oxford Deans.

Despite this concentration on the paraphrase, many articles and no fewer than twenty-four books were to appear while he was at it. One of those twenty-four was *The First Three Gospels* (his sixty-eighth book), published in 1966, on which Principal Michael Green averred, 'I have read no better book by Dr Barclay than this.' It sold out quickly, but Willie delayed working on the promised revised edition for some years, recognizing its deficiencies and the need for careful expansion. This was *his* subject. He meant to make a show of it – usefully – for others. He had preached and lectured on it for years; his mind was replete with its methods and problems, its key exponents. Aware of complaints of the non-academic status of his publications, he determined to rewrite this book at a deeper level. The result was the two-volume work *The Gospels and Acts*, totalling 644 pages, which appeared in 1976 and remained in print for over twenty years.

His Old Testament teacher, John M'Fadyen, used to say that a good teacher is 'an animated question mark'. It was a principle that Willie put into regular and fearless practice – sometimes to the animated responses of his listeners. He was all too aware of the minister whose activities fulfil the words of T. S. Eliot (in *The Wasteland*):

> Where is the wisdom we have lost
> in knowledge?
> Where is the knowledge we have
> lost in information?

He himself questioned ceaselessly, seeking the lost wisdom as well as the erring knowledge – in every aspect of life he touched, 'religious' or 'secular'. The whole world, he asserted, was the arena of God's activity. His pronouncements embodied a this-world emphasis, which displeased the conservative factions with their worldliness – and the liberals with their religiosity. As has often been said, the man who takes a middle-of-the-road stance is liable to be knocked down by traffic from both sides, as Willie was, often.

We have already encountered his comments on nuclear armaments and on the insurance world for its blasphemous imputations. He now took on the judiciary, in his Alex Wood Lecture. This was delivered at Bourneville, Birmingham, one of the great centres of Quakerism in the country. In it he again questioned basic principles, declaring: 'If the principles laid down here are correct, then the whole system of justice in this country is wrong and unChristian.' The gathering pace of the controversy between law and justice, the lack of morality in the former and the doubts of some eminent jurists to include it in the latter – Hart versus Denning *et alii* – greatly concerned him. The lecture was published under the title 'Christian Discipline in Society Today'. It reveals an interesting progression from the time when his view of the ethics of the Sermon on the Mount was that it pertained to 'the inner circle' of Jesus' followers (a view which runs contrary to the statement of Matthew 7:28, but see 5:1; the disjunction evidencing redactional activity). Willie was intent on viewing the world organically – as against the two-state doctrine of traditional reformed theology which opposed Church and State: the whole world was one theatre for God's actions; Jesus was Lord of all, as he was creator of all. God's love and care was for the whole world.

Willie also engaged with another modern problem at this time, calling into question the Church's attitude to buildings. He believed its
work was being paralysed through its possessions, properties it could
not fully use or afford to maintain. This is a very different Barclay from
the one who, at the end of the war, said he wanted more buildings and
better ones for his Church. But times had changed: new perspectives
had become apparent, priorities had altered, techniques were different, and Willie felt the need for revolution. He knew that in raising this
question he was driving at the very heart of church life for most
church-goers, whose commitments are often more focused on buildings than on God; whose leaders are often afraid to take the courageous decision and live apostolically. The Church, Willie declared, was
not meant to be a museum. He had moved on from pre-war concepts,
which went back fifteen hundred years, which denied the great
changes within society. He was looking at present-day realities and –
as always – he was looking towards the future.

He produced yet another, more surprising, challenge in those ecu-
menically sensitive days. In an article headed 'Systematizing the Grace
of God' he denied the validity of ordination at the hands of bishops
and superintendents. These were, he argued, human regulations, a
dictation to God of how man should act – even as 'standardizing' the
conversion experience was another limitation placed on him. This was
followed by a warning to ministers whom he charged with forsaking
their *essential* function as teaching elders. That comment came out of
an invitation which his Church had sent to 820 ministers, inviting
them to gather for a refresher course: 52 applied, and 48 turned up –
a failure rate of about 94 per cent. Willie indicted them for their 'intellectual suicide', but it was their apathy that depressed him most.

Amid all this, he was made Freeman of the Borough of Motherwell,
alongside Sir Samuel Curran, 'vastly thrilled' to be so honoured. It was
the secular equivalent of his Edinburgh DD. Robin Sterling, editor
of *The Motherwell Times*, was deputed to 'chaperone' Willie's friend
Professor W. D. McHardy of Oxford during the two-day celebrations;
someone had obviously been talking about the friends' habits at the
Randolph Hotel!

In the autumn of 1967 his radical views reached their apogee, in
a decision which rocked his Church and, indeed, much of Scotland.
Each year a select committee meets to choose the Moderator of the
General Assembly, whose job it is to chair the Assembly and represent the Church formally, both within and outwith Scotland. The

Moderator is chosen on an alternating basis from men in the parish ministry and from those in academic posts. The post is for one year, and its incumbent is titled the Very Reverend – the ultimate accolade for a life of service. That autumn the Nominations' Committee appointed William Barclay as Moderator Elect. It never thought to ask him. Having ignored his views for so long, it is not surprising that it got things hopelessly wrong.

In breach of time-honoured tradition, and to the committee's consummate embarrassment, Willie turned the honour down flat. It caused uproar in the places of power, disappointment in the minds of the hopeful, delight in the minds of the disrespectful. Even the secular press joined the clamour. 'THINK AGAIN, DR BARCLAY' *The Scottish Daily Express* urged. It, too, perhaps it especially, had not been listening. Pressures were applied: he was informed of the honour entailed in the position, of his admiring readers, the traditions of the Church, and so on. He owed it to them to accept this prestigious appointment. They had no doubt that he would make 'an outstandingly successful Moderator', in a year when the Queen Mother was said to be High Commissioner of the General Assembly (an inaccurate statement). 'Please think again, Professor,' his unthinking editor at the *British Weekly* pleaded, reminding him of his duties, his thousands of admirers, reprimanding him for his 'undue modesty' – and ignoring his consistently stated views of over twenty years.

To say that Willie's point-blank refusal had a stunning effect is to understate the matter. The committee reconvened and a new man was selected; a conspiracy of silence fell over the matter – and the authorities again sought to distract people from the reality of and the reasons for Willie's decision. 'There has been considerable speculation as to who declined to stand as Moderator of the General Assembly,' the Church magazine lied uselessly, of an issue that was known in detail all over Scotland, throughout the UK and far beyond. It continued, 'It is not for *Life and Work* to guess, and Dr Barclay has rightly avoided being drawn into comment.' There is no one more blind than an unfocused churchman.

It was a defining moment for the Church as well as for its principled if outspoken Professor. Professor T. W. Manson of the Presbyterian Church of England (now URC) – the English counterpart to the Church of Scotland – had made a similar point when he declared, to less commotion, 'what the Presbyterian Church needs is not a Moderator but an Accelerator'. Dr Andrew Herron made a similar point when he observed that a moderator is a technical tool for controlling the flow of gas. Willie had long registered his views about ecclesiastical 'gas' by absenting himself from the committees. He never refused to comment on this matter – he wanted his view publicized and was alarmed at the cover-up. A number of people interviewed Willie, most notably David (now Lord) Steel, the son of a former Moderator himself, a lawyer then working as a television reporter.

The interview was hugely important for William Barclay as well as for the Church, ever deaf to his message, as he and Steel both knew. He was more than suspicious that the honour had been meant to quieten him by using him, an old political ploy. The interview was broadcast in Scotland at the end of December – when it was hoped it would be forgotten among the Christmas festivities. Those in the south had to wait until 5 January, when the *British Weekly* printed an (edited) script of it.

Steel asked him bluntly why he had refused the honour. Willie played him like a trout: it would take him away from his University responsibilities, he said; he was particularly worried about his seventeen American postgraduate students. He drew Steel's attention to the costume he would have to wear: 'I haven't got the figure for the traditional moderatorial dress.' Many knew – as the Committee should have known – that this was one of his liveliest *bêtes noires*. He had long amused family, friends, students and parishioners over it. One of them once found him prancing about the room in demonstration of it, an 'hysterically funny performance'. His personal shape had nothing to do with it, of course. His one-time hero, T. E. Lawrence, tersely declared of such outward frippery, 'It is theatrical, and theatre spells circus, and circus spells clown.'

The answers moved up a grade in their seriousnness. It was the *image* projected by it, the unreality of it, which offended him. 'By changing these [antiquated vestments] wouldn't you be divesting the church of its dignity?' Steel queried. Willie's reply was a blow straight from the shoulder. The Church did not need to stand on any such false dignity, and thus he exposed his fundamental arguments: 'It is not dignity but dynamism that the church needs. I would take away the dog collar and the robes and have the minister in ordinary clothes. The church should be a family.' Priorities were the key issue, not the trifles of pomp and circumstance. Thus he could wear the illustrious scarlet of Edinburgh's doctoral robes with enthusiasm, associating with the real world of hard-headed scholarship, not that of the free association of believing people, the family of God.

This was not his only reason. The Moderator's position is non-executive, decorative even. He has no power to *do* anything except tour

the country and make speeches – at no small cost. He cannot even
'control the gas'. The real business of the General Assembly lies in
other hands: in the committees and the way they are manipulated –
the downside of presbyterianism. The presbyters more often than not
run everything, fix everything; they are not necessarily the most
visionary or spiritual of people, as the history of the Church demonstrates. This is not to say that the General Assembly has no power, or
does not at times exert power, but on any scale of proportions it is a
monstrous device with little to show for all the reports, speeches, back-
room dealings and media obsessions that are engendered by its officers. One man with a great heart and a full mind did more for the Kirk
than all this put together, throughout the world – without even a
proper office. He was deaf, to boot.

Willie was simply disinterested in presiding over its processes; he
was only interested in being a conduit for the true dynamic of the
Church, the gospel, which exists on another plane, and for which he
laboured and travelled incessantly – usually at his own expense. We
shall see that on his retirement, no longer needing to tread softly on
others' jokes, he again spoke plainly of it. Others did, too. Peter Clarke,
for example, a detached if somewhat cynical observer, recently put it
this way – the way of the man in the street – in *The Sunday Times*:

> In most churches, however low, you still get a glimpse of something
> transcendent. At the General Assembly the hum of white mackin-
> toshes and gentle snoring leaves no hint of the religious, let alone
> the divine. It may be that this is the essence of presbyterianism ...
> the ingredients of the General Assembly are pettiness, money,
> hypocrisy and a lack of intelligence ... These harmless dumplings
> barely seem the heirs of Thomas Chalmers, let alone John Knox or
> Martin Luther. How lucky we are that religion doesn't matter any
> more.

This judgement was too sweeping, even unfair – and Clarke knew as
much, for he went on to speak highly of the work of individual ministers and their people. But he had an important point, which was
Willie's point also. He knew that away from the establishment circus
genuine religion is found, in a million small, dare we say familial,
ways: the way of the Father and the Son. William Barclay served that
belief all his life. He had no intention of becoming the ecclesiastical
equivalent of a bookend, without whose support religion would fail to
stand up, would cease to manifest its true principle of goodwill.

Moreover, he was concerned at what all those who knew him – who had *listened* to him – would say if he reversed the principle of long years and put on court dress and took time off to moderate the gas. R. D. Kernohan, sometime editor of *Life and Work* and a more honest one (he later retired from his post 'on principle'), who heard what Willie was saying, who knew of his absences from the church 'courts', stated, 'He was probably a better Christian and a better Protestant ... than he was a Presbyterian in the purely literal sense.' That was the point. He was certainly that, and wished for nothing more: he was a Christian, plain and simple; a member of 'Christ's folk' as he translated the *christianoi* of Acts 11:26.

The issue concerned larger and more momentous matters than mere tradition. It turned on Willie's whole view of Christianity, not how one small Church or nation organized it. It centred on the gospel and its liberating, equalizing message, not the timebound, structural shibboleths laid down by clerks and officials; on the realities of goodwill, not merely good ordering. Such 'good order' devotees paid lip service to the comforting words he spoke, the lively illustrations he used, the inspiration he evoked, the publicity he commanded; they rejected his real message, misrepresented it when necessary, and perpetuated their control (even when breaking Church law themselves) to fulfil their ambitions. Outsiders perceived this and voted – with their feet.

TWENTY

THE TELLING PACE

We are not now that strength which in old days
Moved earth and hearth; that which we are, we are.
(Alfred, Lord Tennyson, *Ulysses*)

Could anything be the same after that clash of wills, of interests? Willie had nailed his colours to the mast in a stormy sea; he was forced to do so, indeed, by the Church's own blundering, by its haughty disdain of his views. He knew that his convictions had been rejected by many whom he had befriended and served all his life. They now sought to make him feel *guilty* over this refusal to serve the Church in their way. There is no evidence that they succeeded; quite the opposite.

Some, even those closest to him, were disappointed; they felt let down – and that did concern him. Kate was one, for example, whose finest memory was of her father accompanying the Moderator as his Chaplain in the great Reunion Walk of 1929, which had involved all the religious and civic dignitaries, symbolizing the unification of the two proud church traditions. What an accomplishment it would have been to see her own husband appointed as Moderator! Her sisters thought so, too, and said so, as did many others. Many years later I was informed by some who professed friendship with Willie, who sought to carry his mantle, that this had been a great mistake of his. They still refused to see his point; to hear the cry of society at large.

An undercurrent of resentment remained. The Barclay image had been tarnished: he was best marginalized – if they could achieve that. It is possible that the furore affected him more deeply than he owned. Other changes now took place – not least due to his new image as an iconoclast – sometimes minor, sometimes major. And they were not without their rebounds on his work. For example, his *British Weekly* page – his main organ of outreach to the general Christian public – was reduced; criticisms of him became more open and more vociferous. In the School for Laymen in the *BW* he was expressly criticized for being 'unnecessarily confusing', an astonishing comment against this plain speaker and writer. He had spoken of running a series on the Psalms; it was cancelled at short notice. His comments became even more pungent. He seemed to bait his opponents more openly and deliberately, and exaggerate issues more unduly. Some regarded this as reckless. The times, they said, called for emollition, not stirring. Willie's mood remained upbeat. He was not about to let his answers 'trickle through our heads/Like water through a sieve', to misquote Lewis Caroll. But 'vintage Barclay' no longer quite sparkled; a suggestion of fustiness arose.

This was especially noticeable in the *BW* column 'Seen in the Passing', causeries which had craftily entertained and educated his readers for years. They were now less spicy, less spontaneous, more formal, more backward-looking, as if in defence – unexpected changes. The subjects he handled at this time suggest a mind overtaken by his day job. College and ministry and theological aspects predominated over personal and family incidents – once the central and very engaging feature of his pieces. There is not much that is funny about ordinands – the last one he described had been dismissed for dishonesty! To the average person they were much less interesting – the 'soap' factor declined. Rusty had been put down in old age; Jane was an assertive teenager, not helped by exposure in the press; his grandchildren were still available, but there was a limit to their use and it was very difficult even to poke kindly fun at them, doting grandfather that he was becoming. Most significantly, Kate's health had taken a decisive turn for the worse with migraines and related disorders, suggestive of the old fears and tensions. She and Jane went off to stay with one of her sisters, who noted the change with concern.

It was a time of evident ageing, of loss, of looking back. The 'Old Dalzielians' formed and met – to reminisce, not a classic Barclayan mode. A student, James Gilfillan, interviewed him and plunged him into the past, a willing victim. Willie admitted that he had regretted 'many times' leaving the parish ministry; that he missed the closeness to people such work had afforded; that he was losing too many old friends. A memorial service for Andrew McCosh had been held – significantly on the premises of the Glasgow Y not of the Church of Scotland. Willie mourned the loss of 'my closest friend for thirty years'. He still missed his daughter Barbara, now dead for a dozen years, and said so movingly, unresolved grief resurging. His Faculty colleague Ronnie Gregor Smith died suddenly, and Willie sought to comfort his widow, Kathe, alone in her grief in a foreign land. A colleague in the New Testament Department, Ainslie McIntyre, fell ill also and academic and administrative pressures mounted. Willie again battled alone to keep things going. The grin was becoming a grimace – of pain and effort. It clearly shows on some of the photographs from this time.

Reviews of his work exacerbated the problems. On *The Lord's Supper* (1967), Kenneth Grayston bluntly commented, 'He is out of touch with modern discussion and present needs' – a wounding blow. Even the normally adulatory *New Zealand Messenger* declared in its headline that this was 'Not The Best Barclay'. *The Church in Ireland Gazette* commented that it was 'a disappointing book on an important subject'. His too-easy facility was bearing rotten fruit. His editors were failing him in their inability – or unwillingness – to keep his work in check. One man did like the book, Principal R. E. O. White of the Baptist College, Glasgow, who wrote to say so. Willie replied, thanking him and saying that he was now ready to tackle a subject which had long troubled him: infant baptism. He was, he said, about to be controversial! Something – or someone – put him off. We will never know exactly how or who this was, but the fact that his comments would have driven against a central pillar in his Church's tradition is suggestive.

He had long contemplated doing for the Old Testament what his *DSB* commentaries had done for the New. He had written a number of pieces on it, which I edited and republished in 1986 under the title *Seven Fresh Wineskins*, but this new ambition was something else. A strong body of opinion – Nicoll's 'steady climate of antagonism' (see p. 238) – was rising against the plan. Professionals said 'no'; the public and his publisher said 'yes'. The clash hurt and decided him against it for the present, other duties obtaining.

Denis Duncan sought to rebut his falling stock in an article headed 'William Barclay's Finest Hour'. He stated that 'for over a quarter of a century William Barclay has written every week in the *BW*' (another inaccuracy). The editor's language was sensational and unconvincing. Earlier, such language would have been just; now Willie's ascendancy was being protested too much, and it showed – never more so than with our advantage of hindsight, of course. But Duncan had important things to say: 'There was a time when it looked as if his appointment as Dean had been the straw that broke the man.' The sense of *burden* came through. Duncan spoke of 'the welter of administrative work' that was now laid on him. The burden was intensifying, not lessening, and it was becoming a psychological one as well. At sixty, the merciless industry of this 'dedicated writing machine' was claiming its toll.

The precise reason for Duncan's piece was the publication of the first volume of the paraphrase of the New Testament (1968), which Willie himself referred to as 'my own biggest news'. But it was not that. In an age of proliferating versions it never truly caught on. Being a paraphrase, not a true translation, it was placed outside the interest of serious students and readers. It came rather late in the wake of 'translation fever' which had been rife since the war. The fever had begun shortly before the war, in fact, with James Moffatt (i.e. his revised edition of 1935). Willie's shelves bulged with such publications. Amid this welter of opposing choices and sharpening criticisms, a Dunkirk spirit was called for: defence, consolidation, counter-attack. Willie was too busy to defend himself – and uninterested in doing so. The book had moderate sales for a few years and then became dormant.

It had offered some good things, despite the essential inaccuracies of paraphrastic translation. Others did better, however, and prevailed. Willie's 'biggest news' became almost non-news, a hard pill to swallow after so much effort. He might have taken the hint from the many heated discussions he had had both in the TNT panel of the BFBS and the NEB Apocrypha panel, where he was up against some of the sharpest minds in the UK, or from gauging the market more accurately, but he did not. As with his *DSB* commentaries, he had things to say about the passages he was interpreting, and he declaimed them despite others' views.

That is not the main point, however. His work was winning fewer friends now, with so much alternative scholarships on offer. As we have seen earlier with reference to John 8:1–11 (he indented the passage in his new translation), his heart could rule his head – for the best of reasons, but that is not in accordance with strict academic discipline. His forty-five page appendix 'On translating the NT' is well worth reading (he defends and explains his reasons for dropping 'Thee' and 'Thou' for God, among other things); but it has little to say for the average reader – for whom the paraphrase was meant. His former coeditor Professor Bruce, in *The English Bible*, commented generously when he said of the New Testament paraphrase, 'he never exercised his gift to better purpose'. The signs were otherwise.

He reduced some of the physical pressures on him by going on a crash diet, 'with very considerable success'. In three months he lost thirty-five pounds, i.e. three pounds per week over ten weeks. It shows his strength of will when determined. In this case it was his doctor who did the determining. Willie, who feared doctors and hospitals and all their contrivances, obeyed. We now know that such dramatic reductions in weight can have very harmful affects on the heart; his subsequent cardiac arrest may be put down partly to this heroic effort, which was not counter-balanced by the parallel development of his muscles and circulation through exercise.

This chapter has necessarily been somewhat negative so far, and not just for Willie. In a period of growing negativism, it led to the nihilistic savagery of the seventies. But it was not all gloom. In the New Year Honours List of 1969 he was appointed a CBE: Commander of [the Order of] the British Empire. Though there was no longer an Empire, and certainly no calls for such as he to command it, it was a singular honour, complimenting his Edinburgh DD and his Freemanship of the Borough of Motherwell. So many were the congratulations that poured in that another circular reply was needed – another indication of his pressures, and his courtesy. Appropriately, one letter came from Professor John Ferguson whose book on suffering Willie had found very useful, glad now to return the compliment.

Kate and Jane happened to be with him in London when 'this totally unexpected news' came, so they allowed it to inspire a surfeit of theatre-going – another pilgrimage! Significantly, it was to the comedy shows that they went. 'Laughter,' he declared suggestively, 'is a healing thing.' On their return they visited their friends, the Roses, in Edinburgh, where they had a celebratory meal together at the North British Hotel. Gladys Rose was surprised, considering the *haute cuisine* offered and Willie's reputation as a bon viveur, to hear him order haggis and neeps for himself. But it was that time of year, and Willie was feeling the need to assert his Scottishness against the demands of Empire.

The pressures soon presented themselves again, exacerbated by ongoing concerns over Jane's self-assertions, understandable in those seething years, when flower power was a menacing concept, and hippiedom an alluring way of life – though not, of course, to the average CBE DD and his wife. It was Kate who felt it most keenly, again gaunt of face and anxious of brow. Willie again found respite in his work, escape indeed from a confrontation that he knew only time could solve. It reached a climax in August, and led to Kate's renewed hospitalization. She had changed, too. She was now resenting his work itself, not just the reactions it triggered. Had he not done enough? Could he not see that others were now able and willing to play their part? Why was he not more concerned at her plight? Why did he not do something about the trenchant criticisms being launched at him so often? He was built to carry on; she was not, as her mother had foreseen so long ago, as her sisters now warned.

His final television series took place in 1966 with an unexpected incident. Ronnie Falconer had discovered that the Minister of Lochgoilhead Parish Church was renovating his church. He decided to ask Willie to attend the filming of it and offer some encouraging comments. Despite his recent pronouncements on church buildings he did so – the ever willing, *practical* Professor. During his time there, Falconer recorded, 'a most hostile ... retired naval officer' took Willie to one side, asking him if he knew of his family connections there. Willie replied that he did not – Fort William had always been the centre of his roots. The boat carrying the renovation supplies was due, and Willie was told that it would come in to what was then known as Barclay's Jetty (incorrectly, as we now know), built by his ancestor.

He identified the correct place. It had fallen down, was all but submerged in the waters of the loch. It is the only example from his grandfather's public works known to us. What was even more interesting to Willie was the family's nearby tombstone, which recorded his great-grandfather's and great-grandmother's story; memories of days and hardships long forgotten. Sadly, he found no time to see it for himself. On his return to Glasgow Willie received from the naval officer and his wife – who were in fact far from hostile – a set of photographs of the area, which he said he would treasure.

He had always taken his work home with him; his home *was* his workplace, as much as his office in the university and his 'prophet's chamber' at the Y in London. Work sought him out wherever he was. The post was accordingly heavy, mostly from the public, but also from publishers asking for manuscripts to be assessed, books to be reviewed – and asking why he had not yet dealt with them more quickly. Telegrams came chasing the letters, followed by telephone calls chasing the telegrams (chiefly from Douglas Millard who was becoming something of a nuisance), all demanding more work. Willie still refused to say no; he could not do so, a slave of goodwill.

He had extended his interests again by this time, now being a Council Member of the Glasgow Royal Philosophical Society, and an Executive Committee member of the Scottish Hellenic Society. But the pace was telling. To W. G. Morrice of Motherwell he apologized for declining to supply pulpit for him, a thing formerly unheard of, especially for his much-loved Motherwell (he still found time for its football team). As he admitted:

I have almost given up weekend work during this term time. This is for two reasons: I want to attend the University Chapel as a worshipper (and as an example!) and even more I have discovered that the Bible is right and that it is not possible to work a 7-day week and remain efficient. When I preach on Sunday I come back still tired on Monday ... I have to keep Sundays free except on rather rare occasions.

Nevertheless, he did accept many invitations, some of the most punishing kind. For example, he delivered the Owen Evans Memorial Lectures at the Prifysgol Cymru – the University College of North Wales – in March 1970, on 'Education in the Early Church and its Greek and Jewish Background' – virtually a recapitulation of his Kerr Lectures. He was horrified to hear from the Principal that his visit had been organized around dinners and speeches. He wrote to say that he was actually prolonging his stay in the area 'to try to get caught up with some work', and would they excuse him from the social activities – though he would be 'more than delighted to be at the dinner party on Wednesday'. He found time for the James Reid Memorial Lecture, and for preparing his eagerly awaited Baird Lectures for 1971.

The wanderlust in him was no less now than it had been in his former chief, Professor MacGregor, so from Aberystwyth he drove 250 miles across country – in the days before motorways made such journeying easy – to the Newcastle Y, another home-from-home. It was not his way to admit ill-health, but Kate did this behind his back, writing to its Secretary and pleading that they treat him easily. Before going to Wales he had gone off on tour with his choir, which included a heavy schedule of concerts, meals and services in and around Hawick. She knew how exhausted he was, and was becoming ever more concerned about his evident deterioration.

His three-year stint as Dean completed, the University awarded him one sabbatical term, his first for twenty years. Colleagues from the States were enjoying their second or even their third sabbatical *year*. He spoke of needing to clear 'a mountain of correspondence', not least to former students now scattered around the world, with whom he kept his friendships 'in good repair' as Dr Johnson admonished. He spent the sabbatical in Oxford, his favourite hideaway. He told John Ferguson that he wanted to write the book about baptism there, but other matters squeezed it out. He was content to let them do so. Kate went with him for part of the time, adoring Oxford's spires and colleges, its walks and restaurants. But it was quite a lonely time for her given his lifestyle – essentially a workstyle still. She was worried about Jane, and so returned to Glasgow.

Willie's lifestyle had indeed changed. He lived more than he cared to admit on his reputation; the dynamic was ebbing; he felt extraordinarily tired. He fell asleep often, and – thing of wonder – he had started going to bed at 23.00, where he slept solidly for two (and more) hours before getting up and working (though not always) for two or three hours. He was imprisoned, as he had always been, within the Protestant work ethic; it was not likely to release him now. What to do? His work was his life, his mistress. His friendships included everyone who showed themselves friendly to him: universal goodwill, though he maintained he had very few close friends. They included Glasgow Protestants in their less protesting modes, and Roman Catholics in their more welcoming – Pope John XXIII had opened the windows of his Church, and Willie was delighted at the great-hearted/goodwill expressions that followed. He named fierce atheists among his friends, some from his schooldays; agnostics by the dozen; liberals by the score; plain men by the multitude – and many conservative evangelicals. Some of these had studied under him, but the world was his parish and his incoming post continued, staggering in its proportions; his replies, too, often costly as he frequently sent a book or two to those whose lot touched him (and sometimes whole sets of the *DSB*) – e.g. a lay preacher in India, a poor pastor in Africa, a church sister in the Philippines.

This universality is not an idle claim. He was now read on every continent; his books were translated into over thirty languages; their English editions were found wherever English was spoken. They sold by the thousand. The Russian edition of the *DSB*, the negotiations for which I commenced in 1979, alone had a million copies as its primary target – and that was ten years before Mrs Thatcher claimed to have opened up the Soviet Union to the West. I remember seeing his books on my travels everywhere – in a two-shelf shop in Tiberius, a basement in Athens, at the English bookshop in Cairo, all over Europe, at many downtown stores in the USA and Canada. It says much for his reputation that John Birkbeck found his authorized biography 'all over Australia'.

There was another sense in which the world was his parish: it was so through his *secularizing* dimension; through the way he was seeking to address modern life and problems within the Judeo-Christian ethic, to use non-religious terms – an extension to his 'threshold evangelism' and in line with his old interests in non-church organizations such as the YMCA, the Salvation Army, the Quakers, the BB. At his home church of Williamwood his minister, Colin Campbell, was an adventurous type. He and Willie organized a series of 'open nights' in which secular experts – in medicine, psychiatry, law, education, whatever – would give a forty-five-minute address, after which the floor was thrown open for discussion and debate. It was a repeat, twenty years on and at a different level, of Willie's Young People's Society at Trinity Renfrew; of the many late-night sessions he had held with the young men of the Y, many of whom were themselves involved with scientific or technological studies.

Such engagements had never been far from his mind. In F. F. Bruce's *festschrift* of 1960 he wrote, 'In his missionary approach Paul had no set scheme [or] formula; his approach was completely flexible. He began where his audience was.' As a minister he was necessarily constrained by the practices of the Church of Scotland; as a Sunday School lesson-writer he had to be schematic; so too with his daily reading publications for the Youth Committee, the BB, and the IBRA, as well as with the weekly *BW* diet He had happily restricted himself to doing what was required – to being 'useful' to catch David Edwards' point. Now he was freer to think and write without such inhibitions, and he sought to do so. The tragedy is that he was too tired. That mindset which had been early formed was now too inflexible to maximize its possibilities. He could – and did – listen to others; he saw immense potential in claiming their ideas and seeking to refashion his theology and ethics around them; but, if truth be told, this work now did not amount to much. It never made the breakthrough he intended. And it was heavily criticized – by the liberal fraternity who could see that it was half done; and by the conservative faction who could neither understand what he was doing, nor why he should be doing it. It is a moot point whether his mindset did not undermine it from the start: the dominating personality of WDB still lived in his subconscious.

He was managing to hold his own in some less ambitious areas. Frederick Franklin of Sweden wrote of an international congress at which Willie spoke, his 'large audience, spellbound with the simplicity of his language, his colourful descriptions of the situations, questions and problems of our present time'. The *World Communiqué* which followed spoke of a 'spiritual and educational, never-to-be-forgotten experience ... a privilege and a highlight of the Fifth World Council'. It always had to be spiritual *and* educational, and the spiritual had to underpin the educational. But the two together constituted his natural aim: the world for God; God's world for man – and that in simple, colourful language, Willie's hallmark. Others had been doing so 'unintelligibly' – i.e. in specialist terms, decipherable only to the specialists, in areas which became faddish and 'in' – such as Barth in theology, Tillich in Philosophical Theology, Heidegger in Philosophy, de Chardin in Mystical Science, Merton in Eastern Spirituality.

A spark of this may be seen in his autobiography. He took to task the Nobel Prize-winner Jacques Monod for his *Chance and Necessity*. Willie had been intrigued by such books from his youth, if at the fringes. It was under Mitton's editorship of *The Expository Times* that this interest was more fully developed. Now he opposed Monod's operonic (i.e. gene-linked) determinism, acknowledging that 'in these matters I am a child', yet boldly suggesting that 'the progess of evolution has been due, not to chance, but to invitation and response': a specific moral and theistic argument. He rejected chance and espoused purpose – as he had ever done. He was never more religious, never more Judeo-Christian; perhaps never taken less seriously. I raise this here to show with what his mind was engaged, what was exercising him intellectually – when it was not caught up in the rush of others' schemes and requests that were his usual lot.

These were matters that his peers had considered when his name came up for the Professorship. Known for explosive statements, for outré views, could this man be trusted? Was he not too outrageous? Too little the measured thinker? Too ready to rush into print? Some derided him as the Professor without an unpublished thought. It is interesting to consider such things in the light of Alexander's criticism that 'he had failed to grow mentally' – a grotesquely untrue judgement, as we have seen. Within his own discipline (and outside it) there was much evidence of such growth. We should remember that his was a mind grounded in the Classics – in their primitive science as well as their mythologies, linguistics and history. He understood as few others did the philosophies of the Epicureans, Stoics, Cynics, Sceptics and Cyrenaics. His was a mind that had assimilated just as easily the economic theorizing of Adam Smith, Alfred Marshall and Sydney Webb – a mind that his friend Duncan Black, the Cambridge Professor of Mathematics, had descibed as 'genius'. A multifarious mind that *had* grown, too much so for many of his less gifted colleagues.

It is always dangerous to occupy oneself with the might-have-beens of history. But what might have been William Barclay's effect on the Church had he been offered the job he really wanted, the job those closest to him in 1945/6 knew he wanted? It is the Church's loss that he was not given the Practical Chair he so earnestly desired, that he was placed in a position which failed to stimulate his mind in the ways he most wished and for which he believed himself best suited. Can we doubt that he would have used it to brilliant, even startling effect? John Buchan, one of his heroes, referred to 'the audacity which has always characterized our communion' in his booklet *Presbyterianism: Yesterday, Today and Tomorrow*. Can we doubt any less audacious activity from Barclay in the light of what we have seen? What, for example, would his 'Church of the Air' suggestion have led to, given his vigour and power of imagination? Certainly not to the wishy-washy fare that is so often broadcast today. Perhaps those who considered him for that Practical Chair divined him only too well. The Church has always been wary of the adventurous. It still resists radical change.

One of the books that came to me from Willie's library illustrates very well his adventuring with ideas. It was Sybille Bedford's two-volume biography of Aldous Huxley, a superb work. Willie loved such books. He admired the blind Huxley for his vision and foresight, as well as for his exquisite prose, his great-world view, his ripe and luminous humanity, his ability to think boldly, his liberation from belittling constraints. Willie, as usual, marked his text for its emphases; some are worth noting:

> The wise man does not think of death lest it should spoil his pleasures.

> The more you think, the more obscure and mysterious [existence] becomes.

> It takes a certain amount of intelligence and imagination to realize the extraordinary queerness and mysteriousness of the world in which we live.

> Salvation is not in the next world; it is in this ... here and now. 'The Kingdom of God is within you...':

> If [materialism] means preoccupation with the actual world in which we live – it is something admirable.

He had ever loved the natural world – what Highlander cannot do so? He was moved by its power and beauty, its order and its chaos; views which also included humankind's response to the world – in poetry, music and literature, and in that literature which expressed humanity's place in the world. Was Huxley's emphasis on mystery a reference to the numinous, man's first step towards an appreciation of divinity? Or was there more afoot for Willie in his comment? Willie was aware of Rudolf Otto's classic emphasis on the *mysterium tremendum et fascinans* – the awful and fascinating mystery – but how was the scientist in Huxley interpreting this? Through intellect *and* imagination, which were Willie's emphases, too, and he wished to exercise the point more and more.

Huxley's fourth comment is pure New Testament (though not the whole of its message); it has the virtue that the previous points lacked; which so many of Willie's early influences lacked – the other world is too dominant; that 'other-worldliness' is a false manifestation of man's humanity, a denial of it in fact. Browning's view of this world as mere preparation for the next (one of WDB's great emphases) is essentially un-Jewish and un-Christian. His fifth point obviously tickled Willie's cosmic Christology, but only that? We could have done with more of this – the discovery of a fuller meaning of the incarnation, for example, in which spirit became flesh – and what that means for materiality and existence.

Alongside the work of Huxley came other thinkers, some specifically theological ones, such as Dietrich Bonhoeffer, Harvey Cox, Paul van Buren, who were all essaying forms of 'secular Christianity'. To Keith Snow of Canajoharie, who had informed Willie that he was going to work outside the normal ministry of the Church, in secular teaching, he wrote, 'I entirely agree with you. If I were starting out over again – unfortunately at 62 this is impossible! – I would go either for Religious Education in a Secondary School or I would go for teaching Biblical Studies as an Arts subject in a purely secular university.' However radical he felt, he nevertheless reaffirmed his central subject – the Bible.

What he wanted to do, he stated, was to view it in a secular context, without the constraints that his Church or its ordination vows applied. Ironically, Willie's own son had just secured a teaching place at Jordanhill Training College – to which Willie himself had applied in the forties, though unsuccessfully. There can be no question that he felt increasingly uneasy about the role of the Church as part of the establishment – 'a pillar of society', within an unfree historical continuum, bound by the many compromises it had to make – from within and without. His biblical loyalty may suggest conflict with such secular ideas, but he could do no other; he was pledged to seek out 'decided answers' to the questions that were erupting all around him, and most of all within him.

Kate had a pleasing expression of Willie's generosity just now: she was given her first car, a Rover 2000, which caused some less elevated minds to fret and carp. She was now freer to do as she wanted, Jane having gone to work in France. Their lives had taken a more individual rhythm. Both unwell and sleeping fitfully, they occupied single beds and slowly went their own ways discreetly. Kate was always there for him, his meals cooked, his laundry ready, but something of their former togetherness had gone – and was noticed by their friends. They both felt it, and suffered from it. She could no longer share his work; he could not reduce his commitment to it.

Willie took off yet again, this time to host the first American Summer School of Studies at St Andrews, an event that gave extra shape and spice to his annual routine for the next few years. By now his anti-American attitudes (an effect of wartime reactions) were long gone, save in his humorous chafings. He was experienced in dealing with American students, both under- and postgraduates; the latter now formed an important part of his work. Moreover, many of his former students worked in the States, most of his books were published there, from whence he drew a large segment of his income. He admired the Americans for their openness, their no-nonsense approach, their lack of class-related restraints, their freedoms and easy friendships. This conference was followed by a Bible Week in the East Neuk of Fife. Despite its sparse population, he drew crowds of between six and eight hundred every evening. It was followed by his preparations for the Reid Memorial Lecture (at Cambridge), the St Giles Lectures (at Edinburgh), and his forthcoming Baird Lectures (at Glasgow; in which he was to set new records). This was all on top of the ongoing College work and his literary activity for the *British Weekly* and *The Expository Times* and his various publishers.

It all came to a shattering halt in December 1969. Kate and he had driven down to London to spend Christmas – he, as usual, at the Y, Kate to shop and visit one of her sisters (a medical doctor who, to Willie's voiced displeasure, had disposed of her Scottish accent). Willie had started out with a heavy cold which worsened acutely, but he refused to take time off. Kate became more worried; his responses became slow and confused. She called in Howard Williams, their old friend, asking him to give Willie a talking-to. Seeing him gasping for breath, Howard realized that he was very ill and called in a doctor. Pneumonia was diagnosed and Willie was rushed into the local hospital. Lady Collins heard of it and insisted that he be transferred to the prestigious London Clinic, for treatment at her own expense. As Lord

Moran said of Winston Churchill, 'When a man approaching his seventieth year gets pneumonia, it is, broadly speaking, the heart and not the lungs that decide the issue.' It was true of Willie, who was placed on the danger list as a cardiac arrest intervened. At one stage they actually gave up hope. Ronnie was flown down from Glasgow to support his mother. Willie quietly got on with his own ultimate battle.

The Christian world responded as the news broke; special prayers and even vigils were arranged, and a torrent of letters and get-well cards poured in. 'Bible Man Barclay ordered to Rest' proclaimed one newspaper. Its journalist, Vincent Donnelly, provided the unusual comment that Willie had become incoherent. Others similarly passed on the worst to their readers. Elton Trueblood, a key news-shaker in the USA, published his obituary in *Quaker News*! Willie defied their fears, as he had defied their warnings, and slowly recovered. But not without getting a shock: his doctors gave him six to eight years before his heart would give out completely, thanks to the damage his lifestyle had inflicted on it. Charles Duthie went to visit him, finding him looking 'really feeble', an extraordinary understatement for he was still at death's door. During the medical examinations, in addition to his weakened heart and lungs (emphysema was diagnosed), it was found that he had Parkinson's Disease, an irreversible neurological ailment. He was now a marked man, about to learn in fuller meaning the Orphic tag, 'the body is a tomb'.

Highly strung, unwell as she was, it proved too much for Kate, who came close to a complete breakdown. The history of them both from now on was to be one of unrelenting physical disability, now one ill, now the other. It was not helped by the sheer insensitivity of some colleagues and publishers. Willie's Holy Week Lectures at St Giles were never given, and other work was cancelled. 'I am being very obedient,' he wrote meekly to Braidwood, adding, 'Kate sees to it that I am.' But there were to be very many artful manoeuvres along the way, not least in the preparation of his Baird Lectures, which he was determined to fufil. He still insisted on typing many of his letters, despite the strenuous attempts of Kate and Mrs Gow, his secretary, to stop him. The typing of this 'handless creature' had not improved. To Millard he wrote, 'I hope to go off to Troon [to one of Kate's sisters] tomorrow for a week or ten days torecup erate [sic].' This last was typical of his typing, to which was added an abundance of overstrikes and even grammatical errors. The doctors forbade him to conduct the College Choir, which he continued to do, though he did accept their ban on preaching ('for which I am devoutly grateful').

He disclosed his true attitude (which was not at all obedient) when he said, 'The doctors tell me that if only I can learn to say No I shall live to be 100. I doubt if anyone would want to live to be 100 spending their time saying No.' He was not about to alter the habits of a lifetime, which Kate recalled had been apparent on their honeymoon and earlier. It was the familiar artifice of their 'holidaying'. He would make half-promises not to work, or at least to do very little. She would then find the boot of his car stuffed with books and papers, which would slowly infiltrate their bedroom wherever they were staying. His 'disobedience' concerned other matters, too. He wrote this to another correspondent anxious for his well-being, 'I have not smoked since Christmas Day. Fortunately there are other pleasures which the doctors have not forbidden!' The reference was to his love of nature, of food – but chiefly to a growing dependence on whisky, which he said he needed in order to facilitate his reduced lifestyle, unwisely taken with his pills. It relaxed him, it helped him sleep. Kate worried increasingly. She was hospitalized in the spring of 1970 repeatedly, for 'stomach disorders' and chronic depression.

By the end of the year Willie had regained some of his ebullience; he had proved that he was indestructible. He suggested publicly that unmarried women should be allowed the contraceptive pill, which was met by a howl of disagreement. His critics labelled it 'a capitulation to permissiveness', which was to remain part of his label to the end, ethically and theologically, as his opponents continued to miss his point. (On this topic unwanted children were his focus, not casual intercourse.) The General Assembly of the Church of Scotland ruled against allowing the pill to 'unmarried promiscuous women'. He disagreed with it decisively. In this, as in other practical things, he was often ahead of his contemporaries. Their obscurantism (as he saw it) only served to alienate him further from the Church's centralized leadership, along with the common man.

It was at the point of no return. He wrote, for example, to Bill Christman concerning a challenging manuscript Christman had written about his ministerial experiences at Craigmillar, an area of great social destitution near Edinburgh. Willie was anxious to find a publisher for him. 'There is of course the St Andrew Press,' he opined, 'but if we could get a national [sic] publisher to take the manuscript it would obviously be far better.' (I did publish it – to resounding success – after it had been turned down by the Press's 'expert' reader.) To another he wrote, 'I am sorry to appear to be disloyal but I would really regard the St Andrew Press as a last refuge.' Willie was indignant for the marginalized people – and those who failed to serve them. He had to speak out.

He was particularly disappointed to learn that Howard Williams' liberalizing journal *The New Christian* had failed. He loved its daring. Orthodox doctrine was now under constant pressure, which Willie handled with panache, often disagreeing with its exponents for their wooden views. Although given to making earcatching statements, he was essentially a middle-of-the road man, actually conservative on many issues. The conservatives could not understand him; the true radicals did not wish to. He was against the idea of miracles occurring for 'their own sake'. He was not interested in their historicity, but in their present-day meaning. 'What do they mean for us today?' was his challenge.

His old friend Charles Duthie stirred things by commenting on the Virgin Birth; Willie fanned the flames of controversy a little further. He was very aware of Edwyn Bevan's dictum, 'Argument ... in religion can do no more than clear the track; it cannot make the engine move.' Willie loved railway engines! He wanted to see them moving. In the rush to criticize him, the subtlety of his viewpoints was usually bludgeoned out of sight, his bold faith in the power of Christ and his gospel slighted, his clear message of love as the dominant gospel motif ignored, along with its corollaries of tolerance and respect. He recognized that many denigrated and misrepresented him deliberately, too often fearful for their own faith. They were the opposite of the messengers of goodwill; they could not see his point of relevance, too often energized by *wilful* unkindness – they who could not love God because they did not love their brother, still less preach for him effectively.

Other issues seethed. Pope Paul VI created a ferment in his encyclical *Humanae Vitae*, which even senior Catholics found disappointing. Willie added his voice to the dissent. John Allegro caused a commotion when his *Sacred Mushroom and the Cross* was published – 'an academic practical joke' according to one commentator. Willie ignored this issue completely, content to work at his 'iron rations'. He was pressing on, ever adventurously, if now much less dynamically.

TWENTY-ONE

OF FAITH AND WORKS

> There is an imperative which immediately dictates
> a certain mode of behaviour ... [it] may be called
> that of *morality*.
>
> (Immanuel Kant, *Outline of the Metaphysique of Morals*)

Critics of his theology frequently ignore Willie's deliberate gadfly technique, an historical and useful means of provoking thought, though not a safe one – as Socrates proved. Willie was unconcerned about matters of personal prestige; names would never hurt him. But the provocations he made from time to time stimulated discussion in the wrong direction by making of them a subsidiary point, and diverting attention from the main emphasis.

He was charged by some with being a turncoat; vilified by others as a *trahison des clercs*. It cannot be doubted that he led with his chin on a number of issues: pacifism, alcohol, nuclear disarmament, tobacco, church dress, contraception, women clergy, even Church union when understood as uniformity. Such were some of the practical issues on which he pronounced and for which he became well known. Outsiders loved him for it; they bought him drinks and cigarettes, and were open in their admiration. Larger issues – some elements of the New Testament, the nature of Christ, the secularity of God's working, the status and priorities of the Church – were frequently overtaken by day-to-day issues. As he aged he became more combative, his sense of proportion less noticeable; the press made hay by using him now as goad, now as an Aunt Sally. He was still glad to be found useful!

The growing problem of ministerial shortages was affecting chaplaincy appointments. It was raised at a Chaplains' Conference. Willie judged the proposed solution unfair, 'This is bad for the Air Force and bad for the Church of Scotland. If we do not get Church of Scotland Chaplains the jobs will go to Methodists. I have nothing against Methodists, but I prefer a first-division team when I can get it,' he said provocatively. It was similar to his earlier condemnation of theological students who refused to study Greek: only the linguistically trained can truly understand the New Testament; *ergo*, only they are really worthy of the job. It is an overstatement to say that denominational labels had no meaning for him beyond the descriptive, but he had little patience for their dated shibboleths. He was notably free of the *odium ecclesiasticum* that pervaded the attitudes of many, that diminished his call for excellence, which he ever sought to exercise. A *free* churchman to the core, he was never happier than when serving in non-church or inter-denominational activities. He despised religious imperialism.

His was a highly practical approach – ever the very practical Professor. At this very time he wrote to the Superintendent of Fabric at the University, ticking him off about the state of the road outside his Faculty building. His mundane caring was also apparent in his attendance at the Hutchenstown and Gorbals Youth and Community Association's committee meetings. This reputed non-committee-man was ever willing to throw his weight behind *real* schemes, to get *real* work done – an integral part of his goodwill attitude, which brooked neither doctrinal nor denominational tyranny, still less procedural obfuscation.

Major Fred Brown of the Salvation Army was roughly ousted from his position, due to statements allegedly antithetical of the gospel. Willie, an intense admirer of the SA, was grieved. He knew Brown well, had often preached for him when in London, and knew the real motives behind his courageous book, *Secular Evangelism* – a title dear to his own methods. He reviewed it with great sympathy, arguing Brown's cause for him – and cheerfully getting himself entangled in the crossfire. He knew that many of the critics who attacked him would never be seen caring for drug addicts, talking prostitutes away from their work, offering bowls of soup to the destitute, or carrying drunks back home. Brown was willing to 'dirty his hands' in the cause of the Kingdom of God; in such work superficialities had to be let go – as Jesus had let them go. Willie honoured Brown for his stand; more, he challenged his readers to emulate him. He selected four principles from Brown's book, which might be termed his own:

1. His search for a new *language* to reach modern man.
2. The traditional *expression* of evangelical belief to be recognized as failing the great cause.
3. Lifestyle, rather than belief, to be our preoccupation: 'by their *works* shall you know them...'

4. Genuine involvement with *society*, in specific actions, not the idle repetition of creeds, prayers or hymns.

The second St Andrews Summer School was organized for 1971, which drew 166 attenders. After one session Willie was found asleep by Professor Best and an American colleague. 'Gee, what a worker that man is!' exclaimed the visitor, unaware that a wee dram had more than one beneficial effect. To Howard Williams, anxious about his refusal to obey doctors' orders – Kate had gone off on holiday – Willie wrote, 'I myself have more or less recovered ... I am pretty normal again.' It was not an entirely true statement: he *felt* that he was normal again, and so he must be. Later, the family took a holiday together, grandchildren and all – though without Jane, who was flexing the muscles of her independency again. They spent the time at their then favourite watering hole, the Marine Hotel, Elie. The weather was beastly, but Willie was unfazed: he had taken his books and typewriter with him... While they weathered the inclemency, he worked contentedly.

He opened the academic year by attending a conference of the SSSU at Largs, speaking twice on the same day. His next major event, faculty work apart, was to deliver two lectures under the auspices of the Royal Philosophical Society of Glasgow on 'Situation Ethics', a subject taken from the influential book of that title by Professor J. Fletcher of Philadelphia. They were virtually a rehearsal for Willie's Baird Lectures, which provide a neat example of his readiness to comply with others' wishes – goodwill ever operative. He had proposed for a title 'The Christian Ethic in the Twentieth Century', which was rejected by the television managers as being too egg-headed. So 'The New Testament Way of Life in the Twentieth Century' was suggested. That, too, was vetoed. Ronnie Falconer then suggested 'Jesus Today: the Christian Ethic in the Twentieth Century', to be advertised simply as 'Jesus Today', which Willie found acceptable – perfect indeed. The Lectures were eventually published as *Ethics in a Permissive Society*. This is not the place to engage with the detail of these lectures, but I note their headings to adduce their focus:

1. The Cradle of Christian Ethics [the Old Testament]
2. The Ethics of Jesus
3. 'Situation Ethics' [i.e. Are ethics absolute?]
4. Work
5. The Christian and the Community
6. Person-to-Person Ethics

These headings are not merely representative of the interests of the seething sixties, about to topple into the winterish seventies, but of the whole thrust of William Barclay's teaching – biblically based, centred on Jesus, contemporarily oriented, and *practical*. That focus is particularly his when questions of changelessness are raised, when issues of work erupt, when community interests collide with those of the individual. But the range limited by the lectures was unsatisfactory to him. As usual, he had too much to say, i.e. too much which needed saying. On publication he added three extra aspects: on the ethics of Paul, of pleasure, and of money.

The thoroughness of his preparation is reflected in the list of books 'which have been especially helpful to me' for the lectures. They number over eighty titles – the equivalent of ten to a chapter. He had carefully secreted them in a case to take on holiday, which Kate, unknowing, tried to put in their car boot. She could not even raise it from the ground, it was so heavy. Her reaction has not been recorded. His booklist covers the best treatment of his themes for the last hundred years, from Selby-Bigges' *British Moralists* (1870) to the just-released paperback edition of D. J. Allan's *The Philosophy of Aristotle*. Moreover, they looked at every ethical theory of note, whether Jewish, Greek, Roman or modern.

Significantly – and nothing is more significant for his method than this – he had reread the New Testament in its entirety ('and most of the Old,' he added), in order 'to come to a *scriptural* understanding of the Christian ethic'. Most men of his experience – theologically trained, ministerially experienced, a lecturer for twenty-five years – would not feel a need to do this afresh for a course of lectures; they would already have the matter firmly outlined in their minds; as he had, in English and in Greek. All they would need to do is to rub up the latest theories, think a little, polish the views being aired, examine the critiques and so on. Nothing defines William Barclay's attitudes better than this continual and detailed recourse to his fundamental text, the Bible, even when that text was already firmly in his mind. He returned to it in order to sound it afresh, to listen newly to it – a learning and discovering man ever.

It is this attitude which explains Pritchard's characterization of him as 'a hard man' ethically – far from the wishy-washy liberal so many described. 'It may be,' Willie uncompromisingly declared, 'that what the Church needs to get the people back is not compromise, but a message of uncompromising purity.' The basis of some moderns – Bonhoeffer, Tillich, Robinson, Fletcher, *et alii* – was that man was now mature, come of age; he did not need the old props of precept and commandment. Not so, Willie asserted, against the tide. In that simple assertion he destroyed much that was taken for granted in the sixties, seventies and eighties. Pastorally he was 'soft' (in his sympathies); ethically he was 'hard' (in his standards). But he was never moralistic: the situation, the circumstances, the person, were always to be taken into account.

He was totally committed to morality being an intrinsic part of religion, an assumption then under increasing threat. At a more austere level it was being argued by such as Lord Denning and Professor Hart. Willie was not one to throw the baby out with the bathwater. His ethics had not ground to a halt on the old systems, biblical or otherwise; they were dynamically ordered. The Ten Commandments and the Sermon on the Mount formed the backbone of his ethics, as they did his religious focus. He knew the main systems of Aristotle, Kant, *et alii.*; he devoured the books which expounded them, such as Philippa Foot's *Theories of Ethics* or J. Hospers' *Human Conduct*. He was *au fait* with their critiques, not least from modern writers such as Marx, van Buren, Bishop Barry, Galbraith and Fletcher. He welcomed the British Council of Churches' *Sex and Morality* report (though not without criticism), which had caused such an outcry. He had his answers to the questions raised, yet he refused to offer them as definitive statements. His present lectures were merely 'to provide avenues for further thought', specifically 'not to offer any solutions'.

Five times in the last forty years he had been asked to address the matter of credal affirmation: in 1932, at his ordination, when he signed *ex animo* the subordinate Standards of his Church (*The Westminster Confession of Faith*, etc.); in 1940, when he presented 'A Faith for our Times' a.k.a. 'The Faith of a Christian'; in 1951, when he wrote *One Lord, One Faith, One Life* for the BB – actually reordering Paul's affirmation of Ephesians 4:5 to obviate denominational tension; in 1955, when he expounded *A Draft Catechism for Use in Sunday Schools*; and in 1967, when he dealt with the Apostles' Creed. The Baird Lectures provided the balance for this doctrinal concentration; the polarities of his faith were thus served: faith and practice, doctrine and behaviour, God and man. Their fulcrum, their standard and test, was always the Bible.

Almost all the great influences on his life were now dead, along with some of his closest colleagues. Retirement was firmly on the horizon, especially in view of the medical opinion of 1969 that he had but six years left, eight if fortunate. External matters changed, too. One was of great concern and sadness to him – the new editorship of the *British Weekly*. This had been of the greatest help to his career, in which the brilliance of Shaun Herron had played a notable part. The support, if not the genius, of Denis Duncan followed Herron's departure, but he had now retired, leaving it in the hands of John Capon, an able journalist but not one possessed of the great soul vision that had inspired Herron and Barclay. Across the top of the first letter from him Willie had written, 'Keep this for name' – a novel reaction from this man of incredible memory; his 'Dear Editor' letter – name forgotten – followed almost immediately.

The old style and warmth that had fed generations of *BW* readers were gone. Worse, the paper was being steered in a narrow, party direction. The conservative factions (the plural is necessary) were winning; the lurch to the right, though presently cautious, was under way. The bold, radical vibrancy of its early days, always underpinned by a strong biblical thrust, was now exchanged for the panaceas and superficialities of modern evangelicalism. Willie's views were subordinated to others'; his articles received lower-case headlines, and were printed in smaller type. The man whose journalistic flair had raised the paper to the heights was relegated to a corner. Willie's interests and emphases conflicted with that navel-gazing so much loved of the evangelicals. On 2 April 1971 Willie published a piece entitled 'When Everything's Gone'; his swansong.

This change was symbolic of a more general change taking place throughout western Christianity. Experience mattered more than knowledge; activity more than being. The easy believism of mass evangelism was popular – and populist. Why study the Bible when you can sing choruses that give an immediate buzz? Why risk abrasive reaction to your message when you can sit in a safe ghetto and pray? Protestant Christianity was more sharply divided than ever; small minds had taken over much of its leadership, some of them frankly worldly, even ashamed of its name, some timid, some venal. A General Secretary of the Inter-Varsity Press dared to publish material he knew to be controversial – but under a pseudonym! Men of the calibre of F. F. Bruce – who had spearheaded an intellectually rigorous biblicism – were regarded (when they were not being judged 'dull') as 'unsound'; they were no longer acceptable to the new evangelicalism. Willie's subtleties stood no chance in all this – a mind which was rich in the humanities, which sought to grapple with that love which is 'broader than the measures of man's mind', a memory which teemed with the learning and the adventures of mankind, a man whose view of God's grace was panoramic, who sought to speak boldly and think bravely: such a man was not acceptable.

The seventies took an increasingly defensive line in religion. Martyn Lloyd-Jones, doyen of the Reformed faction, who could preach for an hour on a split infinitive, called Willie 'the most dangerous man in Christendom' – a one-eyed judgement which entirely lacked goodwill, let alone soundness. Christendom had long ceased to exist, not least thanks to such men as Lloyd-Jones, ardent opponents of Church union – of anything, indeed, that did not have the stamp of Calvin (i.e. their idea of Calvin) across it. Barclay was too easy a target for moderation or even for facts to matter, and the ungodly smear wreaked its designed effect. 'Pelagian!' was an epithet loosely thrown at him by this faction, like an old cabbage at a man in the stocks. That it meant next to nothing for the average person was irrelevant; they were speaking to their own, when not speaking to themselves; others did not matter; 'goodwill to all' had been abandoned.

Willie did what he had always done under pressure: he pressed on. In April 1972 the annual choir tour took place in Fife. It was a special occasion for him, marking his twenty-fifth year as choir leader. Many changes had taken place over the years, not only the inclusion of modern pop songs in their repertoire (he had seen behind them, as others did not, to their aspirations and hopes which could be made a peg for greater thoughts) but also in the inclusion of young women and the use of guitars. He was not a man to let the grass grow under his feet: 'Forwards, not backwards.' At the end of the concert at Methil a surprise presentation was made to him: a silver chalice and a silver baton. In June 1972 he finally quit the *British Weekly*, leaving the paper, once a world-leader, to fizzle on – and then fizzle out. Duncan had commented that Willie's work was 'one of the most extraordinary pieces of output in religious journalism', but few *BW* readers were still there to read or understand it; they had abandoned a sinking ship.

He had spent thirty-two of his sixty-four years in the University: seven as student, seventeen as lecturer, eight as Professor. He was now one of the senior men, perhaps the last of the old breed. He bemoaned the lack of students proficient in Greek; real learning, for its own sake, had largely disappeared; the pulpit was being downgraded; the man who had always worked for the 'common man' regretted the empty populisms. He had even been an unwilling aid to this, for his *DSB* and other books were now shamelessly used by ministers, despite the books' design as a *devotional* daily aids. They wanted quick fixes, and

their people got them – second-hand. Willie, against his better judgement, had agreed to a first-degree Divinity course being introduced, in
which neither Greek nor Hebrew was required. He was still doing all
the first-year work himself, the newly revised syllabus requiring twenty different examination papers to be prepared and marked. His help
had been increased: John Riches had joined Neil Alexander (now
Senior Lecturer) as Junior Assistant, bringing a knowledge of German
to the department which, Willie admitted, 'we do not really possess'.

He decided to retire at the end of the session, five years earlier than
necessary. 'I flourish,' he informed a former student, 'but grow shorter in breath.' But it was Kate's health that now caused the greater anx-
ieties. A martyr to constant migraines, she lost more weight and had
to be hospitalized three times during this year; then she fell and broke
her hip, which failed to respond properly to treatment – until they
found that she had broken her pelvis as well. Given drugs to alleviate
the pain, she developed an allergy which exacerbated her condition.
After three months and barely recovered – they found a cracked rib in
the investigations – she fell again and broke three more ribs; a little
while later she broke her finger.

To their great consternation, their house was put under a
Compulsory Purchase Order, to make way for road widening. Unwell
and struggling, ageing and exhausted, they had to start looking for a
new house, with all the upheavals that entails – not least of which was
Willie's large library. Once again friends and students benefited from
his generosity; over a thousand books were given away in the move.

It now took him forty minutes to dress each morning, a painful
ordeal, frail before his time – as was Kate. The years of personal neglect,
chiefly in the six years of the war, and the regime of one hundred
working hours a week over many years had all played their destructive
part. To this was added his heavy smoking and his heavy drinking –
twin evils – plus his much-loved chocolate biscuits and cheese, which
had kept him going for others. (He later told Richard Mulkerne that his
diet consisted of chocolate and whisky.) He of the photographic memory was now becoming forgetful. Doors were left open, lights on, fires
unguarded, the cooker lit, and cigarettes smouldering – a nightmare
scenario, especially to one of Kate's nervous disposition. She again
altered her own lifestyle to take care of his, waiting up late, half dead
with fatigue, until he had gone to bed – merely to ensure that everything was safe before she herself retired; knowing that he was likely to
get up in the middle of the night, and expose them again to danger. The
glorious ministry celebrated around the world was fast coming to an

inglorious end, while they were still being hounded by publishers, self-serving friends and students, few really *caring* for them in their plight – to Kate's expressed indignation.

Willie gamely plodded on, going on tour with the College Choir in the spring of 1973, happily around Ayrshire, Kate's home ground. The American Summer School had now developed into 'the American Institute', its numbers having grown to 180 (346 applied). Its popularity was very largely due to the esteem in which he was held, Willie admitting that he was 'no longer efficient'. In October he commenced his final academic year. His department saw an increase in student interest: there were fifty-four in all, fifteen of which were women, from England. The great change had moved up a gear. Curiously, his 1947 hopes of teaching RE were now partly fulfilled, though in very different circumstances. He still found that teaching the first year was 'an exciting proposition', a mutual discovery, though he had 'the odd sensation of doing things for the last time'.

News of his retirement had broken earlier, in the spring, to worldwide acclaim, though some of the reporting was predictably negative, predictably lacking in goodwill. *The Scottish Daily Express* spoke ambiguously of his 'forthright Christian views' – as if a preacher/prophet should not be forthright; *The Glasgow Herald* happily commented that 'he has strived throughout his career to be an ordinary man, and has succeeded so brilliantly as to have become an extraordinary one'; *The Daily Express* muttered that 'controversy has always dogged his steps'; a New Zealand paper spoke of 'the prowling, growling television personality' as if he had no worthier attributes. The same paper rewarmed an old matter when it reproduced his defence of the rejection of the Moderatorship: 'I've never been a member of the establishment,' he reaffirmed.

And so Willie 'got finished up' as he put it to Bill Telford, a former student. He gave his last lectures at Trinity College, and then went across to New College, Edinburgh, to give a course of lectures to its students, following which he gave three lectures on Christian ethics to the Association of YMCA Secretaries. Then he returned to St Andrews for the 1974 Summer School, attended by over two hundred ministers: his way of finishing, as of starting.

If it was a quieter summer than usual, even though he admitted working twelve hours a day, the autumn started with a bang. He was appointed to his second Professorship – at the University of Strathclyde, Glasgow. It had come about through the good offices of Sir Samuel Curran, Principal and Vice-Chancellor of the University,

with whom Willie had been made a Freeman of the Borough of
Motherwell in 1967; also through the efforts of Professor William
Fletcher (not Joseph, above), a biologist and an active member (unlike
Willie) of the Royal Philosophical Society of Glasgow. It was a Visiting
Professorship – there were thirty or so of them at Strathclyde – so it
was not deemed too onerous for the plainly exhausted incumbent, ten-
able for five years, renewable annually. Its appeal was that it followed
the adventuring pursuits of the Young People's Society meetings at
Trinity Renfrew and those at Williamwood with Colin Campbell. Sir
Samuel commented:

> He was supposed to work mainly in this seminar fashion, and cer-
> tainly it was hoped that he would encourage a mutual interest in
> the wide variety of disciplines found in universities. We did not
> want to see him as a theologian, but rather as someone who was
> very widely informed and very willing to talk with experts in a
> considerable range of expert disciplines.

There could have been few accolades more cheering than this to
William Barclay, who all his life had sought to make a uni-verse of his
beliefs and experiences, whether in the greenwood hopes of his undergraduate years, the grime and sweat of his Renfrew parish, the high
cosmic theology of his Paul and John studies, or among the wasted
lives of a tear- and alcohol-sodden humanity around him, in Soho, as
in the Gorbals. Once again, aged sixty-seven, 'he buckled right in with
a trace of a grin/On his face...' He said to the Vice-Chancellor, recol-
lecting the earlier rejection, 'in my old age the dream is realized'. Had
it been 'an empty gesture' – a doctorate (several had been offered him
by American universities; some were even awarded to him in his
absence), or a Citation for this or that, he would have responded kindly, gladdened, but wondering what the *relevance* or the *usefulness* was.
But this was *real* recognition, among experts, in a multi-discipline
situation, which owned that the gospel had something relevant to say
to it, and which concerned itself with Jesus and *his* world-view.

He was formally fêted at the University of Glasgow by Sir William
Gray, Lord Provost of Glasgow, and Sir Charles Wilson, Vice-
Chancellor. Two former students, presently engaged in editing a
festschrift volume in his honour – J. Miller and J. McKay – also spoke. It
was followed by a less formal celebration, chaired by James Martin:
'The Plain Man's Tribute to William Barclay', at which a number of
friends from the UK and the USA gave speeches. *The Bush* presented

him with a cheque 'representing the people of Glasgow', and Kate was also given a gift. Sixty of the ministers present organized themselves into an impromptu choir and sang for him. Willie growled in the background, 'You were aye good at singing, but not so good at listening!' – his definitive judgement on them. The General Assembly played its part, too, honouring the one who had been unwilling to honour it by his leadership – a moment flawed by the behaviour of Jack Glass, a 'reformed' minister, who pointedly turned his back on the proffered hand of friendship Willie extended to him before the press; ill will triumphant, *plus ça change...*

Willie celebrated his own severance from the University in his preferred way: by publishing another book, the first volume of his two-volume work, *The Gospel and Acts.* It was a happy moment. Technically, it was a revision of his *The First Three Gospels*, published in 1966, itself a revised and expanded edition of his *BW* articles of 1962. Principal Michael Green had heralded its original publication as one of the best things Willie had ever written; many now endorsed that claim, not a little glad that he had at long last made a solid contribution to his own academic field. It brought his views up to date, adding a chapter on redaction criticism and one on historiography; best of all it extended the range of the original book to include John and Acts. It was the largest introduction to its subject in English, and has lasted for over twenty years.

Among those interviewing him at this time was the sports commentator, Arthur Montford, for Radio Clyde in its *Meeting Place* series. Few things of this time exhibit Willie so well as this broadcast, which Radio Clyde kindly allowed me to republish as a music cassette (under the title *A Man and his Music*) in 1986. The interviewer outlined Willie's life, reminded his interviewee of its salient points, and evoked some lively comment, both spicy and humorous. Between these exchanges his favourite music was played: the Highland pipes; Tchaikovsky's *Romeo and Juliet*; Kenneth McKellar singing *All the Things You Are*; Ravel's *Bolero*; The Beatles singing *Yesterday*; Gilbert and Sullivan's *Iolanthe*; Russ Conway on the piano playing *Misty*; the slow movement from Antonín Dvořàk's *New World Symphony* which brought the delightful session to an end. Willie emphasized in this selection his abiding interests, as he bullishly projected his principles, finding the good in each, after the manner of Philippians 4:8 – almost his personal motto.

In the exchanges with Montford he said much more. One point concerned the BBC, which had 'lost hope of me' in broadcasting –

which had nevertheless swept the world; another, more significant, concerned his disappointment when the Church turned him down for the Chair of Practical Theology, a rejection which still rankled. There were fond memories of his and Kate's 'blissful happiness' at Trinity Renfrew; of its huge Sunday School where he had baptized every child personally by the time he had left; of the one thousand homes he could enter to visit, laugh and pray.

He offered some parting advice: to ministers to take big subjects and preach them, avoiding big words; to do away with 'the hymn-sandwich' habit of worship (today we should call it designer religion, a genuine opiate, never more so than when in the hands of 'the corporate speakers of smooth things'); to church members to give up their selfish ways and experiment in worship and service. He warned that the Church of Scotland was sure to become much smaller – a prophecy which is being abundantly fulfilled, thanks not least to the rejection of his methods. Finally, he emphasized two main points: his method of 'threshold evangelism' and its place in his literary work and ethical perceptions; and his present new work, which was continually thrilling him.

The work that was thrilling him most, however, was not his new Professorship, much as he enjoyed it, but 'a new office and a new job'. For years he had spoken of doing for the Old Testament what his *DSB* had done for the New. The earliest published reference to it appears in an interview he gave to James Gilfillan in 1966, but he had long cherished the idea, and even longer expounded the Old Testament itself. His very first sermon, in 1925, was on Isaiah 9:6, and the IBRA Notes I republished as *Seven New Wineskins* in 1986 were a continuation of it. He had preached from it all his life, of course, regarding it as an integral part of Scripture. His New Testament commentary is full of Old Testament references – over 2,500 of them. But the opportunity to write on it more formally (not least from the Westminster Press in America who had been pressing him for years) was never grasped; he was too preoccupied, too ready to say 'yes' to projects on which he had already given his last word.

It has to be said that some of his Old Testament colleagues were not amused at his intentions to work in their area. It was not merely professional jealousy. His Hebrew was deficient; his knowledge of ancient customs second-hand and dated; his involvement with some of the more recent movements – we have already observed it with regard to the Dead Sea Scrolls – was all but absent. Worse, he had not revised some of the old ideas of his conservative upbringing – his trinitarian explanation of the plural of majesty at Genesis 1:26 mentioned earlier is a case in point. Nevertheless, it cannot seriously be doubted that he had something important to say on it. The opposers were up to their old tricks, saying yet again that 'it couldn't be done' – because they could not do it.

By 4 January 1972, Willie was already embarked on the project afresh, ensconced in an office placed at his disposal by William Collins & Sons Ltd in Glasgow specifically to facilitate his Old Testament work. The Saint Andrew Press was not amused. They had been toying with the idea for years. I found some of the correspondence referring to it when I became its manager. Their problem all along – apart from commercial timidity – was that they could not find a William Barclay willing to do the job for them. In other matters they had blotted their copybook with him. Their Old Testament advisors were unanimous in *not* allowing Willie to do it. The American publishers of the *DSB* took umbrage at Collins' move, and patented the title under his name – to prevent them from usurping it.

Willie did not always help himself. He told Bill Telford, a former student, 'I know nothing about the Old Testament,' when he informed him of the new scheme. To a reporter from *The Glasgow Herald*, with the pessimistic medical report of 1969 still ringing in his ears, and with stylish logicality, he commented, 'It will be a Schubertian situation ... I'll be dead before it's finished.' He did, indeed, find himself struggling with the project; but this came as much from the *extra* labours he now undertook for Collins (to say nothing of those of his new Professorship) as from the problems he encountered in the work itself. Further, his health again received some extremely serious, even life-threatening, setbacks. But we must retrace our steps a little.

In 1975 Mowbrays published *Testament of Faith*, which was not originally envisaged as an autobiography, though that had also been asked of him. It was intended to be a statement of belief under the title *What I Believe*. Willie said to Richard Mulkerne, A. R. Mowbrays' commissioning editor, in replying to the invitation:

> I am sadly aware ... that I am no theologian. I mean this. I know what I can do! I am a good linguist and a good student of New Testament background and history, but I fall down very badly on the theological side and on what Tillich used to call 'conceptualization'. It may be that like Miles Coverdale when he started to

translate the New Testament ... I should take this [invitation] as a
sign that I should do it because, as I said, since no one else will do it
this poor creature must try.

He added that he was saddened by the tendency of many scholars 'to
continue to give us works which would be entitled *WHAT I DON'T
BELIEVE* rather than *WHAT I DO BELIEVE*', a stroke against such as
John Robinson of Woolwich, whose obfuscating books sold well but
shed less light than the heat they engendered. He promised to start
writing by the end of 1971 – he was still under strict medical supervision – and to finish it within eighteen months. 'It would be very simple,'
he continued, 'and in any case the philosophers and the theologians
would smile, if not laugh, but it would be interesting to see what I do
believe. I have often wondered and this might be the chance to find out.'
The teasing comment bears consideration. In effect he is reiterating the
view of Bishop Barry who argued that the creeds were *corporate* statements of the Church, not personal ones; he is suggesting that in his
doctrinal expositions he had been working for that purpose – speaking
for others. Now was the time for something new: personal affirmation.
     Graham Green said of autobiography, 'It begins late and it ends
prematurely ... Any conclusion must be arbitrary.' The arbitrariness in
Willie's 'autobiography' marks the book from cover to cover. It was sig-
nalled in another letter to Mulkerne six months later (in reply to one
of those chasing letters which were so angering Kate), in which Willie,
his mortality confronting him, suggested the change of title – to
Testament of Faith. The correspondence is worth noting, for it reveals
not only 'arbitrariness' but confusion. He has moved from personal
witness to autobiography: '...unless it contains some passages of autobiography it will not really explain such faith as I have. I think it must
be partly a personal story and partly a personal testament.' Mulkerne
was delighted, but he was becoming anxious, very aware of the deterioration in his author's health. Another chaser (in which an outline of the book was asked for) elicited another reply: 'It will not be
easy for me to supply an outline because I am afraid I have a bad habit
of writing books without making an outline except in a most brief
way. I find that a book writes itself or it doesn't write it at all, but there
will be some kind of outline, no doubt.' A further six months on he
was again making promises; this time 'to have the book ready for the
autumn delivery to you'.
     In the meantime he accepted more *par erga*. He was asked to speak
on the radio programme 'Thought for the Day', from which developed

'a vast correspondence'. He promised an Australian network ten broadcasts, and an American six – quite apart from fending off John Bowden over the revision of *The First Three Gospels*, stating that his work was under pressure as he was 'the only person left of seniority on the premises'. By March 1973 he was at it again, thanking Mulkerne for being 'unbelievably patient' (those working for Richard had not noticed this); he exempted him from the charge of 'nagging', which Kate did not. A new start date was promised, for September, eighteen months later than the original. In June he confessed to being troubled as to 'what to put in and what to leave out'.

Two weeks after the 1973 St Andrews Summer School concluded, Willie wrote triumphantly, 'I am actually writing the book at the moment and having some pleasure in doing it.' In the writing his beliefs had become merged with personal reminiscence. Two weeks later he was rushed into hospital, once more in intensive care, once more life-threatened, once more beset by pneumonia and at risk of cardiac failure. Mrs Alexandria, his new secretary, wrote to Mulkerne tersely on Kate's say-so: 'His convalescence will be of unpredictable duration.' From around the world correspondence rained down on his office and home; both his secretary and his wife were inundated by it – Kate struggling to control her fears of losing him as well as coping with her own indifferent health. Together they decided, Willie agreeing, that the answer to the endless enquiries and good wishes was a circular letter, the fourth such. While it was being prepared Willie sent a message to Mulkerne, saying that he should not worry, that the manuscript would arrive 'about a month later than he had originally [sic] planned'. But the recovery was slow; other interests were allowed to elbow their way into his life and timetable, and the manuscript lay untouched.

In February 1974, the first three chapters of *Testament of Faith* were delivered, a mere sixty-eight pages in all, and an odd package: chapter 1 'This for Remembrance', which outlined his debts to his family, teachers and friends; chapter 2 'Self-Portrait', a description of the artist as an old man; and chapter 3 'I Believe', an outline of his beliefs, truncated to be sure, which merely included the following headings: God; Jesus; life after death; the home, marriage and family. Though the points were well made, and include much beyond the headings themselves, the weariness and arbitrariness were obvious. One only has to think of the absence of the Bible, which he expounded in virtually everything he wrote, or the Church, which he served all his life, to realize that this was the effort of a drained man, during the writing of which he had almost forfeited his life: iron rations now mixed with clay. The proportions are worth noting: the first chapter was of eighteen pages; the second fifteen; the third thirty-five – a ratio of 33:35 in terms of faith and practice (i.e. ethics). It was disappointing, yet still impressive when we read an admission to a fellow minister of this time, 'I can hardly cross the road now [so bad were his leg ulcers].'

In sending these chapters to Mulkerne, Willie was at pains to apologize for the delays. The rest would follow quickly – a mere chapter, which would show how his beliefs were expressed in his work. He added a new, if exasperating, point: he was having, in this final year at the University, 'to write lectures for an honours student who is taking a course which was never taken before and which we never expected anyone to take' (itself a glaring admission; close students of his work will notice a curious ambivalence towards the apocryphal and pseudepigraphical writings). That is, he was writing the equivalent of a book – for one student. He said in concluding, 'If you want a commentary on *[The] Wisdom [of Solomon]* I could supply it almost overnight, but it has stopped other things.' The final chapter would be delivered in 'ten days or a fortnight'. Two and a half months later it arrived: chapter 4 'The Day's Work' – plus a new proposal, for a final-final chapter, 'Summing Up', which he decided must now be added and which he would write soon. He suggested that Mulkerne should visit him, which he did, flying to Glasgow – and all but flying back down the garden path in retreat as Kate, caught on one of her bad days, saw the anxious publisher off the premises.

On May 15 Willie wrote, 'At last the end has been reached.' He had completed the final chapter, the fifth, his 'Testament of Faith'. He had reread the whole, and found it somewhat repetitious, but he was content. 'Don't forget that meal together, when you come north,' he added, guilty over Mulkerne's expedited exit. But it was not the end of the matter. A former editor for SCM Press, Kathleen Downham, had been asked to prepare the manuscript for publication. She had long known Willie's capacity for sending in unfinished material (as well as his delight over good food and fine claret), and had done much to improve the finished quality of his work. She found this one too much – or, rather, its opposite. She listed the problems, admitted that it was 'not a literary production ... entirely personal to William Barclay', but nevertheless managed 'to pull some sentences together', adding that 'one cannot make it too neat a thing'.

John Stockdale, Mowbrays' chief editor, took the matter further and asked Willie for a bibliography of his work to put in the book. He was denied it in no uncertain terms. Willie said he could not remember what he had written! He commented testily to his secretary, a sign of his exhausted condition, 'If people don't know I write books they haven't been reading much.' Eva Jesse, Mowbrays' marketing manager, sent him a questionnaire; he refused to fill it in. The book limped to its conclusion. David Edwards, now Speaker's Chaplain at Westminster, was sent the heavily edited typescript and asked for a Preface – which Willie found 'embarrassingly kind'. He was asked to proof-correct it quickly, but held on to it as 'Kate must see it first'. It was even further delayed by one of her accidents; this time in the kitchen, when a pan of hot fat fell over her feet.

Mowbrays sent him a proof of the cover, which had already been delayed by his not having a photograph for it (eventually an old still was provided by the BBC). Horrors! Due to a fault in the separations his thin white hair did not show at all; his granddaughter's playful taunt of 'old bald-head' came painfully to light. Kate was dismayed; Willie merely growled, 'Horrible. I admit to being no oil painting, but I am not a Prussian Colonel.' His American publisher, W. B. Eerdmans, more aware of bad imaging, was anxious. He cabled Willie 'for a new photograph – or a new hairpiece!' He got it, and the people of America were able to enjoy his book *and* his silver locks.

So the long-delayed, not-so-neat thing went to press – and then around the world: his testament, borne of an ultimate labour, of invincible goodwill; his life as well as his labour; his practise as well as his belief: his uni-verse, his holistic integrity. His beliefs were not merely intellectual expressions, but practical (and devoted) statements, through soul-wrenching experiences. He made two attempts at defining his doctrinal position. This is not the place to deal in detail with the individual elements, but they are worth comparing. Their proportions – measured here only by page extent – are especially interesting: his iron rations.

'I believe'	'Testament of Faith'
1. God (pp. 37–41)	1. God (pp. 106–7)
2. The world (pp. 41–2)	2. The world (pp. 109–11)
3. The love of God (pp. 43–5)	3. God cares (p. 107)
4. Prayer (pp. 46–8)	
5. Jesus (pp. 48–53)	4. Jesus (pp. 107–9)
	5. The Holy Spirit (p. 109)
	6. Work (pp. 111–12)

Willie commented at the book's end, 'And so to the end – and if I were to begin life over again, I would choose exactly the same service.' It was ever that: a ministry, a service; one of consummate goodwill.

TWENTY-TWO

WEARY, BUT UNDEFEATED

*You have played enough; you have eaten and drunk enough.
It is time you went home.*

(Horace)

'It is very interesting,' Willie wrote to David Anderson, a former student working in the USA, of his work on the *DSB: Old Testament*, the first volume of which was to be on the Psalms. But he admitted that he was making 'very slow' progress. To another he was more explicit: 'In about two years something will happen' – a very long time, contrasted with his battery-hen habits of the fifties.

He had scarcely left the University but was already given to telling his friends that he no longer had news of his old Faculty, which disappointed him. He was having trouble letting go. He not only needed to be useful, he needed to be *seen* being useful. He was still having trouble saying 'no' to invitations, despite his arduous commitments to Collins and Strathclyde University. Aubrey Smith of the IBRA wrote to him, happily re-establishing old links – and asked for a book. Its title was to be *The Nature of God*, a follow-up to his *Testament of Faith*. Willie accepted the invitation, and 'cobbled it together' (his words) quickly. But it was not done well. His hand was losing its cunning, as Dean Inge said at a similar point in his own life. He offered to rewrite it, and the offer should have been taken up, but Smith was aware of the ebbing tide and published it more or less as it stood. At sixty-four pages it is Willie's shortest book – even shorter than his apprentice piece, *New Testament Studies* – and very far from his best work. His doctrine of God, his devotion to God, was infinitely richer than that presented here. It is curiously reliant on H. E. Fosdick, the passé American preacher-writer who played a very notable part in making liberal evangelicalism acceptable in the States, not least through his life-centred style: a *practical* theologian, whose booming Riverside Church, New York, activities influenced Willie from afar. Willie's mindset by this time no longer seems able to rise above past habits and conceptions; he was working on the spent capital of former years.

Another view of this may be seen in an interview he gave to Denis Duncan. His former editor wished to explore the influence on him of Highland evangelicalism, which historically had been conspicuously Calvinistic, and had led to some decidedly odd expressions of the love of God. Duncan asked what he thought the sovereignty of God had to do with prayer. Said Willie, 'I'm afraid I don't think much of the sovereignty of God. I think almost altogether of the fatherhood of God ... I don't think much of God as King so much as I think of him as Father. I'm not thinking so much of the control of God as I'm thinking of the love of God and the arrangement of my life and the enabling of me to lead life as it is.' At first glance it looks like a typical overreaction – his habit of exaggerating a point to emphasize another point he believes more important; a Barclayan trait. But those who work with people at any depth will be familiar with their practice of mis-answering questions, i.e. answering those which were not actually put to them, dealing instead with questions in their own minds. Willie does something like this here. He wants to assert a positive view, not a negative one, which was ever his preference: goodwill assertive. His mind was fixated on the love of God. He believed the Calvinist – the WDB – exaggeration of sovereignty needed to be offset by a heightening of the divine love and caring – and of humanity's responsibilities.

There are times when he appears to suggest a preference for Jesus over God. Jesus is 'our elder brother'; he is easier to understand; we relate to him more readily. Willie had problems with the doctrine of God, as all deep thinkers do. If God be God, he is by definition beyond our ken. He acknowledged those difficulties candidly. His own life had been cauterized by great suffering, as he knew others had. Easy palliatives were unuseful, almost blasphemous in their denial of God's ineffable nature. The letter from Ireland following Barbara's death, referred to earlier, is an example of another, if related, aspect: the superficial, black-and-white opinions of easy-believism, of fundamentalism. 'Your God is my devil,' he commented of it in *Testament of Faith*; the very exaggeration being an indication of his anger at such belittling of the divine nature. He loved the word 'Father' (*Abba*) when applied to God, and reasserted it with abandon. It had a meaning of particular significance to him – the loving sensitivity he had never received from his own father, perhaps. He aspired to that relationship, and taught others to do so. He reflected it in his own family life, being 'soft' and 'overgenerous' with his children in compensation. It represented to his mind something good and wholesome; ultimate caring; something more elevated than credal affirmations of 'God', or the harsh figure of a despotic Calvinism.

Prayer was the link, the fourth element of his beliefs given in his testament of faith. It follows the third – 'the love of God' – and shows the true centre of his faith. He offers four 'rules of prayer' in explanation, which are worth noting:

1. God will not do for us what we can do for ourselves.
2. We should not pray for material things but be content with what we have.
3. Prayer is not the evasion of difficulties, but a conquest over them.
4. Essentially, prayer is simply *being* in the presence of God.

His critics, and many of his readers, ignored the frequency with which he referred to his prayers, prayer life and his ministry of prayer. These are among the most outstanding of his characteristics, yet they were almost totally omitted from the obituaries and the many statements that have been made about him since. Curiously, church leaders are often embarrassed by prayer's reality; their compromises neutralize it.

When the Upper Room honoured him (see p. 298) it emphasized prayer as the second most important characteristic of Willie's life and work – below his Highland origin, his New Testament expertise, his ability to teach ministers and teachers, and his ability to write. Chronologically it was an obvious characteristic before these other points came to fruition, as the good people of Trinity Renfrew knew well. He taught tens of thousands throughout the world to pray. It is perhaps the hardest job of all in the ministry – one at which most ministers fail. Many write beautiful prayers, and say prayers beautifully. Very few make prayer a living reality in their lives and in that of their congregations. Their body language often demonstrates this: it is not the carriage of humble men who walk with God.

It was different with William Barclay. He lived, he walked and talked, as one who knew God. One should look carefully at his Rules of Prayer in *A Plain Man's Book of Prayers*, although they do not express his entire views on the subject. They positively ache with the burden of putting right that false concept of control which many have about prayer. Many of the rules are about ourselves, not God – our responsibility, our duty. 'Know thyself' echoes through them. His understanding of prayer is governed by natural order, natural law, as became a one-word exponent. They are 'secularist' in tone. In prayer we reshape ourselves to the mind of God; we do not ask him to reshape the world to our way of thinking or wanting. Yet – and it is a big yet – his prayers are saturated with love and goodness, with *Abba's* concern and caring.

Our theologizing is more personal than we imagine. The Church has frequently split on personality conflicts in the name of doctrine and truth; schisms of the deepest sort have their roots in such conflicts, and Church history demonstrates it. Willie's strengths rarely showed themselves in conceptualization, or in the field of systematic thinking. It partly explains why *The Nature of God* is such an inadequate book – why his comment about God's sovereignty comes across as lopsided. He could analyse and discriminate brilliantly, but he was never interested in constructing overall views, not least of God. His interest had ever been to live life as it was – in his presence.

There is evidence that by now his mental faculties had deteriorated; they had in fact been waning since the great collapse of 1969, which is not surprising given his major health problems. The details of his life are now if anything more ominous: his short-term memory lapses, his forgetfulness, his occasional logical confusion. Early information was still readily available to him, wondrously so; his memory for such was still phenomenal. Would we not call this Alzheimer's Disease today – or at least an incipient stage of it? Many of its symptons are classically present. It may well have been triggered by the uncovering in his weakness of his painful past – the rows with his father, the latter's tempestuous temper, his mother's cancerous and his daughter's watery deaths, the unending (and unfair) criticisms he had faced since starting to teach, and so on: all these had unsettled him very deeply. They raised questions about God's love and caring, for which 'decided answers' were not easy. Was this why Kate became so enraged when Richard Mulkerne pressured him to complete *The Testament of Faith*? Was she actually observing the damage it was doing to him even as he wrote it? Was this why its follow-up volume, *Why I Believe*, was never started, let alone finished? Those who wish to berate Willie with a large stick should pause for thought – and for charity.

In late April 1975 William Braidwood received a letter from Kate which was full of distress:

Dear Bill,
I simply don't know what to do!
    My husband is in the Royal Infirmary in a side-ward with an oxygen mask and heavily doped. I have been so worried about him for weeks as his breathing was getting so laboured. And what a struggle he was having walking, dressing, etc etc!

If you knew him the way I do, you would know that he never admits to being ill, and I had to take the law into my own hands and phone our doctor. When he came, he sent for a specialist, and within an hour an ambulance arrived and he was in Victoria.

I see him for about fifteen minutes [each day], but he is so doped I can't bother him with anything...

Pneumonia had struck again and Kate, also unwell, supporting herself by a walking stick, was once again having to cope with 'so many letters that my mind is more or less a blank by now'. Even those who praise Willie's work little know of the costs to him and to his wife. On some visiting days now he failed to recognize her, or his son Ronnie, reminding us again of the likelihood of Alzheimer's Disease. He could scarcely breath unaided, his heart condition was giving rise to additional concern, and his Parkinson's Disease prevented him from holding even his newspaper. They faced an uncertain future. Kate now admitted what she had long feared, what the specialist asked her to come to terms with, 'that Bill was the type who would die in harness'. Hopes of some quietness, some togetherness in the evening of life were banished. 'What comfort,' she cried, heartbroken, 'is that to me?'

The present crisis had been precipitated by an unusual event. The American publishing company The Upper Room, which produced daily reading matter akin to the IBRA scheme, organized each year a presentation to one or more of its leading figures for 'notable contributions in Worldwide Christian Fellowship'. This was made formal by means of an illustrated Citation which outlined the contributions of the recipients. Willie had long been known to its directors; they had published the American edition of his Laird Lectures for 1968 under the curious title *Meditations on Communicating the Gospel* (the style was declamatory not meditative). He and Professor James Stewart were presented with their Citations in Edinburgh, on 18 April 1975. The official photograph shows Willie *shrunk* in his suit, shoulders hunched as he sought to steady himself, his lips tight with effort, no trace of a grin possible. He greeted the Citation as a great honour – he was thereby placed, he reminded them, in that line of Christian communicators which included John Mott, Ralph Cushman, John Mackay, Helen Kim, Billy Graham and Elton Trueblood.

Noting that he was a native of Wick, the Citation isolated twelve areas of his work (listed as seven, but theologians are rarely numerate) which they had selected as the main elements of his work:

- Early master of New Testament studies / and teacher of preachers
- Prolific and disciplined writer with insight and power on the meaning of prayer
- Translator of the New Testament / and expositor of relevant biblical applications
- Appreciator of music / trainer and director of choirs
- Lover of persons / whose focus is upon interpretations vividly and strikingly stated
- Effective and versatile communicator of the Scriptures
- Faithful disciple of Jesus Christ / and untiring witness of his love for all the world

The presentation was made in the Edinburgh Assembly Rooms, in the presence of Archbishop (now Lord) Coggan of Canterbury (Anglican), Cardinal Gordon J. Gray (Roman Catholic Archbishop), Bailie John Gray, Neville Davidson (Church of Scotland), James Taylor (Baptist), William O. Weldon (Editor, The Upper Room), John Birkbeck (UK Editor and Organizer for the Upper Room), and several other notables representing, Willie said later, 'every credal colour in the rainbow in Britain': 480 people in all. A Loyal Message to the Queen was read, as was her Gracious Reply. The Salvation Army Singers offered musical entertainment, and a fine meal followed. Some wags wondered why Poachers' Broth had been offered at this arch-popularizer's celebration, but as it was followed by Edinburgh Fog – apparently a culinary delight – theological propriety was maintained.

Word of the celebrations proved to be too much for the religious kill-joys, whose decision to disrupt the occasion as an 'act of witness' came to the notice of the police. They had to provide uniformed and plainclothed escorts for these preachers of peace and goodwill. Jack Glass, whose religious enthusiasms (allegedly Reformed) outran his intellect, led the protesters on behalf of his party, as was his wont. The Very Reverend James Stewart, whose title was adorned by the man himself, of genuine Reformed faith, arrived in his own car. His attempts to park it near to the Assembly Rooms were stopped by an unknowing constable: 'I'm sorry, Sir, but these spaces are reserved for the VIPs.' Without more ado the Doctor of Divinity for whom the event had been organized drove off and parked it elsewhere. It was against such rare men that Glass and his minions fulminated. The attending police officers, who were not Churchmen, were nonetheless duly unimpressed – and said so.

The celebrations closed on a high note, with speeches by several of the leading men, including James Stewart and Willie. The latter spoke in clear and unambiguous terms on a subject he knew to be near to the heart of those present – and those shouting outside: justification by faith, the term being an unusual use for him of unplain language. 'This is a new William Barclay,' declared Donald Coggan, the Archbishop of Canterbury, a former Secretary of the Inter-Varsity Fellowship, one of the most conservative evangelical groups in the country, who had also failed to read his Barclay judiciously.

Jack Glass, locked outside and unable to hear what was being said, later added his own comments in *The Scottish Protestant* regardless of truth or charity, to be sure. He called Willie 'one of Scotland's most evil apostates ... False Professor William Barclay...' He went on to speak of 'this apostate ... a crafty emissary of hell ... a contaminator of the Gospel ... [and referred to his] blasphemies' – a spate of meaningless judgements, written with ungodly venom. Its determined ill-will may be judged by the fact that seven years later this sheet was still being handed out in Glasgow. I was given one myself, during my researches for this book. Such is the corrupted mentality of the theologically uneducated.

Willie, who saw through this particular glass clearly, sadly waved aside such attacks. He did not feel defensive towards people whose understanding of the law of love was so superficial; whose actions contradicted the very tenets they pretended to serve; who were motivated by a fear they could not name and a hatred they could not control. Willie suffered for those who were hurt by such, one of whom was his own wife, who was even now desperately holding on to her own equilibrium, fearful of the damage she believed the criticisms and hatred were doing to her husband of forty-two years.

'I don't know how he managed to get through that citation,' she later wrote. In fact, he very nearly did not. He was light-headed with fever, his body taut with pain, his strength all but spent. They got back to Glasgow, and Willie was rushed straight into intensive care. Two weeks later, at his hospital bed, Kate heard him repeating that the specialists had ruled out all summer work, that it must be cancelled. She dared to agree with them. 'That's nonsense!' he roundly declared. He was determined to go to the American Summer School in July, and to resume his literary work on returning. 'I can't stop Bill,' Kate wrote sadly. 'He loves every aspect of his work ... If only he would content himself with his new subject the Daily Bible Studies of the Old Testament ... but I know he won't.'

By 3 June he was up and active, promising books to several publishers – a volume of prayers 'very soon' to one; to another the steady continuance of the *DSB* project; to a third a six-month stint of weekly readings. Collins themselves delayed their own project by asking him to provide the introductory comments to their new edition of the *Revised Standard Version* – which, Willie said, 'reintroduced' him to Old Testament criticism! But he was only working half days, and struggling at that. The intake for the Summer School that year was 206, and Willie was there as promised. 'They almost kill you with kindness,' he commented, exhausted by the greetings and general bonhomie, which he loved. He was now taking nine different pills each day in an effort to control his various ailments. 'I rattle when I walk,' he observed, embarrassed at his pill-popping. He spoke frequently of the projects he had in hand, of those he was yet to embark on. But Kate and he knew it was not to be; the six ('perhaps eight') years promised to him by his doctors after the 1969 collapse were nearly up and they both felt it keenly.

There was still enjoyment in their lives. Keats once observed, 'A man's life of any worth is a continual allegory.' It is so with this man Barclay. His life symbolized the good life; a life shot through with goodwill, and with its natural enjoyments. Chief among the enjoyments this summer was their new motorcar, always a pleasure to Willie who, to Jane's annoyance, still 'drove down the middle of the road at 28 mph'. They had taken delivery of the Vauxhall Magnum 1800cc Automatic – 'a lovely vehicle'. It took them on their summer holiday to Arbroath, for which Willie said Kate had developed an addiction: its 'smokies' are world famous, and the crisp, eastern sea air was ideal for Willie's congested lungs. As usual his boot contained many books, though Kate did notice that they were fewer than hitherto. Thanks to his now prolonged cat-napping he was slowly recognizing his limitations. They had a custom of inviting former students to share some of their meals with them when staying in their districts. This year it was the turn of Robert Glover and his wife, particularly welcome to Willie and Kate, for Robert has a distinguished musical ability and there was much to talk about.

In October, at Strathclyde University, he began his work on Professional Ethics. Over 240 students gathered to listen to him: *not* religious students studying Divinity or New Testament, as he enthusiastically emphasized, but *secular* students, studying Production Engineering and allied subjects. Willie was 'thrilled'; 'rather more than half of them were Japanese, Chinese and Malaysians,' he wrote later.

Some excerpts from the lectures were published in *Life and Work* under the title 'Religion and Life'. He was at last engaged in a genuine secular involvement of the gospel and its ethic, and he loved it. This was real work! He used this and other opportunities to speak his mind on a wide range of general subjects. He even turned on his own university colleagues, who were presently withholding the examination results in order to gain higher pay. 'It hurts the wrong people,' he exclaimed.

To Senator Norman Paterson of Canada he commented – untactfully ignoring the former's concerns over his country's loss of its traditional trade – how glad he was that Britain was a member of the Common Market (as the EU was then called). He criticized Harold Wilson, the British Prime Minister, for being too much under the power of the trade unions, though emphasizing that he was himself pro-union in principle. A Salvation Army officer wrote calling him a socialist; a term which Willie said flattered him and his views. He had long forgotten his membership of the Liberal Club as a student, and his enjoyments of the National Liberal Club with Douglas Millard, though he did confess to being 'very far from being a supporter of the Labour Party'. He declaimed against Scottish devolution, and criticized Princess Margaret's marriage difficulties. He commented on the Queen's Jubilee celebrations, the Watergate scandal, even nudism. ('...nothing wrong with nudism itself ... I am sure a beach set apart for nudism and nudists would very soon become a very commonly accepted thing'). Many of his letters involved political matters, for example those between him and Malcolm Mackay, a former Minister of War in the Australian government at the time of Vietnam – a big enough problem for any man, let alone one with Moral Rearmament sympathies, a stance which intrigued Willie whose ethics were now questionably absolute. He regretted the lack of 'a Churchillian voice' in British politics, though he would doubtless have had much to say against the pseudo-Churchillian voice that erupted over the country in the name of monetarism shortly after his death. Behind all this lay his oft-repeated conviction that a preacher should be doubly armed – with his Bible in one hand and a newspaper in the other.

Medical mishaps plagued Kate and Willie afresh. 'She has cracked everything,' he wrote to Braidwood of his wife's brittle bone disorders, adding that she was also continuing to suffer from migraines. In February 1976 he went down with influenza, which developed into a new outbreak of his so-called 'bronchitis' (actually emphysema). Kate then went down with 'nettle-rash', clearly a neurological response to the unrelenting pressures. The gloom was lifted on the publication of

Biblical Studies in Honour of William Barclay, edited by J. McKay and J. Miller. Some of the best biblical scholars of the day had been invited to contribute to it, men whose own ministries had overlapped with Willie's – Hugh Anderson, Ernest Best, Robin Barbour, Matthew Black, George B. Caird, Robert Davidson, A. M. Hunter, George Johnston, W. D. McHardy, William Neil, J. C. O'Neill, Charles Scobie *et alii*. The range of articles was well balanced and served Willie's own interests: three on general introductory matters, two on the Old Testament, six on the New Testament, and two on doctrinal elements (politics and Christology). Professor J. C. O'Neill highlighted Willie's work by commenting, 'Professor William Barclay ... has done more than most New Testament scholars to keep open the traffic between scholars who argue – who must argue – about words and ordinary Christians who simply want help to pray and live.' Happily he noted the importance of prayer, even among such cerebral company.

Their joy was savagely ended by the destruction of their car and garage a few weeks later. A mentally disturbed youth had found their garage door open – presumably left so by Willie – and found within it a can of paraffin. He started a fire with it, which very nearly spread to their house and their neighbour's. The newspapers got hold of the story and soon their readers were reeling at the exaggerated comments being disseminated. 'Fire-Bomb Inferno' declared *The Scottish Daily Record*. Others saw in the incident the activities of the IRA. One actually had the almost immobile Willie searching for the incendiary device and 'pulled clear by a neighbour with only seconds to spare'. *The Scotsman* reported that he and Kate had been resting in bed at the time, unwell. They were also reported as being in their kitchen, making tea. Kate was said to have seen the lad enter the garage, then they saw the flames start up. Willie went out into the garden as the explosion from the car's petrol tank detonated; an explosion which blew their neighbour, John Langan, across the garden. He prevented Willie, who was worried about the car, having recently sold it, from getting too close to the fire. In addition to the unhelpful excitement, it also engendered more correspondence, and that on an international scale. A by-product of the story was that it became known that the Barclays had been subjected to 'gang slogans' being painted on their garage wall, usually of a sectarian nature. Jack House interviewed Willie for *The Glasgow Evening Times*. He found him in his pyjamas and dressing gown, admitting to delayed shock. He also admitted to writing 'about fifty books' (the number was actually over eighty), on whose royalties he was apparently paying over 80 per cent income tax. That worried

House. 'To tell you the truth,' Willie replied, 'money has become a nuisance to me.'

Richard Mulkerne had been promised another book, on the background to the New Testament (the subject of one of Willie's not yet republished *British Weekly* articles). This project went by the board. His concentration was failing, not only in his much-loved work but generally. Taking a corner too widely at Montrose one day, his car collided with a lorry, and his spotless record of forty-five years received its first blemish. He was taken to court, his license was endorsed, and he was fined five pounds. He and Kate, with their high moral social responsibility, were mortified, Kate especially so. His driving was becoming a matter of grave concern to her. She knew that he frequently drove after drinking alcohol – we must remember that the great campaigns against this of the eighties and nineties had not yet emphasized its dangers – but she feared an incident. It was but one more agonizing pressure.

At about this time Franco Zeffirelli's film *Jesus of Nazareth* created a sensation. It had a galaxy of superstars in its cast: such as Laurence Olivier, Robert Powell, Cyril Cuzack, Peter Ustinov, Michael York, Christopher Plummer, Anne Bancroft and Claudia Cardinale. Collins had purchased the book's publication rights and Willie was once more sidetracked from the *DSB Old Testament* to rework more authentically Anthony Burgess' and Cecchi d'Amico's text. 'Help, Willie; please help,' asked Lady Collins sweetly. The answer was never in question; more difficulty would have been found in stopping than starting him. Here was a marvellous new opportunity, a chance to move forwards! Having espoused the cause of 'threshold evangelism' all his working life, Willie was now offered the greatest possible way of expressing it, in the text of a blockbuster film, whose budget had been twelve million pounds, from whose 5,000 brilliant still photographs his illustrations would be selected. The Old Testament work took yet another back seat. He was given just two months to do the book, and he did it – with more than a trace of a grin. It appeared in 1977 in full colour, to resounding acclaim – and the shrill bleatings of those who cavilled at his daring to be associated with a book written by a secular author, which contained pictures of an actor playing Jesus.

Its appearance found Kate and Willie ill again, the winter having been one of the coldest on record. Influenza claimed them first, then their now usual follow-up disorders – Willie's chest complaints and Kate's nervous disability. He was told that his office at Collins was to be moved from the centre of Glasgow to its outskirts, necessitating a long journey for him. He hated such disruptions, and this one, he confessed, took him a week to recover from.

At the beginning of July 1977, Kate and he celebrated forty-four years of marriage. Together they limped round the corner of their road to a restaurant in Cathcart, Willie hobbling from the increased ulceration of his leg and some arthritis, Kate due to her rheumatic ankles. They had planned a return to Arbroath, but it was put off – they were simply too tired. Instead they took some short day-drives to their favourite spots south of Glasgow: Ayr, Troon and Prestwick. Seeking warmth, Kate became sunburned, which developed into a painful dermatitis. They had reached the stage described in one of Willie's prayers:

> O God,
> I have come to the stage
> when I can no longer work
> when I can no longer look after myself
> I am not ill;
> I am just old.

But he was ill, on several counts, and he refused to come to terms with it. His coordination was going, he was becoming more confused, and his alcohol intake exacerbated the confusion. He was unquestionably depressed, which no one appears to have diagnosed. 'I am thoroughly placed in the geriatric category,' he admitted weakly to one correspondent. His typing was abysmal, but still he pressed on, comforting this person, aiding another. And he continued to turn down invitations to preach, which still came in regularly though he had not preached for some years. He was ever poised to write his first volume for the *DSB Old Testament*, but his powers had all but deserted him. He wrote to David Anderson again, telling him how difficult he found the Psalms: 'After you have written about one or two of them you find yourself repeating yourself over and again.' He does not say so, but one of the aspects of the Old Testament which must have thwarted him is its absence of words for everyday life, its paucity in this respect contrasts with the Greek New Testament. He was also writing on Genesis; it was 'more interesting from the point of view of writing' – an odd comment which merely underlines the confusion.

He made another small advance in his work, which got him into more hot water, not least from Kate. Iain Reid, a commercial artist, had been impressed by the vigour of his New Testament paraphrase. He proposed to the mainly Roman Catholic publishers, Darton Longman and Todd, that he and Willie prepare *A Life of Christ* – a sort of poor man's version of the Zeffirelli film. They agreed enthusiastically. The denominational aspect was a matter of supreme indifference to Willie. He had many friends in the Catholic Church, not least of whom was Priscilla, Lady Collins herself. He was interested in people, in serving them, not in their more superficial affiliations. Predictably, many were scandalized by the book – by the artist's impression of Jesus and his disciples; 'the swingin' Jesus' atmosphere it suggested; the pictures of Willie that occurred almost as often as those of Jesus. In depicting Willie, Reid caught something that many missed: the grin that had become a pained grimace, which interpretation had given him a hard, unfeeling look, a matter of great loathing to Kate. It was a caricature, she exclaimed, a cruel misrepresentation; it was emphatically not her man. As Willie said in his autobiography, she may be his severest critic, but she was also his stoutest defender.

He kept going into the winter of 1977, despite the cold, wet weather and his varicosed ankles. He wrote letters to old friends – former parishioners, students and ministerial colleagues – and to total strangers from around the world. To some he reminisced, to others he spoke wistfully of things he could no longer see or do. His family was a chief source of delight to him, especially his grandchildren. The latter were much more Europeanized than he had ever been, and he was delighted. His seventieth birthday found him writing to Charles Miller of 'the real milestone' he had reached; only 'the borrowed years' remained. James Fearon, a former tennis partner and the one-time secretary of Motherwell Tennis Club no less, wrote and said how well he recalled WDB, which received an appreciative response: 'There are not so many young people [!] left who knew my father.'

Christmas came and went, a Christmas which darkened his future. The directors at Collins had had to face up to the reality: the *DSB Old Testament* was a dead issue, part of the problem having been of their own making. They wrote to Willie kindly, suggesting that they release him from his duties to them. The courtesy was received like a swordthrust: his time of usefulness – that basic ethic of his whole life – was over. This was worse than rejection; for the first time in his life he had been discharged. Great weariness – depression, surely – set in.

Mrs Hamilton, his secretary at Collins, agreed to travel across Glasgow to his home to continue to act as his secretary. Willie had suggested four days each week; Kate intervened and asked for three. But it was an empty gesture. The *business* of life was passing. Mrs Hamilton appeared at the house on 19 January, not knowing it was for the last time. Before the end of their three-hour session she knew that all was far from well. Willie's mind was not on the work, he was distracted, and in evident physical discomfort. Of this he said not a word. She drove away. She noticed that he stood at the window and watched her go, unusually, looking immensely sad. She knew, then, that it was her last day.

He deteriorated rapidly throughout the evening; his doctor was summoned and immediately ordered his hospitalization. He was rushed into intensive care at Mearnskirk Hospital, very seriously ill, where they sought through the night to palliate his condition. Two days later, on visiting him, Kate found him propped up in bed tearfully holding a letter from an old school friend, Walter Henderson, who had read of his return to hospital. Henderson mentioned in the letter that the presentation copy of his book *A New Testament Wordbook*, given by Willie to his old teacher Jimmy Paterson, had been on public display at the DHS prizegiving ceremony that year. It brought back a flood of memories, happy and sad, a process which continued over the next few days.

Willie died in his sleep at 01.00 hours, on 24 January 1978. 'The end was very peaceful,' Ronnie told a reporter of this man of peace. He died as he had written of Paul several years before:

> But in spite of everything there is no defeat ... He has come to the end like a fighter, weary but undefeated; like an athlete, exhausted but triumphant; like a standard-bearer, battered but with his standard still intact.

As he said in his autobiography:

> When I die, I should like to slip out of the room without fuss – for what matters is not what I am leaving, but where I am going.

Of that he was right certain.

ABRIDGED BIBLIOGRAPHY

The main bibliographical information was given in the first edition of this authorized biography. It sought to trace the development of William Barclay's prolific writings – even from the sermons and addresses which formed their basis – from article to first edition, to later editions and their respective translations. It was not wholly successful, as so many aspects had been lost. This one merely lists his books, not his prolific journalism – nor the no less astonishing work for the SSSU (237 full lessons in all; still extant), his management of its Correspondence Courses, the editorship of its magazine *The Scottish Sunday School Teacher*; nor his lesson work for the secular schools of Scotland between 1945 and 1949.

1945
New Testament Studies, SSSU, 82pp [his first book; an introduction]

1948
Daily Bible Studies: the Foundations of the Christian Faith, CoS, 64pp
   [readings for October-December; the precursor of the *DBR/DSB*
   series]

1951
One Lord, One Faith, One Life, BB, xii + 144pp
Ambassador for Christ: the Life and Teaching of Paul, CoS, 171pp

1952
And Jesus Said: a Handbook on the Parables of Jesus, CoS, 215pp
God's Men, God's Church, God's Life, BB, ix + 159pp
Camp Prayers and Services, BB, 113pp

1953
DBR: the Acts of the Apostles, CoS, x + 213pp [the first volume of
   what is now the *DSB* by the Saint Andrew Press. It should be
   noted that in addition to providing introduction and explication,
   these volumes contain WB's own translation from the Greek,
   which was not revised when the 1974 edition was made. This
   had been taken up in his paraphrase of 1968/9, qv.]

The King and the Kingdom, BB, x + 210pp
DBR: the Gospel of Luke, CoS, xvi + 314pp

1954

DBR: Galatians, Thessalonians, Corinthians, CoS, xviii + 403pp
DBR: the Gospel of Mark, CoS, xxi + 390pp
God's Law, God's Servants, God's Men, BB, viii + 169pp

1955

DBR: the Gospel of John, volume I, CoS, xxxix + 267pp
DBR: the Gospel of John, volume II, CoS, 338pp
DBR: the Epistle to the Romans, CoS, xxxi + 244pp
DBR: the Epistle to the Hebrews, CoS, xxi + 231pp
And He Had Compassion on Them: a Handbook on the Miracles, CoS,
    292pp
A New Testament Wordbook, SCM Press Ltd, 128pp

1956

DBR: the Gospel of Matthew, volume I, CoS
DBR: the Epistle to the Ephesians, CoS, xxiii + 136pp

1957

DBR: the Gospel of Matthew, volume II, CoS, 218pp
DBR: the Gospel of Matthew, volume III, CoS, 315pp
Letters to Seven Churches, SCM Press Ltd, 128pp

1958

The Mind of Saint Paul, Wm Collins & Sons Ltd, 256pp
More New Testament Words, SCM Press Ltd [this, with *New Testament
    Words*, was reprinted in one volume in 1964]
DBR: the Epistles of James and Peter, CoS, xvii + 432pp
DBR: the Epistles of John and Jude, CoS, xiii + 258pp
[It was in this year that the *DBR* was renamed as the *DSB*]

1959

DBR: the Epistles of Philippians, Colossians and Philemon, CoS, xi +
    228pp
DBR: the Revelation of John, volume I, CoS, xxxix + 207pp
DBR: the Revelation of John, volume II, CoS, 133pp
DBR: the Revelation of John, volume III, CoS, 164pp
Educational Ideas in the Ancient World, Wm Collins & Sons Ltd, 288pp
The Plain Man's Book of Prayers, Wm Collins & Sons Ltd, 128pp
The Master's Men, SCM Press Ltd, 125pp

1960

The Mind of Jesus, SCM Press Ltd, 190pp
The Promise of the Spirit, Epworth Press, 120pp
DBR: Timothy, Titus and Philemon, CoS, xv + 324pp

1961

Crucified and Crowned, SCM Press Ltd, 192pp
The Making of the Bible, Lutterworth Press, 96pp [the first of the *Bible Guides* series, edited by W. Barclay and F. F. Bruce, which absorbed some of their energies during 1961–66]

1962

Flesh and Spirit: an Examination of Galatians 5:19–23, SCM Press Ltd, 127pp
Jesus As They Saw Him: New Testament interpretations of Jesus, SCM Press, 429pp
More Prayers for the Plain Man, Collins-Fontana, 160pp
Prayers for Young People, Collins-Fontana, 95pp

1963

Turning to God: a Study of Conversion in the Book of Acts, Epworth Press, 103pp [reprinted with additions in 1978, ed. Clive L. Rawlins, The Saint Andrew Press, 104pp]
The Plain Man looks at the Beatitudes, Collins-Fontana, 124pp
Many Witnesses, One Lord: a Study in the Diversity of the New Testament, SCM Press Ltd, 128pp
Epilogues and Prayers, Collins-Fontana, 224pp
The All-Sufficient Christ: Studies in Paul's Letter to the Colossians, Westminster Press USA, 142pp
Christian Discipline in Society Today, The Fellowship of Reconciliation, 42pp

1964

The Plain Man Looks at the Lord's Prayer, Collins-Fontana, 128pp
Prayers for the Christian Year, SCM Press Ltd, 176pp

1965

A New People's Life of Jesus, SCM Press Ltd, 96pp
In the Fullness of Time, BB, x + 118pp
The Epistle to the Hebrews [a *Bible Guide*], Lutterworth Press, 96pp
Ed. [with H. Anderson] *The New Testament in Historical and Contemporary Perspective: A Memorial Volume in Honour of G.H.C. MacGregor*, Basil Blackwell Ltd, viii + 280pp

1966

The First Three Gospels, SCM Press Ltd, 317pp [revised and expanded
    into two volumes in 1976, 644pp]
Fishers of Men, Epworth Press, 113pp
The Old Law and the New Law, BB, xiii + 123pp
The Plain Man Looks at the Apostles' Creed, Collins-Fontana, 384pp
Seen in the Passing, ed. Rita Snowden, Collins-Fontana, 158pp

1967

The Lord's Supper, SCM Press Ltd, 128pp
God's Man, BB, 86pp
Thou Shalt Not Kill, The Fellowship of Reconciliation, 24pp

1968

Communicating the Gospel, The Drummond Press, xii + 106pp
Prayers for Help and Healing, Collins-Fontana, 124pp
The New Testament, volume I: The Gospels and the Acts of the Apostles,
    Wm Collins & Sons Ltd, 352pp [reprinted with volume II as a
    single volume, in 1976]
Ed. *The Bible and History: Scriptures in their Biblical Setting*,
    Lutterworth Press

1969

The New Testament, volume II: The Letters and Revelation, Wm Collins &
    Sons Ltd, 350pp

1970

God's Young Church, ed. James Martin, The Saint Andrew Press,
    120pp

1971

[This year saw the commencement of the partly revised edition of
    DSB, ed. James Martin; it was completed in 1975. In 1978 its
    Index to the Daily Study Bible was published, compiled by Clive
    L. Rawlins)
Ethics in a Permissive Society, Collins-Fontana, 222pp
Through the Year with William Barclay: Devotional Readings, ed. Denis
    Duncan, Hodder & Stoughton, 316pp

1972

Introducing the Bible, IBRA, 155pp

1973

The Plain Man's Guide to Ethics, Collins-Fontana, 205pp

Every Day with William Barclay: Devotional Readings, ed. Denis
    Duncan, Hodder & Stoughton, 285pp
Marching Orders: Devotional Readings for Young People, ed. Denis
    Duncan, Hodder & Stoughton, 192pp
Jesus Christ for Today [Luke's Gospel], The Methodist Home Mission,
    22pp

1974

By What Authority?, Darton, Longman & Todd Ltd, 221pp
Marching On: Daily Readings for Young People, ed. Denis Duncan,
    Hodder & Stoughton, 223pp

1975

Testament of Faith, A. R. Mowbray Ltd, xii + 124pp

1976

The Men, the Meaning, the Message of the Books, The Saint Andrew
    Press, 149pp [studies in the New Testament]

1977

Jesus of Nazareth, Wm Collins & Sons Ltd, 285pp
More Prayers for Young People, Collins-Fontana, 160pp
The Character of God, Robert Denholm Press/National Christian
    Education Council, 64pp

1978

Men & Affairs, ed. Clive L. Rawlins, A. R. Mowbray Ltd, ix + 149pp

1979

Great Themes of the New Testament, ed. Cyril Rodd, T. & T. Clark Ltd,
    116pp

1980

Arguing about Christianity, ed. Iain Reid, with a Foreword by Ronnie
    Barclay, The Saint Andrew Press, 70pp
The Lord is my Shepherd [selected Psalms], ed. Allan Galloway,
    Wm Collins & Sons Ltd, 153pp

1985

Seven Fresh Wineskins [readings in the Old Testament], ed. Clive L.
    Rawlins, Labarum Publications Ltd, 196pp
Ever Yours [letters from William Barclay], ed. Clive L. Rawlins,
    Labarum Publications Ltd, xii + 292pp

1991

Daily Readings with William Barclay, ed. Ronnie Barclay,
HarperCollins*Religious*, 124pp

1998

William Barclay: Diary Readings, ed. Clive L. Rawlins,
HarperCollins*Religious*, 224pp